THE FORGING
OF AMERICAN SOCIALISM

The American Heritage Series
OSKAR PIEST, FOUNDER

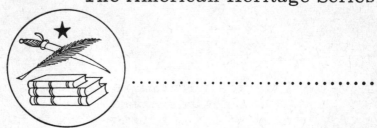

The American Heritage Series

THE FORGING
OF
AMERICAN SOCIALISM

Origins of the Modern Movement

HOWARD H. QUINT

Professor of History, University of Massachusetts

. . . .

The American Heritage Series

published by

THE BOBBS-MERRILL COMPANY, INC.
A Subsidiary of Howard W. Sams & Co., Inc.
Publishers • Indianapolis • New York • Kansas City

To
ELEANOR

PREFACE

Today the United States remains the last great citadel of capitalistic democracy. An organized and institutionalized American socialist movement as such, moreover, is virtually a matter of past history. Of course, some contemporary Jeremiahs insist that the nation is drifting into socialism through the extension of governmental power into spheres of activity hitherto virgin to it. With such persons I should take sharp issue if that were the purpose of this book. But it is not. Nor do I propose to deal with the present dilemma of socialism in the United States and the moribund condition of the Socialist Party of America.

Instead, this study aims to investigate the socialist movement of the last decades of the nineteenth century, when it was in its infancy and full of hope for the future. Specifically, it attempts to show both the European influences and the distinctly American elements that affected the movement, since it should be borne in mind that the upsurge of socialism in the United States at this time was only in part inspired by the classic doctrines of the European Marxists. In point of fact, it came primarily as a protest against the social iniquities resulting from the tremendous economic concentration taking shape in these hectic years of industrial growth. I should say that it owed more for its inspiration to Edward Bellamy's *Looking Backward* than it did to Karl Marx's *Das Kapital*.

The historian has a certain privilege of being arbitrary in establishing the time limits of a study. I have exercised that privilege by setting the years between 1886 and 1901 as the boundaries of this monograph. In fairness to the reader and to the events that transpired during these years I have sought to compress in an opening chapter the developments of the earlier period from 1870 through 1886. In many respects I feel that they are merely anticipatory to the more important story which is related in the ensuing ten chapters.

Making acknowledgments is one of the more pleasant aspects of scholarly endeavor, in some measure because they are usually written after the toil is finished, but more importantly because they afford the opportunity to pay publicly debts which are in many instances long overdue.

First, I want to thank the Faculty Research Committee of the University of South Carolina and the Social Science Research Council. They have extended to me generous financial grants which facilitated and expedited the completion of this study.

Second, I want to thank the librarians. Every scholar knows that with rare exceptions librarians are the most helpful, the most resourceful, and, may I add, the most grievously underpaid of mortals. To single out any one of them for special recognition would do injustice to the many others who assisted me in the preparation of this book. Therefore I wish to bestow collective praise on the librarians of the following institutions: the Library of Congress, the Department of Labor, the Wisconsin State Historical Society, the Rand School of Social Science, the New York Public Library, the Boston Public Library, Yale University, the Johns Hopkins University, Harvard University, Stanford University, Duke University, the University of South Carolina, and the University of Michigan. I am also indebted to the John Crerar Library which made available to me many rare periodicals and newspapers.

Third, I want to thank my fellow scholars. To Professor Charles A. Barker of the Johns Hopkins University, a generous friend and a constructive critic, I am under special obligation. Professor C. Vann Woodward, also of the Johns Hopkins, has offered many valuable suggestions. If Professor Barker has widened my horizons on Henry George, Professor Woodward has helped me to clarify my ideas on the relationship between socialism and Populism. I have profited greatly from the advice, counsel, and criticism of Professors Robert H. Wienefeld and William A. Foran of the University of South Carolina, Francis W. Coker and Morrell Heald of Yale University, and Chester McArthur Destler of Connecticut College. I want to acknowledge, too, the help given me by Frederic Heath, Fred D. Warren, and Algernon Lee, three venerable veterans and scholars of the American socialist movement. And finally, a word of gratitude goes out to Mr. Sol Gilbert for the splendid translations which he made for me from the New York *Jewish Daily Forward*.

Most important, I want to thank my wife, Eleanor D. Quint. Not only has she lived with this study for many years now, but also she has typed it, edited it, and, when necessary, shamed me into rewriting more pages than I should care to admit.

For that which is of value in this book, much credit is due to others; its defects are entirely my own.

Howard H. Quint

University of South Carolina

May 20, 1952

A NOTE ON THE SECOND EDITION

Publication of this second edition has allowed me to make a few minor factual corrections and to eliminate the errors in spelling, punctuation, and syntax that invariably find their way into printed works irrespective of the most diligent efforts to avoid them. I am particularly grateful to those book reviewers who have called them to my attention. Most of them were kind enough not to mention such errors in their reviews.

But the book, as written in 1952, stands. I have had no good reason till now to re-examine or to revise my original findings.

For the history of American socialism after 1901, I refer the reader to David A. Shannon's *The Socialist Party of America* (New York, 1955). Professor Shannon and I planned our volumes to dovetail and his study consequently takes up where this one leaves off.

H. H. Q.

University of Massachusetts
August 1, 1963

CONTENTS

PREFACE   vii

A NOTE ON THE SECOND EDITION   x

THE FORGING
OF AMERICAN SOCIALISM

   I   Marxism Comes to America   3
  II   Failure of Boring from Within   37
 III   Bellamy Makes Socialism Respectable   72
 IV   The Christian Socialist Crusade   103
  V   DeLeon Molds the Socialist Labor Party   142
 VI   Wayland Plants Grass Roots Socialism   175
 VII   Socialism Faces Populism   210
VIII   Non-Partisan Socialism   247
 IX   The Communitarians' Last Stand   280
  X   American Socialism Comes of Age   319
 XI   Socialist Unity Achieved   350

      BIBLIOGRAPHICAL ESSAY   389

      INDEX   395

THE FORGING
OF AMERICAN SOCIALISM

I. Marxism Comes to America

AT THE instigation of Karl Marx and Friedrich Engels, the headquarters of the first International Workingmen's Association, mortally ill from the wasting disease of Bakunin anarchism, was transferred in 1872 from London to New York, to let it die in peace and obscurity. The communist leaders left the unhappy task of administering the last rites and burial to Friedrich A. Sorge, their faithful American adjutant. But Sorge proved to be more a physician than a mortician, and by incredibly hard work and constant attention he kept the patient alive for four more years. Not until July, 1876, did a congress of American socialists finally pronounce the International officially dead. Few Americans probably took the time to read of the International's demise in those rare newspapers which saw fit to carry its obituary notice.

The International's presence in the United States, while a matter of public record, was hardly one of public knowledge or concern; and, indeed, the same might be said of the entire socialist movement during the two decades after the Civil War. The persistent efforts of immigrant proselytizers and their converts to give the transplanted and dissension-wracked American movement organizational permanence and public reputation had pathetically little success. In fact, it was not until 1886 that socialism suddenly and indelibly shocked itself upon the American consciousness. In that year, a populace, which basked in the complacency of the Gilded Age, was generally misinformed by the press that "socialist" agitators were to blame for the bloody Chicago Haymarket Square Riot. And a few months later, the same public learned, this time correctly, that the socialists were playing a major role in Henry George's great New York mayoralty campaign. For uneasy conservatives these were not happy portents for the future.

During the Paris commune of 1871 some American newspapers, to be sure, had raised the specter of socialism's threat to the United States, causing some momentary and vocal apprehension.[1] A few conservatives, like Joseph Cook of Boston Monday Lecture Series fame, thrilled at the prospect of some American "Thiers or McMahon" who would quench "the Gehenna-flames of socialistic revolution" by force of arms.[2] But the great mass of Americans during the 1870's were happily oblivious of the growing socialist movement in Europe and of any menace it might have in store for capitalism and democracy.

Nor was the average American much more aware of the small group of self-acknowledged socialists in the United States. Where cognizance did exist, little fear was held for their doctrines. Americans of the 1870's were surer than their descendants some eighty years later that their democratic institutions could withstand ideological attack. Mere contemplation of the socialists in the United States seemed sufficient in itself to eliminate cause for alarm. A few home-grown radicals were in the lot, but in the main the socialists were recently arrived immigrants—primarily Germans, who had invariably turned out to be solid citizens. Andrew Carnegie nicely summed up the general late nineteenth-century American attitude toward the socialists when he held them to be "a parcel of foreign cranks whose communistic ideas" were "the natural growth of unjust laws of their native land." In other words, the best cure for foreign "isms" was exposure to American democracy.[3]

Carnegie was hitting close to the mark. The socialists faced formidable difficulties in the United States. They could not follow the example of the English Chartists and European social democrats in identifying themselves with the struggle to achieve political democracy; for political democracy had been substantially attained in the United States, and radical middle-class reform parties catered to still unfulfilled democratic needs. Furthermore, few Americans, irrespective of their

---

[1] George L. Cherry, "American Metropolitan Press Reaction to the Paris Commune," *Mid-Century—An Historical Review*, XXXII (1950), 9-11. Also see Samuel Bernstein, "American Labor and the Paris Commune," *Science and Society*, XV (1950), 144-62.

[2] Joseph Cook, *Socialism: With Preludes on Current Events* (Boston, 1880), p. 51.

[3] Andrew Carnegie, *Triumphant Democracy: or Fifty Years' March of the Republic* (New York, 1886), p. 348.

position in society, were willing to accept the implications of the class-struggle theory, the mainspring of Marx's approach to problems of social organization. The class-struggle concept simply ran counter to the grain of the American individualistic, democratic tradition, which stressed in theory, even if it did not always reflect in fact, the equality of all men and the non-existence of classes. Even those who could find some cogency in the socialist critique of capitalism could point out that class stratification was notably less rigid in the United States than in Europe. Nor could it be denied that the United States was still a land of unlimited opportunity for the able and the daring, whose successes were more admired and heralded than envied. American living standards were generally higher than those of any other country in the world, a fact that was not lost on either the native-born or the thousands of immigrants who poured into the United States during the 1870's and 1880's.[4] If the latter, perchance, were willing to accept the permanency of an inferior class status in American society, the same could rarely be said of their sons. Second generation Americans, formed by the leavening of the public school system, were invariably determined to raise themselves from the slough of the sweatshops, the mills, the ghettos, and the slums, and to partake in the abundancy of American life. True, the socialist mirage of the future was undeniably attractive to many of these immigrants and their offspring, and some placed their faith in it. But the bulk of them preferred the American Dream which had proved itself a present day actuality.

Nevertheless, the United States in the 1870's possessed a rich socialist tradition, if one chooses to use the term broadly. Prior to the Civil War and as early as the seventeenth century, it had been the location of several religious, secular, and perfectionist communitarian settlements. The social theories of the benevolent Welshman, Robert Owen, and the noted French utopian, Charles Fourier, had gained practical application largely on the American frontier. Generally, such experiments in community living attracted far more than their share of the intellectual elite

---

[4]Werner Sombart, *Warum Gibt es in den Vereinigten Staaten Keinen Sozialismus?* (Tübingen, 1906), *passim*; Jean L. Burnett, "Socialism and the Republic," *American Journal of Politics,* II (1893), 63-66; Morris Hillquit, *History of Socialism in the United States* (New York, 1903), pp. 153-54.

of the nation and received perhaps undue publicity—much of it extremely favorable. Those choice souls who participated in them were convinced that, as pathfinders and guides to the future, they were offering a peaceful alternative to an inequitable and intolerable existing social order. Their common philosophy was rooted deep in the eighteenth-century concepts of natural law which held that since both the universe and society were governed by certain immutable laws, the defects of a social system were attributable neither to the evil genius of any individual or group nor to fundamental changes in the means of production. Rather, the defects were institutional violations of the laws of society. To live in accordance with these laws, to remold existing social institutions around them, to achieve their goals rationally, collectively, and peacefully, without resort to class warfare were the laudable aims of the secular communitarians.[5]

To establish a direct organizational relationship between the early utopian societies and the socialist political movement of the latter decades of the nineteenth century would be difficult if not impossible. Yet the two should not necessarily be sharply divided one from the other, since the utopian spirit and in particular its ethical ideals were to permeate the American reform, labor, and radical movements for many years to come. It was to come into full recrudescence in the Nationalist movement, which ensued upon the publication of Edward Bellamy's utopian novel, *Looking Backward*, and in the host of communitarian settlements that suddenly floriated during the 1890's. The last stand of utopianism in organizational form came in 1897-1898 with the meteoric rise and fall of the Brotherhood of the Cooperative Commonwealth and the Social Democracy of America. But the utopian vision of the better world is both part and parcel of the great American liberal tradition.

Also forming an integral part of the American pre-Civil War socialist tradition were the activities of the German radicals who flocked to the United States during the 1840's, particularly

---

[5]The literature on communitarian settlements in the United States is copious. For an analysis of the secular communitarian viewpoint, see Arthur Bestor, *Backwoods Utopias: The Sectarian and Owenite Phases of Communitarian Socialism in America, 1663-1829* (Philadelphia, 1950), pp. 3-16. A discussion of the Owenite and Fourierist movements and their relationship to the idea of progress appears in Arthur A. Ekirch, *The Idea of Progress in America, 1815-1860* (New York, 1944), pp. 132-65.

after the unsuccessful uprising of 1848.[6] The best known among them were Wilhelm Weitling,[7] Joseph Wedemeyer, and Friedrich Sorge. Weitling, who for a brief period beginning in 1850 published a little paper, *Die Republik der Arbeiter*, was hardly less utopian than the secular communitarians. While recognizing that Marxist theories, based on the European working class, had little application in the vast and heterogeneous United States, he could not abandon broad, sweeping solutions to the challenging problem of inequitably distributed wealth. His principal social and economic panacea was the labor-exchange bank, but when he failed to make progress with it, he turned to communitarianism. Wedemeyer and Sorge, both close friends of Marx, were better grounded in the theories and principles of scientific socialism. In 1853 Wedemeyer was instrumental in founding the German Workingmen's Alliance, which during its short existence emphasized the class-struggle thesis, the necessity for trade-union activity, and the desirability of wage-earner politics. The intellectual Sorge, along with Conrad Carl and Siegfried Meyer, organized on October 25, 1857, the Communist Club in New York, whose members were well versed in the essentials of Marxism as outlined in the *Communist Manifesto*.[8]

While the abolitionist and free-soil agitations of the 1850's overshadowed all other reform movements, and the German Socialists supported the early Republican party and the Union cause during the war,[9] small socialist groups maintained a separate, if little noticed existence. The socialists lived in a little

---

[6]Accounts of the early German socialist and labor movements may be found in Hermann Schlüter, *Die Anfänge der deutschen Arbeiterbewegung in Amerika* (Stuttgart, 1907), *passim;* A. Sartorius Freiherrn von Waltershausen, *Der moderne Socialismus in den Vereinigten Staaten von Amerika* (Berlin, 1890), pp. 20-36; F. A. Sorge, "Die Arbeiterbewegung in den Vereinigten Staaten, 1850-1860," *Die Neue Zeit*, Vol. IX (1890-1891), No. 2, pp. 193-202, 232-40; Carl Wittke, *Refugees of Revolution* (Philadelphia, 1952), *passim,* especially pp. 166-75.

[7]Carl Wittke, *The Utopian Communist; a Biography of Wilhelm Weitling, Nineteenth Century Reformer* (Baton Rouge, 1950), pp. 120 ff.

[8]Hillquit, pp. 167-70; John R. Commons (ed.), *History of Labour in the United States,* II (New York, 1918), 204-7.

[9]Hermann Schlüter, *Die Internationale in Amerika: Ein Beitrag zur Geschichte der Arbeiter Bewegung in den Vereinigten Staaten* (Chicago, 1918), pp. 13-14; Carl Wittke, *Against the Current, The Life of Karl Heinzen, 1809-1890* (Chicago, 1945), pp. 178-81; Richard T. Ely, *The Labor Movement in America* (New York, 1886), p. 223; Hillquit, pp. 170-72.

world all of their own. Psychologically, socially, and politically divorced from the main stream of American life and from
the traditions of the republic, they were little more than a
parochial group of displaced Germans and other Europeans.
For the most part they were already confirmed socialists before
coming to the United States. And their converts were usually
other immigrants who, contrary to rule, had not found America
the land of unlimited opportunity.

Yet these socialist colonists, as it were, warrant preliminary
inquiry since, beginning in the 1860's, it was they who ripped
away American socialism from its old utopian moorings and
brought it face to face with a thorny problem: whether to place
primary emphasis on trade-union penetration or on political
action. This problem was dividing European socialists into
two opposing camps: the Marxists, who advocated economic
organization preliminary to political participation, and the
Lassalleans, who believed that political victories would gather
wage earners into the socialist fold. Marx insisted that the
socialist commonwealth of the future would have firm foundations only if erected on trade unions and co-operative groups
made up of class-conscious socialists. Lassalle saw the trade
union as a corruptive influence on socialism. He maintained
that it helped, in fact, to anneal the interests of the workers
and the capitalists in a common bread-and-butter end. He
therefore placed his faith in straight political action.

In Europe these opposing views were propagandized by the
International Workingmen's Association, founded by Marx in
1864, and by the Lassallean political agitation, which com-
menced in Germany the year before. In the American socialist
movement Marxism was to enter a similar conflict—not only
with transplanted Lassalleanism, but also with a native American reformist tradition, which with its faith in political action
was Lassallean in spirit. Fully familiar with the internecine
quarrel of European socialism, the American Marxists recognized this native opposition as being essentially similar to its
European foe. Perhaps unwittingly, they made the reformers
more clearly aware of their own particular role in the dynamics
of modern socialism.

The International was not immediately successful in implanting its own sections in the United States. Until late in the sixties it sought to gain the affiliation of the sprawling and catch-all National Labor Union, chiefly by advocating the regulation of European immigration to the United States and by offering to assist the Union during strikes. With the ascendency of William H. Sylvis to the Presidency of the NLU in 1868, it appeared that direct ties with the International would be established, for Sylvis advocated union with the Marxist organization. But Sylvis died in July, 1869; and while in 1870 the NLU did vote to join the International, a formal relationship was never established. The NLU, like the International, was in a state of deterioration, and it did not long survive its leader.[10]

Sorge's Communist Club declared its union with the International in October, 1867, but the first organization of any size or importance to affiliate was the General German Workingmen's Union, founded in New York in 1865. That the charter members of the Union were Lassalleans would indicate that German socialists in the United States did not at this point consider the question of socialist tactics a vital one. Indeed, in 1868 the Lassallean Union and the Marxist Communist Club formed together the Social Party of New York, choosing the Marxist Sorge as its head, but at the same time running candidates in the fall elections on a reformist rather than a socialist platform. In joining the International in December, 1869, the General German Workingmen's Union became Section 1 of New York City.[11]

By the end of 1870 several sections of the International had been established by radical immigrants in New York and Chicago, though socialists in the latter city tended to be more favorably inclined toward a Lassallean course of policy. Native-born come-outers like William West, founder of a society called "The New Democracy," and Stephen Pearl Andrews, a philosophical

---

[10]Schlüter, *Die Internationale in Amerika,* pp. 50-72; Sartorius von Waltershausen, pp. 45-50; Charlotte Todes, *William H. Sylvis and the National Labor Union* (New York, 1942), pp. 85-93; Commons, II, 131-32.

[11]Schlüter, *Die Internationale in Amerika,* pp. 80-115; F. A. Sorge, "Die Arbeiterbewegung in den Vereinigten Staaten, 1867-1877," *Die Neue Zeit,* Vol. X (1891-1892), No. 1, pp. 391-92; Commons, II, 209.

anarchist, organized Sections 9 and 12 in New York City for their fellow American radicals. The two most spectacular members of Section 12 were the resourceful sisters, Victoria Woodhull and Tennessee Claflin, whose radicalism was inclined primarily toward women's suffrage and sexual freedom. However, the sisters were also sympathetic to socialism, and it was in their journal, *Woodhull and Claflin's Weekly*, that the first English translation of the *Communist Manifesto* of Marx and Engels was published in the United States.

The association of the German and American sections in New York was brief and turbulent. The Germans in Section 1 did not take kindly to the meanderings of the American reformers into fields not directly related to the labor movement—notably their advocacy of greenbacks rather than free banking. This did not mean that the Germans themselves were straight-laced Marxists, for they, too, were not unwilling to espouse such broad reformist measures as state help to relieve unemployed workers.[12] But they insisted on socialist discipline. The effort of the German-dominated Central Committee of the International in New York to impose discipline, and the desire of the American sections to try their hand at politics, brought about a split in November, 1871. Upon complaint of the Central Committee, the General Council of the International in London suspended Section 12.[13]

Section 12 did not go down ingloriously, however, for its last official act was to summon a convention of all "male and female beings of America" to meet at the Apollo Theater in New York City on May 10, 1872. An assorted group of some 500 radicals from 22 states answered the call; and, after discussing no end of social reform topics, they formed the short-lived "Equal Rights" party and nominated Victoria Woodhull and Frederick Douglass for the Presidency and Vice-Presidency of the United States, respectively.[14] Considering the other candidates in the

[12]Joseph Dorfman, *The Economic Mind in American Civilization,* Vol. III, *1865-1918* (New York, 1949), p. 43.

[13]Schlüter, *Die Internationale in Amerika,* pp. 151-64; Sartorius von Waltershausen, pp. 73-75; Commons, II, 211-15.

[14]Emanie Sachs. *The Terrible Siren, Victoria Woodhull, 1838-1927* (New York, 1928), pp. 157-62; Schlüter, *Die Internationale in Amerika,* pp. 164-67; Hillquit, p. 198.

field, conceivably the American people might have done well to elect Mrs. Woodhull.

Granted that not a few of the members of Section 12 were rather unstable individuals of the type invariably found on the fringes of all reform movements, their conflict with the obdurate Germans of the Central Committee nevertheless revealed a fundamental difference in outlook between the imported brand of radicalism and the home-grown variety. Equally repugnant to the native-born, who had been nurtured in a relatively fluid and free social order, were the entire concept of political discipline and the working-class program which the immigrant Marxists proposed to follow at a snail's pace. Even the most proletarian of the American radicals looked upon reform as transcending the general barriers of class. And, in a mood reflecting the romanticism of the age, they believed that both social and economic change could be achieved cataclysmically and along several fronts. Hence, they were willing to leave the long, narrow, and tortuous highway of working-class socialism for side roads that seemed to offer short cuts to the promised land.

Despite the purging of Section 12, the International Workingmen's Association made slow but steady growth in the United States between 1871 and 1873, particularly in Milwaukee, St. Louis, Cincinnati, Baltimore, Philadelphia, Pittsburgh, Newark, Buffalo, and Detroit[15]—all cities possessing large German populations. Most of the newly organized sections were composed of German immigrants, though scattered here and there were Bohemian, French, Irish, Scandinavian, and American groups. One French section in New York was made up entirely of Paris Commune refugees. The transference of the headquarters of the International from London to New York in 1872 gave the movement real vitality for a brief period and helped to keep it alive after it had all but expired in Europe.[16]

The temporary vigor of the International found expression in a memorable convention in Philadelphia in April, 1874. At one of its sessions a resolution was adopted which clarified the organization's position on the question of political action. Co-

[15]Sorge, *Die Neue Zeit,* Vol. X (1891-1892), No. 1, p. 390.
[16]Schlüter, *Die Internationale in Amerika,* pp. 202-3.

operation with capitalistic parties was spurned and participation in them denied to all members of the International except by express authorization. Political action was in order only when a true workingmen's party was "strong enough to exercise a perceptible influence" at the polls. All legislative measures sought were to be solely in the interest of the working class. Most important of all, "the economic emancipation of working-men" was the "great end to which every political movement ought to be subordinated as a means."[17]

Failure to aid the working class at a critical juncture, how-ever, helped to lead to the International's undoing. Following the panic of 1873, several trade-unionist members of the Inter-national insisted that the organization relax its unbending attitude toward the labor movement and seek to harmonize its objectives with those of the non-socialist workers. But the German Marxists, particularly those of Section 1 of New York, would have none of it. This internal conflict, together with the increasing demands for the organization of a socialist polit-ical party by German and American workingmen alike, sapped the vitality of the International and rendered its continued existence precarious.

Emerging from the 1870's was a pattern of socialist behavior which corresponded closely to the rises and falls of the business cycle. In years of relative prosperity when employment was steady, the socialists who emphasized an economic program and a policy of "boring from within" the trade unions domi-nated the movement. In such an atmosphere the International gained temporary vigor in the United States. The years of de-pression brought forward the socialists who habitually endorsed political action, usually independently, although sometimes in alliance with radical bourgeois parties, in order to attract dis-contented workers to their movement. The panic of 1873 and its aftermath of depression hence threatened the International and provided the soil out of which was to grow the first real socialist political party in the United States. If the Marxists enjoyed the fruits of prosperity, it was the Lassalleans whose views were to prevail during periods of depression.

---

[17]*Ibid.*, pp. 293-94; Commons, II, 218-19

In 1874 two socialist political parties were organized, the Labor Party of Illinois with headquarters in Chicago and the Social Democratic Workingmen's Party of North America which was centered in New York. Full of enthusiasm, the Lassalleans of the Labor Party entered candidates in the Chicago municipal elections of the spring of 1874, only to poll less than a thousand votes. In the congressional elections of the fall, the Labor Party fared even worse, with the result that the Chicago socialists took stock and temporarily refrained from further political action.[18] In the East, the Social Democratic Workingmen's Party, whose membership consisted less of orthodox Lassalleans than of dissidents from the International, held back from plunging into political contests. Within a year's time it shelved its Lassallean platform which called for concentration on political action and state help to democratically constituted co-operative societies, and adopted a new program similar to that of the International Workingmen's Association. Significantly, the party chose for its national officers several prominent trade unionists, including two future American Federation of Labor leaders, Adolph Strasser and P. J. McGuire.[19]

Thus, three pygmy socialist organizations struggled for survival in 1875: the Social Democratic Workingmen's Party, which claimed a membership of 1500; the International Workingmen's Association with 635 members; and the Labor Party of Illinois with 593 followers.[20] Each had a predominantly German membership, and none differed fundamentally from the others. Common sense, if nothing else, dictated a union of forces. On the initiative of the Social Democratic Workingmen's Party a convention was called at Philadelphia in July, 1876, to bring about the merger.

The meeting accomplished its purpose, and a new Workingmen's Party of the United States was formed. Smoothing the way for the new party was the decision of the congress of the International, which had met in Philadelphia only a few days before, to disband the Association. By their action the ten

---

[18]Schlüter, *Die Internationale in Amerika*, pp. 317-25; Commons, II, 227-30.

[19]Schlüter, *Die Internationale in Amerika*, pp. 297-307; Sartorius von Waltershausen, pp. 97-99; Commons, II, 230-33; Hillquit, pp. 207-8.

[20]*Verhandlungen des Einigungs-Kongresses der Arbeiterpartei der Vereinigten Staaten, Philadelphia, July 19-22, 1876,* p. 4.

American members of the International and one representative
from Germany officially recognized the moribund state of the
IWA.[21] Moreover, the new party was to cater to their own
particular ideological bill of fare. Its platform was Marxist
rather than Lassallean, in that primary emphasis was placed
upon developing socialist strength within the trade-union movement rather than in dissipating it by sporadic sorties into politics.[22] However, local sections, with permission of the party
leadership, might enter into political campaigns where prospects
for success appeared extremely favorable. In structure the new
Workingmen's Party was highly centralized, a characteristic of
future socialist political organizations. Control was placed
in a seven-man national executive committee, all of whose members were residents of a given locality. Their actions were subject to correction by a board of control consisting of five party
members from some other city.[23] Chicago was ultimately selected as the site of the national executive committee, while New
Haven served temporarily as the seat of the first board of
control.

The seventeen months between the time of the formation of
the Workingmen's Party and its first national convention in
Newark, New Jersey, in December, 1877, again swung the socialist pendulum back to politics. During the fall of 1876 and the
spring of 1877 socialist candidates for the most part had done
surprisingly well in municipal elections in various parts of the
country.[24] The outbreak of the vicious class warfare in the
Pennsylvania coal fields between the desperate Molly Maguires
and the obdurate mine operators, the violent eruption of the
railroad strikes of 1877, and their suppression in some localities
by Federal troops provided socialist agitators with a golden
opportunity to propagandize sullen and desperate workers.
These iniquities of capitalism, they contended, proved the necessity for a political party that would obtain justice for the wage
earner.[25]

[21]Schlüter, *Die Internationale in Amerika,* pp. 365-72.
[22]*Verhandlungen des Einigungs-Kongresses der Arbeiterpartei,* p. 13.
[23]*Ibid.,* pp. 16-17.
[24]Commons, II, 272-73, 277; Hillquit, pp. 261-62.
[25]Sartorius von Waltershausen, pp. 139-43.

The Newark convention found the trade-unionist element in the minority, and the political actionists proceeded to alter the party's platform to accommodate it to the new conditions. While socialists were urged to support the labor movement and to assist in the formation of new trade unions along socialist lines, the main purpose of the party was declared to be political. The party's headquarters was transferred from Chicago, where trade-unionist and political factions were equally divided, to Cincinnati, a hotbed of socialist political action. Philip Van Patten, the party's American-born secretary and a partisan of socialist politics, was retained in office. The party's organizational structure was revamped to make it more suitable for participation in local, state, and national elections. And the party name was divested of all association with the policies of the old International. (The Workingmen's Party now became the Socialistic Labor Party.[26])

By the fall of 1878 the political actionists within the Socialistic Labor Party were in the saddle and riding high. The party had gained electoral victories for state and local representatives in Chicago, the nerve center of the socialist movement,[27] and in St. Louis, where the socialists had particularly distinguished themselves during the 1877 strike. Yet at this very time the SLP leadership was actually tottering on the brink of disaster. Returning prosperity was to make workingmen less willing to listen to socialist agitators and vote the socialist ticket.[28] Socialist newspapers and journals were finding it increasingly difficult to continue publication, and several were obliged to suspend either temporarily or permanently. The only new and important addition to the socialist press was the daily *New Yorker Volkszeitung*, founded in 1878 and edited by Dr. Adolph Douai and Alexander Jonas.[29] Within the party itself the dissident Marxist trade unionists were waiting impatiently for an opportunity to steer the SLP back to a trade-union course. Finally, the party came face to face with the problem posed by

---

[26]*Ibid.*, pp. 149-51; Commons, II, 277-79

[27]*Report of the Proceedings of the National Convention of the Socialistic Labor Party, Allegheny City, Pa., Dec. 26-Jan. 1, 1879-1880*, p. 12.

[28]*Ibid.*, p. 5.

[29]Louis Stanley, "Fifty Years of the *Volkszeitung*," *New Leader and American Appeal*, May 12, 1928; Hillquit, p. 227.

the increasing tendency among socialists to bring forward the resort to violence, both as doctrine and as a technique of action.

Beginning in the early months of 1879 a swarm of embittered German socialists came to the United States to escape from Bismarck's "exceptional laws," which were designed to eradicate socialism from the Reich. In many cases the new immigrants repudiated both orthodox political action and trade-union penetration for a policy of achieving the revolution by physical force.[30] Also, certain German socialist trade unionists, apart from the new immigrants, began to organize *Lehr und Wehr Verein*, particularly in Chicago and Cincinnati. These armed "Educational and Defensive" societies were formed to protect socialists from police brutalities, and trade unionists from the bayonets of the state militia.[31] Neither of the social revolutionary groups, apostles of violence essentially through Old and New World circumstance rather than doctrinal conviction, was associated initially with the Bakunin anarchists, with whom they are sometimes confused.

Both the National Executive Committee of the Socialistic Labor Party and its American sections deplored the growing tendency to emphasize armed action. Through party secretary Van Patten, the National Executive Committee disclaimed all SLP connection with the *Lehr und Wehr Verein*, ordered all party members to withdraw from such associations, and informed the Chicago sections not to participate in armed demonstrations. This last bit of advice was promptly and impudently ignored, and the Chicago socialist papers, *Vorbote* and *Arbeiter-Zeitung*, both of which opposed the party's political tack, increased their editorial criticisms of Van Patten and the National Executive Committee.[32]

The *Bewaffungsfrage*—the question of arming—was merely one of several developments that were bringing to a boil the conflict between the politically oriented National Executive

[30]Henry David, *The History of the Haymarket Affair: A Study in the American Social Revolutionary and Labor Movements* (New York, 1936), pp. 59-60.

[31]*Ibid.*, pp. 56-58; Sartorius von Waltershausen, pp. 158-60; Commons, II, 280-82.

[32]*Report of the Proceedings of the National Convention of the Socialistic Labor Party, 1879-1880*, p. 16.

Committee and the powerful trade-unionist group. While many adherents of the latter were no less opposed to the *Lehr und Wehr Verein* than Van Patten and his followers, they were nevertheless willing to ally with the social revolutionaries to bring about a change in the party leadership and a new course of policy. It was for this reason that the Chicago editor, Paul Grottkau, for example, could go along with the social revolutionaries.

The first real challenge by the trade-unionist–social-revolutionary faction came at the party's national convention in December, 1879. There it succeeded in pushing through a vote of censure of the National Executive Committee for giving the Chicago sections unauthorized advice.[33] But the delegates upheld the party leaders in their opposition to armed socialist groups, with Section Philadelphia threatening withdrawal from the party unless this policy was confirmed.[34] Also, Van Patten was re-elected secretary, though he was denounced both by Albert R. Parsons, later of Haymarket Affair fame, who spoke for the Chicago trade-union faction, and by one M. Bachman, a delegate from New York City.[35] Finally, the convention went on record as favoring participation in the 1880 presidential campaign.[36]

Having come out of the Allegheny City convention badly shaken though still in control, the political-action group—along with the Socialistic Labor Party itself—was nearly destroyed by two election fiascos in 1880. The first of these was in Chicago where Frank A. Stauber, a socialist candidate for alderman, was fraudulently counted out by the election judges after he had won a close victory. The trade-union element, anxious to stigmatize socialist politics, seized upon this incident to demonstrate that the politicians of the old parties would not willingly relinquish their offices to victorious socialist candidates.[37] The SLP's dizzy antics in the presidential election were even more discrediting to its leaders and to their program. After

---

[33]*Ibid.*, p. 25.
[34]*Ibid.*, pp. 25-26.
[35]*Ibid.*, pp. 43-44.
[36]*Ibid.*, pp. 18-19.
[37]David, pp. 60-61; Commons, II, 287.

a party referendum had decided against independent Socialist Laborite participation in the campaign, Van Patten and several other prominent members of his faction attended the Greenback Party convention in the hope of "socializing" its platform. Though failing miserably in this objective, they nevertheless had the audacity to ask the SLP membership to support the Greenback presidential candidate, General James Baird Weayer.[38] In Chicago this request brought open revolt by the trade-union faction.[39] In New York the chief protest came not from the trade unionists, many of whom had already left the party during the preceding two years, but from the social revolutionaries, whose number had been greatly augmented by recently arrived radical German immigrants.[40]

Dark days for the Socialistic Labor Party now lay in the offing. Prosperity was returning, with the result that enthusiasm for socialism and, for that matter, Greenbackism, waned. The worker was eating well, and his interest in socialism corresponded inversely to the contents of his dinner pail. In the winter of 1881 flagging spirits were lifted temporarily when F. W. Fritsche and Louis Viereck, two socialist deputies to the German Imperial Diet, made an agitational tour of the East and the Middle West. But internal disaffection on the trade-unionism–politics issue was weakening the party, and new strength in the form of converts was not forthcoming. In fact, the party's never robust membership was shrinking alarmingly. The SLP felt compelled to eschew participation in both the spring and fall elections because of its inability to reach the American voter. In December the party's third national convention met in New York City with nearly all of the seventeen delegates hailing from Manhattan, Brooklyn, and the general metropolitan area. Under these circumstances, the business of the convention was extremely limited and it speedily adjourned.[41] The only solace Van Patten could derive from the

---

[38]Sartorius von Waltershausen, pp. 162-64; Commons, II, 286; Hillquit, pp. 267-69.

[39]Van Patten to George Schilling, Aug. 2, 1880, and Sept. 24, 1880. Schilling Papers, Illinois State Historical Library. Also see Sartorius von Waltershausen, pp. 164-65; Commons, II, 287.

[40]Commons, II, 287-88.

[41]Hillquit, pp. 228-29.

convention was his own re-election as party secretary—due in no small measure to "the difficulty in getting anyone who could write correct English"—and the "harmonious" nature of the gathering which reflected the absence of "the thick-headed dyspeptic element."[42] It was in this weakened condition that the Socialistic Labor Party was obliged to withstand the assaults of both the social revolutionaries and the Bakunin anarchists.

The social revolutionary group had organized, in Chicago, Boston, Philadelphia, Milwaukee, and elsewhere, various "Revolutionary Clubs," which, along with resort to violence, had been completely repudiated by the SLP. The dissident radicals who formed them did not purposely, for the most part, desert socialism for anarchism. In general political philosophy they continued to remain Marxists. But discouragement with the slow, constitutional, parliamentary methods of the Socialist Labor Party tempted them to seek their goals by force and violence. Convinced that the power of the possessing class rested on force, they found themselves ready to combat capitalism with its own weapons.

The formation of the anarchist International Working People's Association, the so-called Black International, in a congress at London in July, 1881, had the effect of magnetizing the social revolutionary movement further away from its Marxist foundations. Several American delegates attended the London congress, though none appear to have figured prominently, and in October, 1881, a convention of social revolutionary clubs at Chicago formally endorsed the new International. This action did not necessarily mean that the social revolutionaries had become converted to the doctrines of anarchism itself but rather that they felt that the anarchist emphasis on force would dramatize both the socialist movement and the need for societal change. Too, the social revolutionary clubs, reacting against the tight-knit, rigid control of the Socialistic Labor Party, were attracted by the loose, federative principle of organization espoused by the anarchists.[43] Indeed, lack of organizational

---

[42] Van Patten to Schilling, Jan. 12, 1882. Schilling Papers, Illinois State Historical Library.

[43] For excellent treatments of the relationship of the American social revolutionaries with the IWPA, see David, pp. 62-76; Commons, II, 290-93.

as well as doctrinal cohesiveness characterized the social revolutionaries.

Indicative of the lack of agreement amongst the social revolutionaries on dogma and tactics was the New York club's general disapproval of the Revolutionary Socialist Party which had been organized at the Chicago convention. The very idea of a party suggested hesitation, compromise, and retreat to the New Yorkers, who after December, 1882, were under the complete domination of the recently arrived German apostle of anarchist violence, Johann Most. Nor did the Gotham social revolutionaries condone the policy of the Middle Western clubs, particularly that of Chicago, of seeking to work through the trade-union movement.

Curiously enough, the distinction of being the first affiliate of the Black International in the United States fell to the International Workingmen's Association, organized in July, 1881, by the erratic Burnette G. Haskell of San Francisco, a nonpracticing attorney, a Chinese baiter, and an editor and publisher of a little radical weekly paper, *Truth*.[44] Haskell's association, commonly referred to as the "Red International" because of the red cards issued to its members, acknowledged spiritual kinship with the defunct Marxist International and was directly affiliated with the anarchistic International founded in London in 1881. Yet the IWA, which grounded its philosophy in the natural rights tradition, rejected both resort to the ballot and deeds of violence as methods for achieving the co-operative commonwealth. Rather it placed primary emphasis on a long campaign of socialist education and agitation. Haskell's ultimate goal, insofar as he had one, was a form of state socialism rather than a loose confederation of autonomous groups of producers, the aim of anarchists like Most.

Though secretly organized, the International Workingmen's Association openly publicized its doctrines and methods. The Association was divided into two branches, one a Pacific Coast division and the other in the Rocky Mountain states. The latter

---

[44]David, pp. 146-48; Commons, II, 298-300; Joseph R. Buchanan, *The Story of a Labor Agitator* (New York, 1903), pp. 254-89; Chester M. Destler, *American Radicalism, 1865-1901, Essays and Documents* (New London, 1946), pp. 78-82.

was led by Joseph R. Buchanan, prominent in the Knights of
Labor and publisher of the Denver *Labor Enquirer.* Each division was completely autonomous. Probably at no time during
the IWA's seven or eight year history did its membership exceed
6,000.

An ideologically more authentic branch of the International
Working People's Association was formed in Pittsburgh at a
conference of social revolutionaries in October, 1883, mainly
through the efforts of August Spies and Albert R. Parsons of
Chicago.[45] It was suggested at the time that a union between
the new organization and the Haskell group be consummated,
but this failed to materialize.[46] Spies and Parsons also made
an effort, with only partial success, to bring the Chicago and
New York social revolutionary factions into closer harmony.
The dynamic Most, now thoroughly in control of the Eastern
movement, as noted, had little patience with their program to
work through trade unions, a course of policy that led ultimately to anarcho-syndicalism. On the other hand, he realized that
he would have to make some concessions if he were to get his
own ideas adopted. Thus, while the Congress adopted a Spies-
proposed resolution to the effect that socialistic trade unions,
which were fighting for the eradication of capitalism, ought to
be the foundation of the future social order, its Manifesto to
the workingmen of America completely ignored trade unions.[47]
The main feature of the Manifesto, an important landmark in
the history of American radicalism, was its assertion that the
only recourse of the wage-earner class against its capitalist overlords was to resort to force.[48]

The Pittsburgh Congress and its ideologically confused but
basically anarchist-oriented Manifesto had the result of sorting
out the socialist sheep from the anarchist goats and of destroying the social revolutionary movement. The more moderate
social revolutionaries like Paul Grottkau wended their way back
into the Socialistic Labor Party.[49] The radicals went over to

[45]David, p. 95; Commons, II, 296.
[46]Destler, pp. 78-104.
[47]David, pp. 95-100; Commons, II, 294-95.
[48]David, p. 103.
[49]Hillquit, p. 241.

the anarchists who continued to flourish until the Haymarket Affair and who maintained a state of constant ideological warfare with the socialists.

The anarchist emphasis on violence was poorly received by American workingmen, who found it completely alien to their own psychology. And it was likewise anarchist propaganda, calling for the employment of insurrectionary deeds, that sent shivers of fear up and down the spines of American businessmen. Until the early 1880's business leaders had been disposed to treat foreign radicals and their doctrines with a certain degree of disdain. But the social revolutionary and anarchist proposals to employ violence brought alarm and a widespread demand for suppression of both socialism and anarchism, the two usually being indiscriminately linked together in the public mind. Said one industrial trade paper of the radical menace:

> The last few years have opened our eyes to the fact that from the off-scourings of Europe we have acquired some very bad citizens; men who are not in sympathy with our institutions, but are enemies of society in general; who would overthrow law and order and apply the torch to property and the sword to slaughter. They are fortunately not formidable in numbers, for the doctrines they preach are too odious to be listened to with patience, and much less embraced. But in the larger cities they are in a position to take advantage of any great uproar or riot and do incalculable injury to life and property before order could be established.[50]

Even Richard T. Ely, the Johns Hopkins economist, whose poverty as a young man caused him to take a vow to write in behalf of the laboring classes,[51] sounded the clarion of alarm against the direct actionist radicals. In his book, *Recent American Socialism*, published in April, 1885, Ely warned of the seriousness of the situation:

> If it were known that one thousand men like the notorious train robbers, the James boys, were in small groups scattered over the United States, would not every conservative

---

[50]Quotation from the May 14, 1885, issue of the *Age of Steel* appears in Morrell Heald's "Business Attitudes toward European Immigration, 1861-1914" (Ph. D. dissertation, Yale University, 1951), p. 233.

[51]R. T. Ely to Joseph Labadie, Aug. 14, 1883. Joseph A. Labadie Papers, General Library, University of Michigan (cited hereafter as Labadie Papers).

and peace-loving householder be filled with alarm, and reasonably so? Yet here we have more than ten times that number educated to think robbery, arson, and murder justifiable, nay even righteous; taught to believe that the slaughter of the ruling classes a holy work and prepared to follow it with all the fanaticism of religious devotion, ready to die if need be, and prepared to stifle all feelings of gratitude and natural affection, and to kill with their own hands every opponent of the grand cause. It is indeed . . . an anomaly that it is lawful for a man like John Most to preach wholesale massacre, while it is criminal for A to incite B to slay C. And this Most is the lion among the extremists in the United States; this man, who on account of his excessive violence, was repudiated by his own countrymen and almost unanimously expelled from the Social Democratic Party of Germany.[52]

Amidst the furor created by the anarchists and social revolutionaries, the Socialistic Labor Party maintained a precarious existence. Its membership in 1883 had shrivelled to approximately 1,500, concentrated in only thirty sections. Political efforts were all but abandoned, as were the attempts to work through the trade-union movement. But the blow which crowned the party's misfortunes came on April 22, 1883, with the sudden disappearance of its American-born national secretary, Philip Van Patten. Disgusted with his German socialist companions, who didn't "seem to care to make Americans understand them," Van Patten left a farewell note telling of his intention to commit suicide. At the time he wrote the note, he was undoubtedly sincere, but a brief period of soul searching convinced him that the cause wasn't worth it. He found a haven and anonymity in the Federal bureaucracy and later became an enterprising, successful, and respected merchant in Hot Springs, Arkansas.[53]

Van Patten's desertion removed from the Socialistic Labor Party one of its conservative bulwarks. Though not personally popular among the party rank and file, he had helped to steer

[52]R. T. Ely, *Recent American Socialism* ("The Johns Hopkins University Studies in Historical and Political Science," 3d Ser., Vol. IV [Baltimore, 1885]), p. 63.

[53]Van Patten to Geo. Schilling, Apr. 11, 1893. Schilling Papers, Illinois State Historical Library. Also see Sartorius von Waltershausen, pp. 223-25; Hillquit, p. 239.

the SLP clear from entanglement with the radical revolutionary incendiaries. The absence of his hand from the party helm was soon evident in the abortive attempt of several prominent Socialist Laborites to bring about a union with the International Working People's Association following the 1883 Pittsburgh Congress. However, the cold reception of the socialist overtures by Spies, speaking in behalf of the International, made it obvious that such a union was completely inadvisable. Bluntly, Spies demanded that the Socialist Laborites disband their party and organize autonomous groups which could then seek admission to the International.[54]

The fourth national convention of the Socialistic Labor Party at Baltimore in December, 1883, nevertheless veered toward a more radical course of policy in the hope of appeasing its social revolutionary element and preventing it from gravitating into the camp of the anarchists. The sixteen delegates present at the convention sought to meet the demand of the social revolutionaries for greater party decentralization by abolishing Van Patten's deserted national secretaryship, by curtailing the authority of the National Executive Committee, and by conferring greater autonomy on local sections. The party's platform was revamped, with new planks calling for constitutional amendments which would abolish the Presidency and the Senate, adopt the referendum, and protect minority parties on the ballot. The delegates also went on record as favoring political action more for propaganda purposes than for legislative ends.[55]

In a manifesto to the workingmen of America, the convention countenanced the use of force in bringing about the socialist revolution. "Look around you and heed the lessons of history," it said. "History shows us that the privileged classes have almost never yet given up their privileges without being compelled to do so by force." This, however, was as far as the convention was willing to go, for a statement of historical prophecy and the actual use of force were two different things. "We do not share the folly of men who consider dynamite bombs the best means of agitation," said the manifesto. "We know full well that a revolution must occur in the minds and in the

industrial life of men before the working class can achieve
enduring success." Warning was also voiced against efforts
to effect a common front with Johann Most and the anarchists.
Most, they held, was "a demagogue who in his agitational efforts only had an eye for making money."[56]

The two years between 1884 and 1886 constituted a drab yet
on the whole recuperative period for the Socialistic Labor Party.
The depression that began in 1883 had the usual effect of sending new members into the party, and though still dwarfed by
the Internationals, it tripled its membership and doubled the
number of its sections.[57] Another indication of vigor was the
addition of many new journals and newspapers, and the publication of dozens of pamphlets, a large number of them by the
John W. Lovell Company of New York City. Among the new
magazines was an official German-language weekly, *Der Sozialist*, edited first by Joseph Dietzgen and subsequently by W. L.
Rosenberg. Dietzgen, who had been known in Germany as "the
philosopher of social democracy," had been editor of the Chicago
Arbeiter-Zeitung.[58] Rosenberg, a man of academic inclination
and training, had been associated with Dietzgen on the same
paper.[59] He was also to occupy the restored office of national
secretary of the Socialistic Labor Party, as the socialists were
soon to discover that the decentralized plan of organization
adopted at Baltimore was impractical. For several years the
SLP leadership bewailed the absence of an official English-
language publication, but this matter was finally resolved in
November, 1886, when the New Haven labor paper, the *Workmen's Advocate*, edited by J. F. Busche, was adopted as a party
journal.[60]

The middle eighties also saw the emergence to prominence in
the party councils of a New York City group associated with
the daily newspaper, *New Yorker Volkszeitung*. The paper was
now under the joint editorship of Alexander Jonas, who had
been with it since its founding in 1878, and Serge Schevitsch.

[56]*Ibid.*, p. 229.
[57]*Ibid.*, p. 254.
[58]*Ibid.*, p. 255.
[59]*Ibid.*, p. 267.
[60]*Workmen's Advocate*, Nov. 21, 1886.

Jonas, a native Berliner with a pleasing un-Prussian sense of humor, was an able Marxist theoretician and journalist. Schevitsch, handsome and versatile, lent the young American socialist movement a certain amount of glamor, since he was an exiled Russian nobleman and the husband of Helena von Racowitza, the beautiful countess for whom Ferdinand Lassalle had fought his famous and fatal duel.[61]

In 1884 the importance of the *Volkszeitung* group within the Socialistic Labor Party was indicated by the removal of the National Executive Committee to New York City. It was also demonstrated when Jonas and three other members of the party's editorial staff toured the country to combat the influence of the anarchists.[62] At the same time, the *Volkszeitung* lecturers, who had the official approval of the party, reiterated time and again the futility of socialist politics and stressed, conversely, the necessity of "boring from within" the labor unions. They singled out in particular the recently organized Federation of Organized Trades and Labor Unions and especially the Knights of Labor, which at this very time was experiencing a tremendous increase in membership.

Socialist infiltration into the labor movement, however, was blocked at almost every turn, and only in New York City, where there were several completely German unions, was there any real evidence of success.[63] Few trade-union officials wanted any close association with the socialists, though at times there was a tendency to take over, without acknowledgment, the latter's critique of capitalism. Many prominent members of the Federation of Organized Trades and Labor Unions were former Marxists who had become dissatisfied with the inability of the socialist program to achieve concrete gains for the average wage earner. Well versed in the technique of "boring from within," they maintained a close vigil against the socialists. Within the Knights, the socialists, although quite frequently a disruptive element, were hardly more successful.[64] The leaders of the

---

[61]Morris Hillquit, *Loose Leaves from a Busy Life* (New York, 1934), pp. 41-44.

[62]Sartorius von Waltershausen, p. 255.

[63]*Ibid.*, p. 264.

[64]Norman Ware, *The Labor Movement in the United States, 1860-1895* (New York, 1929), pp. 104-12, 184-85, 222-23.

Knights, much further removed from Marxism than those of the Federation, followed a strictly American brand of radicalism. Bypassing socialism and the class struggle, their program called for such traditional remedies as additional free homesteads, cheap money, shorter working hours, producers' co-operatives, and legislation against "the money power." The almost amorphous character of the Knights, rather than sophistication of its leaders in Marxist technique, made socialist penetration here extremely difficult. The mass of Knights, two European socialist observers agreed, "knew no more of the teachings of socialism" than they did of "their own supposed principles."[65]

Yet, increasing protests from a widening group of social reformers, akin to the Knights in spirit, against the growth of industrial monopoly, actually aided the socialist agitators. American industrialism, which was to sweep to world-wide leadership in the next decade, was already in high gear, and large-scale, nation-wide organization had become its distinguishing characteristic. Out of the intense competition in the markets, the trusts had already begun to emerge. This tendency was early and effectively analyzed by the Fabian socialist Henry Demarest Lloyd, one of the first of that peculiar variety of American reformers known as "muckrakers." In a widely read article published in 1884, he contended that competition had been stifled by pools, trusts, or pricing agreements in such industries as lumbering, slaughtering, packing, bituminous coal mining, and in the manufacture of stoves, matches, nails, wall paper, burial vaults, crackers, pig iron, barbed wire, southern textiles, and whiskies. In addition, Lloyd claimed that there were well-established monopolies in anthracite coal mining and in petroleum refining.[66]

Ever alert to social protests from outside their own ranks, the Socialist Laborites at their 1885 national convention in Cincinnati sought to fashion their program so that it would appeal to anti-monopolists. The monopoly system, read a plank in the SLP platform, "runs counter to the interest of humanity, to the

---

[65]Edward Aveling and Eleanor Marx Aveling, *The Working Class Movement in America* (London, 1890), p. 139.

[66]Lloyd, "Lords of Industry," *North American Review,* CXXXVIII (1884), 535-53.

principles of justice, and to true democracy; it destroys those values to which, according to the text of the Declaration of Independence, every man has an inalienable right, namely, life, liberty, and the pursuit of happiness."[67] A few years later, in 1887, when the prospects of socialist success appeared not only better but more immediate, the SLP opportunistically changed its platform to read:

> This system . . . carries within itself the germs of a new organization of humanity in the modern industrial states both economically and morally. By the evolution of this system to its highest pitch, the dispossessed working masses will at last become opposed to a comparatively few despotic chiefs of industry, and by reason of the unbearable uncertainty of existence, the former will find themselves compelled to abolish the wage system and establish the co-operative society.[68]

In the same year that Lloyd was calling attention to the "trustification of American industry," the Boston firm of Lee and Shepard published Laurence Gronlund's *The Co-operative Commonwealth*. This was no ordinary book, since it was the first attempt by an American socialist to write in English a comprehensive yet simplified analysis of Marxism for the man in the street. Gronlund's exposition of "German socialism" was faithful to orthodox dogma except on one important point' an ethical idealist, he refused to accept the class-struggle thesis. The Danish-born author, who was also an attorney, teacher, and lecturer, could not lower himself to vindictiveness against persons "who are from circumstances what they are."[69] In this respect Gronlund, who had emigrated to the United States in 1867, placed himself squarely in the main stream of American tradition.

With characteristic Marxian thoroughness Gronlund examined the American social and economic scene against the background of *Das Kapital*. He asserted that the tendency toward industrial concentration and combination, everywhere apparent in the United States, was a confirmation of Marx's analysis of

---

[67]Sartorius von Waltershausen, p. 259.

[68]*Report of the Proceedings of the 6th National Convention of the Socialistic Labor Party, Buffalo, N. Y., Sept. 17-21, 1887*, p. 14.

[69]*The Co-operative Commonwealth* (Boston, 1884), p. 9.

the development of modern capitalism. In a capitalistic economy, he maintained, the very idea of competion was fraudulent, since those persons who exerted most influence over industrial production were intent on controlling or capturing the market for themselves. "These gentlemen," said Gronlund, "have already found that while Competition is a very excellent weapon against their weaker rivals, Combination pays far better in relation to their peers. It is evident, that it is combination they mainly rely upon for their future aggrandizement."[70]

Gronlund contended that only social anarchy could result from continuing the existing planless system of American private enterprise, which was plainly gravitating toward the complete control of the instruments of production by a relatively small but powerful plutocracy. The new industrial capitalism was producing a group of "parasites and vampires." It was destroying, if indeed it had not already destroyed, "the patriarchal, idyllic relations" formerly existing among men, leaving in their place only one bond—"cash payment." Human dignity had been replaced by "exchange value" and freedom had given way to license. The physician, the jurist, the poet, and the scientist had become nothing more than the retainers of plutocracy.[71]

Gronlund rejected popular "remedies" offered to improve both the operation of the capitalistic system and the lot of the workers under it. All efforts on the part of American producers to obtain new foreign markets would inevitably bring them into conflict with European competitors. To meet such competition the producers would not hesitate to lower the wages of their workers. Thus, no solution existed in widening the market for the products of American factories. Profit-sharing and co-operation also failed to provide an answer to the problem of a more equitable distribution of wealth. Profit-sharing meant that workers would compete against each other. Co-operation offered no panacea because few groups of workers could amass sufficient capital to compete with established corporations. An increase in the amount of circulating currency, said Gronlund, taking note of the Greenback movement, would be

---

[70]*Ibid.*, p. 48.
[71]*Ibid.*, p. 53.

of no help to the worker because any increase that might be forthcoming in wages would be more than compensated for by a rise in prices. Trade unionism was admittedly a necessity for the wage-earner class, but the labor movement in its present stage of development was far too weak to take a determined stand against the plutocracy. The eight-hour-day remedy was at best wishful thinking. Eight-hour-day statutes, when passed, had proved to be "dead letters" because of willful lack of enforcement by capitalist-controlled governments.[72]

Socialism, proclaimed Gronlund, was the only solution to the workingman, whose decreasing real wages gave him an ever more limited share of the social product. And socialism was coming, because capitalism and the established order which it supported were destined to fall to pieces by their own weight. When the culmination of capitalism's decay was reached, "the reins" would drop "from the impotent hands of our autocrats" and be taken up "by an impersonal Power, coeval with human nature: The STATE" or "organized society."[73]

The Co-operative Commonwealth was by no means a record-breaking best-seller. There is little evidence to suggest that it was widely read outside socialist circles at the time of its publication. But it was an important work if for no other reason than that it made a deep and lasting impression on the mind of Edward Bellamy, who incorporated much of its socialist message into his own more famous utopian novel, *Looking Backward*, which appeared in 1887. Indeed, it was only after *Looking Backward*'s sensational success that *The Co-operative Commonwealth* began to have a more catholic reading, and this in spite of the fact that Gronlund ordered its sale halted in order to push the sale of Bellamy's book.[74]

The year 1886 was an important one for the socialist movement in the United States. During that year Wilhelm Liebknecht, Eleanor Marx Aveling, and her English husband, Dr. Edward Aveling, toured the country under the auspices of the Socialistic Labor Party; the Haymarket Affair in Chicago brought American radicalism to a crossroads; and Henry

[72]*Ibid.*, pp. 62-70.
[73]*Ibid.*, pp. 76-77.
[74]Arthur E. Morgan, *Edward Bellamy* (New York, 1944), p. 389.

George, with enthusiastic socialist backing, made his great bid for the mayoralty of New York.

Liebknecht was the veteran and beloved leader of the German social democratic movement and Eleanor Aveling was the daughter of Karl Marx. To the throng of socialists who greeted them at Brommers Park in New York City on Sunday, September 19, 1886—estimated by the *Workmen's Advocate* at 25,000 and by the *New York Times* at 3,000—Liebknecht declared: "The German social democracy would not have granted me this furlough were they not convinced of the importance of the movement here for the future of labor." Aveling, a clean-shaven, blue-eyed young man, with brown hair hanging loosely down his neck, spoke in a similar vein and predicted the ultimate triumph of socialism in the United States. Mrs. Aveling, whom the *New York Times* reporter described as generously built, rosy cheeked, and good-natured, but with a "bump of self-esteem," did not speak but promised to do her part at subsequent meetings. Like Liebknecht and her husband, she was cheered by the crowd which waved little red flags.[75]

Wherever the three visitors went, they were warmly greeted by socialist groups. The Avelings wrote a series of articles for the *Workmen's Advocate* on conditions of life in the United States. Many of these were later revised and incorporated into their book, *The Working Class Movement in America*. The condition of American laborers they found comparable to that of English wage earners in the 1840's.[76] Particularly was Mrs. Aveling appalled by the extent of woman and child labor in the United States. American factory girls, she believed, appeared more worn-looking than their English counterparts. "As to the children," she wrote, "I cannot trust myself to speak of them."[77] Yet there was considerable hope for the American worker who "had the benefit of forty years' experience of his European brethren to teach him." And since in the United States it took but ten months to do what in Europe required ten years,[78] the present debility of American socialism offered a challenge to American radicals rather than a cause for despair.

[75]*Workmen's Advocate,* Sept. 26, 1886; *New York Times,* Sept. 20, 1886.
[76]Edward and Eleanor Aveling, p. 25.
[77]*Workmen's Advocate,* Nov. 7, 1886.
[78]Edward and Eleanor Aveling, p. 25.

Liebknecht returned to Germany with socialist hosannahs ringing in his ears, but the Aveling tour ended on a sour note. While the Socialistic Labor Party's National Executive Committee was impressed with Aveling's proletarian eloquence, it was less happily disposed toward his bourgeois expense accounts, which it had committed itself to pay. The Committee found the very first bill "too exorbitant,"[79] and from then on there were complaints and recriminations between the SLP directors and the visiting English scientist, who strongly denied any propensity toward "luxurious living."

The matter was brought into the open when party secretary W. L. Rosenberg dispatched a letter to all of the SLP sections on February 26, 1887, calling on them to pass resolutions of censure against Aveling. From London, where he had returned, Aveling promptly sent to the same sections a handsomely printed letter criticizing the action of the National Executive Committee. "This is an attempt to snatch a verdict based on a one-sided representation of the facts of the case, a verdict with regard to which the accused is placed in a position where it is virtually impossible to defend himself," he said. "If this is the kind of judicial procedure to be introduced into the Socialistic Labor Party, I, for my part, should ask to be tried before a Chicago jury."[80]

The 1887 national convention of the SLP upheld the party Executive Committee, though a reminder was served on the latter to be more careful in the future in making arrangements with visiting agitators so "as to avoid cases like this."[81] The unfortunate conclusion of the Aveling tour did not, however, lessen its propaganda value nor strain in any appreciable respect the ties between the American and European socialist organizations.

The guilt of those who were tried and convicted of throwing the fatal bomb on the night of May 4, 1886, in Chicago's Haymarket Square, during the course of a strike against the Mc-

[79]*Report of the Proceedings of the 6th National Convention of the Socialistic Labor Party, 1887*, p. 21

[80]Joseph A. Labadie Labor Collection, General Library, University of Michigan, Ann Arbor, Mich.

[81]*Report of the Proceedings of the 6th National Convention of the Socialistic Labor Party, 1887*, p. 21.

Cormick Harvester Company, has never been satisfactorily established. Suffice it to say, the inflammatory utterances and appeals to force by Chicago social revolutionaries and anarchists, both in the five years preceding the affair and during the course of the strike itself, were enough to associate them with the deed in the public mind. Four anarchists, August Spies, Albert R. Parsons, George Engel, and Adolph Fischer, paid with their lives on the gallows on November 11, 1887, after a trial which cast considerable doubt on the character and processes of American justice. Louis Lingg, also sentenced to die, cheated the hangman by committing suicide in his jail cell. Michael Schwab and Samuel Fielden escaped the noose by having their sentences commuted to life imprisonment upon an appeal for executive clemency. Still another anarchist, Oscar W. Neebe, received a fifteen year prison term. Schwab, Fielden, and Neebe were to be pardoned six years later by the courageous Governor John Peter Altgeld.

Apparently, the Haymarket bomb itself killed only one man —police captain Mathias J. Degan—though several policemen and workers were slain and wounded in the melee and the wild and indiscriminate shooting that ensued. Yet the whole affair, according to its most able historian, brought about "the first major 'red-scare' in American history, and produced a campaign of 'red-baiting' which has rarely been equalled."[82] The socialists, usually lumped together with the anarchists despite their mutual and intense antagonisms, were targets for attacks by editors, politicians, and professional patriots. More than one newspaper referred to the bomb throwing as "socialist" inspired.[83]

The Socialistic Labor Party, well aware of the propensity to assign guilt by association, practiced discretion during the first burst of anti-radical hysteria and then throughout the trial. However, as the day of execution approached, the party press took a more forthright stand in behalf of the doomed anarchists. The SLP national convention in September, 1887, adopted the following resolution which, among other things, pointed up the

---

[82]David, p. 528.
[83]*Ibid.*, pp. 206-18.

knotty and persistent legal problem of distinguishing advocacy
from positive action:

> The Congress of the Socialistic Labor Party assembled
> at Buffalo, although neither agreeing with the tactics nor
> the principles of the anarchists, nevertheless declares the
> confirmation of the judgment against the eight Chicago
> anarchists to be unjust, to be dictated by prejudice and
> class hatred, and to be an act of class justice.
>
> It was generally admitted that none of the condemned
> men threw the bomb, and our conception of right and jus-
> tice is not so developed, as that we could find any connec-
> tion between the teachings of one individual and the acts
> of an unknown person, for it is a fact that even to-day
> nobody knows who threw the bomb.
>
> We cannot understand how it is possible to know the
> motives of an unknown person.
>
> The meeting at which the bomb was thrown was, accord-
> ing to the evidence, a peaceable one, and would have ended
> peaceably, if the police had not illegally interfered to dis-
> perse the meeting.
>
> We therefore declare that the decision is an attack upon
> free speech, and the right of the people to freely assemble,
> and that its execution would be judicial murder.[84]

The party's official English-language newspaper greeted the
news of the execution of the anarchists with the following blaz-
ing headline:

FOULEST MURDER—BRAVE MEN DIE BRAVELY
FOR LABOR'S CAUSE — THE LYING PUBLIC
PRESS ADDS INSULT TO INJURY—ONE WRONG
BEGETS ANOTHER — LOATHSOME HYPOCRISY
OF MODERN SOCIETY—NOT ENDED.

The news story that followed, as was characteristic of the socialist press, was written essentially as an editorial. It held that
the deceased anarchists, being sane in mind, had no intention
of destroying society or of indulging in murder and rapine.
"Quite on the contrary . . . they had murderers and thieves opposed to them." Their crime lay in denouncing a social system
which allowed "cold blooded robbery of laborers, men, women

---

[84]*Report of the Proceedings of the 6th National Convention of the Socialistic Labor Party, 1887,* pp. 16-17.

and children; a system that drives young girls to prostitution and young men to vice."[85]

The immediate effects of the Haymarket Affair upon the Socialistic Labor Party are not easy to gauge. There is little evidence that the party suffered any loss of membership as a result of generally adverse public opinion. It is not improbable that many supporters of the Red and Black Internationals, both of which were to disintegrate rapidly after 1886, came over to the more moderate SLP. The Haymarket incident undoubtedly helped to kindle interest in radical doctrines,[86] a condition that was to the advantage of the socialists, whose greatest agitational difficulty was public apathy and ignorance. And it must be remembered that the socialists played a leading role in the famous New York 1886 mayoralty election which saw Henry George nearly upsetting a Tammany–G. O. P. election pattern of many years standing.

As of 1886 the Socialistic Labor Party had been in existence for nearly a dozen stormy years without having made any appreciable headway or having achieved any notable successes. The frequent see-sawing on the question of tactics produced constant irritation and dissension and had the effect of alienating from the party many who sincerely believed in the desirability of the co-operative commonwealth. The party's membership consisted predominantly of German immigrants and, more often than not, meetings on both the national and local levels were conducted in the German language. Convention proceedings were invariably written in German rather than in English,—a condition that was greatly deplored by both Marx and Engels. The latter wrote to Sorge that the most salutary thing that could happen to the socialist movement in the United States would be the disappearance of the belligerent, uncompromising, and unrealistic "alte Genossen" Germans who so completely dominated it.[87] Admittedly, there was an ever-present realization on the part of the leaders of the necessity of "Americanizing" the movement. But efforts to attract native-born workers and

---

[85]*Workmen's Advocate,* Nov. 19, 1887.

[86]David, p. 531.

[87]Karl Marx and Frederick Engels, *Selected Correspondence, 1846-1895* (New York, 1942), p. 467. Also see pp. 464, 502.

members of the middle class were conspicuously unsuccessful. The unwillingness of middle-class reformers in particular to succumb to the socialists' loving embrace was clearly seen in the matrix of events both during and after the New York 1886 mayoralty campaign.

II. Failure of Boring from Within

DURING the seven years between 1887 and 1894 the socialists faced two crucial tests which, if hurdled successfully, could assure them an important and positive role in the American labor movement. The first involved maintaining a position of influence in New York City's United Labor Party which had sponsored Henry George's candidacy in the 1886 municipal elections. The second concerned the much more ambitious effort to commit the American Federation of Labor to a full-fledged endorsement of government ownership of the means of production and distribution. The decisive points in both tests came at times that were undeniably propitious. The question of the socialists' status within the United Labor Party was decided in 1887, when organized workers were still reacting to a series of disasters suffered by the labor movement during the previous year. The high point in the all-out struggle to win the American Federation of Labor to the co-operative commonwealth came in the midst of the deepening depression that followed the panic of 1893.

Henry George's bid for the New York mayoralty, a well-chronicled milepost in the history of American social protest, was an event of no little importance for American socialism. The "prophet of San Francisco," as the Duke of Argyll had contemptuously dubbed the earnest and righteous George, had the complete backing of the city's small but aggressive group of socialists. Indeed, the latter had helped to create the ground-swell of wage-earner discontent out of which his candidacy had developed. It was the socialists, more than any other group, who had urged upon the city's Central Labor Union in 1886 the creation of an independent workingmen's party.

The formal founding of the United Labor Party, as was true four years earlier of the Central Labor Union itself, was largely engineered by Socialist Labor Party[1] leaders who, significantly, were accepted as accredited delegates at the organizational meetings.[2] The socialists did not obtain high executive positions in the new party. Nor did they infuse their principles into its platform to any appreciable extent. Yet, on the whole, they were satisfied with the progress made.

In seeking a mayoralty candidate the United Labor Party settled on Henry George, who had taken up residence in New York. George's reputation was already firmly established by his fervent and messianic treatise in political economy, *Progress and Poverty*, published in 1879. His economic doctrines were conditioned by what he had observed on the still raw frontier that was California in the 1860's and 1870's and by what he had read in the works of the British classical economists. He was also under tremendous indebtedness to Thomas Jefferson and Herbert Spencer. From the great Virginian he received inspiration for a society in which all men would have the opportunity for self-development and advancement. From Spencer, the Victorian apostle of laissez faire and the "synthetic philosophy," George gained sanction for his belief that all men had a natural right to the use of land. Like Gronlund, George rejected as inadequate the leading proposals of the day aimed at achieving a more equitable distribution of wealth. Unlike Gronlund, he included socialism among them.

Enough truth existed in the Marxist critique of modern society to allow George, at the time that he wrote *Progress and Poverty*, to take an open minded, if not necessarily sympathetic, view of socialism's "grand and ideal" objectives.[3] Insofar as the latter stood for the dignity of the individual, human brotherhood, and international comity, he gave it his hearty approval. And in agreement with the socialists, he acknowledged that the

---

[1] This change in name appears for the first time in the Dec. 17, 1887, issue of the *Workmen's Advocate*. It was not authorized at the party's convention of that year, when a long discussion was held on the feasibility of changing the party name.

[2] *Workmen's Advocate*, July 25 and Aug. 8, 1886. On origins of the Central Labor Union, see Peter A. Speek, "The Single Tax and the Labor Movement," *Bulletin of the University of Wisconsin, Economics and Political Science Series*, Vol. VIII, No. 3 (Madison, 1917), pp. 24-26; John R. Commons (ed.), *History of Labour in the United States*, II, 441-44.

[3] *Progress and Poverty* (San Francisco, 1879), pp. 269-94.

growth of monopoly necessitated increased state functions. But he feared a society in which the competitive principle would cease to be a primary motivating factor. He wanted no man to be beholden to the state for preferment. As a true son of the eighteenth-century enlightenment and as a believer in man's intrinsic goodness, he could not countenance the class-struggle doctrine which reduced human relations to the laws of the jungle. He saw socialism creating a leviathan state which would not only dwarf man but also lower him to the dead level of mediocrity. Whatever good existed in socialism could be realized more effectively, George maintained, by the far more simple and less disrupting process of land taxation.

George's inquiries into the realm of political economy, undertaken at a time when the nation groaned under the first of the major post-Civil War industrial crises, were prompted by a burning determination to discover why both wealth and poverty increased concomitantly in a civilization capable of accommodating basic human wants and needs. His answer to this age-old paradox in its simplest terms was the monopolization of land. In *Progress and Poverty* he analyzed the process by which the best lands of the nation had been pre-empted, before the wave of settlement, by speculators and monopolists who sold or rented them at huge profits to themselves.[4] As the land increased in value because of the influx of people and the erection of a civilization upon it, the poverty of the actual users grew, since the owners kept the rent—i.e., unearned increment—for themselves. High rents, which the owners could charge because of their monopolistic position, had the effect of decreasing wages on the one hand and profits on the other. Thus, while possessors of land waxed ever richer, those having to pay for the privilege of using it received a correspondingly smaller proportion of the returns of production. Civilization and poverty, hence, advanced side by side.[5]

To destroy land monopoly and to give producers their rightful share of the wealth—and here George mutualized the interests of the entrepreneur and wage earner—he advocated expropriation of all rent by taxation, a method which would in effect,

---

[4]*Ibid.*, pp. 346-54.
[5]*Ibid.*, pp. 305-7.

if not in actual title, socialize land and return to the people their collective birthright. Such a tax would stimulate industry, since producers could now use money paid out in rent for new enterprises. The workingman would benefit, too, by the increase in production. Also, it would have the effect of decreasing, if not eliminating, other forms of taxation. The beauty of George's solution of the problem of poverty amidst plenty was that it was as simple as it was fundamental.[6]

George's candidacy was satisfactory both to himself and the labor party leaders. Politically ambitious, George would have an opportunity to test his strength with the assurance that 30,000 pledged labor votes would protect him from an ignominious defeat. Also, he could use the campaign to publicize his social and economic gospel, which, as he was well aware, had its greatest attraction for persons living in urban communities like New York. On the other hand, the labor party had in George a man with an established international reputation. He was renowned as a champion of the economically less privileged, a humanitarian, and an advocate of political honesty and civic righteousness. Particularly was he popular with the powerful bloc of Irish voters, since his criticism of land monopoly drove directly to the root of Ireland's economic difficulties. Though George was not a member of the working class, he was, and always had been, an outstanding defender of labor unions. He could attract wage-earner support, furthermore, by his strong indictment of monopoly. Middle-class reformers could flock to his banner because his solution to industrial ills by-passed radical collectivism, while socialists could tolerate him because they were willing to accept land nationalization as the first step along the road to the co-operative commonwealth. Even though Marx himself had once described George's ideas as "utterly backward," the New York socialists turned a deaf ear upon the pontification of the master.

If some socialists desired that the new labor party had nominated some one other than George, there was no evidence of it in the party press. The *Volkszeitung* vigorously supported his campaign. The *Workmen's Advocate* called his nomination a

---

[6]*Ibid.*, pp. 362-66.

"preliminary warning to land thieves."[7]   Socialist agitators
were out day and night speaking on street corners in his behalf.
The "prophet" could not complain of lack of co-operation from
the socialists.   There was, if anything, too much of it for his
more conservative followers.

In agreeing to become the candidate of the United Labor
Party—the official name of the new organization—George also
undertook to rewrite its platform.   By this simple procedure
the party's character was subtly and substantially changed. Not
surprisingly, he advanced his taxation plan to the fore, though
at this time it was not named, or presented as, "the single tax."
The labor demands were bunched together into one of the platform's seven planks.   To cater to both the anti-monopolists and
the socialists, government ownership of railroads and telegraphs was espoused.   And to appeal to the politically upright,
greater honesty in government was demanded.[8]   On the whole,
the United Labor Party platform was quite moderate in the
character of its demands, but it was enough to raise the fears
of the conservative and property-owning elements and also the
hierarchy of the Catholic Church.

It is a political truism that mayoralty contests, even in the
larger urban communities, are not distinguished by the high
calibre of the candidates.   The 1886 New York election was
a conspicuous exception.   George's opponents were the millionaire iron manufacturer, Abram S. Hewitt, Democrat, and a
young, conservative, Harvard-educated gentleman and cow-
puncher, Theodore Roosevelt, Republican.   This was one race
in which Roosevelt found himself completely overshadowed, a
condition hardly flattering to his already well-developed ego.
Hewitt and George were the two real antagonists in the campaign, with the former fighting "to save society" and the latter
to make the social order more equitable.

The election vote, tabulated in round numbers, gave Hewitt
90,000; George, 67,000; and Roosevelt, 60,000.   New York elections were not famed for their pristine purity and honesty, and

---

[7]*Workmen's Advocate*, Sept. 12, 1886.

[8]Louis F. Post and Frederic C. Leubuscher, *An Account of the George-
Hewitt Campaign in the New York Municipal Election of 1886* (New York,
1887), pp. 12-15.

this particular one was in all probability even more malodorous than others. The Tammany machine, faced by a serious challenge to its traditional ties with the working class and the Irish bloc, operated with efficiency and dispatch at the polling places and in the purchase of doubtful votes. Rumor had it that thousands of George ballots found a watery grave at the bottom of East River. But the principal cause for George's defeat— and there should be no mistake about it—was the opposition of the Catholic Church which, according to its spokesman, the Right Reverend Monsignor Thomas S. Preston, Vicar-General, never interfered directly in elections except when "the best interests of society" stood in danger. Such a peril apparently existed in 1886, for the Vicar-General on October 25, in answer to an inquiry from a Tammany Hall leader, wrote:

> The great majority of the Catholic clergy in this city are opposed to the candidacy of Mr. George. They think his principles unsound and unsafe, and contrary to the teachings of the church. I have not met one among the priests of this archdiocese who would not deeply regret the election of Mr. George to any position of influence. His principles, logically carried out, would prove the ruin of the workingman he professes to befriend.[9]

The Right Reverend Preston's letter was reprinted and widely circulated by Democratic Party henchmen to Catholic parishioners as they left their churches the following Sunday. It tended to offset the ardent support given to George during the campaign by the "single tax priest," Father Edward McGlynn.[10] Many George partisans, particularly among the Irish, sorrowfully but obediently felt obliged to desert his standard.

The 67,000 United Labor Party votes that had been polled and counted, sweetened the bitterness of defeat for the socialists and for George. It was an impressive total, considering that the party was making its maiden political effort with an inexperienced and undeveloped organization, a meager treasury, and a hostile press. It brought to light a sharpening public awareness of the social dislocations and abuses caused by the new post-war industrial capitalism. Even conservative men of af-

[9]*Ibid.*, p. 133.

[10]*Ibid.*, pp. 129-32; Henry George, Jr., *The Life of Henry George* (New York, 1900), pp. 465-66.

fairs were alarmed at the calloused and grasping behavior of the new industrial magnates. "Those 67,000 votes," said the *Workmen's Advocate*, "are a standing menace to the monstrous capitalistic system which not only robs labor but corrupts laborers."[11] George himself looked upon the campaign as only the beginning for bigger things to come. All over the country local "union" or "united" labor parties were being organized. George set his sights on the presidential election only two years off.

The first problem was to weld the United Labor Party into a permanent organization and to eliminate from its ranks those elements which might prove a cause for embarrassment in the future. The party could not cater to the group for which *Progress and Poverty* was written—the middle class and the skilled wage earners—and at the same time permit the socialists to use it for their own devices. George peered into the future and saw the socialists striking for party control as soon as the ULP was in a position to win political power. Consequently, the anti-religious, materialistic Marxists, with their foreign doctrines and accents, figured high on the list of those to be weeded out of the party.

The socialists held their peace for several months, though dissatisfaction was expressed with the re-affirmation of George's 1886 election platform at a county meeting of the party on January 13, 1887. The *Workmen's Advocate* complained of its concentration on the land and currency problems. While "great things" had been expected, said the paper's New York correspondent, all that had resulted were "hackneyed platitudes" and "labor chestnuts."[12] A week later the party adopted new resolutions from platform chairman Daniel DeLeon which made concessions to the socialists and trade unionists. These characterized the existing economic system as "perverse" and as robbing "the producer of a large share of the fruits of his labor."[13]

During the campaign the hostility of the non-socialist press obliged the Central Labor Union and a few individual unions to found a newspaper of their own, *The Leader*, in order to

---

[11]Nov. 7, 1886.

[12]Jan. 22, 1887.

[13]Speek, *Bulletin of the University of Wisconsin, Economics and Political Science Series*, Vol. VIII, No. 3, p. 95.

give George's views a hearing and a fair presentation before
the public. The paper's editor was Louis F. Post, a onetime
carpetbagger in South Carolina, an attorney, and an experienced
journalist. George had no direct association with it and apparently wanted none.[14] He was anxious, however, to have his
own paper, particularly in order to pursue his quarrel with
Archbishop Corrigan, who had cracked the lash of ecclesiastical
authority on the unbending back of Father McGlynn.[15] As a
consequence, George founded *The Standard* on January 8, 1887,
and became its editor-in-chief.

This development coincided with the capture of the *Leader*
by the socialists, though not a result of it. Early in January
the socialists succeeded in getting control of the paper at a stockholders' meeting and appointed Serge Schevitsch to succeed
Post as editor.[16] The latter immediately went over to the
Standard in the capacity of associate editor. For two or three
months the two papers co-existed as official party organs without overt evidence of hostility. But beneath the calm on the
surface, ripples of tension were developing between the socialists and the single taxers. The former took decided exception
to the efforts of the middle-class single-tax element to drop the
term "labor" from the party name and to minimize the wage-
earner demands in the platform.[17] Late in June the *Leader*
editorially praised Laurence Gronlund's sharp attack on the
single tax in his little pamphlet, *The Insufficiency of Henry
George's Theory*. The *Standard* did not answer Gronlund's criticism.[18] But rumor became rife that the single-tax element
would attempt to drive the socialists out of the United Labor
Party at its state convention in August.

In early August most socialists in the New York area were
still disposed to believe they could work harmoniously with
George.[19] But the disquieting rumor and the call for the state

[14]*Leader,* Dec. 10, 1886.

[15]*Standard,* Feb. 5, 1887; Speek, *Bulletin of the University of Wisconsin,
Economics and Political Science Series,* Vol. VIII, No. 3, pp. 101-3; Henry
George, Jr., *Henry George,* pp. 486-96.

[16]Speek, *Bulletin of the University of Wisconsin, Economics and Political
Science Series,* Vol. VIII, No. 3, pp. 98-99.

[17]*Ibid,* pp. 104-6.

[18]*Workmen's Advocate,* Aug. 6, 1887.

[19]*Ibid.*

convention were bad omens. The convention summons, written by George himself, mentioned only three principal issues to be placed upon the agenda: taxation of land values, currency reform, and government ownership of railroads and telegraphs.[20] The apparent jettisoning of all labor demands led the socialists to presume, with good reason, that George and the single taxers were seeking to complete the transformation of the ULP from a militant wage-earner organization suitable for socialist propaganda purposes into a vapid middle-class reform party.

The socialists worked feverishly to solidify their position within the United Labor Party in view of the coming convention and the crisis it gave promise of producing. On July 24 the county executive committee accepted unanimously a socialist resolution which held that affiliation with the Socialist Labor Party did not disqualify one for membership in the United Labor Party.[21] The committee accepted the socialist contention that the SLP was not a political party within the accepted meaning of the term, since its participation in elections was solely for propaganda purposes. It was also pointed out that members of the Socialist Labor Party had been accepted as accredited by the Central Labor Union. Furthermore, it was noted that when the United Labor Party was first formed, the SLP's unique character was specifically recognized.

Fortified with this ruling, the socialists proceeded to campaign for the election of their partisans to the various delegations to the party convention. Rumor was now bruited that the socialists were on the verge of capturing the United Labor Party just as they had gained control of the *Leader*. Schevitsch sought in vain to squelch such reports. He termed them "malicious" and "ludicrous." "It is but natural that in voting for delegates to the Syracuse Convention they [socialists] should select men holding the same views as they do on social and economic questions," said Schevitsch. "But these men have not the slightest intention of 'capturing' anything or 'sitting down' on anybody."[22]

---

[20]*Leader*, May 5, 1887.
[21]*Ibid.*, Aug. 5, 1887.
[22]*Ibid.*, July 28, 1887.

The aggressive actions of the socialists coupled with increasingly harsh criticism of the single tax brought a bristling reaction from George and his intimate associates. George declared publicly that one of the principal tasks of the coming state convention was to define the party's stand with respect to "the State or German socialists" who were seeking to force their own "peculiar views" on the United Labor Party. Evading the issue would afford the party's enemies a "specious pretext" to smear it with the brush of socialism.[23] He insisted that the party had no place for those who maintained that the "burning social question" was not a land tax but rather "the abolition of all private property in the instruments of production."[24] "The truth is," said George, "that state socialism, with its childish notions of making all capital the common property of the state . . . is an exotic, born of European conditions that cannot flourish on American soil."

Implementing George's verbal condemnation of the socialists was the action taken by county general committee chairman John McMackin. At the committee's meeting of August 5, McMackin reversed the decision of the county executive committee, to which he himself had acceded, and now ruled that membership in the Socialist Labor Party constituted disqualification for eligibility in the United Labor Party.

McMackin's decision fell like a bombshell. Civil turmoil broke out openly in the United Labor Party ranks. The *Workmen's Advocate* condemned the act of "Black Thursday" and declared that George, "attacked by egotistical insanity" and "drunk with fulsome praise and unstinted worship," was seeking to sack the socialists in the hope of insuring his own political success and that of the "Tammany heelers" who surrounded him. In similar vein an editorial in the same issue remarked that the socialists were indeed lucky to have had the "weakness of the 'new prophet' so early demonstrated."[25] The *Volkszeitung*,

---

[23]*Ibid.*, Aug. 4, 1887.

[24]*Standard*, Aug. 13, 1887.

[25]Aug. 13, 1887. The national executive committee of the SLP issued an appeal in pamphlet form to "all trade unions, socialists, and members of the Socialistic Labor Party." It pointed out that the socialists were the true founders of the ULP and claimed that they had gathered workingmen "routed and cowed by the Chicago bomb and the New York boycott decisions" into a party that could defy "the overbearing insolence of the possessing class."

more circumspect in its utterances, regretted that George had not seen fit to confer with leaders of the Socialist Labor Party to define the relationship between it and the United Labor Party. The German daily still expressed willingness to support George on the basis of the 1886 mayoralty campaign platform. It denied any desire on the part of the socialists to impress their views on the United Labor Party.[26] Much the same position was taken by Schevitsch in the *Leader*. He suggested that the United Labor Party leaders accept on its own weight and merit the statement of the SLP that it was not a political organization in the sense of a bona fide labor party.[27]

In reality, the fate of the socialists within the United Labor Party was settled before the Syracuse Convention was called to order on August 17 at Alhambra Hall. If George was determined on nothing else he was resolved to rid the party then and there of the socialists. He was convinced that he could recoup any losses in party strength suffered among New York City workingmen from new adherents among the farmers and wage earners of the smaller upstate cities. The single-tax element, largely on the basis of representatives from the recently organized Land and Labor clubs, had a majority of the delegates.

From the start the single taxers took the offensive by electing Louis Post temporary convention chairman. Next they supported a majority report of the convention's credentials committee which recommended against the seating of six delegates who were still affiliated with the Socialist Labor Party.[28] It was in this debate that the entire ideological battle was refought by partisans of both factions. The Georgites raised the usual condemnations of government ownership of the means of production and distribution. Socialist morality was questioned, particularly for the benefit of George's Irish Catholic followers, in the light of the Socialist Labor Party's 1885 platform which contained a demand that divorce be granted "on mutual consent upon providing for the care of children."[29] Henry George him-

[26]*New Yorker Volkszeitung,* Aug. 15, 1887.

[27]*Leader,* Aug. 10, 1887.

[28]*New York World,* Aug. 18, 1887.

[29]*Leader,* Aug. 18, 1887.

self called for the expulsion of the socialists at the same time
that he conceded their contributions in the past. "The greatest
danger that could befall this party," he said, "would not be the
separation of its elements—but would be a continuance within
its ranks of incongruous elements."[30]

The socialist contingent, spearheaded by Richard J. Hinton,
George G. Block, Laurence Gronlund, Hugo Vogt, Walter Vrooman, and Serge Schevitsch, appealed against the creation of a
schism in the party. They marshalled all of their familiar arguments on the nature of the Socialist Labor Party. Some of them
threw caution to the winds and sharply criticized overweening
concentration on the single-tax issue. Schevitsch, who had attempted in vain to bring about a *rapprochement* with George
on the train which carried them from New York to Syracuse,
made no apologies for past socialist criticism of the latter's
theories. "The very life of a great idea," he said, was "discussion and criticism." And he prophesied that the United
Labor Party would seal its own doom by ridding itself of its
loyal, "self sacrificing and hard working" socialist adherents.
"If you want one of those soap bubble parties which have exploded so often on the surface of our political ocean, then drive
us out," Schevitsch declared.[31]

The single taxers did precisely that; the socialist delegates
were rejected. While George acknowledged that the socialists
would be badly missed during the course of campaign work, he
did not believe that the vote of the United Labor Party would
suffer appreciably. Furthermore, the convention proceeded to
adopt a platform that not only specifically repudiated socialism
but also made the single tax the party's focal issue. Against his
better judgment, George permitted himself to be put up as the
party's candidate for the relatively unimportant office of Secretary of State in the coming November elections.[32]

The socialists never doubted the sincerity of George's beliefs,
for no man who knew him could arraign him on that charge.
He took his role as "prophet" in dead earnest. Yet they had
legitimate right to resent the treatment which he had meted out

[30]*New York World*, Aug. 19, 1887.
[31]*Ibid*.
[32]*Ibid*., Aug. 20, 1887.

to them. He had refused even to discuss the situation with their leaders, despite their faithful service to him during the campaign. By George's own admission, they had been among his most effective workers. They had asked for little and received less from the United Labor Party, which they had been largely instrumental in founding. George, indeed, was the interloper, the "borer from within," who had succeeded in converting the party from one that catered to the grievances of the working class into one which sought to save the middle class from extinction. Even after the election they had been willing to support him, because George's land program struck at one of the very foundations of capitalism; but they had been summarily and presumptuously rejected.

Under these circumstances, it could be no surprise to find the socialists opening a barrage of hostile criticism against George and their erstwhile single-tax allies. While the convention was still in progress, George Block, one of the expelled delegates, accused George and the single taxers of having packed it with dummy delegates. If George was throwing the socialists overboard to win farmer support, said Alexander Jonas, he was making a colossal mistake. "George can't hoodwink the farmers," he quipped, because "they can never understand his theories."[33] Another socialist, interviewed by a *New York World* reporter, declared bitterly: "We worked like dogs for that man last election. We gave him our money. We didn't ask for any political position . . . . The deeds of a renegade are viewed with scorn."[34] In the *Workmen's Advocate*, the veteran Marxist journalist, Dr. Adolph Douai, wrote: "It is less our loss than it is Henry George's loss. He might have turned out one of the celebrated persons of history, as the redeemer of labor in America from its Egyptian bondage."[35]

The socialists had a case against Henry George. But those persons who seek equity must come into court with clean hands, and this was hardly true of the socialists. Like George and his single-tax followers, the socialists had sought to use the United Labor Party for their own purposes. Had the socialists

---

[33] *Ibid.*, Aug. 19, 1887.
[34] *Ibid.*, Aug. 20, 1887.
[35] *Ibid.*, Aug. 27, 1887.

gained control of the party, they undoubtedly would have manipulated it with their own ends uppermost in mind. If non-socialists had objected, they could have left or, more likely, been expelled. And if the party had ceased to be useful to the socialists, they would have cast it aside like an old shoe.

Acceptance of political catastrophe rarely comes with good grace. The New York socialists would have been the exception to the rule had they taken their defeat at Syracuse in acquiescence and docility. Besides, the United Labor Party had now changed in character. It was as much a foe to be opposed as the Republican and Democratic parties. In fact, it was to be combatted even more vigorously, since it still made the pretense of being a workingmen's party and hence competed with the socialists for the proletarian vote. The socialists could do battle with the United Labor Party both in the spirit of revenge and on the grounds of political and ideological honesty.

They formulated their plans at a series of conferences in New York City. At a Webster Hall meeting on September 8, attended by both socialists and anti-George trade unionists from the Central Labor Union, a Progressive Labor Party was organized, and a platform catering primarily to labor union demands was adopted. The platform also advocated high taxes on land, incomes, and corporations as well as government ownership of telegraphs, railroads, and public utilities. The new party had been established because the United Labor Party was "now under a despotic ring."[36]

A slate of candidates was nominated for the November elections at a state convention of the Progressive Labor Party held at Webster Hall on September 28. John Swinton, the aging labor journalist, was offered the honor of opposing George, of whom he was highly critical. But he declined because of ill health and lack of time and money, and the nomination went to J. Edward Hall, a machinist. All but one of the other candidates were associated with the labor movement. This contrasted sharply with the United Labor Party ticket which was completely devoid of working-class representation. The social-

---

[36]*Workmen's Advocate*, Sept. 17, 1887.

ists had a point in saying that the name, United Labor Party, was a misnomer.[37]

The Socialist Labor Party, as such, did not associate itself with the Progressive Labor Party. Its Lassallean faction would have preferred straight socialist politics under the banner of the SLP to the hybrid and splinter Progressive Party. The *Workmen's Advocate*, knowing whereof it spoke, presaged internal SLP doctrinal and tactical difficulties by noting that not all socialists in New York were supporting the Progressive Labor Party, though there was unanimous opposition to the George party. Refusing to become unduly excited about the forthcoming campaign, the paper's editor wrote:

> The fact is, this excitement about politics is entirely too ephemeral and superficial to captivate thoughtful socialists. Down at the bottom there must be education and conviction. After that the political action of those who are converted to socialism will not require to be drummed up with the paraphernalia of old party tactics or such 'church-revival' methods as characterize the land tax anti-povertyites.[38]

In the radical movement a political campaign often finds the left-wing parties slugging harder at one another than at their common enemies to the right. The New York elections in the fall of 1887 were typical. George and Schevitsch publicly debated the merits of land taxation and socialism before a capacity audience at an Eighth Avenue theater. In the *Standard*, George vigorously attacked the socialists, and the latter answered in kind. Their biggest blast came after George expressed belief that the condemned Haymarket anarchists had received a fair trial.[39] While George may have been sincere in his opinion, it was a particularly unfortunate and objectionable statement, because he had previously expressed a contrary view. It left the sturdy little reformer vulnerable to the charge of hypocrisy. His socialist foes could argue that he was seeking to disassociate himself from the proletarian movement in order to gain middle-class support.

Neither the single taxers, who had lost much of their erstwhile support from among Irish workers, anarchists, and

---

[37]*Leader*, Aug. 23, 1887.
[38]*Workmen's Advocate*, Oct. 22, 1887.
[39]*Ibid.*, Oct. 15, 1887.

Knights of Labor, nor the socialists with their skimpy organization, could derive great satisfaction from the election results.
The United Labor Party polled 72,000 votes as against 480,000
for the victorious Democrats and 459,000 for the Republicans.
The Progressive Labor Party obtained only 5,000 votes, nearly
all of which were cast in New York City. The 72,000 votes
which George received were not completely unimpressive, but
his decline in popularity in the metropolis was evidenced, in
part, by the loss of 31,000 votes from his 1886 mayoralty total.[40]
Contributing largely to George's loss of strength was not only
the socialist defection but also the fact that the orthodox parties
had literally robbed the United Labor Party of its *raison d'être*
by enacting into law nearly all of its platform demands at the
1887 session of the New York State Legislature. The *Workmen's
Advocate* expressed satisfaction to see the George "craze" reduced by almost half. "Still," it said, "the 35,000 votes cast for
their demi-god shows what enthusiasm will do even if reason
is absent." As for the meager vote of the Progressive Labor
Party, the paper declared that it was accepting it "philosophically."[41]

The electoral debacle of the Progressive Labor Party, followed
by a somewhat similar situation in Milwaukee the next year,[42]
resulted in a new and dreary round of doctrinal stock-taking
by Socialist Laborites. The party's Lassallean wing had never
been reconciled to either concentration on trade-union penetration or co-operation with the new labor parties. Nevertheless,
it had gone along with the trade-union faction and dutifully
supported the socialist-backed labor parties during the 1886
and 1887 political campaigns. At the SLP national convention
at Buffalo in September, 1887, the Lassalleans succeeded in
watering down a Marxist-sponsored invitation to Haskell's
crumbling International Workingmen's Association to affiliate
with the SLP. But at the same meeting they held their peace
when the following resolution was adopted:

---

[40]Speek, *Bulletin of the University of Wisconsin, Economics and Political
Science Series,* Vol. VIII, No. 3, p. 140.

[41]*Workmen's Advocate,* Nov. 12, 1887.

[42]Bayrd Still, *Milwaukee, The History of a City* (Madison, 1948), pp.
285-86.

To recommend to the members wherever one or more labor parties are in the field, to support that party which is the most progressive; that is, the platform and principles of which comes nearest to ours, and at least recognizes the conflict between capital and labor; but members shall not be permitted to participate in the founding of new parties, when there is no well-founded reason to believe that the same shall fully recognize our principles.[43]

This resolution differed notably in spirit from a similar one approved at the party's 1885 national convention affirming independent SLP political action and condemning all other parties as "reactionary."[44]

The near calamity of the Progressive Labor Party provided the Lassalleans with a potent argument for the Socialist Labor Party to act independently. They maintained that the creation of the former was a mistaken effort to wreak vengeance on George and his followers. They refrained, however, from open disparagement of SLP tactics until the spring and summer of 1888, when political fever symptoms were already burgeoning forth in anticipation of the fall elections. Then party national secretary W. L. Rosenberg and his friend J. E. Busche, who were strategically placed as editors of the official organs, *Der Sozialist* and the *Workmen's Advocate*, began to reprimand the trade-union faction and to censure its policies.

Their attack opened simultaneously on April 28, with editorials in both papers deprecating the time and effort which socialists had put into the trade-union movement for the scanty results obtained. Busche acknowledged that a trade-union policy of "one step at a time" might not be out of order, but he insisted that the labor movement had to have a socialistic rather than merely an opportunistic direction. On June 2 another *Workmen's Advocate* editorial cautioned against socialist enthusiasm for "booming so-called labor parties," which had been found so unprofitable in the past. A more positive editorial on August 18 suggested that the purely propaganda activity of the Socialist Labor Party would have to be directed, as in France and Germany, into independent social-democratic pol-

---

[43]*Report of the Proceedings of the 6th National Convention of the Socialistic Labor Party,* p. 11.

[44]*Workmen's Advocate,* Apr. 2, 1887.

itics. "Mere fault protesting and fault finding is becoming altogether too wearying," wrote Busche. On September 15 the *Workmen's Advocate* was still more emphatic. In an editorial entitled, "Where We Stand," Busche wrote: "The Socialist Labor Party finds that it cannot remain alone towering in the realm of theory while they [*sic*] are still young in practice in the United States." Socialists were called on to sponsor their own candidates for the coming fall elections. The time had come for the Socialist Labor Party to extend the hand of leadership to the wage-earner class.

The Lassallean argument for independent political action was designed to appeal to the small minority of native-born socialists in the party. It was extremely difficult to convince Americans of the efficacy of a political party which was not, in fact, a political party at all. The Marxist tactic of infiltrating a reform party seemed a roundabout approach to effective political participation. Besides, the Lassalleans were more attuned to the American tradition in their desire to extend the horizons of socialism past the wage-earner class. They maintained that scientific socialism appealed to all persons irrespective of race or class distinction and that the Marxists, by dedicating their major efforts to the discontented few who were organized in trade unions, were cutting themselves off from mass support. They considered trade unions purely for the enhancement and defense of the organized workingman. And they saw only humiliation and disaster in directly associating socialism with the numerous failures of strikes and boycotts that developed out of trade-union action. To encourage the formation of labor unions was one thing; to integrate them into the socialist political movement was another; and to tie the destinies of socialism to them was still another—and one to be avoided.

The plea of the *Workmen's Advocate* for socialist participation in the 1888 New York elections was received sympathetically by the Busche-led "American" sections of the party and vigorously opposed by the Marxist *Volkszeitung* faction. The latter sought in vain to prevent a move to commit the party to independent politics on the ground that it was too late to organize properly for the campaign.[45] But the American sections pushed the issue before the Central Committee of Section New York and just succeeded in getting a favorable response. Then, in a gesture of socialist solidarity, the party nominated a *Volkszeitung* stalwart, Alexander Jonas, for mayor, and J. Edward Hall for governor.[46] As 1888 was also a presidential election year, the New York socialists decided to assert themselves in the realm of national political policy. But as their platform called for the abolition of the presidency they found themselves in a dilemma. They cleverly escaped this apparent cul-de-sac by nominating a full ticket of presidential electors who were instructed to vote, if chosen to the electoral college, "No President."

At the same time that the American sections in New York were committing the Socialist Labor Party to a course of independent political action, they were also taking steps to convert the national party into a social-democratic organization. Accordingly, they requested the National Executive Committee to submit to the general membership a constitutional amendment substituting the following political resolutions for those adopted at the 1887 national convention:

> Whereas, the Socialist Labor Party of the United States is a propaganda party and
>
> Whereas the participation in municipal, state, and congressional elections is a good means of agitation,
>
> Resolved that the Socialist Labor Party hereby declares itself to be an independent political party for the purpose of participating in such elections and
>
> Resolved, that faithful allegiance to the Socialist Labor Party and severance of all connections with other political parties be a condition of membership in the Socialist Labor Party—all other parties being considered as forming one reactionary mass.[47]

The amendment was adopted as presented, and the Rosenberg-Busche faction seemed firmly in control.

---

[45] *Ibid.*, Sept. 22, 1888.

[46] *Ibid.*, Oct. 27, 1888.

[47] A printed form of this amendment, dated Sept. 14, 1888, is in the Socialist Labor Party Papers, State Historical Society, Madison, Wis. Also see *Workmen's Advocate*, Aug. 10, 1889.

This control remained effective during the first months of 1889 despite the party's poor electoral showings in the fall. The 2,645 votes which Jonas received in the New York election were more than a disappointment to Rosenberg, Busche, and their followers. The returns were a decided jolt, especially when contrasted with the preceding fall. Nor did the paucity of Socialist Labor Party ballots in Milwaukee and New Haven give cause for rejoicing. Yet Busche sought to derive some balm from the results, and at the expense of his opponents in the party. He rationalized the smallness of the SLP vote as evidence of the failure of socialist propaganda to permeate the working class. At its best, propaganda through trade unions was not enough. The socialists' biggest problem was to agitate and educate the great mass of the populace through the medium of politics.[48]

Between January and August of 1889 the political and trade-union factions of the Socialist Labor Party struggled to build up strength for the inevitable showdown between the unreconciled *Volkszeitung* group and the party leadership. The former occupied a powerful position in the party, since it strongly influenced the German socialist movement in New York City which, in turn, dominated the Socialist Labor Party organization in the general metropolitan area. And since the combined sections of Greater New York were empowered by the party's constitution to choose or depose the National Executive Committtee, the Rosenberg faction's control over the party was at best precarious.

Early in August, the *Volkszeitung* faction began a campaign designed to dispossess Rosenberg and his supporters from positions of authority in the party. The Central Committee of the New York German sections drew up a list of fifty itemized charges against Rosenberg and National Executive Committeemen Adolph Gerecke, Joseph Sauter, and William Hintze. The party officers were accused of systematically antagonizing trade unions and labor leaders and of maliciously opposing the American Federation of Labor's campaign for the eight-hour day. Rosenberg, in particular, was denounced for dictatorial conduct in office, incompetence, dishonesty, and drinking the beer of a

---

[48]*Ibid.*, Nov. 10, 1888.

boycotted brewery. When the four men refused to resign after presentation of these charges, the German Central Committee arbitrarily declared their offices vacant.[49]

The party's Board of Supervision, which sat in Philadelphia, found this action illegal under the SLP constitution.[50] But this opinion merely caused the *Volkszeitung* group to adopt a new maneuver. It induced the SLP Central Committee for the Greater New York area to call a special meeting on September 10 in order to conduct a "legal investigation" of the complaints filed against the National Executive Committee. Some two hundred were present when the meeting opened at Clarendon Hall, though many of Rosenberg's supporters were said to have withdrawn under threats of personal violence. The gathering was outwardly harmonious and united in opposition to Rosenberg and his friends; by the end of the evening they were shorn of their offices.[51]

Irrespective of the competence or the views of Rosenberg and his followers, their ouster from office savored of the coup d'état. This in itself warranted them some sympathy from many socialists who disagreed with their basic policies. The German Marxist group in New York never enjoyed the full confidence of its socialist brethren in other parts of the East and Middle West, and its disposal of the party leaders by steam-roller tactics did not enhance its reputation. The arrogant action of the New York Germans recalled a similar situation some fifteen years earlier when the International Workingmen's Association fell apart largely because of the domineering attitude of its New York German Section 1.

The big question now for the *Volkszeitung* element was whether the party membership as a whole would sanction its coup. The Board of Supervision apparently decided that under the circumstances acquiescence was the better part of valor and approved the change in the party leadership. Moreover, the Rosenberg forces were placed at a distinct disadvantage by the seizure of the *Workmen's Advocate* and *Der Sozialist* by *Volks-*

[49]*Ibid.*, Aug. 10, 1889; *Manifesto of the National Executive Committee of the Socialist Labor Party, Sept. 21, 1889.*
[50]*Workmen's Advocate*, Sept. 7, 1889.
[51]*Ibid.*, Sept. 14, 1889.

zeitung adherents. Since former treasurer and national committeeman Reinhardt Meyer had refused to turn over the party funds to Rosenberg and Busche,[52] they could not afford to publish their side of the case through a newspaper medium. They were obliged, therefore, to issue a manifesto to the national party membership in which they reviewed the entire controversy with the *Volkszeitung*. They refused to recognize the legality of the coup and called on socialists everywhere to repudiate the "usurpers."

Both the Rosenberg and trade-union factions hurriedly summoned conventions in Chicago during the following four weeks. It was no accident that the Midwestern metropolis was chosen, for each side was anxious to enlist to its banner that city's considerable number of socialists. However, neither convention really produced anything more than strong restatements of the ideological and tactical issues that divided the Marxists from the Lassalleans. The Rosenberg group sought to mollify trade unionists by adopting resolutions calling for support of wage-earner organizations in their efforts to combat "employer encroachments" and to gain shorter hours of work and higher pay. But it insisted that the emancipation of labor could be achieved only through political action leading to a socialist society.[53] The trade-union faction, on the other hand, went on record against independent political action and advocated supporting progressive labor parties. It maintained that socialists were duty bound to join existing trade unions or to help found new ones, to make workers see the "irreconcilable conflict between exploiters and their victims," and to support without stint efforts of labor leaders to achieve the eight-hour day.[54]

For approximately a year and a half the Marxist-*Volkszeitung*-trade-union faction and the Lassallean-Rosenberg-political group battled tooth and nail for acceptance among the nation's strife-weary socialists. Gradually the former, better organized and in possession of the more important newspapers, won out.

---

[52]*Appeal to the Sections of the Socialist Labor Party from the National Executive Committee, New York, Sept. 5, 1889.*

[53]*Proceedings of the National Convention of the Socialist Labor Party, Chicago, Sept. 28, 1889,* pp. 4-5.

[54]*Workmen's Advocate,* Oct. 26, 1889.

But the Rosenberg element stubbornly refused to concede defeat. Though reduced to a skeletal organization, often referred to as the "perambulating faction" because of frequent changes of headquarters, it continued to maintain that it was the bona fide representative of organized socialism in the United States.

The sequel to the expulsion of the Rosenberg-Busche faction from the leadership of the Socialist Labor Party provided one of those curious paradoxes which have cropped up so often in the socialist movement. The *Volkszeitung*-led coup had been justified on the grounds of the Lassallean group's preference for political action over trade-union penetration, its generally unfriendly attitude toward organized labor, and its arbitrary leadership. Yet, within a few years after Rosenberg and Busche were removed from the party helm, the Socialist Labor Party embarked on a strenuous course of independent politics, found itself increasingly at odds with the trade-union movement, and entrusted its fortunes to the leadership of a small New York clique headed by brilliant, dogmatic, and intolerant Daniel DeLeon.

The first straw in the wind indicating that the new party chieftains might not, after all, desert the political arena for trade-union penetration came in September, 1890, when the Socialist Labor Party of New York nominated Dr. Franz Gerau for Judge of the Court of Appeals. To the pleasant surprise of the SLP leadership, Gerau polled 13,704 votes—a strong contrast with the miserable showing that the party had made in 1888. "We confess that while we always held that the wage workers of the cities were by no means as conservative as their so-called leaders would have us believe," said the elated Lucien Sanial, "we were not ready for such a widespread manifestation of socialist sentiment in villages and sparsely settled districts." Sanial, a former Parisian journalist who had succeeded Busche as editor of the *Workmen's Advocate*, believed that the New York state SLP ought to ponder the advisability of creating an organization for political action and suggested a party referendum on the matter.[55]

Political action took on a greater attraction in the light of stiffening resistance by the American Federation of Labor

[55] *Ibid.*, Nov. 22, 1890.

leadership to socialist efforts to "bore from within." This opposition rested on firm historical and doctrinal grounds. The
founders of the AF of L, not a few of them former Marxists
and Socialist Labor Party members,[56] premised their organization upon an acceptance of modern industrial capitalism and a
willingness to advance the interests of organized labor both
through and under it.[57] They accepted implicitly the fact and
the inevitability of corporate bigness. Nor did they see any
cure for the trust, although they acknowledged that political
prescriptions might be concocted to help curb the disease of
unbridled corporate power. They exalted "pure and simple"
wage-conscious trade-unionism over the class-conscious variety
characteristic of European labor organizations. They considered the trade union an end in itself, rather than an agency to
assist in the abolition of the wage system or to foster the interests of any particular group, socialist or otherwise. In this latter
regard they maintained a constant vigil against efforts to divert
the Federation from its basic trade-union objectives. Thus,
once again a paradox existed wherein a group of men, nurtured
on Marxist doctrines, stood as the principal bulwark against
those professedly seeking their realization.[58]

The socialists were a vocal though hardly a disruptive minority within the American Federation of Labor, which was
founded in 1886, and in its parent organization, the Federation
of Organized Trades and Labor Unions of the United States
and Canada, which had been established five years earlier. At
the 1885 convention of the latter organization, the socialists
presented a resolution advocating the formation of an independent workingmen's political party which would sponsor
trade unionists as candidates. The resolution was beaten,[59]

[56]Samuel Gompers, while not a socialist, was well read in Marxist theory.
See his *Seventy Years of Life and Labor: An Autobiography*, I (New York,
1925), 381-402.

[57]See Selig Perlman, "The Basic Philosophy of the American Labor Movement," *Annals of the American Academy of Political and Social Science*,"
CCLXXIV (1951), 59-61.

[58]David Saposs, *Left-Wing Unionism: A Study of Radical Policies and
Tactics* (New York, 1926), pp. 15-17.

[59]*Report of the Fifth Annual Session of the Federation of Organized
Trades and Labor Unions of the United States and Canada, Washington,
D. C., Dec. 8-11, 1885*, pp. 17-18.

though in the next year, when the AF of L was organized, the convention went on record as urging "most generous support to the independent political movement of workingmen."[60] Socialist resolutions were introduced thereafter at subsequent conventions and though they were almost systematically rejected, the socialists themselves were still in good grace. The defeat of the Lassalleans for control of the SLP brought the belief that closer relationships might be forthcoming between the trade-union-inclined Marxists and the labor organization.

In 1890, however, a situation was developing in New York City that was to dramatize the socialism versus trade-unionism issue and to make the name of American Federation of Labor president Samuel Gompers an anathema in hundreds of socialist households. The Central Labor Union, weakened by internal wranglings engendered by the Henry George campaigns, had fallen on evil days. It had slipped into the control of none too scrupulous political opportunists and partisans of the Knights of Labor who were generally in bad odor because of their opposition to the eight-hour day movement. As a consequence, several socialist-dominated unions decided to withdraw from the Central Labor Union and to organize their own Central Labor Federation. The new body, which was founded on February 12, 1889, applied for and received a charter from the AF of L.[61]

In the course of the year, efforts were made to effect a reconciliation of the two groups and from December, 1889, to June, 1890, a temporary union was achieved. During this period, the Central Labor Federation went out of existence, and its secretary deposited the organization's charter with Gompers for safekeeping. When in June, 1890, the Central Labor Federation was resuscitated, it requested the return of its charter. This Gompers refused. With the backing of the AF of L's Executive Committee, he maintained that the old charter had been surrendered. And he refused to grant a new charter, on the grounds

---

[60]*Report of Proceedings of the First Annual Convention of the American Federation of Labor, Columbus, Ohio, Dec. 8-12, 1886,* p. 16.

[61]See *Report of Proceedings of the 10th Annual Convention of the American Federation of Labor, Detroit, 1890,* pp. 12, 17, 23-26. The account that follows is based primarily on this source. Also see *Workmen's Advocate,* Dec. 20, 1890; Gompers, I, 384-87; Nathan Fine, *Labor and Farmer Parties in the United States, 1828-1928* (New York, 1928), pp. 137-40; Hillquit, *History of Socialism in the United States,* pp. 298-99.

that one of the organizations affiliated with the new Central Labor Federation was the New York American Section of the Socialist Labor Party. The AF of L constitution, said Gompers, prohibited political parties from affiliation with the order, and hence the Central Labor Federation could not legally be granted a charter. This decision enraged the New York socialists, since it had been common practice for working-class parties to be represented in local central labor union bodies.[62] They served notice that they would appeal the decision at the 1890 convention in Detroit.

Samuel Gompers was rarely the man to be unprepared for a fight or to shy away from one. The socialists had raised their storm signals and he was ready for the gale of protest which he knew would sweep into the convention. In his presidential report, which came early on the convention's agenda, he took great pains in reviewing his quarrel with the in-again, out-again Central Labor Federation. And just in time, for he had scarcely finished when the gathering storm broke. It came in full fury when the credentials committee reported adversely on seating Lucien Sanial, who was present not only as the delegate of the Central Labor Federation but also as a Socialist Labor Party representative in that body.

For the greater part of two days, socialists and pure-and-simple trade unionists exchanged angry recriminations or, in more temperate moments, traded expositions on the philosophy of the American labor movement. Rightly, the two principal antagonists were Gompers and Sanial, who was permitted to plead his case on the convention floor even though his credentials had been rejected. Sanial stoutly contended that the Socialist Labor Party was not a political party either as understood by American workingmen, or in the light of European practice, where trade unions were branches of socialist parties. Gompers, in reply, denied that the European labor movement ought necessarily to be emulated and observed that unions had been in existence in the United States long before the founding of the Socialist Labor Party. He also pointed out that to give the socialists special privileges within the AF of L would bring similar de-

---

[62] Saposs, p. 22.

mands from other political and economic groups. Such would have the inevitable effect of splintering the Federation into fragments that could never possibly be welded back together. Forcefully and repeatedly, he warned against deserting "pure-and-simple" objectives for socialism's alluring but intangible returns.

When the matter was finally placed before the convention as a whole, the credentials committee was upheld 1,574 to 496. This decisive socialist defeat was followed by three others. A resolution demanding abolition of the wage system was beaten. Another resolution recommending affiliation with the SLP by all AF of L members was reported upon adversely by the resolutions committee and no further action was taken. Finally, Thomas J. Morgan, the Welsh-born Chicago machinist, attorney, and socialist who had ably seconded Sanial in the general debate on the Central Labor Federation issue, was overwhelmingly beaten by Gompers, 1,716 votes to 194, for the presidency of the Federation.

The Socialist Labor Party, as such, was not concerned with the trade-unionism versus socialism controversy at Detroit and hence was under no obligation to take official cognizance of the socialist defeat. However, attacks on "pure-and-simple" trade unionism were perceptibly more in evidence in its official English-language publications, and in August, 1891, Sanial left for Brussels to plead the case of the Central Labor Federation before the International Labor Congress.[63] To counter this effort to embarrass the AF of L, Gompers produced an opinion solicited from the veteran Marxist, F. A. Sorge, which upheld his trade-union political policy.[64]

The socialist rout at Detroit occasioned still another inquiry into the Socialist Labor Party's trade-union tactics. It was now all too clear, at least to the party leadership concentrated in Sanial, Daniel DeLeon, and Hugo Vogt, that Gompers and his associates were intent on betraying the working class by acceptance of, and subservience to, capitalistic wage-slavery. To overcome the entrenched "pure-and-simple crooked labor fakers" in the AF of L was not worth the effort and the struggle

---

[63]*People*, Aug. 2, 1891.
[64]Gompers, I, 388-89.

involved. Hence, not only was the Federation written off as past saving through socialist redemption, but a war to the death had to be fought against it for the allegiance of the American wage earner. Admittedly, this was a radical departure from past trade-union policies by the party, and it involved open antagonism with the country's strongest labor organization. But it was deemed imperative if the working class was to be won over to socialism.

The new trade-union policy did not find general acceptance by the party rank and file, particularly socialist members of the American Federation of Labor. The latter did not slacken appreciably their "boring" tactics despite harsh criticisms, first in the *Workmen's Advocate* and then in its successor, *The People*. But "boring from within" came hard, and for the next two years the socialists were unable to claim any notable advances. In 1892, for example, the Federation's convention at Philadelphia overwhelmingly defeated a Morgan-proposed resolution calling for government ownership of the means of production and distribution.[65] That the delegates went on record in favor of public ownership of the telephone and telegraph systems was no particular victory for the socialists, as this intrinsically anti-monopoly demand was being advocated by many non-socialist reform groups.

The panic of 1893 sent socialist stock soaring in the American Federation of Labor. In the face of several disastrous strikes, a declining labor market, and a series of adverse judicial decisions, the Federation's policy of sharing capitalism's fruits lost appeal. Despair was etched on the faces of hundreds of cold, hungry, and homeless unemployed workers, who wandered aimlessly through the industrial cities begging for food or shelter from the economically more fortunate. Ominous rumblings of dissatisfaction arose against an industrial system that had brought such a state of affairs to pass and against the politicians and the black-robed jurists who apologetically defended it.

The industrial unrest, moreover, was framed against a background of agrarian discontent of some half-a-dozen years' standing. Only a year before, the agrarian People's Party, which had

---

[65]*Report of Proceedings of the 12th Annual Convention of the American Federation of Labor, Philadelphia, Dec. 12-17, 1892, p. 39.*

arisen to protest the farmers' plight, had given its presidential candidate, James Baird Weaver, over a million votes. This in itself was evidence that new remedies to old problems would receive a hearing. Radicalism, if not necessarily socialism itself, was definitely in the air, and not a few highly placed leaders of the AF of L were willing to flirt with the Populists with the view of consummating a farmer-labor marriage.[66] If the times were out of joint, they were not inauspicious for the socialists.

In his report to the 1893 AF of L convention at Chicago, Gompers gave expression to the general temper of inquietude. "To struggle to supplant such a system by one in which 'man's inhumanity to man' shall be a thing relegated to and regarded as the barbarian of the past," he declared, "is the duty of every man who loves his kind, and is the mission of organized labor."[67] In "supplanting the system," however, Gompers was by no means peering into the future to seek out the Nirvana of the co-operative commonwealth. He would not junk the capitalistic mode of production. Rather, he would close the gap between the ability of industrial capitalism to produce and the inability of the wage-earner class to consume. His solution was to spread employment by reducing the number of working hours of the average laborer.[68] From the time that Ira Steward first broached the eight-hour day in the 1860's[69] through President Franklin D. Roosevelt's New Deal, this constituted the "pure-and-simple" trade unionist's alternative to socialism.

Historians have been prone to point out that the farmer during the 1880's and 1890's was disposed to accept increased intervention by the state into the economic and social life of the nation. In noting this general agrarian acceptance of what may be termed roughly "the welfare state," they have tended to gloss over labor's similarly strong demands for positive governmental action. The 1893 convention of the AF of L showed clearly that the individualistic trade unionist was not unwilling to see the extension of governmental authority, especially when exer-

---

[66]Commons, II, 510.

[67]*Report of Proceedings of the 13th Annual Convention of the American Federation of Labor, Chicago, Dec. 11-19, 1893*, p. 11.

[68]*Ibid.*, p. 12.

[69]Commons, II, 90.

cised in his own behalf. The convention adopted a resolution sponsored by Thomas J. Morgan which condemned "as inhuman and destructive of the liberties of the human race," a societal system which denied work to the man who was willing and eager to labor, treated him as an "outcast," arrested him as a "vagrant," and punished him as a "felon." The resolution also asserted

> that the right to work is the right to life, that to deny the one is to destroy the other. That when the private employer cannot or will not give work the municipality, state or nation must.

The aroused delegates did not stop there, for they accepted still another Morgan proposal, a political program which both implicitly and explicitly committed the Federation to a socialist course of policy. The program's preamble acknowledged doctrinal indebtedness to the trade unionists of Great Britain who had adopted, with considerable success, "the principle of independent labor politics as an auxiliary to their economic action." The eleven-point political program, of which Article 10 was to engender a storm of controversy, contained the following demands:

1. Compulsory education.

2. Direct legislation.

3. A legal eight-hour workday.

4. Sanitary inspection of workshop, mine, and home.

5. Liability of employers for injury to health, body, or life.

6. The abolition of the contract system in all public work.

7. The abolition of the sweating system.

8. The municipal ownership of street cars. and gas and electric plants for public distribution of light, heat, and power.

9. The nationalization of telegraphs, telephones, railroads, and mines.

10. *The collective ownership by the people of all means of production and distribution.* [Author's italics.][70]

11. The principle of referendum in all legislation.

---

[70]*Report of Proceedings of the 13th Annual Convention of the American Federation of Labor,* p. 37.

While the convention voted down, by the close vote of 1,253 to 1,182, that part of the resolution which recommended "favorable" consideration of the program by American labor organizations, the platform as a whole was overwhelmingly accepted by a vote of 2,244 to 67.[71] Unions affiliated with the AF of L were requested to instruct their delegates to the 1894 convention as to what action ought to be taken on the program.

During 1894 Morgan's political program found almost complete acceptance among the various craft unions, state labor federations, and city central labor unions affiliated with the AF of L.[72] Only the bakers' union rejected it completely.[73] The typographical and web-weavers' unions turned down Article 10, while the carpenters' union insisted on tacking on to it the amendment, "as the people elect to operate." In some instances, local AF of L organizations went into politics on the basis of the program, usually in close co-operation with the Populists and socialists. Such political ventures were conspicuously unsuccessful and gave powerful ammunition to the Gompers "pure-and-simple" faction.

The American Federationist, which made its debut in March, 1894, under Gompers' editorship, provided an editorial medium for the Federation's members to air their views on the political program. It was a somewhat muted sounding board, however, because Gompers had little desire to give the question additional publicity. In the first issue of the *Federationist*, Morgan and Frank K. Foster, editor of the *Boston Labor Leader*, argued the cases for and against the political program, particularly Article 10. Foster contended that endorsement of Article 10 would mean "hara-kiri" for the labor movement and its annexation by the Socialist Labor Party. He also feigned ignorance of the type of political party that supporters of the program expected the Federation to endorse.[74] Morgan set him straight on this score. The program contemplated endorsement of socialism and action through a socialist political organization. If trade-union leaders accused the socialists of "chasing rain-

[71]*Ibid.*, p. 38.
[72]Saposs, p. 24.
[73]*American Federationist*, I (1894), 130.
[74]*Ibid.*, pp. 5-6.

bows," said Morgan, what was their alternative? He couched
his answer in the realistic terms of the labor movement's recent
failures:

> Better stay with the Carnegies, Fricks, and such, nothing
> like our trusty weapons, the strike, boycott and political
> pull. See how we have reduced the hours of labor! See how
> we have raised our wages! See our successes at Home-
> stead, Buffalo, Coeur d'Alene, Tennessee! See the labor
> laws we have placed on the statute books as a result of the
> political help we gave to candidates who were friends of
> labor! See how we over-awe the State and federal courts!
> Aye, see the starving multitude, see the blind leading the
> blind, and the knaves feasting with the enemy.[75]

Other articles in the *Federationist* were in some cases more,
and in others less, sanguine than those of Morgan and Foster.
Joseph Buchanan and Charles Sotheran, both veterans in the
labor movement, thought that the People's Party, rather than
either of the old parties or the socialists, deserved the Federation's support. The Populists, said Sotheran, "could solve satisfactorily the labor question without the aid of the so-called
socialist marplots, casuists, irreconcilables, disruptionists, falsi-
fiers, and boodlers, who have been too long leading our German-
American wage earners through a slough of despond that not
only handicaps and cripples them, but seriously affects the entire labor movement.[76] Sotheran's sourness toward the Socialist Labor Party was understandable, for only four months before
he had been expelled for "circulating malicious and libelous
statements" against the party leaders.[77]

The socialists within the American Federation of Labor had
a big inning at the 1893 convention. They anticipated even
greater success at the Federation's 1894 general meetings to be
held in Denver. Their partisans could come to Colorado with
the knowledge that an overwhelming majority of the AF of L
general membership had endorsed the Morgan program. Furthermore, the industrial crisis which had advanced their cause
in 1893 showed no sign of abating. On the contrary, working-
class unrest had continued to swell. This was dramatized by

---

[75]*Ibid.*, p. 7.

[76]*Ibid.*, p. 193.

[77]*People*, Aug. 5, 1894.

the formation of "industrial armies" which marched on Washington seeking redress of the grievances of their tattered members, and also by the Pullman Strike, which resulted in a complete defeat for the American Railway Union. The contemptuous treatment of the industrial commonwealers at Washington and the crushing of the Pullman Strike by a federal court injunction lent weight to socialist arguments that the workingman's sole salvation lay in the co-operative commonwealth.

While the socialists were well aware that in Samuel Gompers they had an opponent of both skill and determination, they were unprepared for the consummately artistic job of sabotage that he and a small group of allies perpetrated upon Morgan's political program at the Denver convention. Gompers centered the attack directly on Article 10. His strategy called for amending it to the point where it became a mockery. Accordingly, when the controversial article came up for discussion, his friends were ready with amendments. One such amendment called for "the collective ownership by the people of all means of production and distribution by confiscation without compensation." Other amendments would substitute anti-land-monopoly, single-tax, postal-savings-bank, and direct-legislation planks. No wonder, then, that in the welter of amendments, the delegates lost sight of Article 10's original proposal. When the final showdown came, the Gompers group carried the day and by a 4-to-3 majority voted out the disputed, amendment-laden article. Then, to rub a little salt into the wounds of the socialists, the "pure-and-simple" forces put the convention on record as approving each of the other articles of the Morgan program individually but refusing to support them as a whole.[78]

All things considered, it was an effective performance by Gompers, who obfuscated the entire issue by ridicule, as he frankly admitted in his somewhat self-righteous autobiography.[79] But Gompers did not escape completely, for the socialists were not without spite. They teamed up with some

[78] See *Report of Proceedings of the 14th Annual Convention of the American Federation of Labor, Denver, Colorado, 1894*, pp. 37-39; Saposs, pp. 25-26; Fine, pp. 144-46.

[79] Gompers, I, 393.

of his trade-union foes to knock him out of the presidency for the first and only time during his thirty-four years' affiliation with the AF of L. His successor for a year was John McBride of Massillon, Ohio, a member of the United Mine Workers. McBride lacked Gompers' capabilities and was no more attached to socialism than his predecessor. But the socialists preferred him, in 1894 at least, to their inveterate and more formidable foe. It must have been with delicious satisfaction that Daniel DeLeon, only a few weeks after the Denver convention, read a postcard from a poverty-pleading Gompers, requesting that his name be placed on the complimentary mailing list of the *People*.[80]

Henry Demarest Lloyd complained bitterly of the "treachery" of the "labor fakirs" to John Burns who, along with another British socialist, David Holmes, had represented the Trade Union Congress of Great Britain at the Denver convention.[81] But the truth of the matter was that if there was such "treachery," the rank and file of the AF of L either did not detect it, or if it did, failed to raise a hue and cry against it. Moreover, at subsequent Federation conventions during the 1890's, the socialists became increasingly weaker and were unable to do more than annoy the regnant Gompers clique. In 1902 the socialists made their last great challenge but again failed.

Since the Socialist Labor Party leadership had written off the American Federation of Labor as a lost cause some four years earlier, the Denver debacle did not surprise or affront it. Rather, the proceedings at Denver confirmed what it already knew—namely, that socialists could gain nothing through and would only be compromised by, a trade-union movement which philosophically accepted a program based upon acquiescence and expediency and which organizationally placed great emphasis on individual trade-union autonomy. As events proved, the Socialist Labor chieftains were correct in believing that the officialdom of the AF of L would not tolerate socialists "boring from within," once such a tactic threatened to undermine its own leadership and its "pure-and-simple" trade-union approach.

---

[80]Gompers to DeLeon, Dec. 31, 1894. Daniel DeLeon Papers, State Historical Society, Madison, Wis. (Cited hereafter as DeLeon Papers.)

[81]Lloyd to Burns, Feb. 6, 1895. Henry Demarest Lloyd Papers, State Historical Society, Madison, Wis. (Cited hereafter as Lloyd Papers.)

Had the socialists triumphed over Gompers in 1894, conceivably the whole course of American labor development and political history might have been altered. Though the socialists remained active in the AF of L for several decades after the Denver convention, they were never able to change its capitalistic orientation. Their efforts in this direction tended to grow feebler through the years. The failure of an independent labor party to take shape in the United States may be attributed, in part, to the fateful choice that was made at Denver. Unlike that of Great Britain, where the trade-union movement helped to create a labor party of its own, organized labor in the United States, with only occasional divergences, followed the Gompers opportunistic political line. It eschewed independent working-class politics and rewarded its political friends and punished its political enemies irrespective of party labels. As a consequence, the workingman was left frequently with little choice other than to vote either for labor-baiter Tweedledum or for anti-labor Tweedledee.

III. Bellamy Makes Socialism Respectable

THE CHRISTIAN Socialist Reverend W. D. P. Bliss wrote in 1898: "It is doubtful if any man, in his own lifetime, ever exerted so great an influence upon the social beliefs of his fellow beings as did Edward Bellamy."[1] Bliss's views coincided with those of Henry Demarest Lloyd, who stated: "There is no writer of modern times who has done as much as Mr. Bellamy to awaken the world to the necessity of justifying its inheritance from the progress of the past by making a little progress of its own along the lines of economic brotherhood."[2] Dr. H. P. Peebles, who was active in the reform movement in California, wrote of Bellamy: "History teaches that every special cataclysm finds a master mind . . . and Bellamy may have come to answer the cries of oppressed humanity . . . . Bellamy is the Moses of today."[3]

Vida D. Scudder declared that under the impact of *Looking Backward* "the fading emotions of the old Abolitionist era flamed again . . . with the incandescence of a social hope reaching beyond the Negro, to the working classes,—to all the children of men."[4] Even one of Bellamy's severest critics conceded that "until *Looking Backward* appeared many thoughtful Americans did not fully realize the utter chaos with which production is at present conducted; the almost hideous struggle for an existence everywhere prevailing, and the advantages to be derived from cooperation."[5] The ordinarily taciturn Thorstein Veblen waxed enthusiastic over *Looking Backward* and

---

[1] *American Fabian,* IV (June, 1898), 1.

[2] Lloyd to Frederick Bellamy, Nov. 12, 1898. Lloyd Papers.

[3] H. P. Peebles, "The Utopias of the Past Compared with the Theories of Bellamy," *Overland Review,* XV (1890), 574, 576.

[4] Vida D. Scudder, *On Journey,* (New York, 1937), p. 165.

[5] Arthur H. Dodge, *Socialist-Populist Errors: An Exposition of Popular Political Theories* (San Francisco, 1894), p. 39. Also see Nicholas P. Gilman, *Socialism and the American Spirit* (Brooklyn, 1893), p. 200; Carlos Martyn, "Churchianity vs. Christianity," *Arena,* II (1890), 154; "The Success of *Looking Backward,*" *Journal of the Knights of Labor,* Feb. 6, 1890.

his sensitive young wife, Ellen, said of the book: "I believe it was the turning point in our lives because it so affected me."[6]

American socialism's debt to Bellamy was readily acknowledged. Daniel DeLeon, while deploring Bellamy's political "tactical errors" during the nineties, heralded the great service *Looking Backward* performed in the "cause of human progress."[7] J. A. Wayland, the Kansas socialist newspaper editor, wrote that Bellamy was one of the few men who had not lived in vain, since *Looking Backward* "popularized socialism, made it interesting, and started millions to thinking along lines entirely new to them."[8] Similarly Eugene V. Debs's paper commented: "He did a wonderful work because he brought to the limited intelligence of that very dull person, the average 'practical man,' a picture of the 'practical working' of socialism."[9] The 1898 convention of the Social Democratic Party passed a resolution stating that no more effective work had been done for socialism in the United States than that by Bellamy. The party's official paper said that *Looking Backward* had "pierced the gloom of economic slavery and prepared people to accept the emanating truths of socialism."[10] The great French socialist leader, Jean Jaurès, considered *Looking Backward* "an American masterpiece" that did "wonders toward dissipating hostile ignorance against our ideas."[11]

Raised in the supercharged atmosphere of the Civil War years, Edward Bellamy, the man who was contemplated by many as the new social prophet of the day, wanted desperately as a youth to be a soldier. Failure to pass the physical examination for admission to West Point turned him reluctantly to law, journalism, and finally literature. In the literary field he toiled in virtual obscurity until 1887, the year in which his tremendously popular utopian romance was published. Indeed, when Frances E. Willard wrote to the publishers of *Looking Backward* to learn "who, when, and what this Edward Bellamy

[6]Joseph Dorfman, *Thorstein Veblen and His America* (New York, 1934), p. 68.

[7]*People,* May 29, 1898.

[8]*Appeal to Reason,* June 4, 1898.

[9]*Social Democrat,* June 2, 1898.

[10]*Social Democratic Herald,* July 9, 1898.

[11]*Ibid.,* May 26, 1900.

might be," she received a reply which stated: "We do not know except that his letters are mailed from Chicopee Falls, Massachusetts."[12]

Indeed, from his boyhood, except for brief periods away, Bellamy spent his entire life in Chicopee Falls, which he watched develop from a small rural town into an industrial community. The third son of the Reverend Rufus King Bellamy who for thirty-five years served as minister of the local Baptist Church, he was also descended from the Edwardian thinker, Joseph Bellamy, and a long line of New England preachers. Bellamy's early Puritan environment unquestionably influenced his strong sense of social justice.[13]

The public schools of Chicopee Falls furnished the bulk of Bellamy's formal education. At Union College he spent two semesters of desultory study, which were followed by a year's travel in Europe, particularly in Germany. Upon returning to the United States he "read law" but never practiced. Instead, he turned to newspaper work, serving briefly on the editorial staff of the *New York Post* and then for a longer period on the *Springfield Union*.

Always a frail youth, Bellamy at the age of twenty-five developed the tuberculosis which was finally to take his life. During the year 1877-1878 he sought to regain his health in Hawaii, and upon his return he decided to give up the strenuous routine of journalism for the less tiring one of literary writing. Bellamy was a shy, serious, self-contained man. While possessing strong humanitarian sympathies, he had not particularly exhibited them in his early literary works or in his public activities. This fact makes *Looking Backward* that much more impressive.

By most literary standards *Looking Backward*, on which Bellamy rocketed to fame, was a good, though hardly great, novel. Some of his earlier writings, such as *Dr. Heidenhoff's Process*

---

[12]Frances E. Willard, "An Interview with Edward Bellamy," *Our Day*, IV (1899), 539.

[13]Arthur E. Morgan, *Edward Bellamy*, pp. 9-29. This is the definitive biography of Bellamy. Excellent brief discussions of Bellamy appear in Daniel Aaron, *Men of Good Hope: A Story of American Progressives* (New York, 1951), pp. 92-132; Charles A. Madison, *Critics and Crusaders* (New York, 1948), pp. 134-54.

and *Mrs. Ludington's Sister*, novels concerned with psychological plots, outshone *Looking Backward* in artistic craftsmanship.[14] But none of his prior works brought his readers so squarely face-to-face with the unpleasant realities of American industrial life. Bellamy's critique of the growing concentration of industry, albeit in a fanciful manner, made *Looking Backward* an important social document instead of a mere work of commonplace literary merit. It faced head-on the problems of economic consolidation and the frequent failure of the competitive principle to operate equitably in the society of the Gilded Age. Like Henry George, Bellamy offered a panacea to an American people accustomed to listening to, if not always ready to accept, prefabricated solutions to social and economic problems. Bellamy's cure-all called for complete abolition of the competitive principle in social and economic relationships.

Looking Backward related the story of Julian West, a young Bostonian who awoke in the year 2000 A. D. from a hypnotically induced sleep begun in 1887. Introduced to his new surroundings by one Dr. Leete and his daughter, Edith—who provided the pale, romantic interest in the story—the former Back Bay gentleman discovered a revolutionary change in American life. The foremost feature of the change was that in all phases of human activity the principle of co-operation had been substituted for that of competition. West observed almost miraculous differences, produced by the new spirit of co-operation, in both the people and their physical surroundings.

To his great surprise, West learned that the new state of affairs had evolved directly out of the capitalistic system. As the wealth of the nation and the instruments of production and distribution had come almost entirely into the possession of a few individuals during the early years of the twentieth century, the state, without recourse to violence or bloodshed, had taken control of all private industrial enterprise and consolidated it into one huge trust. This was operated by the nation in the interest of the citizens. By its ever-increasing tendency toward

---

[14]For an analysis of Bellamy's writings, see Robert L. Shurter, "The Literary Work of Edward Bellamy," *American Literature*, V (1933), 229-34; Herbert W. Schneider, *A History of American Philosophy* (New York, 1946), p. 198.

concentration and monopoly, capitalism had sown the seeds of its own destruction.[15]

All responsibility for production and distribution lay in the state. The workers of the country were members of the "Industrial Army." Membership was compulsory for all persons between the ages of 21 and 45,[16] and all received equal pay regardless of the nature of their labor.[17] After twenty-four years of service, the worker retired and devoted himself to "the intellectual and spiritual enjoyments and pursuits which alone mean life."[18]

As the core of the economic life of the nation, the Industrial Army was divided and subdivided into hundreds of trades, vocations, and professions. Men and women were allowed to use their natural abilities in directions which gave them the greatest degree of personal satisfaction and, at the same time, to employ them in a manner most profitable to the nation.[19] Honor and prestige for a job well done were the primary motivations for work.[20] Since all workers received equal pay, incentive to labor did not rest on a materialistic basis.

Despite the totalitarian nature of the society portrayed in *Looking Backward*, the activities of the government were reduced to a minimum. A strong syndicalist spirit pervaded the political institutions of Bellamy's proposed social order. Governmental power resided in workers who had completed their terms of service in the Industrial Army. Their leader was the president of the nation. State, territorial, and local administrative divisions were swept away. Little need was felt for legislation since society had perfected its political institutions on the basis of co-operation. The functions of the National Congress, which met once every five years, were largely of a perfunctory nature.[21]

Perfect international comity existed in 2000 A. D. In 1887, said Bellamy, the public enemies had not been England, France,

---

[15]Edward Bellamy, *Looking Backward, 2000-1887* (Boston, 1889), pp. 56-58.
[16]*Ibid.,* p. 63.
[17]*Ibid.,* p. 93.
[18]*Ibid.,* p. 196.
[19]*Ibid.,* p. 66.
[20]*Ibid.,* p. 164.
[21]*Ibid.,* pp. 207-8.

Germany, or any other country but cold, hunger, and nakedness.[22] In the new world-civilization these conditions did not exist. Amity among the nations of the world, all of which had become industrialized, facilitated international trade. International economic relations were supervised by an international council. All barriers to immigration and emigration had been abolished.

Bellamy, shaken by the Haymarket Affair in 1886, carefully pointed out that the transition from the old competitive society to the new order of co-operation and brotherly love had not been accomplished by labor parties or by anarchists. In the 1880's, he said, radicals by their inflammatory talk actually had hindered the cause of social and economic reform and, for this reason, had been subsidized by the opponents of reform.[23] He said that the new era had begun only when the majority of the American people had been won over to the ideas of the "Nationalist Party." This party, he explained, appealed not to one class, as had many of the earlier shortsighted and self-professed radical groups, but to the highest ethical aims of all classes. It had taken its name from the fact that it advocated the "nationalization," or the ownership by the state, of all of the means of production and distribution. With the assumption of power, the Nationalist Party had begun at once to revolutionize the entire social and industrial system.[24]

Looking Backward closed with a grand vista of progress in all phases of human activity. It portrayed an era of unlimited human happiness, of intellectual achievement, of scientific conquest of nature. It pictured a Golden Age of peace and plenty, of leisure and freedom. The wastes and social blunders of the past were gone. Humanity had reached social, intellectual, and political maturity as the twenty-first century dawned.[25]

Such, in brief summary, was the blueprint of Bellamy's society of 2000 A. D. His appeal to the highest ethical aims of all classes was, in essence, a message to those middle-class Americans who were disturbed by the increasing hardening and

22*Ibid.*, p. 59.
23*Ibid.*, p. 252.
24*Ibid.*, pp. 253-54.
25*Ibid.*, p. 292.

stratification of society along class lines. His utopia developed
out of the existing chaotic capitalism without the bitterness of
class strife. Its leaders were neither members of the plutocracy
nor working-class radicals. Bellamy's society, moreover, differed from that of any of the literary utopias which had pre-
ceded it in that it was the first to reach the millennium along the
new highways of historical and evolutionary theory.[26] Bellamy
did not create an abstract substitute for the existing social order.
Rather he suggested an alternative direction to the social and
economic trends of the day.[27] Just as Henry Drummond's
Natural Law in the Spiritual World sought to show the middle
class that Darwinian evolution was not in conflict with its
religious beliefs, so *Looking Backward* attempted to demonstrate that the great impending changes would not imperil its
regnant position in society.

At the time that Bellamy wrote *Looking Backward*, he had
not read Marx, Engels, or any of the other well-known socialist
theorists. In the summer of 1888 he wrote to William Dean
Howells: "I have never been in any sense a student of Socialistic
literature, or have known more of the various Socialist schemes
than any reader of newspapers might."[28] Undeniably, however,
he had been introduced to some of the main facets of "scientific
socialism" through Laurence Gronlund's *The Co-operative Commonwealth*. Bellamy, like Gronlund, gagged on the class-struggle thesis. But he was in complete accord with Marx's analysis
of the development of industrial concentration under a system
of capitalistic production.

Bellamy's social reconstructionism went considerably beyond
that of his contemporary social reformer, Henry George. Like
him, he was willing to use the government as an instrumentality
for achieving social change. Unlike George, he could see no
good whatever in the competitive principle. Bellamy was ready
and eager to eliminate it from all phases of human activity.

---

[26] See Joyce O. Hertzler, *History of Utopian Thought* (New York, 1926),
p. 228; Richard Hofstadter, *Social Darwinism in American Thought, 1860-
1915* (Philadelphia, 1945), pp. 93-94.

[27] For a contemporary criticism of Bellamy's views, see Morgan, pp. 385-409.

[28] Bellamy to Howells, June 17, 1888. A copy of this letter was shown to
the author by Mrs. Marion Bellamy Earnshaw of Springfield, Massachusetts.

But as a humane revolutionist, he rejected the use of force or coercion for the attainment of this end.

Looking Backward's immense sale indicated that its social message struck a resonant chord in the hearts of many Americans.[29] More copies were sold than of any other American novel since Harriet Beecher Stowe's *Uncle Tom's Cabin*.[30] Written in a simple, direct, and indeed almost conversational style that contrasted with the more ornamental prose of most contemporary novels, *Looking Backward* was pervaded with a sense of immediacy and urgency. Its appeal was especially great to humanitarian-minded members of the urban middle class who, by the late 1880's, were becoming visibly alarmed at the grasping tycoons of finance and industry and by the militant leaders of organized labor.[31]

Among those impressed by Bellamy's easy approach to the brotherhood of humanity were two young Boston newspapermen, Cyrus Field Willard, a labor reporter for the *Boston Globe*, and Sylvester Baxter, an editorial writer for the *Boston Herald*.[32] Willard and Baxter, men of taste and refinement, were interested in Theosophy.[33] Independently of each other, the two men conceived the idea of organizing a society in Boston to work for the realization of Bellamy's Nationalist society. Through the intermediation of Bellamy, to whom each had expressed his views, Willard and Baxter became the guiding spirits behind the formation of a "Nationalist Club" in Boston during the autumn of 1888.

In addition to interesting other Theosophists of the metropolitan Boston area in Bellamy's ideas, Willard and Baxter

---

[29]Morgan, p. 245. Also see Elizabeth Sadler, "One Book's Influence: Edward Bellamy's *Looking Backward*," *New England Quarterly*, XVII (1944), 530-55; Joseph Dorfman, *The Economic Mind in American Civilization*, III, 141-42, 154, 159; Ralph H. Gabriel, *The Course of American Democratic Thought* (New York, 1940), pp. 210-12; Boyd C. Shafer, "The American Heritage of Hope," *Mississippi Valley Historical Review*, XXXVII (1950), 443.

[30]Vernon L. Parrington, *Main Currents in American Thought*, Vol. III, *The Beginnings of Critical Realism in America, 1860-1920* (New York, 1930), p. 302.

[31]*Ibid.*, p. 315. Also see John Chamberlain, *Farewell to Reform* (New York, 1933), p. 55; W. D. P. Bliss, *Handbook of Socialism* (London and New York, 1895), p. 144.

[32]*Nationalist*, I (1889), 16-17.

[33]Morgan, p. 261.

found fellow enthusiasts among a group of retired Civil War officers who frequented a reading room in Boylston Street. Conceivably, the army officers, among whom were Captain Charles E. Bowers, Captain E. S. Huntington, and General Arthur F. Devereaux, "the hero of Gettysburg," were more interested in commanding the industrial army than in achieving the brotherhood of humanity.[34] Nevertheless, Theosophists and army men joined forces; and in January, 1889, after three months of preparation, the Boston Nationalist Club was launched on the rough sea of social and economic reform. While Theosophists, and in lesser degree army men, dominated the club, its membership over a period of years included such distinguished men and women as Edward Everett Hale, William Dean Howells, W. D. P. Bliss, Thomas Wentworth Higginson, Hamlin Garland, Julia Ward Howe, Frances E. Willard, Laurence Gronlund, Mary A. Livermore, Abby Morton Diaz, Lucy Stone, Helen Campbell, Thaddeus B. Wakeman, Solomon Schindler, and John Boyle O'Reilly.[35] The club's membership, while perhaps not including men of the intellectual stature of George Bernard Shaw or Sidney Webb, on the whole compared favorably with that of the London Fabian Society, founded some five years before.

From Chicopee Falls, Bellamy followed closely yet detachedly the organizational moves of the club. He commended Willard's efforts to convert to Nationalism the "cultured and conservative class . . . for which *Looking Backward* was written."[36] He appeared among his new disciples at the third preliminary organizational meeting on December 15, 1888, and was elected the club's vice-president. But for a year and a half Bellamy, who was a poor public speaker and not a leader either by nature or by inclination, took only a passive interest in the affairs of the organization.[37] If he was the prophet of a new order, he refused to be its priest. He was not even a regular contributor to the club's official publication, *The Nationalist Magazine*, which first appeared in May, 1889. Taking pride in Bellamy's

[34]*Ibid.*, p. 248.
[35]*Ibid.*, p. 251.
[36]*Ibid.*, p. 249.
[37]Henry Austin, "Edward Bellamy," *National Magazine*, IX (1898), 70-71.

retiring modesty, the Nationalists liked to contrast him with the forceful and energetic Henry George.[38]

The Declaration of Principles of the Boston Nationalist Club, adopted in January, 1889, amalgamated the ethical, mystical, other-worldly Theosophist social thought of Helen Blatavsky with the gas-and-sewage immersed Fabian Socialist economic theory of Sidney Webb. It asserted:

> The principle of the Brotherhood of Humanity is one of the eternal truths that govern the world's progress on lines which distinguish human nature from brute nature.
>
> The principle of competition is simply the application of the brutal law of the survival of the strongest and most cunning.
>
> Therefore, so long as competition continues to be the ruling factor in our industrial system, the highest development of the individual cannot be reached, the loftiest aims of humanity cannot be realized.
>
> No truth can avail unless practically applied. Therefore, those who seek the welfare of man must endeavor to suppress the system founded on the brute principle of competition, and put in its place another founded on the nobler principle of association.
>
> But in striving to apply this nobler and wiser principle to the complex conditions of modern life, we advocate no sudden or ill-considered changes; we make no war on individuals; we do not censure those who have accumulated immense fortunes simply by carrying to a logical end the false principle upon which business is now based.
>
> The combinations, trusts and syndicates of which the people at present complain demonstrate the practicability of our basic principle of association. We merely seek to push this principle a little farther, and have all industries operated in the interest of all by the nation—the people organized—the organic unity of the whole people.
>
> The present industrial system proves itself wrong by the immense wrongs it produces; it proves itself absurd by the immense waste of energy and material which is admitted to be its concomitant. Against this system we raise our protest; for the abolition of wage slavery it has wrought and would perpetuate, we pledge our best efforts.[39]

[38]*Nationalist*, II (1889), 34.

[39]W. D. P. Bliss (ed.), *Encyclopedia of Social Reforms* (New York, 1897), p. 918.

The Boston Nationalists initiated their drive for economic and social salvation with the evangelical fervor of missionaries seeking new converts. "It is a holy war, which we, who begin the struggle, must wage as a sacred duty," declared the *Nationalist*. "But with the consciousness of right, and that we are working for our fellowmen," it continued, "we can fight bravely on like soldiers, regardless of whether we ourselves shall live to the hour of triumph so long as the army presses on to final victory."[40]

The Boston Nationalist Club laid down the tenets of the new reform movement and served as parent organization for a chain of clubs extending from coast to coast and beyond to Canada, England, and New Zealand. Almost every city of consequence had at least one Nationalist club and many a sun-baked prairie town became a hotbed of "Bellamyism." In California, which Laurence Gronlund found "nearer ripe for the co-operative commonwealth than anywhere else in the country"[41] and which Nicholas Paine Gilman classified "the most excitable state in the Union," the seeds of Nationalism fell on fertile soil that needed little irrigation. By October, 1889, five Nationalist papers were being published in the Golden State.[42] In November, 1890, one hundred and fifty-eight Nationalist clubs were organized and flourishing in twenty-seven states. Of these, sixty-five were scattered throughout California and sixteen concentrated in New York City. The Nationalist movement was in full flower in February, 1891, when one hundred and sixty-five clubs were known to have been chartered.[43] Thereafter enthusiasm for Nationalism began to wane, and by 1894 the movement was all but played out.[44] The reform press in the late nineties still referred on occasion, however, to the formation of Nationalist clubs.

The clubs attracted a variegated membership. Many veteran fighters for social justice joined them; for not a few younger men and women the clubs were starting places for careers in

---

[40]*Nationalist,* III (1890), 110.

[41]*Commonwealth,* II (Mar. 2, 1895), 6.

[42]*California Nationalist,* Vol. I, No. 16 (May 24, 1890).

[43]John Hope Franklin, "Edward Bellamy and the Nationalist Movement," *New England Quarterly,* XI (1938), 754.

[44]*American Fabian,* I (Dec. 1895), 3.

the socialist and reform movements. Theosophists figured large in organizing the first Nationalist club and in publishing the *Nationalist*. Likewise, they appear to have played an important role in the affairs of some of the other clubs, notably in California. Names of members of the Protestant clergy and of the Hebrew rabbinate were conspicuous on club rosters. In San Francisco, Rabbi Samuel Freuder resigned from his synagogue to devote himself "to preaching to both Jew and Gentile the gospel of Nationalism."[45] Attracted by the Nationalists' emphasis on equality between the sexes, hundreds of women joined the clubs and in not a few constituted the bulk of the membership.

Many clubs, as has been noted of the Boston group, could boast of distinguished memberships. Present at the initial meeting of New York City's first Nationalist club were such diverse personalities as Daniel DeLeon, Lucian Sanial, and Thomas Davidson, the eminent philosopher and founder of The Fellowship of the New Life, the ethical organization out of which the London Fabian Society had developed. Other New York Nationalists included General Abner Doubleday, remembered neither for his social views nor his military exploits but as the "father of baseball"; Imogene Fales, who wrote scores of articles on social reform during the 1890's; Florence Kelly, who was on the road to fame as a social worker; and Charles Sotheran, a biographer of Horace Greeley.

In Newark, Eltweed Pomeroy, champion of direct legislation, was an enthusiast for Nationalism. Jesse Cox and Corinne Brown, who were to be members of the National Executive Board of the Social Democratic Party during the late nineties, belonged to a Chicago club, as did the famous lawyer, Clarence Darrow. A. S. Edwards, editor of several socialist papers, and Algernon Lee, a future director of the Rand School, played prominent roles in the Minneapolis Nationalist club. N. O. Nelson, a leading advocate of profit-sharing and direct legislation, was active in Buffalo Nationalist activities. Dr. C. F. Taylor, editor of *Medical World* and an indefatigable fighter for social justice, was among the reformers who joined the

---

[45]*Nationalist*, II (1890), 146.

Philadelphia club. Burnette G. Haskell, former leader of the
International Workingmen's Association, sought to recoup his
waning fortunes in a Nationalist club in San Francisco, and H.
Gaylord Wilshire, "the millionaire socialist," was a frequent
speaker at Nationalist meetings in and around Los Angeles.[46]

The diversity of interests of these people would imply that
the Nationalist clubs imposed few membership restrictions.
Since leaders of the movement had not set up a rigid doctrinaire
position to uphold, almost any social malcontent could comfort-
ably place himself under the Bellamyite standard. Largely
because of the Theosophist origins of the movement, the Nationalists shied away from a clear-cut program of political and
economic action. They exhibited unity of purpose only on the
issue of municipal ownership of public utilities. Differences
of opinion on methods and objectives, part and parcel of the
varied membership, kept the Nationalists from achieving the
cohesiveness necessary for a strong reform movement. Thomas
Wentworth Higginson, who early perceived these defects, deserted the Nationalists and became one of their most telling
critics. He described Nationalism as "a statue with feet of clay
and limbs of iron, and forehead of brass, and crutches of
splintered reeds."[47]

The middle-class character of the Nationalists was stressed
repeatedly in "club notes" in the *Nationalist*. Like the British
Fabians, they refused to consider "middle class" and "bourgeois" as terms of reproach. One Michigan correspondent reported that "Nationalism has several enthusiastic advocates
in this city, and they are not among the poor, ignorant, or visionary, but educated and talented and some of the wealthiest people
in town."[48] Both the Fall River, Massachusetts, and Fort
Dodge, Iowa, clubs sent word that Nationalist meetings were
attended by "the best people in town."[49] Mrs. Kate Buffington

---

[46]California Nationalists were sharply divided into two factions—the San
Francisco group, which published the *Pacific Union*, and the Los Angeles
group, which got out the *California Nationalist*. See *Workmen's Advocate*,
May 3, 1890.

[47]Thomas Wentworth Higginson, "Edward Bellamy's Nationalism," *Our
Day*, V (1890), 337.

[48]*Nationalist*, II (1890), 207.

[49]*Ibid.*, pp. 118, 146.

Davis, secretary of the Minneapolis club, took pride that its membership included "manufacturers, bankers, ministers, and capitalists."[50] A group of "wealthy ladies" from the Fifth Avenue district of New York City were reported to have organized a club.[51] The Chicago Nationalist club's membership was said to be composed of "lawyers, bank officers, merchants, and other people of the middle class." Its meeting of May 6, 1889, was held at the Palmer House, and admission was by written invitation only.[52]

Men and women from the working class and from the poverty-stricken segment of society rarely joined the Nationalist clubs. The clubs, therefore, were in the main free from any infusion of persons whose grievances they were seeking largely to correct. On the first anniversary of the founding of the Boston Nationalist Club, Willard noted that the organizers had made it an "unwritten law" that membership be limited as much as possible to "men who had been successful in the present fierce competitive struggle" and not open to the "crank and the uneducated foreigner importing ideas declared to be 'exotic.' "[53] A second Nationalist club in the South End section of Boston may have been a reaction to the character of the membership of the original organization,[54] though probably it catered more to women. Miss Leila J. Robinson, "the celebrated lady lawyer," was its president and one Miss Forsyth its secretary.[55]

Generally, little real effort was made to bring members of the working class into the Nationalist ranks. In the San Francisco Bay area, the Nationalists attempted to enlist trade unionists largely because of the influence of Haskell, who dominated the movement briefly.[56] In Philadelphia, P. J. McGuire, the general secretary of the American Federation of Labor and a former member of the Socialist Labor Party, was active for a time in the local club. A disillusioned Knight of Labor, L. P.

---

[50] *Ibid.*, p. 183.

[51] *Ibid.*, III (1890), 113.

[52] *Ibid.*, I (1889), 92.

[53] *Ibid.*, II (1889), 38.

[54] Morgan, p. 252.

[55] *Nationalist,* I (1889), 266.

[56] Ira B. Cross, *A History of the Labor Movement in California* (Berkeley, 1935), p. 215.

Wild, importuned members of the Knights to take up the cause of Nationalism, without any visible evidence of success.[57] Such cases were exceptions to the rule and, as General Francis A. Walker noted, "while a large amount of intellect has gone into the movement, comparatively little muscle has been enlisted in the service."[58] While the Nationalists always professed to the worker that his interests were theirs, they desired no close association with him.[59]

The prairie-fire spread of Nationalist clubs impressed Socialist Labor Party leaders, particularly those associated with its American sections. The party desperately needed native-born, respectable, middle-class backing, something Nationalists could furnish in abundance. Not surprisingly, the *Workmen's Advocate* displayed more than a passing interest in the spring of 1890 when the Boston Nationalist club circularized member organizations on the feasibility of forming a league for Nationalist political action,[60] a referendum that was to be of no consequence. During this same period the official Socialist Labor paper gave considerable sympathetic publicity to Nationalist organizations and literature. Typical was Daniel DeLeon's article: "Nationalism—Aspirations that Gave it Birth and Forces that Give it Strength." *Looking Backward*, said DeLeon, condensed and asserted "all of the cardinal principles of the most advanced economic thinkers."[61]

For the most part, the Nationalists rejected the flirtations of the Socialist Laborites. They desired to give their own particular brand of collectivism a distinctly "American" basis in both ideology and tactics. They feared contamination from the class-conscious, "European" radicalism of the Socialist Labor Party. Largely on this score, Bellamy and his followers refused to refer to themselves as "socialists." The very term "socialism," said Bellamy, brought into the mind of the average American —of which Bellamy himself was a splendid representative— ideas of atheism, revolution, and "sexual novelties."

[57]*Journal of the Knights of Labor,* May 23, 1889.
[58]F. A. Walker, "Mr. Bellamy and the New Nationalist Party," *Atlantic Monthly,* LXV (1890), 260.
[59]*Nationalist,* III (1891), 559.
[60]*Workmen's Advocate,* Mar. 29, 1890.
[61]*Ibid.,* Mar. 15, 1890.

In an article appearing in the December, 1889, issue of the *Nationalist*, Sylvester Baxter made the first effort on the part of any Nationalist leader to differentiate Nationalism from Marxian Socialism. He asserted that Nationalists were unlike Marxists in their refusal to condone class conflict, in their emphasis on reform in the United States rather than in the world, and in their willingness to work slowly through municipal and state reforms, such as public ownership of utilities.[62] Succinctly stated by Baxter, these constituted the main ideological distinctions between Nationalism and Marxian Socialism. Nationalist writers, including Bellamy, subsequently elaborated on Baxter's analysis. Nearly always, however, they agreed substantially with it.

The Nationalists and Marxists differed principally on the class struggle, a doctrine which, according to Laurence Gronlund, "never obtained among Anglo Saxons."[63] Reared in a tradition of equality of opportunity, the middle-class Nationalists could not think in terms of the class struggle, let alone accept it as a law of history. Nor would they concede that society's virtues resided in the proletariat. Appeal to the interests of a single class, they maintained, showed pettiness of outlook and lack of faith in man's intrinsic goodness. In a complex society lacking rigid class lines, it was necessary to solicit the aid and good will of progressive-minded people of all classes. There had always been in the United States, Gronlund noted, "noble hearts both among the rich and comfortable classes who had a true sympathy with the toilers and some even who were willing to sacrifice all to right their wrongs." Only with a broad basis of support could the co-operative commonwealth be ushered in equitably and peacefully.[64] Bellamy believed it unreasonable to denounce the wealthy in the name and interest of the poor since both were products of the same system.[65] The system, rather than any individual or group of individuals,

---

[62]*Nationalist,* I (1889), 82-83.

[63]*Ibid.,* II (1889), 3; Laurence Gronlund, "Nationalism," *Arena,* I (1890), 157; F. I. Vassault, "Nationalism in California," *Overland Monthly,* XV (1890), 660.

[64]Gronlund, *Arena,* I, 157.

[65]*Nationalist,* II (1889), 2.

needed to be changed.[66] "Until we call a man names, there is always the chance that we may convert him but afterwards none at all," said Bellamy.[67]

Similarly, the working class could not attain the new co-operative commonwealth by its own efforts. "The proletaire can never right matters," wrote one Nationalist, "because people regard any attempt on its part to be what it is, an effort to level society downwards. Nationalism is the converse. It aims to level upwards, always upwards, by educating the people in the principles of the brotherhood of humanity and the methods of exemplifying that relation in our daily lives."[68]

Like the English Fabians and in the vein of *Looking Backward*, the Nationalists insisted that the transition from competitive capitalism to co-operative collectivism could be made gradually and peacefully. It would come as a result of the evolutionary process of capitalistic development, because the increasing tendency toward industrial concentration meant the ultimate destruction of the existing order.[69] Here the Nationalists were in substantial agreement with the Marxists, but from there on they parted company. The Nationalists, again in accord with the Fabians, saw the evolutionary tendency speeded by the people, acting through the agency of their government. And especially ought local government be utilized, since it was most sensitive to democratic pressures. Bellamy maintained that the true Nationalist society would not be realized until all industries were under the direct control and ownership of a centralized national government.[70] But in practice, he and the Nationalists were willing to attain their ends piecemeal through municipalization of local utilities and transportation facilities.[71] Most orthodox Marxists frowned on such a utilitarian approach.

The Nationalists repudiated independent political action. Realistically, they considered the great mass of Americans both

[66]*New Nation*, III (June 24, 1893), 315.

[67]*Nationalist*, II (1889), 2.

[68]*Ibid.*, III (1890), 559.

[69]Edward Bellamy, *Equality* (New York, 1898). pp. 322-47. Also see *Nationalist*, III (1890), 87-89.

[70]*New Nation*, II (Jan. 9, 1892), 17-18.

[71]Edward Bellamy, "Progress of Nationalism in the United States," *North American Review*, CLIV (1892), 742-52.

unready for and hostile to radical change. They deemed it imperative, therefore, to prepare the minds of the people for the co-operative commonwealth by an intensive educational program. "A great many things will have to be unlearned, and a great many lessons will have to be patiently drilled into the minds of the people before they will be ripe to take matters into their own hands and go even to the extent of nationalizing railroads, telegraph, etc.," said Boston rabbi Solomon Schindler.[72] Education, organization, and agitation, methods of the British Fabians, were in order rather than political action.

The Nationalists were patriotic, in some cases to the extent of chauvinism. Here, too, they were at variance with orthodox Marxist theory. Patriotism ought to be encouraged rather than discouraged, said Bellamy, because it was "the grandest and most potent form under which the enthusiasm of humanity had yet shown itself."[73] "We are proud of Uncle Sam," Laurence Gronlund stated fervently. The Nationalists rejected, too, the Marxist contention that a closer bond existed among the wage-earners of the world than among the capitalists and proletarians of any one country. The international brotherhood of humanity loomed as a distant objective compared to the immediacy of effecting a Nationalist program in the United States. Nationalists were firm believers in the "mission of America" to guide the rest of the world, although some were willing to admit Great Britain into a partnership for the dissemination of social righteousness. They maintained that because the Anglo-Saxon countries possessed political systems which could bring about peaceful change, they would inevitably be the pathfinders to a new and better social order.[74]

Bellamy insisted that the realization of a Nationalist society would not be through efforts of foreign malcontents who came to the unguarded shores of the United States. Leadership rather would come from Americans "descended from generations of Americans"—people like Bellamy himself. Such men and

---

[72]Solomon Schindler, "First Steps to Nationalism," *Arena*, XIII (1895), 27-28. For a biographical sketch of Schindler, see Arthur Mann, "Solomon Schindler; Boston Radical," *New England Quarterly*, XXIII (1950), 453-76.

[73]*Nationalist*, II (1889), 3.

[74]*New Nation*, I (May 16, 1891), 245; Gronlund, *Arena*, I, 158.

women were better able to contrast and to judge "how strongly things were tending from good to bad," and thus ultimately assume leadership in the "counter-revolution against the growing plutocracy."[75]

Bellamy held that all men should be paid equally. This assumption, which was not shared by Gronlund, W. D. P. Bliss and many other Nationalists,[76] was in direct variance with the Marxist principle: "From each according to his powers; to each according to his needs." British Fabians, too, considered equal rewards as utopian. But to the Yankee puritan, Bellamy, equality of wages was an ethical rather than economic question. "All men who do their best do the same," he said in *Looking Backward*. "A man's endowments, however godlike, merely fix the measure of his duty."[77] Equal pay represented the only means by which distinctions among men, not based upon ability, could be abolished. "Under the present system," he declared, "it is tolerably notorious that the hardest workers and the chieftest [*sic*] producers are the poorest paid and the worst treated, while not only idlers share their product with them, but get the lion's share of it."[78] Sylvester Baxter, who was, next to Bellamy, the most able theoretician of the movement, agreed that a Nationalist form of social organization would make impossible the contemporary system of payment for services. No standard could measure an individual's contribution to society. Since all men and women were partners in the national community, he argued, they ought to share equally in their livelihood.[79]

During the early days of the movement several proposals were made suggesting "practical fulfillment" of Nationalist objectives through either an individual communitarian settlement or a league of such colonies. The "Letters to the Editor" column of the *Nationalist* published various communitarian schemes or invitations to establish colonies in many parts of the country.[80] Among the principal Nationalist leaders, Cyrus

---

[75]*New Nation*, III (Feb. 18, 1893), 94

[76]*Dawn*, III (Feb. 12, 1891), 4; Gronlund, *The New Economy* (Chicago and New York, 1898), p. 93.

[77]P. 94.

[78]Bellamy, "Looking Backward Again," *North American Review*, CL (1890), 360.

[79]*Nationalist*, I (1889), 11.

[80]*Ibid.*, III (1890), 47, 190-91; III (1891), 478-79.

Field Willard alone was sympathetic to the communitarian idea. "It is a cherished thought of mine to devise some method by which all the scattered communities could be brought together and use their united force to overthrow the present competitive system," he had written to the veteran Fourierist Alcander Longley in 1889.[81] Bellamy harbored no such ideas. "We should consider the cause of Nationalism more advanced by a single step taken by the city, state, or nation towards its ideal, and embodied in the law of the land," he wrote, "than by the complete success of some small colony founded on the full nationalist plan."[82] Yet, in the face of Bellamy's outspoken opposition to communitarian settlements, the press rarely missed an opportunity to editorialize the failure of a "Bellamy colony" as an example of the fallacy of the "socialist principle."[83]

The literature of Nationalism illustrated the class basis of the movement and its relationship to the Marxists; it also gave the movement intellectual meaning and thus provided the basis for a middle-class, non-Marxist socialist tradition. In explaining the economic, political, and ethical implications of Nationalism, its spokesmen left several definitions. In basic assumptions nearly all leading Nationalists were in agreement. In particular aspects they all differed considerably among themselves. Since Bellamy was their most important theoretician, his views on what Nationalism was and how it would evolve constitute to all intents and purposes the gospel of the movement.

Nationalism's economic meaning in terms of its lowest common denominator, said Bellamy, was in "making all production for use, and not for profit."[84] Every nationalized business was a step in the right direction insofar as it eliminated the profit motive. In the conflicting economic forces and the business crises of the day Nationalists saw not merely an unintelligible chaos but a "stream of tendencies through ever larger experiments in concentration and combination" which ultimately would integrate the economic and political forces of the nation into one.[85] Nationalists aimed, therefore, "to put an end to

[81]*Altruist*, X (Dec., 1889), 44.
[82]*New Nation*, III (Sept. 23, 1893), 434. Cf. Bellamy, *Equality*, p. 351.
[83]*Arena*, XXI (1899), 529.
[84]Bellamy, "The Programme of the Nationalist," *Forum*, XVII (1894), 86.
[85]Bellamy, *North American Review*, CLIV, 746.

the present irresponsible control of the economic interests of the country by capitalists pursuing their private ends, and to replace it by responsible public agencies acting for the general welfare."[86]

Political democracy in which the people collectively controlled their government, without economic democracy in which the people collectively controlled the means of production and distribution, was worthless, according to Bellamy. And economic democracy constituted the chief objective of the Nationalists. Said Bellamy:

> Nationalism . . . is the doctrine of those who hold that the principle of popular government by the equal voice of all for the equal benefit of all, which, in advanced nations is already recognized as the law of political organization, should be extended to the economic organization as well; and that the entire capital and labor of the nations should be nationalized and administered by their people through their chosen agents, for the equal benefit of all, under an equal law of industrial service.[87]

If political democracy, only, were to exist, great capitalists could still exercise irresponsible economic power in behalf of their own private interests. Neither individual nor community would be spared by the plutocracy in its drive to control both the economic and political power of the nation. "The industrial system of a nation, like its political system," Bellamy asserted, "should be a government of the people, by the people, and for the people. Until economic equality shall give a basis to political equality, the latter is but a sham."[88]

Nationalism meant something more than a political and economic system. It involved an ethical way of life. "Nothing can be in the long run or on a large scale sound economics which is not sound ethics," said Bellamy, expressing sentiments similar to those of the founders of the American Economic Association. It was no mere coincidence but a logical necessity that equality should be of basic importance in both economics and ethics.[89]

---

[86]Bellamy, *Forum,* XVII, 81.
[87]Bellamy, *North American Review,* CLIV, 742.
[88]*New Nation,* III (Apr. 15, 1893), 35.
[89]Bellamy, *Equality,* p. 195.

In giving the title *Equality* to the sequel of *Looking Backward*, Bellamy went straight to the heart of his social beliefs.

The transition from a competitive, capitalistic society to a co-operative Nationalist order would be slow, orderly, and in accord with the innate workings of economic evolution under capitalism. On this point all Nationalists were fundamentally in agreement. In words which might easily have been written by Sidney Webb, Bellamy declared:

> They [the Nationalists] propose no revolutionary methods, no hasty or ill-considered measures provocative of reaction, no letting go of the old before securing a hold on the new; but an orderly progress, of which each step shall logically follow the last, and shall be justified to the most shortsighted by its immediate motives and results without invoking any considerations of ultimate ends. Those who wish to go only a step at a time, we welcome as allies, and we pledge them a co-operation which is not the less cordial and considerate because of the fact that results which they regard as ends seem to us but means to ends.[90]

Bellamy explained further that Nationalists planned to effect their program gradually, "first embracing certain semi-public businesses and extending to others as indicated by their special conditions; the controlling idea being always to avoid derangement of business and undue hardship to individuals." Confiscation was definitely not a method of Nationalism,[91] said Bellamy, who strongly respected personal property rights. When private plants were taken over by a city, state, or nation, compensation would be paid to the owners. The basis of valuation would be "the present cost of a plant of equal utility."[92]

The broad theoretical generalities of the Nationalist leaders failed to satisfy the rank and file. The former considered themselves primarily as interpreters and teachers; the latter was more interested in action. Bellamy was aware of the frustration among many Nationalists who, after having been inspired by *Looking Backward*, felt the need of a program for practical implementation. In response to persistent demands for such a program, he listed five realizable objectives for which

---

[90]Bellamy, "First Steps toward Nationalism," *Forum*, X (1890), 183.
[91]Bellamy, *North American Review*, CL, 362.
[92]Bellamy, *Forum*, XVII, 89.

members of the movement could work. He refused, however, to give any one priority over the others.

First, Bellamy advocated a new school system which would raise the age limit of compulsory education. Children would not be employed during school hours, and families of the poor were to be partially supported by the state. Economically underprivileged children would thereby be able to attend schools without placing a financial burden on their parents. The second objective of the Nationalists was the public ownership of municipal heating, lighting, and street car facilities. All further municipal franchises to individuals or private corporations were to be discontinued. Third, Bellamy asked for nationalization, or ownership by the Federal government, of all telephone and telegraph lines, express offices, railroads, and mineral deposits which might be discovered in the future. Coal mines, for some inexplicable reason, were to be controlled but not owned by the Federal government. The fourth part of the program called for the employment of 1,500,000 additional men and women in the public services. And lastly, he urged Nationalists to campaign against political office holders who retained positions with industrial concerns.[93]

Whereas in *Looking Backward* Bellamy had predicted the rise of a great Nationalist political party, in actual practice he opposed political activity to carry out the aims of the Nationalist clubs. His objections to Nationalist political action were much like those of Marxist leaders during the 1870's and 1880's. Formation of a Nationalist political party, he feared, would corrupt and weaken the movement; the lure of public office was enough to turn the most ardent reformer into a scheming politician. Nationalists could garner only a few votes at the polls, which were controlled by the smooth-running machines of the two old parties. A poor showing would only serve to discredit the real aims of the movement in the eyes of the people. Bellamy's fears were eminently justified by events. In Rhode Island and in California, local Nationalist groups had sponsored candidates in elections and in both instances the results had been disastrous.[94]

[93]Bellamy, *North American Review*, CL, 362-63.
[94]*New Nation*, I (Mar. 14, 1891), 101, 103; *ibid.* (Apr. 11, 1891), p. 165; *ibid.* (Oct. 24, 1891), p. 615; *ibid.* (Apr. 25, 1891), p. 203.

Nationalists figured impressively, however, in the reform movement during the years between 1889 and 1894. Hardly an issue of the *Nationalist*, or its successor, *The New Nation*, which Bellamy personally edited, appeared without notice of a Nationalist group's participation in some local agitation, be it for pure food and drug laws, for public ownership of utilities, or for more democratic government. In agitating for reform and in publicizing many of capitalism's social defects, the Nationalists have their real significance. After the early nineties, thanks largely to their efforts, the great majority of Americans was no longer to be a stranger to collectivist ideas, as had been true in the 1880's. Nationalists, moreover, gave these ideas a respectability hitherto lacking. In the words of the fastidious Harry Thurston Peck, *Looking Backward* and Nationalism "brought Socialism up from the workshops and beer-gardens into the libraries and drawing rooms."[95] No longer were the demands for public ownership of the means of production and distribution voiced almost exclusively by a small group of working-class radicals. The Nationalist movement brought the middle class into the struggle for public ownership. After the turn of the century when the reform tide was running high, "Muckrakers" and Progressives were to follow along trails blazed by the Nationalists.

In California, the Los Angeles Nationalist clubs, which were organized by wards, worked principally for direct legislation, the Australian ballot, and abolition of private municipal franchises;[96] the Oakland club, composed mainly of women, championed a child labor bill.[97] In New York City, where the evils of the tenement house and "sweating" system were notorious, the Nationalist clubs agitated for improved social and school laws and "proper factory legislation for children."[98] The New York Nationalists also sought a municipally owned rapid transit system. Samuel Gompers recalled in his autobiography that the initiative for the organization of a Labor Press Association

---

[95] Harry Thurston Peck, *Twenty Years of the Republic, 1885-1905* (New York, 1906), p. 735.

[96] *California Nationalist*, Vol. I, No. 16 (May 24, 1890); *Nationalist*, II (1890), 146.

[97] *Nationalist*, II (1890), 275.

[98] *Ibid.*, p. 148.

in New York came from a group of Nationalists including Cyrus Field Willard and Henry Austin.[99]

A Nationalist correspondent in Kansas City, Missouri, wrote: "There is already a clean-cut issue between the people here and a private water-monopoly. We hope to see that pushed to a finish and to at least enter the wedge at other vulnerable points against monopoly."[100] A year later Nationalists in Kansas and in other prairie states were co-operating with the Farmers' Alliance and various radical groups in congressional elections.[101] In Philadelphia the Nationalist club was widely and favorably publicized for its investigation of public works deficiencies and industrial conditions, even to the extent of commendation by some of the more conservative local papers.[102]

In Massachusetts, the nerve center of the movement, Nationalists campaigned aggressively for cheaper power rates and for municipal ownership of public utilities. In 1889 Nationalists in the area of Boston, which Charles A. Dana caustically referred to as "Bellamyville," circulated petitions for the passage of a bill by the state legislature permitting municipalities to construct and operate their own gas and electric plants. The bill was pushed through the House but defeated by the Senate which, according to the Nationalists, was controlled by the state power-trusts. Undaunted, Nationalists resumed their campaign the following year and obtained more than 13,000 signatures on a petition favoring the measure. The bill was brought up before the legislature again and, after a bitter fight, was passed.[103] Nationalists did not carry on the struggle single-handed; they were backed by labor organizations and by strong public sentiment. Yet they undeniably led the campaign for the enactment of the measure despite the determined opposition of a combination of electric and gas companies which, by Bellamy's reckoning, represented $35,000,000 in capital.[104]

---

[99]Gompers, *Seventy Years of Life and Labor,* I, 442-43.

[100]*Nationalist,* II (1889), 79.

[101]*Ibid.,* III (1890), 114.

[102]*New Nation,* II (Apr. 2, 1892), 217.

[103]Henry Winn to H. D. Lloyd, Feb. 14, 1895. Lloyd Papers. Gilman, *Socialism and the American Spirit,* p. 218.

[104]Bellamy, *North American Review,* CLIV, 742 ff.

Boston Nationalists also carried on a vigorous "muckraking" campaign. They produced statistical data to demonstrate that the city was being charged an exorbitant rate by private power companies for services to public buildings. The *Nationalist* accused the Board of Aldermen of smothering a bill for public ownership of municipal utilities because of personal interests in the Great Bay Gas monopoly.[105] Boston Nationalists also waged a spirited fight for pure food and drug reform. Using statistics compiled by the Massachusetts Board of Health, they showed that 30.9 per cent of the state's food, 39.6 per cent of its milk, and 26.4 per cent of its drugs had been adulterated.[106] "Only by making the manufacture of food supplies and drugs public business," said the *New Nation*, "could pure food be assured and adulterations completely prevented."[107]

Like social reformers of the ensuing generation, the Nationalists warned against the danger of plutocracy and sought to show the interlocking of big business and political interests. Anticipating the famous Congressional Pujo Report of twenty-three years later, the *Nationalist* said that fifty men in the United States could control the commerce and currency of the country and bring economic life to a standstill, if they so saw fit.[108] Repeated attacks on the influence of corporate business in government appeared in the *Nationalist* and the *New Nation*. Industrialists were condemned for sponsoring hand-picked candidates, and lobbyists were assailed for helping to secure legislation favorable to trusts and monopolies. "When your legislators are mere puppets in the hands of the money kings, what have you left of a Government of the People, by the People, and for the People?" asked a *Nationalist* article addressed to the citizens of Massachusetts. "Do you consent to this? Shall your state become a permanent plutocracy?"[109] Public officials, it noted, declined re-election in order to become lobbyists, as more money could be made in such an occupation. The lobby of the 1889 Massachusetts legislature was alleged to include ex-

[105]*Nationalist*, I (1889), 59.

[106]*Ibid.*, p. 263.

[107]*New Nation*, I (May 30, 1891), 277.

[108]*Nationalist*, III (1890), 195.

[109]*Ibid.*, I (1889), 231-32.

Presidents of the Senate, ex-Speakers of the House, and ex-Governors.[110]

Nationalists shared with other reformers of the late 1890's and practical progressives of the first decade of the twentieth century the conviction that many economic injustices could be corrected by the still further extension of political democracy.[111] They championed adoption of the initiative and referendum, woman suffrage, and direct election of United States Senators. In the initiative, said Bellamy, was contained one of the most potent weapons for "the deliverance of the people from the money power." When the initiative was complemented by the referendum, the people, who in the last analysis were nearly always right, would be in a position to drive the politicians "out of business."[112]

As members of a movement dedicated to general social and economic amelioration, the Nationalists had to face the problem of active co-operation with other contemporary reform and labor groups. If the Boston Bellamyites constituted, in effect, the high command of the movement, the Nationalist policy was to oppose all alignments with other groups and full commitments on their programs. "Nationalists should adhere firmly to the principles of Nationalism, pure and simple, and not permit themselves to dissipate their energies taking up minor issues," asserted a blunt editorial in the *Nationalist*.[113] While this statement of policy conceivably satisfied the Theosophist editors of the magazine, it appeared unrealistic to most of the men and women enrolled in the local clubs, the doers of the movement. As a consequence, Nationalists often joined forces with other groups in local situations.

In the early nineties Nationalism shared the reform stage with the single-tax and eight-hour-day movements, but with neither was there wholehearted and mutual co-operation. Bellamy and the Nationalists accepted Henry George's ideas on unearned increment in land values.[114] But they did not agree

[110]*Ibid.*, p. 231.
[111]*Ibid.*, II (1889), 13.
[112]*New Nation*, III (Jan. 21, 1893), 33.
[113]*Nationalist*, II (1890), 414.
[114]Bellamy, *Equality*, p. 191.

with the insistence of many of George's followers—not of George himself—that the removal of unearned increment on land would solve entirely the country's social and economic problems. Associated closely with the land-rent issue were questions of interest and profits, which Bellamy and every other shade of socialist insisted, were equally important forms of unearned increment. If interest and profits from capital investments continued to exist, the single tax would be completely inadequate.[115] While admittedly a step in the right direction, the single tax stopped far short of the final goal. The nationalization of land, the Bellamyites maintained, merely would form the basement of a new social and economic edifice. It was just as important that the Vanderbilts and Goulds should not monopolize the first floor, and the capitalist class as a whole not enjoy the light and comfort of the upper stories.[116]

Little unanimity of opinion was to be found among the Nationalists on the question of practical co-operation with the single taxers. Scores of letters came to the offices of the *Nationalist* and the *New Nation* expressing the hope that the two reform groups would get together even though their ultimate objectives in the form of social and political organization were different.[117] Occasionally the Nationalists and single taxers joined forces to work for such aims as municipal ownership of utilities or nationalization of railroads and telegraphs. But extensive co-operation was never forthcoming, and relations between the two groups were characterized generally by sniping and bickering.

That they were "for" but not "of" the working class largely determined the position taken by Nationalists toward labor organizations. Bellamy asserted that labor unions were necessary, if for no other reason than to combat the already united phalanx of capitalists. But most of his followers, while granting labor's inherent right to organize,[118] were unable to escape their middle-class prejudices and placed little faith in labor unions and their leaders, especially when resort was made to

---

[115]*Ibid.*, p. 192.
[116]*Nationalist*, I (1889), 220.
[117]*Ibid.*, III (1890), 188, 339-40, 477-78.
[118]*Ibid.*, II (1890), 330; III (1890), 99.

the strike. It would not do to substitute the selfishness of the trade union for that of the capitalist, said Bellamy, whose views were to change perceptibly during the course of the nineties.[119] Nor would it suffice, said an editorial in the *Nationalist*, to replace oppressive factory owners with labor leaders who, more often than not, might be "unscrupulous demagogues, ever ready to betray [the members of unions] for . . . selfish advantage."[120]

Uppermost in the thoughts of many labor leaders in the United States during the eighties and nineties was the attainment of the eight-hour workday. It transcended all other trade-union issues. The eight-hour day was the same kind of a panacea for the working class as Nationalism and the single-tax remedy were for the social protestants of the *petit bourgeoisie*. It offered workers an opportunity to improve their lot without the paternalism of the state or the humanitarianism of other groups in society. A more equitable distribution of wealth, ostensibly, would be its ultimate result.

The Nationalist high command equivocated on the eight-hour day. Here, as on other issues, they were plagued by the duality of Nationalism as an ultimate social ideal and as an immediate plan of campaign. Theoretically, they held back their blessing from the eight-hour-day movement because it proposed to operate under the existing capitalistic system.[121] In practice, the same Nationalist leaders acknowledged the advisability of limiting the number of working hours and of supporting this popular labor demand. In 1890 the parodoxical situation existed wherein the Boston Nationalist club, which at its annual meeting had opposed committing Nationalists to advocacy of the eight-hour day, was circularizing the affiliated organizations throughout the country urging their assistance in the obtaining of eight-hour-day legislation.[122]

Considerably more sympathy and understanding were shown to organized labor, however, when Bellamy took personal charge of the Nationalist publication. His approach to labor problems was more realistic than that of the Theosophists who had edited

---

[119]Cf. *Looking Backward*, p. 253, with *Equality*, pp. 209, 318.
[120]*Nationalist*, I (1889), 216.
[121]*Ibid.*, II (1889), 76. Also see *ibid.*, III (1890), 33-35.
[122]*Ibid.*, II (1890), 183.

the *Nationalist*. The outbreak of industrial warfare on a national scale in 1892 sharpened his sympathies for the working class. In the Homestead Strike the *New Nation* stood firm in support of the workers and their union. It scored the Carnegie Company's labor-baiting policies, the use of Pinkertons and strike-breakers, and resort to the state militia.[123] While showing little sympathy for Alexander Berkman, the anarchist who attempted to assassinate company manager Henry Clay Frick, it did not commiserate with Frick, who was described as "particularly brutal . . . an arrogant oppressor of the people and promoter of industrial disorder." The whole affair was designated a "barren victory" for capitalism. It signified the "desperate character of industrial discontent which must soon issue either in anarchy or nationalism."[124]

Nationalism was a movement which exploded in all directions at the same time. That was its principal weakness. Its energies were never channelized. It had little organization, less leadership, and almost nothing in the way of a co-ordinated working program. After the first flush of enthusiasm had passed, it failed to attract new converts and lost the services of several able men who had initially been its sponsors. Even its utopian objectives lacked those elements of imminent expectation and of ultimate fulfillment that won countless thousands over to Marxist ideological doctrines which, in the last analysis, were no less utopian. Perhaps all of this was inherent in the original nature of the movement. Yet Nationalism, organizationally considered, was not destined to fail, for it might have gone the way of British Fabianism, to which it was so similar.

By 1892 Populism had sapped the Nationalist movement of any real vigor it still had. The People's Party had a prospect for immediate success entirely lacking in Nationalism. Hundreds of Nationalists joined the Populists, leaving the clubs virtually hollow shells. Despite a publicized meeting of Nationalist leaders at the Chicago World's Fair in 1893 to discuss new tactics, the disintegration of the movement was apparent.[125] Suspension of publication of the *New Nation* on February 3,

---

[123] *New Nation*, II (July 16, 1892), 453.
[124] *Ibid.*, II (July 30, 1892), 481-82; *ibid.* (Nov. 26, 1892), p. 698.
[125] *Ibid.*, III (Sept. 16, 1893), 428.

1894, was a severe blow to both the Nationalists and to Bellamy, who not only lost a large part of his meager fortune but also impaired his health under the strain of getting out the magazine week after week. Whatever Nationalist propaganda was published thereafter came from a Bureau of Nationalist Literature headed by B. Franklin Hunter of Philadelphia. Hunter vainly sought to keep the spark of Nationalism aglow, but by 1896 the movement as an organization was all but dead. Only a few isolated clubs lingered on in different parts of the country.

Still, the spontaneous formation of Nationalist clubs was one of the more extraordinary phenomena of a troubled decade. Bellamy's followers provided the force behind a mighty ground swell of socialist and reform agitation. They challenged, too, the widely accepted laissez faire doctrines of Herbert Spencer. After the propaganda spadework of the Nationalists, the principle of government ownership and regulation became the favorite solution for the social and economic ills of the United States up to the outbreak of the first World War.

IV. The Christian Socialist Crusade

In THE decades immediately prior to the Civil War, the Protestant pulpit was a bulwark of social stability. Northern Protestant clergymen were among the most active Abolitionists, but only rarely did they see fit to protest against the obvious injustices that resulted from the prevailing economic order. Rumblings of discontent during the Jacksonian period annoyed rather than frightened the clergy, particularly those members reared in the Calvinistic tradition of thrift, hard work, and stewardship. To confront the grumblers and to prove the heresy of their demands, Francis Wayland and other academic doctors of divinity confidently resorted to the Manchester School's laissez faire doctrines, distilling and redistilling them in lectures on political economy in American colleges. The clergy's faith in "natural economic laws," and in the men of affairs who operated under their assumptions, was coupled with a thoroughgoing condemnation of any misguided persons who might question them. Ricardo's "iron law of wages" answered with an indisputable finality those radicals who would obtain more money for workers through strikes. The existence of misery was unfortunate but inevitable since it stemmed from the weaknesses of human nature; it did not inhere in the economic system.[1]

Post Civil War years witnessed the rapid and dramatic inclination of the American economy toward industrial capitalism. The attendant social problems were brought starkly to attention by the unprecedented violence of the railroad strike of 1877, by the Eight-Hour Day strikes and the Haymarket Square incident of 1886, and by the swelling labor unrest during the first half of the 1890's. Likewise, the sprawling urban slum areas, created in large part by the new industrialism, became an

---

[1]For an account of the Protestant church's attitude toward social and economic problems in preindustrial America, see Henry F. May, *Protestant Churches and Industrial America* (New York, 1949), pp. 3-87.

[103]

ugly and socially dangerous malignancy upon the American scene.

The overwhelming majority of Protestant ministers, with eyes turned serenely upward in contemplation of heavenly salvation or gloweringly downward in condemnation of the new infidel Darwinian evolutionary theory, displayed startling incomprehension of the forces behind the new industrialism. Nor did these clergymen appreciate industrialism's human costs, which were explained, if and when at all, not in terms of the economic system as such but on the basis of human depravity. To industrial workers barely existing on subsistence wages, this shopworn explanation of poverty had a patently false ring. Small wonder that they began to stay away in droves from the "rich men's churches."

Keenly aware of the jaded nature of the ecclesiastical defense of the status quo and deeply worried over the growing alienation between the church and the wage-earner class, some clergymen searched for more satisfactory answers. This latter group, generally associated with the Social Gospel movement, sensed a marked divergence between the social ideals of Christianity and the assumptions of the new economic order.[2] The church, they felt, could neither give positive sanction to the new industrial capitalism nor be a passive witness of its social implications. The most radical of these churchmen went still further in deeming it insufficient to speak out against subsistence wages, long hours of toil in dimly lighted and insufficiently ventilated factories, and employment of children in mines and mills. They demanded that the church lead the way to a new ordering of society based on the principles of Christ's gospels.

---

[2]Most complete account of the Social Gospel movement is found in Charles H. Hopkins, *The Rise of the Social Gospel in American Protestantism, 1865-1915* ("Yale Studies in Religious Education," Vol. XIV [New Haven, 1940]). Other important treatments of the movement are found in May, *Protestant Churches and Industrial America;* Aaron I. Abell, *The Urban Impact on American Protestantism, 1865-1900* ("Harvard Historical Studies," Vol. LIV [Cambridge, 1943]); James Dombrowski, *The Early Days of Christian Socialism in America* (New York, 1936); Gabriel, *The Course of American Democratic Thought,* pp. 308-30; Charles and Mary Beard, *The American Spirit* (New York, 1942), pp. 446-63; Merle Curti, *The Growth of American Thought* (New York, 1943), pp. 629-32; M. C. Latta, "The Background for the Social Gospel in American Protestantism," *Church History,* V (1936), 256-70.

If the church were to assume the leadership of a general movement for societal rehabilitation, it would have to take a completely different view of its functions, the Christian radicals maintained. "I am tired of the cant of the churches, touching the necessity of a change of heart," said the Reverend Alexander Kent, a leading Nationalist and pastor of the People's Church in Washington, D. C. "Change of heart that leaves the great body of Christians in all churches in love with the devilish spirit of our competitive system, is a change that will never bring the Kingdom of God to men, and therefore can never take men to the Kingdom of God."[3] Similarly, Wendell Phillips' biographer, the Reverend Carlos Martyn, wrote: "The Church will never rehabilitate itself in popular influence by meretricious expedients. It is not to be saved by broom drills, dairy-maid fairs, and catchpenny festivals. . . . No; the church must interest itself in practical affairs. It must be a leader in good words and works. It must vindicate its right to be by divine helpfulness."[4]

The radical Social Gospelers, notably those associated with the Episcopal Church, were greatly influenced by the writings of the English Christian Socialists, by the tracts of the London Fabian Society, and by the social criticisms of John Ruskin. They were under equal if not greater intellectual obligation, however, to Henry George, Edward Bellamy, and Jesse H. Jones. George and Bellamy, of course, were well known to their own generation, but Jones, though admired by a small group of Protestant clerics, was little recognized by other contemporaries. His reputation rests largely on recent scholarship.[5]

Jones was an eccentric, Harvard-trained Congregationalist minister from North Abington, Massachusetts. He preached an unorthodox and mystical brand of Christian communism, the details of which were set forth in two murky books, *The Kingdom of Heaven* (1871) and *The Bible Plan for the Abolition of Poverty* (1873). In 1872 he inspired the organization of the Christian Labor Union, which for six years sought to educate Boston's wage earners in the principles of trade unionism and

[3]*Dawn*, IV (Dec. 7, 1892).

[4]Carlos Martyn, "Churchianity vs. Christianity," *Arena*, II (1890), 157.

[5]For detailed treatment of Jones, see Hopkins, pp. 42-49; May, pp. 75-79; Dombrowski, pp. 77-83.

labor reform. He also edited the union's two short-lived papers, *Equity: A Journal of Christian Labor Reform* and *The Labor Balance*.

Jones sounded the pitch-pipe for a chorus of social protest that was to peal out from left-wing clergymen in the last decade of the nineteenth century. But during the seventies his radicalism proved either too indigestible or too peppery for the stomachs of even the most socially aware Protestant clergymen. His espousal of government ownership of the means of production and distribution; his demand for abolition of rent, interest, and profits; and his support of the Knights of Labor and the Socialist Labor Party placed him "beyond the pale of respectability."

During the early 1880's the adoption of direct-action techniques by the immigrant social revolutionaries caused many Protestant pastors to abandon their complacency and take note of the challenges of socialism and anarchism. Loyal to social conservatism, the ministry, almost to a man, opposed the radical ideologies. The objections raised against socialism were essentially those which had already become traditional: the dwarfing of the individual in a society dedicated to equality, the immorality of the class-struggle thesis, the atheism and materialism of Marxism, the economic fallacy of the surplus-value theory, the concentration of oppressive power in the state, and the delusion of seeking regeneration through society as a whole rather than through the individual.

Some churchmen, like the Columbus, Ohio, Congregationalist, Washington Gladden, and the New York Episcopalian, R. Heber Newton, agreed that the socialists had raised questions regarding American industrial society that necessitated more cogent explanations than had heretofore been advanced by apologists for capitalism, lay and clerical alike. These early Social Gospelers, while opposing political socialism, recognized a need for greater individual opportunity and social equality. In the mood of reform rather than revolution, they proposed various means for the fulfillment of this need: greater church attention to and sympathy with trade unions and with the problems of the wage-earning class; encouragement of co-operation and profit-sharing; more extensive social and economic planning by the state; and determined efforts to blunt class antagonisms by a heightened sense of social responsibility on the part of the possessing class.[6]

By the end of the 1880's many socially inclined ministers and lay religious leaders were advocating a more radical solution of the industrial problem. Undoubtedly, the tremendous popular success of *Looking Backward* and the acerbity of the industrial warfare of the early nineties had much to do with inspiring clergymen and pious laymen to embrace socialism. Some did so quietly, while others announced their conversion with a vehemence that shocked their congregations and friends. In the main, they did not hesitate to call themselves socialists, though few were willing to be designated as such without the limiting prefix, "Christian." They wanted no association in the public mind with the godless Marxists. With the ardor of recent converts, they preached the gospel of a new order that would be socialistic in its organic collectivism and Christian in its spiritual values. They wished, in short, to achieve the Kingdom of God on earth and the Brotherhood of Man. In an age of industrial buccaneering, they proposed to give society a social and economic ethic based upon the Sermon on the Mount.[7]

Books on Christian Socialism, rolling off the presses of American publishing houses in increasing number, gave evidence of a rising public interest. One of the most widely read of these was the Reverend Franklin Monroe Sprague's *Socialism from Genesis to Revelation*. Sprague, a Congregationalist minister from Agawam, Massachusetts, maintained that the church had to make a clear-cut choice between God and Mammon. Rejecting Gladden's willingness to reform the abuses of capitalism, he held that the church could not continue to serve the Devil and at the same time give lip service to God. The choices were clear: "pro-capitalism or anti-capitalism . . . caste or equality; riches or righteousness; competition or co-operation; self-interest or self-denial; the 'bitter envyings and strife' or neighborly love; anarchistic laissez-faire or mutual protection; plutocracy

---

[6]Hopkins, pp. 65-78; May, pp. 170-203.

[7]For a sharp rejoinder to the Christian Socialist position, see Reverend Lyman Abbott, "Christianity vs. Socialism," *North American Review*, CXLVIII (1889), 447-53; Edward S. Parsons, "A Christian Critique of Socialism," *Andover Review*, XI (1889), 597-611.

or theocracy; in a word Individualism or Socialism." The church, Sprague insisted, could not continue its "temporizing and Pharasaical attitude" toward wealth. "The spirit of the Master and of His gospels" was "uncompromisingly against the possession of riches amid want and suffering."[8]

Sprague found no difficulty in reconciling Christianity and socialism. Each was cosmopolitan, embracing all men everywhere. Equality, "as taught in the Bible," he said, was often more honored by socialists than by the church itself. Socialism upheld the Christian doctrine of stewardship in its recognition that wealth was not for personal emolument but for the benefit of society. And socialism, like Christianity, sought greater social justice and an end to the existing "commercial justice" which glorified the strong and crushed the weak.[9]

Vida D. Scudder, just at the starting point of a distinguished teaching career at Wellesley College, had immersed herself in the New Testament, Sir Thomas More's *Utopia*, the writings of Frederick D. Maurice, and the Fabian Essays. These led her to a magnificent vision of "revolution by consent" and a temperate advocacy of Christian Socialism. She made no claim that socialism would create a race of either heroes or saints. Human nature could not be changed. But socialism, said Miss Scudder, might "produce a race of men ready to enter with new zest the domain of new interests which we today are too heavily burdened freely to explore."[10] Socialism aimed to bring about universal conditions which would make for the best environment and the best work. It would eliminate the helplessly bored— the very rich and the very poor. "It would render possible, for the first time for centuries, literal obedience to the commands of the Master; it would enable men to 'take no thought for the morrow,' for it would remove from them the necessity of constant thought for what they shall eat, what they shall drink, and wherewithal they shall be clothed." The same results could be reached more simply and directly through obedience to the

---

[8]Franklin M. Sprague, *Socialism from Genesis to Revelation* (Boston, 1893), pp. 236-37, 471.

[9]*Ibid.*, pp. 6-7.

[10]Vida D. Scudder, "Social and Spiritual Progress, A Speculation," *Andover Review,* XVI (1891), 62-63.

"lucent words of Christ . . . which history and psychology reveal as a natural law." But she acknowledged that this state had not yet come to pass.[11]

Sprague and Miss Scudder were among the many who advanced intellectual justification for Christian Socialism in the United States during the late eighties and nineties. But its great proselytizer, its Saint Paul who carried the word throughout the length and breadth of the land, was the Massachusetts Episcopal clergyman, W. D. P. Bliss. Like his contemporary, Supreme Court Justice David Josiah Brewer, Bliss was born of Congregationalist missionary parents in Turkey. But that was as far as the parallel between the two men went. Brewer, trained in the individualism of a Kansas frontier society and imbued with the constitutional ratiocinations of his uncle, Justice Stephen J. Field, was to become a bulwark of judicial conservatism and a fierce opponent of socialism in all of its forms. Bliss, spiritually sickened by what he had observed in the bleak New England mill villages and deeply influenced by the economic treatises of Henry George and the British Fabians, became a vocal and fearless critic of the status quo and an exponent of social and religious radicalism.

Bliss was educated for the Congregationalist ministry at Amherst and the Hartford Theological Seminary, from which he graduated in 1882. Originally he had planned to go into the missionary service, but on entering the Congregationalist ministry he knew that his calling was not to convert the heathen of foreign lands. Instead, he dedicated himself to seeking out greater social justice for the less privileged in the United States.

Following a brief pastorate in the little town of South Natick, Massachusetts, Bliss left the church of his forebears for the Episcopal ministry into which he was accepted on October 25, 1885. In making this change in religious affiliation, Bliss was motivated by both doctrinal and social considerations. He believed that the Episcopal Church alone, among the various Protestant denominations, represented the original Catholic idea of ecclesiastical unity. Furthermore, he considered it more sec-

---

[11]*Ibid.*, p. 61. For a more complete exposition of Miss Scudder's social attitude, see Vida D. Scudder, *Socialism and Character* (Boston, 1912).

ular in outlook and hence more concerned with the cause of social reform than any of the other Protestant churches.[12]

Bliss's first official duty as an Episcopalian minister was as licensed lay reader in St. George's Church in the industrial town of Lee, Massachusetts. The three years that he served at Lee were in reality an apprenticeship for the remainder of his life. He formed a warm and lasting friendship with George E. McNeill, the veteran eight-hour-day advocate and one time associate of Jesse H. Jones in the Christian Labor Union.[13] Plunging into the trade-union movement, he joined the Knights of Labor and quickly rose to the rank of Master Workman in the local assembly. In 1887, the young and energetic clergyman, now widely renowned as a champion of the wage earner, was nominated for Lieutenant Governor by the short-lived Massachusetts Labor Party. But most important of all, Bliss's ideas became crystallized at Lee, and he took up the cause of Christian Socialism which had lain dormant since Jones had cried vainly into the capitalistic wilderness in the 1870's.

Bliss's temperate approach to socialism reflected an assimilation of the philosophy and methods of the British Fabians. Sharing their Victorian attachment to the idea of progress, he considered the nineteenth century the greatest period in the development of civilization and fully expected the twentieth and twenty-first centuries to be even better. Christian Socialists, he believed, could build with assurance for the future on the basis of the present. In Anglo-Saxon countries, in particular, they had firm foundations, since well-established, essentially democratic, political institutions facilitated the accommodation of socialism,[14] oversimplified by Bliss as "democracy in business."

Rejecting the rigidity of Marxism, Bliss welcomed the adoption of all progressive measures, not necessarily as ends in themselves but as means to ends. Thus, he favored co-operation, profit-sharing, trade unionism, the eight-hour day, associations of all kinds, ballot reform, civil-service reform, and land re-

---

[12]W. D. P. Bliss, "Socialism in the Church of England," *Andover Review,* X (1888), 496.

[13]*Dawn,* VII (Nov., 1895), 1.

[14]*Ibid.,* I (Jan., 1890), 2.

form. "Through all these practical, gradual, immediate reforms," he declared, "positively, scientifically, constructively,
we would pass towards the future. That must come gradually
and freely which comes to stay."[15]

Again like the Fabians, Bliss stressed municipal ownership
of public utilities as the most important form of socialism. "It,
too, has the advantage of tending most to Democratic Socialism,
and the development of local self-government," he said. "It can
most speedily reach the crying evils of our times, the evil, and
unutterably evil conditions of our large cities." Christian Socialists, in contradistinction to the Marxists, he once stated,
were loath "to turn everything over to Uncle Sam, trusting to
Uncle Sam to realize God's Kingdom in the United States."[16]

In 1887 Bliss went to Boston to take charge of the Mission of
the Grace Church. During the same year he helped to organize
in New York City the (Episcopal) Church Association for the
Advancement of the Interests of Labor, better known as the
CAIL. The CAIL affiliated itself with no political reform
group. Nor did it adhere to any set of rigid political or economic principles. Its chief activities were mediating labor disputes and helping to frame industrial legislation. It represented
the first organized attempt by a church denominational group
to counter the accusation that religious bodies were laggard in
meeting their community responsibilities. The CAIL's president was Bishop F. D. Huntington, and its list of vice-presidents
numbered more than forty other Episcopal bishops, most of
them High Churchmen.[17]

The CAIL was one of many organizations that Bliss was to
have a hand in founding. He was, for example, a charter member of the first Nationalist club organized in Boston in 1888.
Nationalism's espousal of the brotherhood of man and its condemnation of the class struggle made it acceptable to him. But
he had little patience with the impractical Theosophists and
Civil War veterans who formed the nucleus of the club. As
early as February, 1889, he was conferring with other Nation-

[15]*Ibid.*, p. 1.

[16]*Ibid.*, II (July-Aug., 1890), 112.

[17]May, p. 104; Spencer Miller, Jr., and Joseph Fletcher, *The Church in Industry* (New York, 1930), pp. 52-76; Dombrowski, p. 98.

alists on the feasibility of forming a Christian Socialist group similar to that of the Guild of St. Matthew in London.[18] Following a Nationalist meeting on May 7, 1889, Bliss, together with several other club members, including the Reverend Francis Bellamy, a cousin of the author, met at the Tremont Temple in Boston and organized the Society of Christian Socialists. The Society's membership cut sharply across denominational lines. Its president, the Reverend O. P. Gifford, and Bellamy were Baptists; Mary A. Livermore, a vice-president, was a Universalist; the Reverend Philo W. Sprague, another vice-president, and Bliss, who served as secretary, were Episcopalians.[19] Eight days after the formal organization of the Society, a monthly magazine, *The Dawn: A Magazine of Christian Socialism and Record of Social Progress*, edited by Bliss, made its appearance in Boston.[20] It was the first paper devoted exclusively to advancing the gospel of social Christianity in the United States since the *Labor Balance* in 1878.[21] Its motto was: "He works for God who works for man."

The Christian Socialists framed a Declaration of Principles which expressed their evolutionary reformist philosophy and their immediate and long-run aims. It contained the fundamental assumption of the Social Gospelers that an immanent God was the source and guide of human progress and, consequently, that all social, political, and industrial relations should be based on the Fatherhood of God and the Brotherhood of Man. An industrial and commercial system premised on economic individualism was held contrary to God's order, since it meant that the earth's natural resources and man's mechanical inventions were destined for the advantage of the few instead of the many. Such a system divided society into the possessing few and the rest of mankind, who had neither the resources nor the opportunity to advance.

The Declaration of Principles maintained that organized Christianity had no recourse other than to protest against the competitive system and to demand in its place another which

18*Dawn*, I (May, 1889), 3.
19Bliss (ed.), *Encyclopedia of Social Reform*, p. 258.
20*Dawn*, I (May, 1889), 3.
21Hopkins, p. 177.

would benefit all men alike. Happily, the existing highly inte-
grated industrialism provided the basis for a new "social order,
which with the equally necessary development of the individual
character" would be "at once true Socialism and true Christianity." The duty of Christian Socialists was to prove that
socialism and Christianity were fundamentally compatible, and
then to make the church the leader in the establishment of a new
social and socialist order grounded on Christ's teachings.[22]

Subsequent to the formulation of this statement of principles
Bliss called for a general reformation of American Protestantism, both in theology and in social attitude. Traditional theology, Bliss insisted, required simplification, since Christianity, in
its generally accepted form, had little in common with the faith,
love, life, and sacrifice of Jesus. Christianity was a life, not a
creed; a method, not a philosophy; and a "battle, not a dream."
The way to reform was to return to Christ's religion and way
of life: Christ was a workingman who fed the hungry and performed deeds of love for man. The church required a higher
conception of itself and its mission; it had to be powerful, unified, and, above all, democratic, catering to poor as well as rich.
Particularly was there a tremendous responsibility upon the
ministry which, according to Bliss, was too full of "self-seekers,"
more interested in large salaries, impressive rectories, and church
clubs and dinners than in their true spiritual and social obliga-
tions. The church could not be depended upon to exert leadership so long as it was weighted down with clergymen unable
to see the world past the stained glass windows of their houses
of worship. The true churchman of Christ, he maintained, was
one who read, studied, preached, and stood forthrightly for
social Christianity.[23]

While Bliss's approach to socialism followed the already
plowed furrows of Fabian gradualism, his enthusiasm for a
Christianized co-operative commonwealth led him on occasion
to extreme statements about the manner of its realization. "We

[22]*Dawn*, I (May, 1889), 3; Dombrowski, pp. 99-100. The Declaration of
Principles of the Society of Christian Socialists appears in Philo W. Sprague,
Christian Socialism, What and Why? (New York, 1891), pp. 144-45.

[23]*Dawn*, III (Jan. 29, 1891), 8. Cf. Bliss, "The Divine International or:
The Church and the Labor Movement," *American Federationist*, I (1894),
118-19.

say, let there be a revolution," he wrote in April, 1892. "Let us to arms. Let us sing the Marseillaise. Only let it be a revolution that shall go to the bottom of the question . . . . let it be an uprising of not the third or the fourth or the fifth estate, but of all estates, of all God's children against the slavery to Mammon."[24]

Bliss and his fellow Christian Socialists insisted that Christian Socialism was neither an adjunct of Nationalism nor an attempt to realize the society visualized in *Looking Backward*.[25] In fact, they disagreed with *Looking Backward*'s ultimate objectives and with the Nationalists' doctrines and methods. They held that Bellamy's utopian social order contradicted the laws of evolutionary development, in that it was static in character.[26] They looked with disfavor upon its compulsion, regimentation, military organization, and centralization of power.[27] Bellamy's insistence on equal wages was criticized as completely unsound economically and unwise socially. And they chided the Nationalists for refusing to acknowledge themselves as "socialists."[28]

Christian Socialists viewed Nationalism's program as far too passive and as somewhat nebulous. While Henry George's friend, R. Heber Newton, not altogether fairly accused the Bellamyites of seeking to achieve too much with grandiose schemes,[29] Bliss charged that the Nationalists did not go far enough along the road to socialism. He considered the Socialist Labor Party program a more adequate statement of socialist objectives.[30] Christian Socialists asserted also that Nationalists paid insufficient attention to the land and unemployment problems.[31] With good reason, they criticized the Nationalists for failing to work more closely with organized labor.[32] On this score, Bliss condemned those Nationalists who opposed all alliances with trade unionism on the ground that the latter was a

[24]*Dawn*, III (Apr., 1892), 4.
[25]*Ibid.*, I (Aug., 1889), 5.
[26]*Ibid.*, III (Feb. 12, 1891), 4.
[27]*Ibid.*, I (Jan., 1890), 4; II (Nov., 1890), 283.
[28]*Ibid.*, III (Feb. 12, 1891), 4.
[29]*Ibid.*, I (July, 1889), 2-3.
[30]*Ibid.*, II (Feb. 12, 1891), 4.
[31]*Ibid.*, I (Jan., 1890), 4.
[32]*Ibid.* (Sept., 1889), p. 4.

class movement. This was more than an error in judgment; it was a fatal mistake. "Christian Socialists," on the contrary, he asserted, gave a "hearty Godspeed to their brothers of the factory and the plough."

In the bitter industrial conflicts of the early nineties, Bliss, while deprecating the strike as generally ineffective, took a forthright stand on the side of labor. He championed the striking switchmen of the New York Central Railroad in 1890 and defended their resort to adequate protective measures when attacked.[33] "If corporations have the right to arm private detectives and fire upon almost any pretext, why has not organized labor an equal right to form, arm, and drill a similar body to defend themselves?" he asked.[34]

The Homestead Strike in 1892 found the *Dawn* shrilly critical of the Carnegie Steel Company's employment of Pinkerton detectives and the use of the state militia to crush the workers. Those who drew the sword would ultimately perish by the sword, it warned. For ten years, according to the *Dawn*, the Pennsylvania militia had served as "a body guard to Mr. Frick, while he, by process of law" lowered wages.[35] Some good would come from the strike, Bliss opined, since it would turn working-men to socialism. Trade unions, as the strike demonstrated and as Daniel DeLeon was beginning to point out, simply could not control the rising gigantic monopolies and combinations. Only the state could do that. Therefore, said the *Dawn*, the working-man's "one chance" was at the polls. Either "Triumphant Plutocracy, Socialism or the Reign of Terror" lay in store for the future.[36]

The Pullman Strike two years later brought a similar reaction from the *Dawn*. George McNeill wrote an article condemning the Pullman feudalism; and Bliss's support of the American Railway Union and its leader, Eugene V. Debs, was unequivocal.[37] The failure of the 1895 Brooklyn Trolley Strike, after

---

[33]*Ibid.*, II (Oct., 1890), 253.
[34]*Ibid.* (Sept., 1890), p. 197.
[35]*Ibid.*, III (Oct., 1892), 2.
[36]*Ibid.*, IV (Nov. 23, 1892), 2.
[37]*Ibid.*, VI (July-Aug., 1894), 97-98, 101.

considerable violence and bloodshed, led Bliss to make still another appeal to workingmen to accept conversion to socialism:

> Workingmen are learning fast that American justice and American laws exist mainly to keep workingmen down and protect property, while capitalists can disobey the laws *ad infinitum*. It is well. Workingmen must learn that they can gain nothing by appeal either to violence or to legal proceedings. Their only way is to strike through the ballot and overcome the capitalistic ownership of the country.[38]

Bliss and his fellow Christian Socialists of Boston invited all who subscribed to their Declaration of Principles to establish similar fellowships. They volunteered to send out lecturers from among their number to speak on Christian Socialism to any community which might request them.[39] But if they entertained hopes of seeing a repetition of the Nationalist phenomenon, they were to be disappointed. From Chicago, for instance, where memory of the Haymarket bomb was still fresh, the *Dawn*'s local correspondent, the Reverend William E. Sillence, wrote half-apologetically that the Christian radicals hesitated to form a society because of the confusion of anarchism and socialism in the public mind.[40] From other parts of the country Bliss received words of encouragement, but little response to the invitation to organize Christian Socialist societies.

Undaunted, Bliss kept up the campaign for a national league of Christian Socialist societies. In January, 1890, a group of his New York Episcopal clergymen friends partially justified his unbounded optimism by organizing a society.[41] Still, two local organizations were a far cry from a league. In the spring of 1890 Bliss proselytized the message of Christian Socialism while on a lecture tour of the Middle West. The fruits of the tour were the formation of Christian Socialist societies in Chicago and Cincinnati.[42] In the autumn, the Reverend Harry C. Vrooman, one of the famed "Vrooman boys" of Kansas, succeeded in organizing a Kansas State Christian Socialist Society.

---

38 *Ibid.*, VII (Feb., 1895), 2.
39 *Ibid.*, I (Sept., 1889), 7.
40 *Ibid.* (May, 1889), p. 5.
41 *Ibid.* (Feb., 1890), p. 5; *ibid.* (Mar., 1890), p. 6.
42 *Ibid.*, II (June, 1890), 92.

The year 1890 and the brief span of institutional Christian Socialism in the United States drew to a close simultaneously. In November the Boston Society of Christian Socialists had reached the dissolution point, and Bliss was obliged to shoulder alone the financial burden of the *Dawn*'s publication. After the beginning of 1891 notices of activities of Christian Socialist societies disappeared completely from the latter's pages. That Christian Socialism failed to take hold as in England was hardly the fault of the indefatigable Bliss. He had played his role of organizer to the very hilt. The trouble was that there were too few Christian Socialists in 1890 who chose to be organized.

Bliss's efforts to place Christian Socialism on an institutional basis not only ended in failure but also cost him his position with the Grace Church in South Boston. The Protestant Episcopal Mission advised him early in 1890 either to give up the *Dawn* or resign as head of the Grace Church Mission. It felt that he could not do justice to both. Bliss promptly resigned.[43] The Socialist Labor Party paper, the *Workmen's Advocate*, described his action as that of an "honest man and scientific socialist . . . driven from his pulpit for daring to preach the doctrines of the Carpenter of Nazareth."[44]

Bliss proved to the Episcopal Mission authorities that they were in error. He continued to publish the *Dawn* "in the interests of social Christianity." And in April, 1890, with the sympathetic backing of Bishop Phillips Brooks, he again plunged into active church affairs by opening the Mission of the Carpenter in Boston. While divine services at the Mission were carried on in accordance with the forms of the Episcopal Church, no direct affiliation existed between the two. At the Mission's first public meeting, Bliss, George McNeill, and some twenty other men and women agreed to associate to work for practical Christianity under the name of the "Brotherhood of the Carpenter." More specifically, the Brotherhood sought to bring all types of men and women together to consider the application of Christianity to social problems.[45]

---

[43]*Ibid.*, V (Feb. 4, 1893), 1.

[44]*Workmen's Advocate*, May 3, 1890.

[45]*Dawn*, II (May, 1890), 41-42.

The Brotherhood of the Carpenter held regular late Sunday afternoon services, which were followed by ham-and-pickle suppers and an evening session devoted to discussions of social problems or special lectures by Bliss or guest speakers.[46] Eventually, the functions of the Mission and those of the Brotherhood became completely separate, with the former devoting its efforts to religious affairs and the latter concerning itself with the amelioration of social and economic injustices.[47]

Bliss took pride in the Mission's progress, especially since it was almost entirely dependent financially on contributions. In his mind it represented a start in the direction of a social and religious fellowship which he hoped to organize in Boston. When Bliss had gone over to the Episcopal Church in 1885, he had carried with him the hope that some day he might be able to establish a community in which the church would be the focal point in the lives of the inhabitants. In such a community men would work in co-operative industries, and families would live in a true Christian spirit of fraternalism.[48]

Bliss discussed with several friends the establishment of a social-religious community. Some proposed the formation of a settlement, or at least the rental of houses, in a section of Boston, so that persons believing in Christian brotherhood might dwell near one another.[49] A neighborhood community of this nature would be similar to that of the Fellowship of the New Life which Thomas Davidson had organized in London in 1883. At one time, Bliss considered the purchase of a farm near Boston where Christian Socialists could live together in unity, freedom, and piety. Although such a plan bore a resemblance to the Brook Farm idea, Bliss stubbornly denied any similarity between his proposed rural community and the former Fourierist colony.[50]

---

[46]In March, 1891, the Reverend W. D. P. Bliss, "Priest and Socialist," gave the following series of lectures before the Brotherhood of the Carpenter: 1. "Jesus the Learner; or, Christ at the Feet of the Rabbi"; 2. "Jesus the Worker; or, the Lesson of the Workshop"; 3. "Jesus the Teacher; or, the Gospel of the Kingdom"; 4. "Jesus the Victor; or, the Triumph of the Kingdom." *Ibid.*, III (Feb. 26, 1891), 10.

[47]*Dawn*, III (Dec., 1891), 15-16.

[48]*Ibid.* (May, 1892), p. 13.

[49]*Ibid.* (Feb. 12, 1891), p. 2.

[50]*Ibid.* (Nov., 1891), pp. 7-8.

Late in the summer Bliss took what he believed was another step toward the formation of a Christian Socialist fellowship in Boston: he rented a large house to serve as a community center. While never fulfilling its intended purpose, the house, christened the Wendell Phillips Union, served many useful and laudable ends. It became the headquarters for the Brotherhood of the Carpenter;[51] two of its large halls were rented as meeting places for labor unions and social reform forums;[52] religious, economic, and cultural discussion groups were held for those who cared to attend. Among the Union's other activities were the organization of a Purchaser's League[53] and the establishment of a co-operative for the manufacture of children's clothing. The latter venture was most disappointing to Bliss who complained that people were "not interested enough in reform to give us their orders."[54] It ended disastrously when its women operators were discovered violating trade-union standards.

While organizing the Union, continuing his work at the Mission of the Carpenter, and editing the *Dawn* under constant financial pressure, Bliss early in 1892 piled a further burden upon himself by agreeing to go on a three months' lecture tour for the newly founded Christian Social Union. This organization was a Christian Socialist body within the Episcopal Church and was modeled after the Church Social Union in Great Britain.[55] Its objects were "to claim for Christian law the ultimate authority to rule social practice; to study in common how to apply the moral truths and principles of Christianity to the social and economic difficulties of the present time; and to present Christ in practical life as the living Master and King, the Enemy of wrong and selfishness, the Power of righteousness and love."[56]

The tour, the first of many taken by Bliss under Christian Social Union auspices, profoundly affected him. On departing

---

[51]*Ibid.* (Sept., 1891), pp. 3, 12.

[52]*Ibid.* (Dec., 1891), p. 5.

[53]*Ibid.* (May, 1892), p. 16.

[54]*Ibid.* (Oct., 1892), p. 4.

[55]*Ibid.* (May, 1891), p. 10. Also see Miller and Fletcher, pp. 77-89; Dombrowski, p. 98; W. J. Kerby, *Le Socialisme aux États Unis* (Bruxelles, 1897), p. 93.

[56]*American Fabian,* I (Oct., 1895), 8-9.

from Boston he considered political action through the People's Party the surest method of achieving social and economic reform. He was equally certain that the small religious fellowship constituted the best practical approximation of the Brotherhood of Man. When he returned, he knew he had been wrong in both assumptions. He had met several Populist leaders and was impressed by their sincerity but he saw little hope of political uplift through them.[57] And conversations with clergymen in various Middle Western cities convinced him that the religious community plan, though admirable in intent, was too limited both in scope and in character.[58]

For the next year and a half Bliss spurned politics. Even the dark days of the panic of 1893 failed to restore his old zeal for political reform. Articles in the *Dawn* scarcely reflected his Christian Socialist sentiments. He felt that the nation could be saved only by another great spiritual awakening;[59] and, with the exception of participating in a local tenement-house reform agitation, he devoted himself almost completely to religious affairs at the Mission of the Carpenter.

Another trip, this time to Europe, snapped Bliss out of his doldrums and back into the thick of the reform movement upon his return to the United States in 1894. He was exhilarated by the progress of socialism both in Great Britain and on the continent.[60] In Britain he had witnessed firsthand the work of the British Fabians and was impressed by the extent of their educational efforts among the middle class. Could not a socialist educational organization similar in character to the British Fabian Society be established in the United States? Fabian Society lecturers Sidney Webb, Edward Pease, and Percival Chubb when visiting the United States had often commented on the need for such an organization. The Nationalists had made a beginning in the right direction, but their clubs were in a state of advanced decomposition. What better effort could Bliss make for social reform in the United States than to help establish an American Fabian Society?

[57]*Dawn*, III (Apr., 1892), 6.
[58]*Ibid.*, p. 5.
[59]*Ibid.*, p. 8.
[60]*Ibid.*, VI (1894), 162.

True to character as a "champion company-promoter" of reform causes,[61] Bliss went about organizing an American Fabian League. As usual, he began by forming a club and founding a magazine. The Fabian Society of Boston, which included most of Bliss's devoted followers from the Brotherhood of the Carpenter, and a magazine, *The American Fabian*, both made their debuts early in 1895.[62] The aim of the *American Fabian*, according to Bliss's prefatory comments, was "to unite social reformers and lead the way to a conception of Socialism, broad enough, free enough, practical enough to include all that is of value, no matter whence it comes, and replace jealousy between reformers by co-operation for the general good . . . . A narrow, petty, jealous Socialism can never and ought never to win this country."[63] The first issue of the *American Fabian* was hardly distinguishable from the *Dawn*, which continued to limp along by printing articles which Bliss was compiling for his monumental *Encyclopedia of Social Reform*, to be published in 1897.

In the *American Fabian*, Bliss urged the formation of a league of American Fabian societies. He drew up an organizational plan which permitted any club devoted to the study of socialism or to the realization of socialist proposals to be federated into the league. Such a league, he said, would unite those men and women who believed in the efficacy of a gradualist approach to socialism. It could spread socialist thought among the "thinking and studying" people, provide a program of strategy, and develop a thoroughly American socialist policy and program.[64] Once an effective league was established, the time would be ripe for the publication of American Fabian tracts.[65]

On the whole, social reformers showed little more inclination to join an American Fabian League than they had to affiliate with an organized Christian Socialist movement. In New York, the Altrurian League, founded in May, 1894, to inquire into "the applicability to American conditions of the collective own-

---

[61]*Bellamy Review*, I (Feb., 1901), 338.

[62]*American Fabian*, I (Feb., 1895), 5; *Dawn*, VII (Apr., 1895), 5.

[63]*American Fabian*, I (Feb., 1895), 5.

[64]*Ibid.* (Apr., 1895), p. 6.

[65]*Ibid.* (Dec., 1895), p. 5.

ership of all of the means of production and distribution," voted
to change itself into the Fabian Society of New York and to
co-operate with Bliss and the Boston Fabians.[66]   Three members of the League were formerly affiliated with the London
Fabian Society.[67]   Several other ex-British Fabians helped Bliss
establish a Fabian Club in Philadelphia.[68]   At Madison, Wisconsin, Paul Tyner, who spent his time editing magazines, studying the occult sciences, and agitating for social reform, headed
a short-lived Fabian society formed after a lecture by Bliss in
that city.[69]   In the Far West Laurence Gronlund was reported
to have organized a chain of Public Ownership Clubs which
Bliss believed would readily enter a national league having principles identical with their own.   But despite his appeal "to fall
in line with one movement that shall unite East and West and
in which all members shall have an equal voice," the Western
clubs went their own separate ways.[70]

Bliss's selfless efforts were once again largely in vain.   An
American Fabian League was never officially launched; and
another of his eminently worthwhile projects died still-born and
passed into the limbo of lost causes.   Yet the brief agitation for
Fabianism was not a total loss.   The *American Fabian* continued publication until 1900 and provided a journal for the considerable group of unorganized Fabian socialists in the United
States.[71]   It also printed several "American Fabian tracts."

[66]*Ibid.* (Apr., 1895), p. 5. *The Fabian News,* organ of the British Fabian
Society, noted the formation of the Boston and New York Fabian societies
and predicted a "great future in America for Fabian activity." *Fabian
News,* V (1895), 25. Edward R. Pease, secretary of the London Fabian Society, offered to send copies of the *Fabian News* and the *Fabian Tracts* to all
persons whose names were submitted to him by the secretaries of the American Fabian societies. *American Fabian,* I (Dec., 1895), 5.

[67]*The Populist,* Dec. 15, 1894. As far as the author can learn, this is the only
issue of the New York Populists' paper ever published. It was seen in the
W. J. Ghent Manuscripts at the Library of Congress, Washington, D. C.

[68]*American Fabian,* I (Nov., 1895), 10.

[69]*Ibid.,* p. 8.

[70]*Ibid.* (Dec., 1895), p. 5.

[71]In March, 1896, the *American Fabian* (II, 11) outlined a social and political program for Fabians in the United States:
Social Demands: 1. Reduction in working hours proportionately to progress
in production. 2. United States ownership of all railroads, telephone and telegraph systems, canals, and all other forms of communication and transportation.
3. Municipalization of all local ferries, streetcars, water and gas works, electric plants, and all industries requiring franchises. 4. Public lands to be de-

After 1895 Bliss, with some reluctance relinquished control of the little magazine to the New York Fabian Society, which published it until the organization's suspension.[72] Prestonia Mann, a prolific writer on social-reform topics, succeeded Bliss as editor. Poor health soon obliged her to turn the magazine over to William J. Ghent, an intelligent but bellicose young reformer.[73] During the period of Ghent's editorship, which lasted approximately a year, the talented California poetess and gadabout reformer, Charlotte Perkins Stetson, contributed several articles to the magazine.[74] New York Fabians believed Miss Stetson a worthy female counterpart of George Bernard Shaw, an opinion which the latter if he were aware of it, undoubtedly did not share. John Preston, another New York reformer, served as editor of the *American Fabian* from 1898 until the cessation of its publication in 1900. The return of prosperity, said Preston in his valedictory editorial, was disastrous for reform papers.

The failure of Fabianism to develop into an institutionalized movement was another disappointment to Bliss, as was his

---

clared inalienable and lands revoked from individuals and corporations not complying with terms of purchase. 5. Legal incorporation by states of local trade unions without national organizations. 6. United States government to have exclusive right to issue money. 7. Congressional legislation for scientific management of forests and waterways and end to waste of nation's resources. 8. Inventions free to all, inventors to be remunerated by the nation. 9. Progressive income tax and inheritance taxes on large estates. 10. School education for all children under fourteen—such education to be compulsory, free, accessible to all through public assistance in books, food, clothing, etc. 11. Repeal of all pauper, tramp, conspiracy, and sumptuary laws and unabridged right of combination. 12. Official statistics on labor conditions, prohibition of labor for school children and for women in conditions detrimental to health and morality; abolition of convict labor contract system. 13. Employment of jobless by cities, state, and nation. 14. All wages to be paid in lawful money and equal pay for equal work for men and women alike. 15. Occupationl disability and employers' liability laws.

Political Demands: 1. Adoption of Initiative and Referendum. 2. Abolition of Executive's veto power in local, state, and national governments. 3. Municipal self-goverment. 4. Direct and secret vote in all elections; universal and equal right of suffrage without regard to color, creed, or sex; election days to be legal holidays; principle of proportional representation to be used. 5. All public officials to be subject to recall. 6. Uniform civil and criminal law throughout United States; abolition of capital punishment.

[72]*American Fabian,* II (Mar., 1896), 6.

[73]Ghent's books, *Our Benevolent Feudalism* (New York, 1902) and *Mass and Class* (New York, 1904), were powerful indictments of the social aspects of modern industrial capitalism.

[74]*American Fabian,* II (Jan., 1897), 3.

aborted effort to establish a "National Educational and Economic League." If his Fabian League was designed essentially to carry the message of socialism to the middle class, the National Educational and Economic League was to bring it to the workers, particularly organized trade unionists.[75] To leave such a responsibility to the Socialist Labor Party with its gospel of class hatred, Bliss thought unwise, just as it was impolitic to channelize American workers, as yet unprepared for socialism, into that party.[76] "We honor the true proletarian socialists," said Bliss. "Their platform is our platform; but we do not believe the proletarians ought to go ahead of the common people."[77] Admittedly, the SLP stood for socialism, "but neither for that form of socialism nor for those methods of political action" which alone could win Americans. As long as the party continued as it was, it would remain small, "doing some good, perhaps, among German Americans and others, but little more." Socialism would make advances in the United States "in spite of rather than because of the SLP," he declared.[78] Needed, rather, were local, non-partisan workingmen's political-education clubs in which non-socialist proletarians could work for socialist objectives.

The organizational beginnings for such a venture came again in Boston where, in the spring of 1895, Bliss's little band of loyal supporters from the Mission of the Carpenter founded the National Educational and Economic League. The financial angels of the League were the radical Dr. W. S. Rainsford, rector of the wealthy New York St. George's Church, and several of his Gotham friends. President of the League was George McNeill, and its paid secretary and organizer was Harry Lloyd, a Boston American Federation of Labor leader, not to be confused with the wealthy Chicago socialist, Henry Demarest Lloyd.[79]

Bliss hoped that Henry Demarest Lloyd would take the lead in sponsoring the workingmen's educational league. But Lloyd

[75]*Ibid.*, I (Nov., 1895), 11-12.

[76]*Dawn*, VI (Mar., 1894), 35.

[77]*Ibid.*, III (Oct., 1891), 2.

[78]*American Fabian*, I (Feb., 1895), 5.

[79]Bliss to H. D. Lloyd, Apr. 16, 1895. Lloyd Papers.

balked when he noted that McNeill and his own namesake were the titular leaders of the organization. In a "plain and blunt" letter to Bliss, the Chicago Lloyd took him to task for appointing the Boston Lloyd as secretary and organizer, because the latter was reputedly in the bad graces of Boston and Haverhill labor leaders and was also a known opponent of the effort to commit the American Federation of Labor to a full espousal of government ownership of the means of production and distribution. The organizer of any association which had as its primary purpose the indoctrination of socialist principles, said Lloyd, of necessity had to be a socialist. No doubts could be attached to him.[80]

Stung by Lloyd's criticism, Bliss stubbornly defended the League's secretary and organizer as a man whose views "were not for sale" and one who was "completely trustworthy." "I know that he is a collectivist," he wrote to his Chicago friend. Likewise, Bliss, who opposed socialist "boring from within" tactics, vindicated Lloyd's opposition to the controversial Article 10 in the proposed 1894 American Federation of Labor platform. In opposing Article 10, he said, Lloyd was thinking basically of the best interests of the Federation.[81] When Henry D. Lloyd refused to accept this explanation, Bliss wrote pleadingly to him: "Please . . . even if you can't approve, don't throw any cold water on my fine plan."[82] Lloyd obliged by doing nothing one way or the other. However, he wrote to Thomas J. Morgan a pointed and not inaccurate estimate of Bliss. "He is a good fellow; one of the best. But he must be, agitationally, a mere child."[83]

Bliss, ever earnest and nurtured on the highest grade milk of human optimism, did not brood over failure. Nor was he seemingly nettled by the criticism which fell indiscriminately upon him from both the left and the right. The following sample of the abuse to which every moderate reformer is subjected from extremists first appeared in *The Altruist*, the strange little paper of that quixotic St. Louis communitarian mutualist, Alc-

---

[80]Lloyd to Bliss, May 4, 1895. Lloyd Papers.
[81]Bliss to Lloyd, May 28, 1895. Lloyd Papers.
[82]Bliss to Lloyd, July 17, 1895. Lloyd Papers.
[83]Lloyd to Morgan, July 11, 1895. Lloyd Papers.

ander Longley. It was reprinted later with malice aforethought
by Daniel DeLeon in the *People*:

> Reverend W. D. P. Bliss of Boston spent a week in this
> city lately preaching Socialism and Trades Unionism in one
> of the Episcopal churches. It was amusing to see him
> dressed in a long white gown and to hear his denunciation
> of plutocrats and his pitiful appeals for the poor, while
> his slim audience of well-dressed people in their costly
> church made it seem like he was accusing a lot of masters
> in the absence of their servants. It seemed like pouring
> water on a duck's back to ask them to give up their wealth
> for charity or for municipal control, instead of going to
> the poor and telling them to help themselves by combining
> like the rich do. Asking God and landlords and speculators
> to change their tactics is more absurd than trying to make
> a hungry lion lay down in peace besides a lamb![84]

Between 1889 and 1896 Bliss was the principal spokesman for
most of the radical Protestant clergymen. His socialism did
not differ fundamentally from Bellamy's. Both men were
permeated by the gradualist doctrines of the Fabians and the
Brotherhood of Humanity concept of Christianity. Both denied the class-struggle thesis. And both looked on humanity
as an organic whole. Bliss's various organizational efforts
never achieved the success of the Nationalist movement, but they
were important in helping to keep alive the Nationalist tradition
after the Bellamyite agitation had lost its vitality.

Bliss attracted only a fraction of the public attention showered
on his contemporary clerical radical, George D. Herron.[85] This
stormy petrel, who compellingly challenged the social right of
the wealthy to their possessions and vigorously preached a powerful gospel of social redemption, was likened by his admirers
to the Old Testament prophets. In his personality was said
to be combined the fearlessness and social conscience of Amos,
the vision of Isaiah, and the foreboding of Jeremiah. From
early boyhood, Herron was certain of his ordained role in the
regeneration of the world,[86] and the strength of this conviction

---

[84]*Altruist*, XXIX (Mar., 1899), 10; *People*, May 2, 1899.

[85]My account of Herron has depended considerably upon Hopkins, pp.
185-200; Dombrowski, pp. 171-93; and May, pp. 249-56.

[86]Unpublished MS of Dr. J. S. Nollen of Grinnell College. I am under
great obligation to Dr. Nollen for permitting me to see those parts of his
manuscript on the history of Grinnell College which concern Herron.

won him a host of idolizing followers. Contrariwise, it created a sizable number of critics who, in varying degrees of hostility, considered him a menace to established social and religious institutions.

Herron was of the same generation of Hoosiers as those notable American socialists, Eugene V. Debs and J. A. Wayland. He was born in Montezuma in 1862, the son of poor, devout Scottish parents who strongly impressed upon him their own stern Calvinistic morality. Herron's father personally undertook the education of his delicate and mystically inclined son, whose voracious appetite for reading early reflected a scholarly leaning. After an apprenticeship to a printer, Herron spent three years of study at Ripon Academy in Ripon, Wisconsin— the only formal education he ever received. It constituted his training for the Congregationalist ministry which he entered in 1883, the same year that he married Mary Everhard. Yet Herron was not unprepared for the intellectual responsibilities of the pulpit, since he was widely read in theology, philosophy, history, and economics. Nonetheless, he was largely self-taught, and this helped to instill in him a tendency toward dogmatic assertiveness which sometimes annoyed his friends and infuriated his opponents.[87]

Herron's reputation as a clergyman grew slowly, though his tremendous abilities as a preacher were apparent from the beginning of his career in the church. Intense, inspired, emotional, sincere, and to a degree messianic, Herron was able to grasp and hold almost hypnotically the attention of even the most hostile of audiences.[88] Sermonizing upon the pressing social problems, such a purveyor of the gospel did not adhere to logical consistency, cut-and-dried facts, and hard-and-cold statistical analysis. Herron, quite consciously at times, eschewed all three. "Christ did not save the world," he once said, "by a scientific study of the economic conditions of society."[89] Obviously, Herron's crusading and essentially anarchic approach to God's Kingdom on Earth differed from that of Bliss.

---

[87]*Ibid.*

[88]An excellent description of Herron is by Eltweed Pomeroy in *The Social Forum*, I (Aug., 1899), 82-83.

[89]George D. Herron, *The New Redemption* (New York, 1893), p. 11.

Herron's fame first flashed across the Social Gospel firmament in 1890 when, as pastor of the First Congregationalist Church of Lake City, Minnesota, he delivered his famous sermon, "The Message of Jesus to Men of Wealth," before the Minnesota Congregationalist Club in Minneapolis. In this sermon are Herron's seminal ideas with respect to Christianity and its relationship to the individual and society. He elaborated upon them in subsequent sermons and became increasingly radical in discussing their implications but never changed them to any extent.[90]

Bluntly, Herron told his audience that the existing social and religious order was wrong because it placed a premium on competition, self-interest, and material power. Such a civilization failed to secure morality and justice, since it put the weak at the mercy of the strong and at the same time minimized the paramount Christian principles of stewardship and sacrifice. A civilization premised on self-interest was built on a foundation more dangerous than dynamite, warned Herron. It rested on falsehood and contained within it "the elements of anarchy" because it had no basis in "moral realities." It was atheistic because it treated God and His righteousness as external to itself. It was nihilistic because it thrived on destruction.[91]

Civilization could be saved, Herron insisted, by a return to Christ, by the emulation by all Christians of His sacrifice on the cross. Sacrifice was not "life's accident but life's law." No man, hence, could live other than a sacrificial life in a world of sin. Christians were vicarious sufferers for their fellow men. The meaning of the cross was "not a release from but an obligation to sacrifice." The true Christian would follow the example of the Master; for only in this course was there salvation for him and his brethren, since atonement and redemption, to be truly meaningful, had to be social in character and thereby reflect the organic nature of society.[92]

Herron noted for the particular benefit of any businessmen in the audience that the lesson of the cross had much larger ap-

[90]This sermon appears in Herron's *The Christian Society* (Chicago, 1894), pp. 99-122.

[91]*Ibid.,* pp. 103-4.

[92]*Ibid.,* pp. 110-13.

plication to men of wealth, because they had "larger opportunities and possessions to sacrifice." The corporation manager, the merchant, the mill owner, the mine operator, the street-railway president were all admirably suited to become disciples of Christ. Elaborating on this theme of Christian stewardship, Herron declared that the Lord, indeed, gave power to every man of wealth "to be a saviour of his fellow-men." A businessman who failed in this regard "made a disastrous and irreparable business failure." The businessman had no more right to seek out personal profit from his enterprises than did Jesus to bring about miracles for personal gain.[93]

The day was coming, said Herron, in which a truly Christian social order would exist on earth, the fulfillment in the here and now of God's Kingdom of Heaven. In such a society the ordering of things would be in accordance with His divine sanction. Social clubs, newspapers, shops, stores, corporations, homes, political organizations that did not have as their end the making of men divine would have no place in an order redeemed by Christ and one in which an immanent Christ was King.[94]

Widely publicized, Herron's Minneapolis address was like a best-selling novel or a work of original scholarship and profundity in that it definitely established the reputation of its author. Herron could now pick and choose his pulpit, and his selection was the First Congregationalist Church of Burlington, Iowa, where he assumed the duties of pastor in December, 1891. The new minister was almost destined to be a source of controversy in view of his irregular social attitudes. Some of the more prosperous members of the Burlington congregation doubtless developed serious misgivings about their new spiritual leader, especially when he defended labor unions and their leaders. On the other hand, Herron enjoyed the complete support of two of the church's leading parishioners, the extremely wealthy Mrs. E. D. Rand and her daughter, Carrie. Indeed, the latter's infatuation with the slender, raven-haired young minister was scarcely veiled. His responsiveness to her attentions caused much tongue-clacking in the little Iowa community and a growing alienation from his wife.

[93]*Ibid.,* pp. 113-15.
[94]*Ibid.,* pp. 116-17.

In the fall of 1893 President Thomas A. Gates of Grinnell College—then Iowa College—announced that a chair of Applied Christianity had been endowed at the college and that Herron had been appointed to occupy it. The donor of $35,000 to establish the chair was Mrs. Rand, and when Herron left Burlington for Grinnell to take up his new duties, his benefactress and her daughter followed suit. Carrie Rand's appointment as Dean of Women at Grinnell brought her into frequent contact with Herron, who was soon spending nearly all of his leisure time at the Rand home, where he thoroughly enjoyed the luxuries of the household. Despite Herron's strictures on the virtues of Christian poverty, he was at heart a sybarite who delighted in those things that money alone could buy.[95] Under these circumstances, his relationship with his wife became irreparably strained and finally broken.

Grinnell was a beehive of Social Gospel activity and Herron's effect on the college was electric. He enjoyed the confidence, co-operation, and support of President Gates, who figured prominently in the Social Gospel movement himself and successfully parried off adverse criticism of the college and of its professor of Applied Christianity. Moreover, Gates, Herron, and a group of friends took over the publication of the *Northeastern Congregationalist* in 1894, rechristened it *The Kingdom: a weekly exponent of applied Christianity*, and for five years used it to publicize Herron's radical Social Gospel message, which otherwise might have had difficulty in finding its way into the more staid theological reviews. The *Kingdom* was, in fact, the principal sounding board for social Christianity during the 1890's, though its general tone, on the whole, was more moderate than Herron's own.[96]

Herbert W. Gleason edited the *Kingdom*, assisted by an advisory staff which represented nearly every shade of coloration on the Social Gospel spectrum. If the journal teetered on pressing issues of the day, such vacillation simply was representative of the character of the movement itself. When the *Kingdom* was obliged to cease publication in 1899 as a result of a lawsuit occasioned by Gates's exposé of the American Book Company's

---

[95]Unpublished MS of Dr. J. S. Nollen.

[96]Dombrowski, pp. 110-20; Hopkins, pp. 194-95.

textbook monopoly,[97] the Social Gospelers were deprived of their most effective journal of opinion. Although Clarence Darrow ably defended the Kingdom Publishing Company and Gates was not convicted, the legal fees and court costs drove the company into virtual bankruptcy and prevented further publication of the journal. The *Kingdom*'s would-be successor, *The Social Forum*, never came close to approximating the former's popularity.

Herron's doctrine of social salvation through collective sacrifice was largely responsible for the founding in Georgia of the Christian Commonwealth Colony, one of many such settlements established during the brief resurgence of communitarian socialism in the 1890's.[98] Ralph Albertson, a young Congregationalist pastor, was the chief instigator of this enterprise. He wrote a series of articles in the *Kingdom* advocating the organization of a religious community devoted to absolute communism of possession, Christian brotherhood and co-operation, and complete obedience to the teachings of Jesus. Albertson's proposals attracted several come-outers including John Chipman of Florida; George Howard Gibson of Lincoln, Nebraska; and William Damon of Andrews, North Carolina. Together these four men laid the plans for the Commonwealth Community which was launched in November, 1896, in an effort to demonstrate to the world that the Kingdom of God on Earth was at hand if only men were willing to join it.

Not surprisingly, the Commonwealth Colony, which refused entrance to no man, attracted the support of many religious radicals and Social Gospelers both in the United States and abroad. It had a membership of from 350 to 400 persons during its four years of existence. Among its most sympathetic observers was Count Leo Tolstoi, for the members of the colony sought to practice his doctrine of non-resistance. Herron waxed

[97]George A. Gates, *A Foe to American Schools* (Grinnell, 1897); *Social Forum,* I (June 1, 1899), 26.

[98]See Dombrowski, pp. 132-70, for an excellent account of the Christian Commonwealth Colony. The Henry D. Lloyd Papers contain several interesting letters regarding the organizational efforts of the colony: Lloyd to George H. Gibson, Dec. 18, 1895; Herron to Gibson, Jan. 13, 1896; Gibson to Lloyd, Jan. 15, 1896; Albert H. Pease to Lloyd, Jan. 25, 1896; Gibson to Lloyd, Jan. 25, 1896; John Chipman to Gibson, Jan. 30, 1896; Gibson to Lloyd, Feb. 8, 1896; Gibson to Lloyd, Apr. 12, 1896.

enthusiastic over the community and wrote to Henry D. Lloyd, who helped to underwrite the venture, that he hoped to see others like it initiated. "I have a sort of feeling," said Herron, "that if we can get some of these colonies rightly initiated and then arrange for a federation of these co-operative institutions, we may have one key to the situation." Herron indicated that he was willing to make "almost any sacrifice" to inaugurate such a movement.[99]

The Commonwealth Colony disbanded in the spring of 1900 when its leaders, practicing non-resistance, refused to combat slanderous allegations by a few malcontents with respect to the community, including the patently false one of free love. The colony's demise was a real loss to social Christianity, which it had sought to make a living reality.

Meanwhile at Grinnell, the dynamic Herron was preaching before larger and larger audiences, teaching before constantly expanding classes, writing new sermons and strictures for the *Kingdom*, and attracting more and more public attention to the little Iowa college. He also was largely instrumental in the founding of the American Institute of Christian Sociology at Chautauqua in July, 1893. The Institute, of which Richard T. Ely, Josiah Strong, and Herron were the first three presidents, was organized after the pattern of the Episcopalian Christian Social Union. Its purpose was to study the implications of Christianity with regard to existing social and economic conditions and to publish the results of its findings, particularly for the benefit of university instructors and students. In the summer of 1894 the Institute, which claimed at one time over a thousand members in some twelve states, sponsored a series of conferences at Grinnell which attracted leading members of the Social Gospel movement to Iowa.[100]

Herron's services as a lecturer were in constant demand and he filled engagements throughout the country in churches, public forums, and universities. Rarely did he fail to arouse conservatives to furious opposition. At the University of Nebraska, after Herron had delivered the commencement sermon

---

[99]Herron to Lloyd, Jan. 13, 1896. Lloyd Papers.

[100]See Hillquit, p. 321; *Dawn*, VI (June, 1894), 82-83; John R. Commons, *Myself* (New York, 1934), p. 51.

to the 1894 graduating class, he was followed to the podium by
the governor of the state who demagogically denounced him as
an anarchist—a popular smear-term since the Haymarket Affair.[101]   Herron was also attacked the following year after
speaking before the Congregationalist Club of San Francisco.
His assailant there was the Reverend C. O. Brown, pastor of the
First Congregational Church in nearby Oakland who accused the
Middle-Western visitor of being a sincere but dangerous radical,
who taught false economic ideas and heretical religious doctrines.[102]   Attacks upon him by such ecclesiastical conservatives
as Brown strengthened Herron's conviction that the overwhelming majority of Protestant churches in America were spiritually
bankrupt because of subservience to the rich.   The Christ that
was needed, Herron asserted, was "not in the tomb of meta-
physics where theology has stood guard these many ages, obedient to ambition in the church, agreeable to craft in the
state."[103]   Rather he was the living Christ who would lead men
committed to social redemption to the holy society of the Kingdom of God on Earth.

Herron had the most derogatory of opinions on the social pur-
poseness and character of the majority of Protestant churches.
Just before departing for Palestine in 1900 he gave a newspaper
interview in which he expressed the thought that there was no
essential difference between the Standard Oil Company and
the Presbyterian Church.[104]   In similar vein, he had declared
shortly before:

> If I were to stand before any representative religious
> gathering in the land and there preach actual obedience to
> the Sermon on the Mount, declaring that we must actually
> do what Jesus said, I would commit a religious scandal;
> I would henceforth be held in disrepute by the official
> religion that holds Jesus' name. If the head of some great
> oil combination, though it had violated every law of God
> and man, besides the so-called economic laws which neither
> God nor man ever had anything to do with, and though it

[101]Dombrowski, p. 178.

[102]C. O. Brown, *Professor Herron's Teachings Reviewed, Ought the
Church of Christ to Join the Propaganda of Socialism* (Pamphlet; San Francisco, 1895), *passim;* Dombrowski, pp. 179-81; May, pp. 255-56.

[103]*Appeal to Reason,* Jan. 14, 1899.

[104]*Social Democratic Herald,* Feb. 3, 1900.

had debauched our nation infinitely beyond the moral
shock of civil war, were to stand before any representative
religious gathering with an endowment check in his hand,
he would be greeted with an applause so vociferous as to
partake of the morally idiotic.[105]

Herron's attacks on institutional Christianity alienated some
Protestant clergymen who were otherwise sympathetic to his
religious ideas. Bliss, for one, deeply regretted the tone of Herron's assault on American churches.[106]

Herron's eventual espousal of socialism was not essentially
the result of a conviction that Marxism provided in itself a
solution to the ills of humanity or to the abuses of capitalism.
"No political legislation," Herron said, agreeing with Vida D.
Scudder, "ever had or ever would have the power to make men
unselfish."[107] Herron identified himself with socialism because
he believed that a socialist society, with its emphasis on individual sacrifice for the collective well-being and with its quest for
social justice and genuine equality of opportunity, would provide an atmosphere of freedom in which religious spirituality
could best exist.[108] And he maintained that "an industrial
democracy [socialism] would be the social actualization of
Christianity."[109]

From 1892 to 1899 Herron quietly supported the Socialist
Labor Party, but it was not until the emergence of the Social
Democratic Party in 1899 that he was willing to stand and be
counted as a socialist. In 1900 he sent the Social Democratic
Party a check for $500 to help in the coming presidential cam-
paign,[110] which he and the party candidate, Eugene V. Debs,
opened for the socialists at a rally at the Central Music Hall in
Chicago on September 29.[111] After the election, Herron played
a leading role in reconciling the warring factions among the

[105]George D. Herron, *Between Caesar and Jesus* (New York, 1899), pp.
94-95. Cf. *The New Redemption,* p. 60.

[106]*Dawn,* IV (June, 1894), 82.

[107]George D. Herron, *A Plea for the Gospel* (New York, 1892), pp. 145-46.

[108]Herron, *The New Redemption,* p. 34.

[109]Herron, *Between Caesar and Jesus,* p. 99.

[110]*Social Democratic Herald,* June 2, 1900.

[111]*Ibid.,* Oct. 6, 1900.

socialists and in paving the way for the creation of the Socialist Party of America.[112]

The speech which Herron delivered at the Music Hall was a ringing declaration of faith in socialism and a skillful effort to blend together the materialism of Marx and the spirituality of Christ. It sought to weave socialism into the great American tradition of individualism and equality. And it attempted to show the fallacy of any reform which still left intact a system based upon competition.

Herron professed to see three main problems facing American socialism. The first was to create a sense of class consciousness among the workers of the nation and to make them aware that they were the real producers of the earth and hence the rightful owners of the means of production and distribution. When the socialist talked of class consciousness, said Herron, he spoke of that which was clearly apparent. Nothing could "obviate the hideous fact" that one class of human beings was living off another class; that a capitalistic class "was heaping up the produce of the producing class." However, Herron was careful to differentiate between "class consciousness" on the one hand and "class hatred" on the other, a distinction not always made clear by socialists of the day. Socialists had not thought of arraigning one class against another as individuals, he said. The class-consciousness appeal was not "for strife or hostility or antagonism but for manhood, for constructive purpose, and spiritual nerve and genius." Socialists, Herron continued, were not appealing for support on the grounds that they were better than other men, but because socialism was superior to capitalism. And particularly did they want this truth imparted to the working class. Socialism could not be established in the United States until American labor became conscious of its maturity, and undertook "the task of organizing out of the materials of nature and history a coherent and free society in which every man shall equally inherit with every other man the resources and opportunities that open wholeness and gladness of life to the human soul."

The second principal task was to demonstrate the compatibility of socialism with the American democratic tradition. Par-

[112]See Chapter XI, below.

ticularly was it necessary to show that individualism would be
enhanced rather than eclipsed in a socialist society. Individualism, in truth, could only be realized through collectivism, Herron
maintained. Since all persons in common depended on the
sources and tools of production, individual liberty was possible
only when these were collectively owned. No man could be free
so long as he was "dependent upon some other man for the
chance to earn his livelihood." Nor could equality or brotherhood exist so long as the competition of capitalism placed a
premium on inequality and on battles in the market place.

Thirdly, said Herron, it had to be shown that while socialism
may have been grounded originally on materialism, its ends
were essentially spiritual. He went so far as to identify the
material with the spiritual. "All material things," he insisted,
were "intrinsically spiritual values"; they were "the coin of the
spiritual realm." If the universe was sincere and meaningful,
the true goal of history was liberty of the soul. This condition
could never be realized so long as the individual was compelled
to struggle for survival. A rational civilization sought "not
the so-called survival of the fittest, but the fitting of all to
worthily survive." In essence, Herron declared, socialism was
a religion. It represented the "harmonious relating of the whole
life of man"; it stood "for a vast and collective fulfilling of the
law of love." As the socialist movement grew

> its religious forces will come forth from the furnace of
> consuming experience. No matter how materialistic its
> origin, when socialism brings men together in a great pur-
> pose, it soon begins to develop fidelity and tolerance and
> patience and good will, and the noblest human graces. As
> American socialism goes on its way it will become a spiritual
> passion; not a cry for rights, but a call to elemental right-
> eousness.[113]

Herron's espousal of political socialism and his support of the
Social Democratic Party drew a sour reaction from the *Bellamy
Review*, which espoused an extreme brand of non-partisan so-
cialism:

---

[113]*The Speeches of Eugene V. Debs and Prof. George D. Herron Delivered
at Formal Opening of National Campaign, at Central Music Hall, Chicago,
Sept. 29, 1900* (Pamphlet; Chicago, 1900).

His [Herron's] usefulness is much less now than formerly. Since he joined the Debs political party he has ceased to be a prophet. He is now a partisan, standing for one particular method of social evolution. Professor Herron is an ethical idealist, and never should have attempted to be anything else. He knows nothing of practical politics. He should be nonpartisan like, Mayor [Samuel "Golden Rule"] Jones. His genius is of too rare and subtle a quality to catch votes with.[114]

Herron did not cease to be a prophet, however. The Social Crusade, a religious fraternity that was greatly influenced by his social and religious doctrines, was organized by the Reverend J. Stitt Wilson, who was later to become a reform mayor of Berkeley, California.[115] The Social Crusade, said Wilson, was born "after the pangs of years of hunger and prayer for the Eternal Truth concerning Righteousness, Justice and Brotherhood." Its immediate objective was to arouse the conscience of men and women to the wrongs and injustices of the capitalistic system, "to give light to them that sit in industrial darkness and to shatter industrial chains." Its ultimate goal was to bring about such social and economic changes that no man would be denied the right to work.[116]

This weighty burden, which the Social Crusaders shouldered willingly and eagerly, demanded ceaseless education and agitation. They met the challenge by resorting to soapbox, street-corner meetings, by offering to speak before any and every group which would give them a hearing, and by organizing Social Crusade Circles. While encouraging the work of the Crusade, Herron himself did not become a member until January, 1901. Carrie Rand also joined at this time and became its treasurer.

The Social Crusader, a messenger of brotherhood and social justice was the official journal of the movement, and its editorial offering in large measure mirrored the development of Herron's thought. When Herron went over publicly to political socialism the *Social Crusader* followed suit, and thereby incurred

---

[114]*Bellamy Review,* II (1901), 34.
[115]*Social Crusader,* I (Sept., 1898), 7-8.
[116]*Ibid.,* pp. 4-5, 9.

the charge of the Fabian socialist, Eltweed Pomeroy, that it
was an organ of "extreme hero-worshipping socialism."[117]

In the presidential election of 1900, the *Social Crusader*
brought the fraternity directly into politics, as Wilson became
convinced that the solution to the entire social issue ultimately
rested on intelligent use of the ballot.[118] The Social Crusade,
wrote Wilson, was not a political organization, but the application of ethical and spiritual life was concerned not only with
the individual but also with society. "Pure politics" he held to
be "the process of discovering and applying to the actual facts
of our social and industrial life, the truths of the Kingdom of
God. And the ballot is our individual means of expressing our
social and political convictions. The ballot-box is the organ
through which the social conscience speaks. From this field of
activity no citizen can escape, if he would. Even inaction
acts."[119]

In August of 1900, Wilson, though refusing to "enslave himself by partisan politics," told readers of the *Social Crusader*
that he personally was going to vote for Debs, the candidate of
the Social Democratic Party, because he was the "natural nominee of the workers of America."[120] As the campaign warmed
up, Wilson's enthusiasm for Debs and the Social Democratic
Party increased commensurately. The party's records refer to
Wilson's organizing a Social Democratic local in Cedar Rapids,
Iowa;[121] and Thomas J. Morgan wrote to Henry Demarest
Lloyd that the Social Crusade leader was "manifestly stump-
ing" for the Social Democratic ticket in Chicago.[122] In the
October issue of the *Social Crusader*, Wilson wrote that the
Social Democratic Party was a distinct political crystallization
of the various forces in America that were making for a new
social order. It represented the beginning of an effort, designed
ultimately to prevail, to free the masses from social injustice.
Nor was the party chimerical in character or created out of a

---

[117]*Social Unity,* I (Jan., 1901), 9.

[118]*Social Crusader,* I (Feb., 1899), 13.

[119]*Ibid.,* II (Oct., 1900), 4.

[120]*Ibid.* (Aug., 1900), p. 7.

[121]William Butscher to J. S. Wilson, Aug. 8, 1900. Socialist Party Collection, Duke University.

[122]T. J. Morgan to H. D. Lloyd, Oct. 15, 1900. Lloyd Papers.

mélange of demagogues, cranks, and reformers. It was destined
to stay and to usher in a socialist society which would replace
the capitalistic order, already past its climax and doomed to
extinction. "As the new order appears on the horizon," Wilson
predicted, "those who see it live in a new day already. And
they form the advance guard of a new civilization."[123]

While Herron was inspiring the establishment of the *Kingdom*, the founding of the Christian Commonwealth Colony, the
organization of the American Institute of Christian Sociology,
and the launching of the Social Crusade, his conservative critics
on the Board of Trustees at Grinnell were becoming increasingly determined to oust him from the faculty. The press, businessmen, and not a few clergymen looked askance upon the college
for maintaining a professor whose teachings savoured of social
rebellion. Herron's relationship with Carrie Rand made him
vulnerable to vituperative personal attacks. His criticism of
marriage as a "coercive institution" was the last straw. On October 13, 1899, Herron voluntarily submitted his resignation, hoping that it would not be accepted but willing to abide by any
consequences that might ensue. On the whole, his letter of
resignation was marked by moderation of tone. He explained
his action on the ground that the American college, dependent
as it was for financial support on the wealthy, was no place to
disseminate controversial social ideas. He expressed satisfaction
that Mrs. Rand would not withdraw her endowment of the chair
of Applied Christianity.[124]

The acceptance of Herron's resignation by the Grinnell Board
of Trustees hurt him more than he cared to admit publicly. In
a letter to Joseph Labadie, the Detroit labor leader and philosophical anarchist, Herron wrote that he had offered himself
as a sacrifice to the "power of things or monopoly" and thereby
demonstrated the basic issue between the latter and "the freedom
of the human spirit." The acceptance of his resignation, he
said, "makes it impossible for anyone to claim freedom of teaching in our institutions of higher learning; it has always been
a hypocritical boast anyhow, such freedom never did exist.

---

[123]*Social Crusader,* II (Oct., 1900), 4-6.
[124]Herron's letter of resignation appears in full in *Social Forum,* I (Nov.,
1899), 177-80.

Those who take the position of the trustees seem to think there oughtn't to be any such freedom, while to those who take more or less our own position, the incident seems to raise the whole issue of social reconstruction."[125]

The divorce that had long been brewing between Herron and his wife became an actuality in March, 1901. Mrs. Herron, who sued on the grounds of "cruelty, culminating in desertion," was given custody of their five children and later received $60,000 for her own and their support—the personal fortune of Carrie Rand.[126] In May, Herron and Carrie were married by the Reverend William Thurston Brown, a Christian Socialist minister from Rochester, New York, in an unconventional ceremony in which each took the other, for man and for wife.[127] Thus, Herron sought to carry out in practice the opposition which he preached to coercive institutions.

Hard on the heels of Herron's second marriage came his expulsion from the Congregational Church ministry. The Council of Iowa Congregational Churches, which took this action, justified it on the ground that Herron was "guilty of immoral and unChristian conduct."[128] Again Herron was roughly shaken, and in the face of the derision of his critics he issued a dignified statement to the general public. "If the church and society may visit [this decision] on me, in making a protest against a system that seems to me destructive to all true morality, and to the very citadel of the soul's integrity," he said, "then my protest has earned its right to be heard . . . . I cannot speak what I seem to see as truth, without living out all the truth about myself, even though the living of the truth destroy my opportunity to speak."[129]

To the commiserating Labadie, Herron pictured himself as a martyr of socialism. The "unequalled and unthinkable attack" on him, he said, did not stem from any deep interest in his personal problem, but rather resulted from an attempt by the church and the capitalistic press to destroy "his influence as a

[125]Herron to Labadie, Nov. 24, 1899. Labadie Papers.
[126]*Dictionary of American Biography,* VIII (New York, 1932), p. 594.
[127]Hopkins, p. 200.
[128]Unpublished MS of Dr. J. S. Nollen.
[129]Quoted in Dombrowski, p. 173.

socialist and thereby reach the cause itself." During the entire crisis, said Herron, his "deepest suffering" came from the possible adverse effects upon the socialist movement. The "enemies of human freedom" sought to take advantage of the furor to bring about disharmony in the socialist ranks. As for himself and his new wife, he declared: "We two who have gone through this storm together, and through many years of suffering and work before the storm came, have more than ever placed our lives on the altar of human need."[130]

But Herron was trumpeting a swan song and he undoubtedly knew it. While the hubbub created by his marriage gradually subsided, his usefulness to the "cause" was hopelessly impaired. Partially on this account, Herron went to Italy to live permanently with his wife and mother-in-law at the latter's villa at Fiesole. In his passing from the American scene, the socialist movement lost a powerful, compelling, dramatic, and not unsympathetic personality.

Bliss and Herron were in the advance guard of the Christian Socialist movement in the United States. Herron in particular attracted to himself a small but fanatically devoted group of admirers. They and others like them undoubtedly caused many of their fellow churchmen to pause and to take spiritual and intellectual stock of themselves. Yet, there is always the danger of assuming that the views of a small number of forceful, articulate, and liberal clergymen represent those of the pulpit as a whole. For purposes of perspective, it should be re-emphasized that the radical social Christianity of Bliss and Herron affected only a very thin part of the Protestant clergy in the 1890's. Particularly untouched or unmoved by the doctrines of Christian Socialism were the thousands of clergymen in the Bible Belt regions, where urban sophistication was absent and religious fundamentalism held sway.

---

[130]Herron to Labadie, June 15, 1901. Labadie Papers.

V. DeLeon Molds the Socialist Labor Party

IN THE autumn of 1890 when an American electorate was expressing at the polls its dissatisfaction with the "Billion Dollar" Fifty-first Congress, Daniel DeLeon was forsaking the respectability of the middle-class Nationalists for the disreputable and proletarian Socialist Labor Party.[1] It was the crossing of the Rubicon for the erudite, thirty-eight-year-old attorney and former professor, for in embracing socialism he eliminated himself from the opportunities for preferment that his undeniable talents might have obtained for him in a capitalistic society. It was an important event, also, in the history of American socialism; for DeLeon as much as, if not more than, any other man during the 1890's shaped the course of American socialist political development.

DeLeon had been in the United States for eighteen years before he took his position in the socialist ranks. He was born in Curaçao in 1852, the son of Salomon and Sara DeLeon. Unquestionably he was of Jewish stock despite his curious, if not outright ridiculous, claim of descent from a wealthy, aristocratic, Catholic, Spanish family of Venezuela.[2] His father was a surgeon in the Dutch colonial army—hardly an occupation for a Spanish grandee—and, according to some of DeLeon's tormenters, carried the surname "Loeb."[3]

Young Daniel, weak and sickly as a youth, was sent to Europe to be educated. He studied first at a Gymnasium in Hildesheim, Germany, and then at the University of Leyden, from which he was graduated in 1872 at the age of twenty, an accomplished

---

[1]An excellent though brief treatment of DeLeon, who deserves a full length biography, appears in Charles Madison's *Critics and Crusaders*, pp. 470-85. Also see Arnold Petersen, *Daniel DeLeon: Social Architect* (New York, 1941); L. G. Raisky, *Daniel DeLeon, The Struggle Against Opportunism in the American Labor Movement* (New York, 1932); Louis Fraina, "Daniel DeLeon," *New Review*, II (1914), 390-99.

[2]Olive M. Johnson, *Daniel DeLeon, American Socialist Pathfinder* (New York, 1923), p. 9.

[3]Gompers, *Seventy Years of Life and Labor*, I, 417.

linguist and widely read in history, philosophy, and mathematics. In the same year he came to New York, where he took up with a group of Cuban revolutionists and edited their Spanish-language newspaper. This was romantic though hardly remunerative work, so DeLeon began teaching at a Westchester County school. This position helped to finance him through Columbia Law School, from which he graduated with honors in 1878. After practicing law for a brief time in Texas, he returned to New York and in 1883 won a prize lectureship at Columbia in Latin American diplomacy. He retained it for two three-year terms, at the end of which time the University's officials were not reluctant to see him go.

Critics of ivory-tower academics could maintain without excessively great danger of error that DeLeon was not promoted to the full professorship which he believed due him because of his activities in behalf of labor and his participation in the Bellamy Nationalist movement. By popular account, he began to take an active interest in labor affairs during the 1886 Eight Hour-Day strikes, when police brutality against workers aroused his indignation. When Henry George ran for mayor in the same year, DeLeon spoke in his behalf several times. In fact, he was on the committee which nominated George. Here he was in respectable company, since his fellow committee members included the Reverends R. Heber Newton and Edward McGlynn, Professor Thomas Davidson, Charles F. Wingate, James Redpath, and Gideon J. Tucker.

DeLeon was in less reputable surroundings when he spoke the next year before a mass meeting at Cooper Union protesting the death sentences of the Haymarket anarchists. To support Henry George was out of character, though not completely damning, for a Columbia faculty member. But to speak in behalf of men whom newspapers and public spokesmen vied in assigning to the gallows was an indication of emotional instability and of unfitness to teach impressionable young students. It required courage and intellectual integrity for DeLeon to tell a predominantly working-class audience of between three and four thousand: "I come here deliberately and for the good name of our beloved country that its proud record shall not be blood-stained by a judicial crime as the one contemplated in Chicago."[4]

During the next two years, DeLeon skirted the nether edges of the organized socialist movement. He was one of the leading luminaries of the first Nationalist club in the metropolitan New York area, and his services as a speaker—he was an excellent one—were in great demand. As of March, 1890, he considered the Nationalist movement "one of the most important, if not absolutely the most important" of the forces of progress in the United States.[5] He wrote several articles explaining "practical Nationalism" for the Socialist Labor Party paper, the *Workmen's Advocate*, which showed warm sympathy for the Bellamyites throughout 1889 and 1890.

The failure of the Nationalists to adopt a program of political action made DeLeon doubt the long-run value of their agitational efforts. In addition, he had begun to read in the general field of Marxist literature. Marx's scientific determinism completely eliminated Bellamy's visionary utopianism from his social philosophy. In early October, 1890, DeLeon was still introduced as a Nationalist at a Socialist Labor Party reception for John Swinton.[6] But at this very time he stood at the crossroads of his career, and a few weeks later he took the highway into the Socialist Labor Party.

The SLP considered DeLeon a great acquisition, as indeed he was. The party had a few members, like Hermann Schlüter and Alexander Jonas, who compared favorably with him in intellectual stature. But for the most part they were newly arrived and usually clannish Germans unknown to the general public. Few if any Socialist Laborites could match DeLeon's skill in debating and public speaking. On the lecture platform the slightly built and neatly bearded DeLeon could skillfully unravel the most complex ideas into the simplest of generalizations and illustrate them with striking similes and metaphors. And when the occasion arose, he could display an amazing knowledge of Marxist theory despite his relatively recent exposure to it, an attestation of his perceptive and retentive mind.

[4]David, *History of the Haymarket Affair*, p. 412.

[5]*Workmen's Advocate*, Mar. 15, 1890.

[6]*Ibid.*, Oct. 18, 1890.

The Socialist Laborites began at once to use the services of their new convert. With each new responsibility, he acquired a corresponding increase in power within the party's top councils. In the spring of 1891, he became the party's "national lecturer" and went on an organizational tour that took him as far as the Pacific Coast.[7] In the fall elections of the same year, he was the SLP candidate for governor of New York and polled a respectable total of 14,651 votes.[8] But it was as editor of the *People*, the official English-language weekly of the SLP, that DeLeon stamped his personality on the party. In August, 1891, Lucien Sanial, whose eyesight was failing, left for Brussels to attend the International Labor Congress, entrusting the editorship of the *People* to DeLeon.[9] Once ensconced in the editor's chair, he remained there until death removed him in 1914.

Those who knew and admired DeLeon considered him a sincere, benign, hard-working, brilliant man who, at great economic and personal sacrifice, had dedicated himself completely to socialism. Rather than compromise with his principles by working for capitalistic enterprises, he made a miserable and desperate living by editing the *People* and translating socialist tracts. The DeLeon family was well acquainted with poverty, and it was not of a genteel quality. They experienced it in their daily lives and also saw it everywhere around them from the squalid East Side tenement in which they lived.

Even DeLeon's opponents were usually willing to concede that he possessed a tremendous intellectual grasp of Marxism. Those who had suffered under his editorial lashings looked on him as an unmitigated scoundrel who took fiendish delight in character assassination, vituperation, and scurrility. But most of DeLeon's contemporaries, and especially his critics, misunderstood him, just as he himself lacked understanding of people. He was not a petty tyrant who desired power for power's sake. Rather, he was a dogmatic idealist, devoted brain and soul to a cause, a zealot who could not tolerate heresy or backsliding, a doctrinaire who would make no compromise with principles. For this strong-willed man, this late nineteenth-century Grand

---

[7]*People*, Apr. 12, 1891.
[8]*Ibid.*, Nov. 29, 1891.
[9]*Ibid.*, Aug. 2, 1891.

Inquisitioner of American socialism, there was no middle
ground. You were either a disciplined and undeviating Marxist
or no socialist at all. You were either with the mischief-making,
scatterbrained reformers and "labor fakirs" or you were against
them. You either agreed on the necessity of uncompromising
revolutionary tactics or you did not, and those falling into the
latter category were automatically expendable so far as the
Socialist Labor Party was concerned. DeLeon even excommunicated his own son, Solon, from the SLP for questioning
his interpretation of Marx's theory of value.

In the technique of editorial defamation and coarse personal
attack, DeLeon had few equals. Yet he did not engage in bil-
lingsgate for its own sake, for he possessed an excellent command
of language and a facility for clear expression. Rather, he used
personal abuse as a weapon to bring into disrepute those persons
who threatened to befoul the pristine purity of orthodox Marxist
dogma, of which he was the most able and honest interpreter.
The whole matter for DeLeon was not one of personalities but
of principles, and the ends justified the means. Needless to
say, the victims of his vicious and gross attacks did not contemplate them on such a lofty plane.

DeLeon joined the Socialist Labor Party when the smoke of
doctrinal battle between the Marxist trade-unionist and Lassallean political-action elements still hung heavy over the
organization. According to DeLeon, the dispute over tactics
did not come to grips with realities, because each faction, in
concentrating its energies on its own particular objectives, failed
to offer a sufficiently comprehensive plan of attack against
the powerfully entrenched bastions of capitalism. If the socialists were to make any headway in the United States, he
maintained, they would have to assault their opponents simultaneously and without surcease on both the political and economic fronts with no quarter given or asked. A victory in
politics without a corresponding triumph in the trade-union
realm would simply lead to social catastrophe, since the capitalist would still hold the key to power through his continued and
unchallenged possession and ownership of the means of production and distribution.

In substantial agreement with DeLeon were Lucien Sanial, Hugo Vogt, and Henry Kuhn, and under their combined piloting the Socialist Labor Party began to swerve sharply away from its past policies and practices. DeLeon and his friends were determined to make the SLP a truly revolutionary party which rested firmly on a class-struggle base and rejected all compromises with capitalism, be they in industrial warfare or in political action. "If you have an economic organization alone," said DeLeon, "you have a duck flying with one wing; you must have a political organization or you are nowhere . . . . Make no mistake: The organization of the working class must be both economic and political. The capitalist is organized on both lines. You must attack him on both."[10]

Capitalism could not be combatted with desultory forays and half-hearted attacks. This was the fallacy of orthodox trade-union action, which never benefited the working class as a whole and which was becoming progressively less successful as capitalistic ownership tended toward increased concentration. The industrial struggles of the day gave illustration of the uselessness of the strike and boycott as labor weapons. "Local revolts everywhere show that bravery is an attribute of honest toil," wrote DeLeon during the Homestead Strike. But "small bands of heroes" could not stand up against the capitalists, who not only possessed economic power of their own to crush them but also had resort to the government, courts, and militia which they controlled.[11] Revolutionary socialism had to struggle relentlessly with capitalism for political power. True, the chances of success were slim, but the campaign and the election gave the socialist minority an opportunity to place its views before the mass public and to harmonize itself with the American political tradition.

"In all revolutionary movements, as in the storming of fortresses," said DeLeon, "the thing depends upon the head of the column—upon that minority that is so intense in its convictions, so soundly based on its principles, so determined in its action, that it carries the masses with it, storms the breastworks and

---

[10]Daniel DeLeon, *Revolution or Reform* (Pamphlet; New York, 1943), pp. 31-32.

[11]*People,* July 10, 1892.

captures the fort."[12] Just as Bliss saw the American political system offering a golden opportunity to the middle class to bring in socialism peacefully and gradually, so did DeLeon believe in its full utilization by the proletariat. "Thanks to universal suffrage," the proletariat could, if it wished, exercise the powers of the state "peacefully, in our day, by a mere declaration of its will at the ballot box."[13] Thus, he hoped for a bloodless socialist revolution in the United States.

Because of the character of its mission, the socialist political minority had to insist upon and enforce discipline within its ranks. "If you allow your own members to play monkeyshines with the party," said DeLeon, "the lookers on . . . will justly believe that you will at some critical moment allow capitalism to play monkeyshines with you."[14] Those who joined the revolutionary vanguard had to steel themselves against dickering and bargaining, take satisfaction in slow gains, be "wholly insensible to all feelings of shame" at the "comparative smallness" of their number, and not allow themselves to be driven "by the itch for political and party success."[15]

Throughout the spring and summer of 1892, the *People* editorially foreshadowed Socialist Laborite participation in the presidential election of the fall. The spectacular successes of the newly organized People's Party, and the disastrous labor defeats in the strikes of the year—at Homestead, Pennsylvania; Coeur d'Alene, Idaho; Buffalo, New York; and Tracy City, Tennessee—were used to emphasize and dramatize the desirability of political action. An editorial of August 21, entitled "Arouse Yourselves," strongly urged independent socialist politics on the national level:

> Workingmen, quit fooling, be up and doing!
>
> Your brothers are being butchered in Tennessee, bayonetted at Homestead, browbeaten in Buffalo, trampled upon throughout the land.
>
> The capitalist class is bent on destroying the last vestige of your freedom; its reign is that of brutal savagism.

[12]DeLeon, *Revolution or Reform,* pp. 22-23.
[13]*People,* Oct. 16, 1892.
[14]DeLeon, *Revolution or Reform,* p. 25.
[15]*People,* July 2, 1893.

It rifles you of the wealth you alone produce, wheedles your votes out of your hands, and then turns both wealth and office to your destruction.

The power of Government, which you confine to it, is its principal engine of oppression. Wrench that power out of its grip. A Presidential election is on. Cease to be the voting cattle for your plunderers. They masquerade as Republicans and Democrats, Free Traders and Protectionists, to divide, confuse, and deceive you. Set up your own candidates. Vote for yourselves. Conquer at the ballot box the political power of the land. Hold in your own hands, no longer place into those of your fleecers, the legislative, the executive, the judicial,—and the MILITARY POWER.

The day you will it, you are freemen.

Strike next November at the ballot box; strike vigorously.

Time is precious; it may soon be too late.

A week after the appearance of this editorial, a conference of the state SLP committees of New York, New Jersey, Connecticut, Pennsylvania, and Massachusetts met to consider the party's stand on the election. The majority of the delegates favored nominating candidates, although the party's official platform called for the abolition of the Presidency, Vice-Presidency, and Senate of the United States. In the light of the party's new tactics, this provision had no validity. Consequently, it was quietly ignored and in the following year dropped from the platform.

Apparently, DeLeon's first choice for the presidential nominee was Harry W. Robinson, an SLP stalwart from Boston and the party's gubernatorial candidate in the 1891 Massachusetts elections. But Robinson, who had expressed his willingness to serve the party in any practical way, "constitutionally or unconstitutionally," and even to the extent of "open violence," had begged off because of illness.[16] As a result, the conference turned to another Bostonian, a sixty-six-year-old manufacturer of photographic equipment and reproductions, Simon Wing. His vice-presidential running mate was Charles H. Matchett, a New Yorker, Civil War veteran, and employee of a telegraph cable company. The *People*, answering frequently expressed criticisms of the "foreign nature of the Socialist Labor Party,"

---

[16]Robinson to DeLeon, July 8, 1892. DeLeon Papers.

noted with pride the "American backgrounds" of the candidates. It pointed out that Wing had been a former Abolitionist and that Matchett came out of "pure Anglo Saxon" and "genuine New England American stock."[17]

The SLP candidates were on the ballot in only six Eastern states, and their total vote was not such as to cause consternation among the leaders of the established parties. Wing and Matchett polled a total of 21,512 votes, of which 17,956 were cast in New York.[18] Admittedly, the Socialist Labor vote left much to be desired, but the party leaders could take solace from the steady advance of the socialist vote in New York. In 1890, the statewide SLP vote in New York was 13,704; in 1891, it rose to 14,651; and in 1892, as noted, it jumped to nearly 18,000. DeLeon expressed satisfaction with the result. The "solidness" of the party, he said, was encouraging.[19]

Simultaneously with the adoption of an uncompromising socialist political program, the Socialist Laborite leadership, through the medium of the *People* and pamphlet literature, began to espouse what it termed a "New Trade Unionism." This proposed trade-union doctrine, according to its supporters, was firmly grounded on the Marxist class-struggle hypothesis. In any event, it was not spun out of theoretical whole cloth, for it reflected the results of much pondering over the socialist failure to capture the American Federation of Labor and the inefficacy of existing trade-union tactics to benefit the entire working class. In ultimate refinement, it became DeLeon's concept of industrial unionism.

As DeLeon and his circle saw it, the fatal weakness of the existing American labor movement was its lack of class-consciousness. This resulted mainly from its acceptance of the permanency of capitalism in its present industrial form. Moreover, it had come to adopt the middle-class attitude that workingmen and capitalists were united by ties of brotherhood. Once such a concept of status was assented to, it became literally immoral "to fight the boss." Instead of defiantly demanding

---

[17]*People,* Sept. 4, 1892.

[18]Lucien Sanial, *"The Socialist Almanac and Treasury of Facts* (New York, 1898), p. 226.

[19]*People,* Nov. 13, 1892.

the worker's rightful wages from the profits of production, the
pure-and-simple trade-union leaders meekly acquiesced to fleec-
ings by the capitalists for the sake of picking up a few crumbs
dropped from their tables. "Instead of being a militant, class-
conscious organization, ever watchful of the interests of the
workers and ever ready to do battle" against conditions that
tended to degrade them, the trade-union movement had "reduced
itself to a mere benevolent organization, doling out charities
for sick- and death-benefits, thus taking upon itself the functions of an ambulance service on the industrial battlefield,
taking care of the wounded, burying the dead, and stripping
itself of all other functions."[20]

If existing trade unions sought to improve the conditions of
their members, what was their chance of success? Not particularly bright now, and even less so in the future. As capitalistic
industrial ownership became increasingly concentrated, the effects of strikes and boycotts were felt correspondingly less by
the combines and corporations. In trustified industries, where
complete monopoly conditions existed, strikes and boycotts were
absolutely worthless.[21] In those industries where semi-monopoly
conditions prevailed, the strike or boycott might occasionally
be effective in achieving minor gains. In industries where competition was still existent—an ever narrowing group—orthodox
trade-union weapons, employed under the most propitious circumstances, might obtain as often as not temporary concessions,
though hardly permanent advantages.

What, then, was the alternative for the class-conscious, revolutionary members of the proletariat insofar as the organized
labor movement was concerned? Only one alternative existed
—the creation of a trade-union movement organized industry-
wise rather than by craft, and closely affiliated with the Socialist Labor Party. A powerful federation of such industrial
unions, representing all of the American wage earners, would
constitute, in effect, a class-conscious socialist army which would

---

[20]*Proceedings of the 9th Annual Convention of the Socialist Labor Party,
New York, 1896,* p. 10.

[21]In an editorial following failure of the Buffalo Switchmen's Strike, De-
Leon wrote: "Once more it has been shown that no strike could succeed in
industries that have reached a high degree of capitalistic concentration."
People, Aug. 28, 1892.

seek to win not merely local skirmishes but a decisive and final triumph for the proletariat. When the hour of revolution was at hand, or even before, if "capitalist political chicanery" sought to pollute the ballot box, this well-indoctrinated, socialist-led force of industrial workers would be in a position to take over the means of production and distribution with a minimum of dislocation. Capitalists and their minions in the political state dared not defy such an overwhelming show of strength.

The successful implantation of industrial unionism in the United States during the late 1930's gives historical and doctrinal validity to a considerable part of the "new trade-unionism" argument. It was no mere fortuitous development; bigness in industry inevitably spawned bigness in labor. Only through industrial unions of the character of the United Automobile Workers and the United Steel Workers has labor been able to stand up against concentrated corporate power. And, it is generally agreed, industrial unionism has helped to create among workers a sense of class awareness previously either lacking or inchoate, even if it has not developed a militant class-struggle psychology. In the latter respect, institutional forces in American life still provide formidable if not insurmountable barriers.

Yet, like the American Federation of Labor, the industrial unions have completely accepted capitalism. They have pursued the same bread-and-butter goals as the AF of L, with some embellishments to meet new conditions and situations. And in tactics, they still use the strike as the ultimate weapon. Socialists, whether in the AF of L or the CIO, when confronted with the bald alternative between socialism and trade unionism, have invariably given the latter their first allegiance. What DeLeon and his group failed to realize was that the average American wage earner could not live on millennial hope alone, even though he might be sympathetic to the co-operative commonwealth. The revolution was a long time in coming, and meanwhile the worker wanted shorter hours, higher pay, and better working conditions—trade-union goals upon which DeLeon looked almost with disdain.

DeLeon and his lieutenants faced the alternative of developing from scratch a new industrial union structure or of converting the American Federation of Labor or the Knights of Labor

to that end. The latter course of policy was preferable since
it did not involve the difficulties of organizational spadework.
Capturing the AF of L was ruled out, largely because of the
socialist defeat at the Detroit convention in 1890 but also partly
because of the difficulty of manipulating an organization possessing generally autonomous federated unions. The highly
centralized Knights of Labor, on the other hand, was in the
throes of internal dissension. A well-disciplined socialist minority might easily take over the order, which had been declining
steadily since the wave of disastrous strikes in 1886. Under
socialist direction, the Knights could be metamorphosed into a
straight industrial union organization and serve as a powerful
competitor to the AF of L for the loyalty of the organized industrial worker. What the Socialist Labor Party leadership
had to discover, therefore, was a feasible method of gaining control of the Knights of Labor.

The DeLeon, Sanial, Vogt, and Kuhn speedily devised a plan of
strategy. The first and most important step was to infiltrate
the New York District Assembly 49, the strongest and most
influential in the Knights of Labor. Once firmly entrenched
and in authority in District Assembly 49, the socialists would
be in a position to exert pressure in the national councils of the
order and ultimately to take control.

The conquest of District Assembly 49 was carried out according to plan. The drive was spearheaded by a strong socialist
nucleus already within the order and by members of the United
Hebrew Trades, which affiliated itself with the Knights. This
organization, composed mainly of Jewish garment workers,
was socialist-led since its founding in 1888.[22] DeLeon, himself,
joined the Knights in July, 1891, as a member of Mixed Assembly No. 1563, which consisted more of intellectuals, parlor socialists, and reformers than actual wage earners. Unlike the
American Federation of Labor, the Knights did not restrict
themselves to members of the working class. The greatest socialist asset in District Assembly 49 was a jovial, ruddy-cheeked

22Hillquit, *History of Socialism in the United States,* pp. 287-88. A general account of the Jewish labor movement in New York at this time is found
in Abraham M. Rogoff, *Formative Years of the Jewish Labor Movement
in the United States, 1890-1900* (New York, 1945). Also see Charles A. Madison, *American Labor Leaders* (New York, 1950), pp. 199-205.

Irishman named Patrick J. Murphy, who served as its secretary. A loyal Socialist Labor Party member, Murphy was largely responsible for DeLeon's election as the Assembly's delegate to the Knights' General Assembly, or national convention, at Philadelphia in November, 1893.

Reporting on the General Assembly, John W. Hayes, editor of the *Journal of the Knights of Labor*, observed that the new delegates included the world-renowned Daniel DeLeon, whose name was "respected and honored as that of an honest, honorable, and one of the very ablest of the living exponents of the principles labor reformers hold dear."[23] DeLeon, aggressive and assertive as always, made his presence felt at Philadelphia. He led a small group of socialist delegates who combined with supporters of the Iowa farmer editor, John R. Sovereign, to end the feckless Terence V. Powderly's fourteen-year reign as Grand Master Workman of the order. From the socialists' point of view, Sovereign was hardly an improvement over Powderly. While both men professed socialist leanings, each was a warm supporter of the People's Party. DeLeon apparently believed, however, that any change in the leadership of the Knights was for the better. Powderly had been tried and found wanting, whereas Sovereign was unproven as yet. In an editorial in the *People*, DeLeon wrote:

> Powderly was the vestige of an era that is fast passing away . . . . In the seventies and deep into the eighties the natural growth of labor organizations was such that neither character nor positive knowledge was requisite on any hand. The movement took its course, and the 'Accidents' that were raised to leadership were 'leaders' in name only . . . . It was under such circumstances that Powderly rose to leadership in the order.

According to DeLeon, a new era was at hand for the Knights of Labor; it was one in which socialists would be in the vanguard.[24]

The Populists within District Assembly 49 recognized the socialist designs on the Knights before the national officers of the order did. At the meeting of January 13, 1894, during which

[23]*Journal of the Knights of Labor*, Nov. 16, 1893.
[24]*People*, Dec. 10, 1893.

officers were to be chosen for the coming year, District Master Workman George W. McCaddin, a Populist, sought to halt socialist inroads into the Assembly by denying voting rights to Knights affiliated with trade associations outside the order. Such a ruling deprived members of the United Hebrew Trades of their presumed rights and occasioned a stinging denunciation by DeLeon. He appealed to Sovereign, warning that an adverse ruling would render him "equally guilty with those who got up this job." If necessary, said DeLeon, he would "carry the matter beyond" Sovereign.[25]

The affair was settled to DeLeon's satisfaction, but peace and harmony still did not reign within the District Assembly. In July, Charles Sotheran, a Socialist Labor Party member but an opponent of DeLeon, denounced the latter's presence in the Assembly. Sotheran argued that membership in the Knights was denied to lawyers and that technically DeLeon was still a lawyer even if he no longer practiced. Sotheran's objection to DeLeon was overruled by the Assembly and the sole result of the incident was the former's unceremonious expulsion from the Socialist Labor Party. The party had no room, said DeLeon, for "this 250 pound perambulating scrap book and historic junk shop." He was alluding to Sotheran's encyclopedic knowledge of the early socialist movement in the United States.[26]

On the national level, Grand Master Workman Sovereign was discovering that living in the same organization with DeLeon presented its peculiar problems. In May, 1894, the General Executive Board of the Knights advised the membership to scrutinize closely the political "chess board" and to elect no one to Congress who did not "recognize the right of the people to control and issue the money or medium of exchange of the United States."[27] DeLeon declined this advice immediately. He answered in the *People* that the real issue was not the control or issuance of money, as the People's Party maintained, but rather the collective ownership of the means of production. Candidates had to possess greater qualifications than mere advocacy of a money plank, said the fiery editor.[28]

[25]DeLeon to Sovereign, Jan. (n. d.), 1894. DeLeon Papers.
[26]Newspaper clipping in DeLeon Papers.
[27]*Journal of the Knights of Labor,* May 10, 1894.
[28]*People,* May 20, 1894.

When the leadership of the Knights showed little discernible
evidence of being chastened by the professor's editorial lecture,
he prepared a more potent one and delivered it in the *People* a
few months later under the title, "A Word with Grand Master
Workman J. R. Sovereign." The labor movement, said DeLeon,
could be represented politically only by a wage earner's party
standing on an advanced program. "The pitiful sight of . . .
seeing the working class divided against itself, supporting its
enemies, and foolishly abashing one by exalting another" had
been witnessed long enough. "We warn you in the name of the
socialist Knights . . . true to the order . . . against similar blunders." Closing on an ominous note which could not have escaped
Sovereign's notice, he declared: "It matters not whether this
individual or that is laid low."[29]

With the election of national officers in the order coming up
in a few months, Sovereign decided to heed DeLeon's strictures,
at least when he visited New York. He had no desire, certainly,
to be "laid low" by the socialists in the order. In an address to
District Assembly 49 on September 23, he asserted that the
struggle being waged in the country at the time was "between
organized labor and heartless capitalism, between the masses
and the corporations, between the oppressed human souls and
the dollars of Shylock." If this sounded like socialism, said
Sovereign, he was willing to stand and be counted as a socialist.[30]

DeLeon's influence in the Knights was at its peak during the
order's General Assembly at New Orleans, November 13-23,
1894. Powderly's friends were making a determined effort to
restore him to power. With the Sovereign and Powderly forces
evenly divided, the DeLeon-led bloc of eight socialist delegates
held the balance of power. DeLeon pressed home this enviable
advantage by agreeing to support Sovereign for re-election in
exchange for Sanial's appointment as editor-in-chief of the
Journal of the Knights of Labor. The harassed Iowan had
little choice but to agree to this *quid pro quo*, and with the backing of the socialists he was returned to office. His crown of
authority, however, rested uneasily as long as he was under
obligation to the socialist chieftain, whose objectives were now

---

[29]*Ibid.*, Aug. 5, 1894.
[30]*Journal of the Knights of Labor*, Sept. 27, 1894.

completely unmasked.[31] For his part, DeLeon was jubilant;
not only had his support been decisive in Sovereign's election,
he had also heard Sovereign, in his presidential report to the
General Assembly, call for the abolition of the "wage system"
and the establishment of a "co-operative industrial system."
Upon returning to New York, he wrote an editorial lauding the
Knights and offering them full socialist support in emancipating the American people from the "yoke of capitalism."[32]

In a matter of months DeLeon's jubilation was to turn into
white-hot wrath and, even worse for a man of his domineering
temperament, frustration. Sovereign reneged on his agreement
and began to combat the creeping socialist influence within the
order. Early in January he wrote an artless and dissimulating
letter to DeLeon stating that for the moment financial difficulties had made it impossible to give Sanial "a place on the *Journal*."[33] Sensing the double cross, DeLeon replied angrily that
the agreement at New Orleans called for Sanial's appointment
as editor-in-chief so that the *Journal* could be converted "into
what it should be and what it has not been especially during the
past year, a source of instruction to its readers." He demanded
that Sovereign live up to his pledge. The order's financial
straits could be alleviated appreciably, he suggested, if the general officers drastically slashed their excessively high salaries.[34]

If open warfare was not declared between the blunt and outspoken DeLeon and the leadership of the Knights, it nevertheless existed in fact. After an unmerciful DeLeon editorial[35]
ripped to shreds Sovereign's contention that socialists erred in
not supporting the Populist money plank,[36] Sovereign wrote to
the SLP editor: "I want to doubly assure you that any criticism
you may desire to write concerning me or my views on any phase
of the labor question will in nowise detract from my personal
friendship for you."[37] But this was window dressing and, be-

[31]Commons (ed.), *History of Labor in the United States,* IV, 220; Fine, p.
156.
[32]*People,* Dec. 2, 1894.
[33]Sovereign to DeLeon, Jan. 7, 1895. DeLeon Papers.
[34]DeLeon to Sovereign, Jan. 22, 1895. DeLeon Papers.
[35]*People,* Mar. 10, 1895.
[36]*Journal of the Knights of Labor,* Feb. 28, 1895.
[37]Sovereign to DeLeon, Mar. 23, 1895. DeLeon Papers.

sides, personal friendships to DeLeon were always secondary to abstract truths. Both men knew that, eventually, the struggle for power had to be settled once and for all.

Throughout the spring and summer of 1895 the *People* and the *Journal of the Knights of Labor* exchanged barbed editorial comments, chiefly on the issue of the People's Party. Accusations and recriminations came thick and fast, however, on other issues. For example, the *People* expressed displeasure with the K of L support of Democrat A. P. Gorman's candidacy for the Maryland governorship, while the *Journal* charged that some of the locals affiliated with District Assembly 49 had failed to support a boycott against certain New York breweries. DeLeon, himself, was accused of dissuading Arthur Keep, his chief lieutenant in the District of Columbia, from joining a local of the Knights. But the big blow which was to sweep the socialists clean out of the Knights began in September. Sovereign and the other national officers, taking advantage of their control over the organizational machinery of the order, began an investigation of the socialist stronghold, District Assembly 49.

Unrest had been rife in the District Assembly ever since the socialists had begun their "boring from within" tactics. In January, 1895, the socialists succeeded in replacing George McCaddin as District Master Workman with one of their own number, William L. Brower. The election was bitterly contested, and once again the question of the voting rights of trade associations was raised. The defeated Populist element within the District Assembly appealed for a second time to the national officers for a ruling. The latter delayed until nearly the eve of the order's General Assembly and then announced that an investigation of District Assembly 49 would be forthcoming.[38] Its purpose left no one in doubt, least of all the socialists. However, District Assembly 49 at its September meeting defiantly elected DeLeon and six other "uncompromising socialists" as delegates to the coming General Assembly. DeLeon, with characteristic vigor, struck back at the foe through the editorial columns of the *People*. The general officers of the Knights, he wrote, had "degenerated into a band of brigands no better than

---

[38]Fine, p. 156.

those of Powderly's old regime." They were now in "desperate straits" and "ripe to be kicked out."[39]

The General Assembly of the Knights, convened from the 12th to the 22d of November, ended with a crashing finality the socialist efforts to capture the order. By a close 23 to 21 vote, the convention denied the validity of the credentials held by DeLeon and the other representatives of District Assembly 49.[40] The routed socialist delegates had no alternative other than to troop back empty handed to New York where they reported the debacle to their followers. DeLeon called on District Assembly 49 to repudiate the General Assembly.[41]

The meeting of District Assembly 49 on December 1st was, as usual, disorderly. To add to the drama, Sovereign and Hayes were present and heard themselves denounced as "fakirs" and "traitors" to the labor movement. They were accused of having packed the convention with bogus delegates. They were excoriated as implacable enemies of the co-operative commonwealth. There could be no truck with such men, the socialist delegates maintained. Obedient to DeLeon, the District Assembly censured the national leadership of the Knights and withdrew from the "corrupted" order.[42]

Sovereign and the National Executive Board of the Knights replied in kind, first by expelling DeLeon, Patrick Murphy, and others guilty of "disrupting" District Assembly 49[43] and then by granting new charters to thirteen anti-socialist locals which had refused to leave the order.[44] Simultaneously, Hayes began a series of anti-socialist editorials and articles in the *Journal of the Knights of Labor.* He quoted Uriah S. Stephens, founder of the order, as having written:

> You must not allow the socialists to get control of your Assembly. They are simply disturbers and only gain entrance to labor societies that they may be in a better position

---

[39]*People,* Sept. 29, 1895.

[40]*Ibid.,* Dec. 1, 1895; *Journal of the Knights of Labor,* Nov. 28, 1895; Fine, p. 157.

[41]*People,* Dec. 1, 1895.

[42]*Ibid.,* Dec. 8, 1895.

[43]*Journal of the Knights of Labor,* Dec. 5, 1895.

[44]*Ibid.,* Dec. 12, 1895.

to break them up. You cannot fathom them, for they are crafty, cunning and unscrupulous.[45]

According to Hayes, who demonstrably was not unskilled in invective himself, DeLeon was living proof of the accuracy of Stephens' warning. "A fifth rate pettifogger" with a "smart smattering of law jargon," the former Columbia professor had failed miserably to capture and break up the Knights. "Now this adventuresome faker," continued Hayes, found himself "landed high and dry, expelled in disgrace from the organization he tried to destroy." A "little handful of poor, simple, ignorant dupes" was discovering that their leader had "involved them in his own wreck." Such was inevitably the fate of those who followed "this semi-legal blackguard" whose "sole stock in trade" was "falsehood, slander, and deceit."[46]

For DeLeon and his supporters in District Assembly 49 the socialist efforts to bore from within the established national unions were now at an end. If pure-and-simple trade unionists could not be won over by joining them, the alternative was to stand up against them. DeLeon was well aware that such a course of policy involved opposing both the Knights of Labor and the American Federation of Labor, but he was willing to abide by the consequences. He was certain that sooner or later a revolutionary labor organization, based upon irreconcilable opposition to capitalism, would win the allegiance of the working class. The wage earner might be misled some of the time by pure-and-simple trade-union leaders, but he could not be deceived all of the time.

The expulsion of the DeLeonites from District Assembly 49 did not catch them unprepared. In truth, it provided the catalyst for the creation of a new and uncompromisingly socialistic trade-union movement. On December 6, on the initiative of District Assembly 49, a meeting was held in conjunction with representatives of the socialist-dominated Central Labor Federation of New York City, the Brooklyn Socialist Labor Federation, the Newark Central Labor Federation, and the United Hebrew Trades. The result of the session was a rough plan for a militant, class-conscious national labor organization and the issuance

[45]*Ibid.*, Feb. 14, 1896.
[46]*Ibid.*, Dec. 5, 1895.

of an invitation to forward-looking trade unionists to meet at
Cooper Union Hall on Friday, December 13.[47] According to
the invitation, the gathering was to honor the "progressive"
delegates who were attending the national convention of the
American Federation of Labor, currently in session in New
York City.[48] Whether intended as such or not, it gave the appearance that the socialist delegates were sympathetic to the
purposes of the meeting.[49]

For the more superstitious and less scientific socialists, the
Cooper Union meeting, held on such an inauspicious date, boded
ill for the future. And many were to maintain that Friday,
December 13, 1895, marked the beginning of the decline of socialist influence in the American labor movement.[50] Be that
as it may, the meeting was attended by a capacity audience.[51]
Scores of persons, unable to obtain seats, waited outside the
hall. On the speakers' platform, behind which hung a huge
red banner, sat officials of District Assembly 49, several women
distinguished in East Side labor activities, and twelve delegates
from the American Federation of Labor convention.

The speakers for the evening were the young William Brower,
president of District Assembly 49; John F. Tobin and J. Mahlon Barnes, prominent socialist members of the AF of L;
Sanial; and DeLeon. Brower and Sanial, the first two speakers
on the program, established the tone of the meeting by viciously
attacking pure-and-simple trade unionism. Brower said that
after listening for three days to the sessions of the AF of L
convention, he could find little hope for the masses. Sanial,
pointing out that the American Federation of Labor represented
only 200,000 of the "25,000,000 American wage slaves," asserted:
"We are going to organize the working classes . . . to take the
reins of government into their own hands." He boasted that
the French socialists, with their bloc of fifty-eight representatives in the Chamber of Deputies, had been responsible for the
overthrow of four premiers and the resignations of two presi-

[47]*People*, Dec. 15, 1895.
[48]*New York World*, Dec. 14, 1895.
[49]Commons, IV, 221.
[50]*Ibid.*, p. 222.
[51]*People*, Dec. 22, 1895.

dents. "That's what we must achieve in America," he shouted.

Tobin and Barnes were less belligerent, though the former attacked the American Federation of Labor for failing to support working-class political action. Tobin, president of the Boot and Shoe Workers' Union, declared that one good political victory was worth more than all of the resolutions passed at the Federation's conventions. Barnes, of the International Cigar Makers' Union, was introduced as the "Demosthenes of Philadelphia." He proved to be the disappointment of the evening. His half-hour long speech was so rambling and incoherent that the reporter from the *New York World* jokingly termed the introduction a wilful effort on the part of New Yorkers to discredit Philadelphia oratory.[52] Throughout Barne's remarks, the audience impatiently called for DeLeon to take over the podium.

DeLeon was wildly cheered during his brief address. Applause was especially heavy when he declared: "Just as you snatch a pistol from the hand of a highwayman, so you have the right to snatch excessive property from those who hold it . . . . One class does all the work, and the other does nothing save marry its daughters to rotten European princes." The audience enthusiastically approved the following resolution which DeLeon presented at the end of his speech:

> Whereas the issue between the capitalist class and the laboring class is essentially a political issue involving such modifications of our institutions as may be required for the abolition of all classes by transferring to the whole people as a corporate body the land and machinery of production,
>
> Resolved, that we the socialists of New York, in mass meeting assembled, urge upon all our fellow workingmen throughout the United States the necessity of joining the Socialist Trade and Labor Alliance now being organized for the purpose of placing the labor movement in its only true and national lines—the lines of international socialism.[53]

Barnes was to maintain later that he was completely unaware of the true purpose of the Cooper Union meeting.[54] Likewise,

---

[52]*New York World*, Dec. 14, 1895.

[53]*Ibid.; People,* Dec. 22, 1895.

[54]Fine, pp. 167-68.

many opponents of DeLeon within the Socialist Labor Party
were to claim that the organization of the Socialist Trade and
Labor Alliance did not preclude them from "boring from within" the American Federation of Labor. They cited a resolution
by DeLeon, adopted by the 1896 national convention of the
Socialist Labor Party. It called on "all socialists of the land to
carry the revolutionary spirit of the ST and LA into all the
organizations of the workers, and thus consolidate and concentrate the proletariat of America in one irresistible class-
conscious army, equipped with both the shield of the economic
organization and the sword of the Socialist Labor Party
ballot."[55]

Yet the practical and doctrinal aspects of the Socialist Trade
and Labor Alliance were always clear. There was no stealth
in the Alliance, as was sometimes held. Its purposes were open
and aboveboard. If it was to be the economic revolutionary
movement of the labor class, like its political counterpart, the
Socialist Labor Party, then consistency demanded that it oppose
tooth and nail both the Knights of Labor and the American
Federation of Labor. Such opposition would have the inevitable result of dual unionism, and DeLeon contemplated this
policy from the start. As the Socialist Labor Party fought in
the political arena against capitalistic charlatans, so would the
Socialist Trade and Labor Alliance struggle against the "fakers"
of the established unions in the field of labor organization.

Hugo Vogt, in reporting to the 1896 SLP convention on the
Socialist Trade and Labor Alliance, explained its creation on
the basis of freeing the labor movement "from those leeches—
that do not belong to it, that actually have turned the trade
union organization into agencies of capitalism." The tactic of
"boring from within" both the American Federation of Labor
and the Knights of Labor had borne little fruit; for while socialists often had been able to "drive the conservative leaders
into a corner," they had always lost the ground gained "through
the trickery" of the "labor fakirs." It was impossible, said
Vogt, to bring about any change whatsoever in the conduct of
the established national unions.[56]

[55]*Proceedings of the 9th Annual Convention of the Socialist Labor Party,*
p. 30.
[56]*Ibid.,* p. 28.

Four years later, DeLeon, in a memorable New Haven debate with Job Harriman, explained the principles upon which he and his friends founded the Socialist Trade and Labor Alliance. They believed, he said, that the American Federation of Labor and the Knights of Labor could not "be ignored" nor "be bored from within exclusively." They had to be "battered to pieces from without." It was the aim of the Alliance to organize "the unorganized men . . . and with their aid try to reform those unions and bring them over." In pursuit of this policy, "war" could not be avoided. You could not establish a national organization like the Socialist Trade and Labor Alliance, said De-Leon, and imagine that it meant friendship with the American Federation of Labor and the Knights of Labor.[57]

Most trade unionists within the Socialist Labor Party showed no fondness for the new ST and LA offspring. Indeed, they had not been consulted as to the desirability of its being born into the socialist family. They were unready to abandon "boring from within" the American Federation of Labor for the party leadership's revolutionary but uncharted course of action. They were still convinced that the AF of L, by ceaseless agitation and education, could be won over to socialism at the same time that it protected the daily bread-and-butter interests of its members.

The DeLeonites, on the contrary, lovingly nurtured the ST and LA and at the 1896 SLP national convention, they were successful in committing the party to its support. "We hail with unqualified joy the formation of the Socialist Trade and Labor Alliance as a giant stride towards throwing off the yoke of wage slavery and of the robber class of capitalists," said a convention-endorsed resolution.[58] For its part, the Alliance had already exhibited true filial devotion to its parent organization and ally: its constitution provided that all of its officials, both on a local and a national level, be pledged to support the Socialist Labor Party. Sections of the party were invited to

[57] *A Debate on the Tactics of the S. T. and L. A. Toward Trade Unions between Daniel DeLeon and Job Harriman, New Haven, Conn., Nov. 25, 1900* (Pamphlet).

[58] *Proceedings of the 9th Annual Convention of the Socialist Labor Party,* p. 30.

send representatives to the central bodies of the Alliance, in the same manner as the various unions but without paying dues or taking out charters. And "as a sign of recognition and brotherhood," the Alliance permitted three delegates of the SLP to sit in on its conventions with full voting rights.[59] This provision allowed DeLeon to be present at ST and LA conventions as a fully accredited delegate.

Vogt had cautioned the 1896 SLP convention against expecting too much from the new Alliance. Of necessity, its numbers initially would be small in comparison to the membership of the AF of L. But the Alliance would grow "by the gradual working of the experiences through which American labor was passing." It was only a question of time, said the patient Vogt, before the mass of American wage earners, disillusioned with the leadership and tactics of the old trade-union organizations, would come into the Alliance.[60]

Probably at no time in the ST and LA's brief and tempestuous history—it merged with the Industrial Workers of the World in 1905—could it claim a membership of more than 30,000. The largest percentage of its locals was in the metropolitan New York area, though charters were granted to labor groups throughout the country. In the first flush of the Alliance's efforts, charters were issued to more than 200 labor organizations.[61]

The ST and LA inevitably entered into the picture whenever and wherever internal dissension existed in the AF of L. It failed, however, to capitalize on the discontent amongst the socialist-led Western Federation of Miners which in 1897 broke away from the AF of L to form the Western Labor Union. Inroads were made into the ranks of the garment workers, cigar makers, coal miners, glass-bottle workers, and textile workers. Gompers never minimized its menace to the Federation. In his presidential report to the 1896 national convention of the AF of L, he noted that "in a number of instances, local unions affiliated with us have been rent asunder." The purpose of the Socialist Trade and Labor Alliance, he said, "was to undermine

[59]*Ibid.*, p. 29.
[60]*Ibid.*, pp. 28-29.
[61]*People,* July 3, 1898; Fine, p. 161; Hillquit, p. 304.

and destroy the trade unions of the country and of the American Federation of Labor itself."[62]   In the *American Federationist* Gompers had previously written in April that the work of "union wrecking" was "being taken up by a wing of the so-called socialist party of New York, headed by a professor without a professorship, a shyster lawyer without a brief, and a statistician who furnished figures to the republican, democratic and socialist parties." The purpose of the new labor organization which had been launched from "a beer saloon" was to crush every trade union in the country.

Especially among the textile workers did the Alliance challenge the AF of L for power. In Georgia, where the Federation was making a strenuous drive to organize the textile-mill workers, the Alliance adroitly channelized this effort to its own advantage.[63]   During the famous 1898 textile-workers strike in New Bedford, Massachusetts, both Gompers and DeLeon appeared on the scene, the former to appeal for loyalty to the AF of L, the latter to win the millhands over to the Alliance. It was on this occasion that DeLeon delivered his well-known speech, "What Means this Strike?", one of his clearest expositions of the "new trade-unionism." The Alliance enrolled many new members,[64] although not enough to dominate the industry.

In New York City, the ST and LA was a constant thorn in the side of the AF of L. It kept the East Side in perpetual turmoil.[65]   The strike at Seidenberg's cigar factory in March, 1898, brought the most serious collision of the Alliance and the Federation in New York. Alliance, Federation, and non-union men, all employed at the factory, had walked out together in protest against a reduction in wages. The Alliance men were members of Local 141, and the Federation workers were affiliated with Local 90, controlled by anti-DeLeon socialists. According to the Alliance version of the strike, the Federationists

---

[62]*Report of Proceedings of the 16th Annual Convention of the American Federation of Labor, Cincinnati, Dec. 14-21, 1896*, p. 13.

[63]Gompers, I, 419.

[64]Thomas Hickey to *New Yorker Volkszeitung*, Mar. 4, 1898 (telegram). DeLeon Papers. Also see *Report of Proceedings of the 18th Annual Convention of the American Federation of Labor, Kansas City, Mo., Dec. 12-20, 1898*, p. 9; *American Federationist*, V (1898), 11-12; Gompers, I, 419-20.

[65]*Ibid.*, p. 418.

made a backdoor settlement with the firm, which established a closed AF of L shop, and therefore cost the Alliance men their jobs.[66] The AF of L account was that the members of the Alliance had returned to their jobs while the strike was still in progress and hence were scab workers. DeLeon, wrote Gompers, "has made the name socialist synonomous with cheap, unfair workers and strike breakers."[67]

After the middle of 1898 the Socialist Trade and Labor Alliance suffered a steady decline. The most staggering blow was the desertion of the New York Central Labor Federation, after a raucous convention of the Alliance in Buffalo on July 4, 1898. The delegates at the convention had displayed an attitude of independence and truculence not to DeLeon's liking. They deposed his henchman, William Brower, as head of the Alliance and elected an executive board which excluded DeLeon, himself. Furthermore, they showed an inclination to cease fighting the existing trade unions.

DeLeon at once set to work to reverse these actions. He and the other party leaders in New York pressured the newly elected Alliance executive board into resigning. Then they saw to it that the board's new members were undeviatingly loyal. Commenting on this development, Gompers remarked: "Well done, Loeb [DeLeon], as a politician, a manipulator, and as a boss, you can give Platt, Croker, et al., cards and spades."[68] DeLeon's maneuver, he said, served as a warning against allowing a political party to dominate the labor movement. In an outpouring of invective that would have done DeLeon himself proud, Gompers declared that the Alliance "conceived in iniquity and brutal concubinage with labor's double enemy, greed and ignorance, fashioned into an embryonic phthisical dwarf, born in corruption and filth" was now dying "surrounded by the vultures of its progeny ready to pounce on the emaciated carcass of the corpse."[69]

---

[66]*Proceedings of the 10th Annual Convention of the Socialist Labor Party, New York, June 2-8, 1900*, pp. 13-14; Henry Kuhn and Olive M. Johnson, *The Socialist Labor Party During Four Decades, 1890-1930* (New York, 1931), pp. 29-30.

[67]*American Federationist*, V (1898), 37-38.

[68]*Ibid.*, p. 143.

[69]*Ibid.*, pp. 115-16.

DeLeon's critics among the socialists maintain that the Socialist Trade and Labor Alliance created an unbridgeable chasm between socialism and the trade-union movement. Such an accusation is not altogether fair. It cannot, of course, be proved that any real cohesion would have existed between the socialists and the trade-union movement had DeLeon never appeared on the scene. The contrary would appear to be true on the basis of socialist–trade-unionist relations within the AF of L between 1889 and 1896. Furthermore, since American workers in mass-production industries were not organized until the late 1930's— and then not on the initiative of the AF of L—it is questionable whether the Federation was truly representative of the wage-earning class in the United States and hence a proper vehicle for socialist agitation and infiltration. DeLeon, no doubt, minimized the appeal to the worker of a trade-union policy based on higher wages, shorter hours, and better working conditions, but he did recognize that such a program could not provide the dynamic that his brand of revolutionary socialism required.

In molding the Socialist Labor Party into a proletarian and revolutionary organization, DeLeon sought to prune from its membership those middle-class reformers who vacillated on the class-struggle thesis. He felt obliged, also, to rid the party of all who refused to accept socialist discipline or, more accurately, those who refused to subordinate themselves completely to his inflexible will. As a consequence of this desire for party purity, he drove from the party ranks some of its most able members and finally, in 1899, brought about a general rebellion. The end result was the reduction of the Socialist Labor Party into a small sect of simon-pure DeLeonites.

Among those drummed out of the party was Herbert N. Casson, a radical clergyman who had left the Methodist Church in 1894 to found a Labor Church at Lynn, Massachusetts. Casson's expulsion by his local SLP section resulted from his criticism of the *People* as being "too scientific," his objections to the SLP stress on the "exploitation of the proletariat," and his advocacy of a socialist-Populist-labor alliance.[70] For a time,

---

[70]T. A. Brophy to DeLeon, Oct. 29, 1895. DeLeon Papers. Also see *People*, Dec. 8, 1895.

Casson's case threatened to become a *cause célèbre* in the Socialist Labor Party, because the party's Massachusetts grievance committee upheld the minister,[71] and the state central committee permitted him to tour the commonwealth lecturing under SLP auspices.[72] However, when the issue was presented before the party at its 1896 national convention, DeLeon's supporters confirmed Casson's expulsion.[73]

Another Massachusetts socialist who felt the hard boot of expulsion was James F. Carey. An aggressive socialist and ardent trade unionist, Carey had an immense following among the shoe workers of Haverhill. Largely on the strength of their votes, he was elected Alderman in December, 1897, on the Socialist Labor Party ticket.[74] Since SLP electoral victories were few and far between, the *People* took intense satisfaction from Carey's triumph. But Carey's independence of spirit, revealed by his refusal to accept advice from the party moguls in New York or to welcome speakers whom they dispatched to Haverhill, infuriated DeLeon. This was heresy enough, but when Carey voted in favor of a $15,000 appropriation for a new Haverhill armory, he drew upon his head an anathema from "the New York Pope," and formal excommunication.[75]

Albert Sanderson, a St. Louis lawyer, teacher, journalist, and former communitarian socialist, was one of DeLeon's greatest potential enemies. He and Gustav A. Hoehn, a well-known German socialist editor, headed a group of St. Louis Socialist Laborites who harbored ambitions of capturing the party leadership. At the 1893 SLP national convention in Chicago they narrowly missed bringing about the transfer of the National Executive Committee from New York to St. Louis, a move that would have halted, temporarily at least, DeLeon's ascendency in the party.

71Brophy to DeLeon, Nov. 23, 1895. DeLeon Papers.

72DeLeon to Squire Putney, Oct. 10, 1895; Putney to DeLeon, Oct. 20, 1895. DeLeon Papers.

73*Proceedings of the 9th Annual Convention of the Socialist Labor Party,* p. 48.

74*People,* Dec. 12, 1897.

75*Proceedings of the 10th Annual Convention of the Socialist Labor Party,* p. 45.

Equally challenging was Sanderson's attempt to make St. Louis the chief publication site for the party press. Personal motivation was present, since he was publisher and Hoehn editor of a socialist newspaper, *St. Louis Labor*. By means of the Socialist Newspaper Union, which served as a central dispensing agency, local editions of *Labor* were published in some thirty-five different communities, mostly in the Middle West.[76]   In April, 1894, Sanderson's chain of newspapers launched a concerted editorial campaign designed to bring about the discontinuance of the *People* and adoption of *St. Louis Labor* as the official party organ.

Always alert for attacks by "adventurers," the National Executive Committee countered with a well-reasoned appeal to the party membership. It pointed out the organizational difficulty involved in having the party headquarters in one city and the party press in another; it maintained correctly that *Labor* was far inferior to the *People* as an expositor of scientific Marxism; and it accused Sanderson of seeking to establish a monopoly in the field of socialist publication.[77]

For the next two years, ill feeling festered between the St. Louis Socialist Laborites and the party directors. *Labor* was one of the first papers to oppose DeLeon's dual unionism policy. When the matter was finally taken up at the party's 1896 national convention, the delegates dutifully condemned *Labor*, disassociated it from the party, and went on record against the publication of its local issues.[78]   The convention's action settled the publication issue but not the seething dissension in St. Louis. During the next year the St. Louis SLP section was dissolved on a minor pretext by the National Executive Committee.[79] When it was subsequently reorganized, it contained only dutiful and obedient DeLeonites.

---

[76]Frederic Heath (ed.), *Social Democracy Red Book (Progressive Thought* [Terre Haute], Vol. I [Jan., 1900]), p. 116. *Social Democracy Red Book* constituted the entire January, 1900, issue of *Progressive Thought*. It is cited hereafter simply as *Social Democracy Red Book*.

[77]*People*, Apr. 22, 1894.

[78]*Proceedings of the 9th Annual Convention of the Socialist Labor Party*, pp. 58-59.

[79]*Proceedings of the 10th Annual Convention of the Socialist Labor Party*, pp. 10-11.

Cleveland was another center of party disaffection in the Middle West. For years the Cleveland SLP section had been a maverick, for its members showed little disposition to accept the domination of New York in the party councils. In the early years of the nineties, the so-called "Cleveland faction" had shown a strong inclination to co-operate with the People's Party and other reform groups. And when DeLeon and his friends launched the Socialist Trade and Labor Alliance, there was strenuous opposition since the Cleveland socialists, led by Max Hayes and Robert Bandlow, were highly influential in the local labor movement.

In 1895, Section Cleveland committed the cardinal sin of sending representatives to a meeting which had as its expressed purpose the creation of an independent labor party to contest in the forthcoming municipal elections. The meeting was called by the socialist-dominated Central Labor Union, and before adjourning it adopted a platform which was almost a word-for-word replica of that of the Socialist Labor Party. Irrespective of this fact, the section's action contravened the party's general constitution, which banned compromises with other political parties. As result, the National Executive Committee suspended Section Cleveland.

To DeLeon's chagrin, the suspension was reversed upon appeal to the party's Board of Grievances. The latter held that the spread of socialist ideas was more rapid than was the organization of the Socialist Labor Party and that Section Cleveland had fused with workingmen who, while not socialists, were sympathetic to socialist principles. At the party's 1896 national convention, DeLeon warned that such was "a rather dangerous practice" and "fraught with serious complications for the future."[80] But he could not induce the convention to expel Section Cleveland, which remained to snipe at him for the next two years.

Criticism from the "provinces" was more or less a constant source of annoyance to DeLeon, but to be attacked by socialist newspapers in New York City was an unendurable provocation. The offenders were the Jewish daily, *Abendblatt*, and the week-

[80] *Proceedings of the 9th Annual Convention of the Socialist Labor Party*, pp. 19-20.

ly, *Arbeiter-Zeitung.* They were under the control of the Arbeiter-Zeitung Publishing Company, although the Socialist Labor
Party technically had the power to appoint their editors. This
proved to be an unworkable arrangement with constant bickering resulting between the publishing company and the party.

The editorial staffs of the papers consisted largely of men
who were active in the Jewish East Side labor movement. De-
Leon's repudiation of his own Jewishness undoubtedly did not
set well with them, for although many of them had strayed a
bit from the religion of their fathers, they never forgot that
they were Jews. Furthermore, DeLeon's shifting trade-union
tactics annoyed and embarrassed them, and they did not hesitate
to attack the *People*'s editor, first on the ground of his temporary infatuation with the Knights of Labor and later for his
sponsorship of the Socialist Trade and Labor Alliance.[81] De-
Leon replied to these attacks in kind in the *People;* but, as with
the case of Section Cleveland, he was unable at the 1896 convention to crush the Jewish opposition.[82]

When the SLP National Executive Committee could not cope
with local problems without serious danger of losing face, it
habitually resorted to a procedure which rarely failed—namely,
an appeal to the national party membership for support. When
the Jewish socialists, emboldened by their successful stand at
the 1896 convention, persisted in attacking the party's trade-
union policies during the next winter and spring, the National
Executive Committee polled the SLP membership by referendum on the desirability of placing *Abendblatt* and the *Arbeiter-
Zeitung* under direct party control. The results were highly
satisfactory to the Committee, for the referendum approved its
proposal, 1,527 to 538. In New York City, the voting favored
party control 421 to 308.[83]

---

[81] Harry Rogoff and J. C. Rich have written informative articles on the
relationship between the New York Jewish socialists and the Socialist Labor
Party in the 50th anniversary issue of the *Jewish Daily Forward,* May 25,
1947.

[82] *Proceedings of the 9th Annual Convention of the Socialist Labor Party,*
pp. 15-16, 51-53.

[83] *People,* June 13, 1897. For a pro-DeLeon treatment of the controversy,
see Kuhn and Johnson, *The Socialist Labor Party During Four Decades,* pp.
27-28.

Arthur Keep, DeLeon's friend in the nation's capital, wanted an end put to the argument, even if it meant having "every Jew furnished with a padlock to affix on his jaw."[84] But the controversy did not die with the referendum. The dissident Jewish journalists, now free of party ties, began independent publication of the *Jewish Daily Forward*. Perhaps more than any other single factor, it was responsible for weaning away Jewish trade unionists from SLP influence.

Despite rising internal dissensions occasioned primarily by DeLeon's trade-union policies and by his imperious leadership, the Socialist Labor Party experienced a steady growth between 1890 and 1896. Failure of an effort to induce the "perambulating" Rosenberg faction to return to the fold in 1892 was more than compensated for by the hundreds of new recruits who came into the party during the panic of 1893 and the subsequent years of depression. Whereas the party could claim only 113 sections at its 1893 convention in Chicago, it could boast of 200 three years later. While the largest number of these sections was in the Eastern industrial states and in Illinois and Ohio, SLP organizations could be found in twenty-five different states. Only the South was literally virgin country to the party.[85]

Political victories, however, did not come easily. Even if the primary reason for socialist political action at this phase of the party's development was propagandistic, nevertheless both the SLP leaders and the rank and file thirsted for electoral triumphs. In the spring of 1894, when Matthew Maguire was elected Alderman on the Socialist Labor Party ticket in Paterson, New Jersey, the *People* pealed forth:

> Let the proletariat of the land rejoice!
> Light is breaking, day is dawning![86]

---

[84]Keep to DeLeon, July 14, 1897. Socialist Labor Party Papers, State Historical Society, Madison, Wis. (Hereafter cited as SLP Papers).

[85]*Proceedings of the 9th Annual Convention of the Socialist Labor Party,* p. 12.

[86]*People,* Apr. 15, 1894.

The only other political victory of the SLP until 1897 was the election of John H. O'Connor as Councilman in Holyoke, Massachusetts, in 1895.[87]

In the 1896 presidential campaign the SLP ran Charles H. Matchett for the Presidency. Matchett, it will be recalled, had been the party's Vice-Presidential candidate four years before. His running mate now was Matthew Maguire who, if nothing else, was a proven winner. They polled 36,275 votes, a gain of nearly 15,000 votes since 1892. The SLP was now on the ballot in fourteen new states.[88]

The gain in party membership and the slightly improved showing at the polls did not conceal the fact that the Socialist Labor Party had not as yet become a powerful agency for the dissemination of socialist propaganda nor a satisfactory political outlet for American radicalism. The "new trade-unionism," moreover, had alienated both the American Federation of Labor and the Knights of Labor and threatened to disrupt the Socialist Labor Party itself, as indeed it was later to do. Nor had DeLeon really succeeded in "Americanizing" the socialist movement, though undoubtedly he thought he was proceeding toward that end. The difficulty was that DeLeon never understood the American tradition. He did not appreciate the extent to which it emphasized social solidarity as opposed to class antagonism, compromise and pragmatic give-and-take rather than unbending doctrinaire revolutionary determinism, and individual freedom of choice and dissent instead of dictation from arbitrary authoritarian leadership.

[87] *Ibid.*, Dec. 8, 1895.
[88] Sanial, *The Socialist Almanac and Treasury of Facts*, p. 226.

VI. Wayland Plants Grass Roots Socialism

WHILE Nationalism and Christian Socialism floundered during the depression unleashed by the panic of 1893, a grass roots variety of socialism was germinating in trans-Appalachian America. This new and not altogether orthodox socialism has received almost cavalier treatment from scholars, who have usually contemplated it with overly focused Marxist lenses which blur out nearly everything not associated with urban radicalism or trade unionism. And, paradoxically enough, this has been true notwithstanding the fact that American socialism has had its largest following in the Middle West. This new socialism was vocally protestant rather than institutional in character; its chief spokesman was Julius Augustus Wayland, a saturnine, sandy-haired, stoop-shouldered publisher of weekly newspapers, better known to thousands of faithful readers as "J. A. Wayland, The One Hoss Editor."[1]

In the transitional nineties Wayland was a reincarnate Tom Paine for American radicalism. During that and the subsequent decade his weekly newspapers, *The Coming Nation* and *Appeal to Reason*, had wide circulation throughout the United States. Wayland's reputation was so firmly established during the early years of the twentieth century that A. M. Simons, an early Marxist historian in the United States, described him as "the greatest propagandist of Socialism that has ever lived."[2] Time has buttressed rather than weakened Simons' opinion; for the leftist press, with all of its luminaries, has not produced since Wayland's death in 1912 a socialist propagandist of comparable stature.

Wayland's eclectic brand of socialism had certain affinities with radical Populism, Fabianism, and orthodox Marxism,

---

[1] For a somewhat more concise version of this chapter, see Howard H. Quint, "Julius Augustus Wayland, Pioneer Socialist Propagandist," *Mississippi Valley Historical Review*, XXXV (1949), 585-606.

[2] A. M. Simons, "J. A. Wayland, Propagandist," *Metropolitan Magazine*, XXXII (1913), 25.

though certainly it could not be identified with any of them. He never suffered from that extreme self-consciousness that so often affected many of his fellow socialists when discussing doctrinal matters, and he blithely ignored razor-edge distinctions made by Marxist theoreticians. Wayland hankered for the destruction of the capitalistic system and was never overly concerned as to the method of accomplishment. Even at its best, his approach to political and economic problems was vague and lacking in consistency.

Populism was the principal medium through which Western and Southern agrarian radicals voiced their discontent during the early nineties. It allowed the righteous to crusade against the forces of evil personified by the international Wall Street money-changer. It permitted the debt-burdened farmer to go to the polls and cast out of public office men who were little more than the puppets of corporations and monopolies. It accorded, too, with the nation's traditional belief in progress; for once the common people wrested their government from the control of the plutocracy, a new era of political honesty and economic prosperity and plenty would reward them for their struggle against Mammon.

Wayland's socialism had much of Populism's emotional appeal. Men and women who gave sympathetic ear to his advocacy of the co-operative commonwealth were usually possessed with an "emotional craving for a 'new deal' in radicalism."[3] Among his admirers were left-wing Populists who had become disgusted by the tendency of their leaders toward conservatism, notably after the party had been committed to free silver and William Jennings Bryan in 1896.[4] A few were penurious farmers and tradesmen who had read *Looking Backward* and saw in Bellamy's proposed totalitarian society an enviable contrast to their own. Still another group were the escapists who would withdraw from a competitive society to seek a new life in a small communitarian settlement.

Wayland became a socialist at approximately the time that the People's Party was being organized. Previously, he had

---

[3] Commons (ed.), *History of Labor in the United States,* IV, 224.
[4] J. A. Wayland, *Leaves of Life* (Girard, Kan., 1912), p. 29.

found capitalism congenial to his own particular talents.[5] His career had spanned from virtual rags to somewhat more than modest riches. He was born in poverty in Versailles, Indiana, in 1854. Thirty-nine years later, he left Pueblo, Colorado, with suitcases bulging with gold and government bonds.

Wayland had experienced poverty and privation, but he also knew that wealth could be acquired under capitalism. Wayland's mother, widowed three months after his birth, had been obliged to take in washing and do domestic work in order to support herself and her three children. To help augment the always meager family income, young Wayland, with only two years of formal schooling, began a two-dollars-a-week printer's apprenticeship to one J. E. Rebuck, publisher of the weekly *Versailles Gazette*. This job gave Wayland his real education and implanted in him an ambition to become an editor in his own right. In 1873, at the age of nineteen, he gratified that desire by becoming a partner in a printing business and in the publication of the *Ripley Index*. The little paper was put out with great struggle—perhaps the hardest of his life, he later recalled. The *Ripley Index* survived, but Wayland himself did not remain for long in Versailles. The West, virgin and brimming with opportunity, beckoned, and in 1877 he pulled stakes. With his recent bride, Etta Bevan, Wayland settled in Harrisonville, Missouri.[6]

Harrisonville, where Mrs. Wayland had relatives, proved an unhappy choice. The scars of the Civil War were still raw and unhealed, and Wayland's never-concealed Republican views immediately invoked the dislike of all but a few of the town's citizens. Most of the inhabitants were avid Democrats, and not a few were Confederate veterans. Wayland did well financially, however, prospering with another printing establishment and making money by shrewd land-speculation. In addition, he began publication of the *Cass News*, intended to serve the

---

[5]Wayland "had a keen nose for a good business enterprise and was what could be termed a money maker. . . . He could, like a pointer dog, pick out a likely looking piece of business property and sell it later at a profit." Fred D. Warren to Author, Mar. 8, 1947. "It is not recorded of Wayland that he ever lost money in a real estate deal." Henry Vincent, *Wayland: The Editor with a Punch, An Appreciation* (Pamphlet; Massillon, Ohio, 1912), p. 9.

[6]Wayland, *Leaves of Life*, pp. 7-19.

small group of Republicans in the county. His popularity in Harrisonville reached its nadir when President Rutherford B. Hayes rewarded him for his services to the Administration party with a postmastership, a position which he did not really want and subsequently resigned.

Wayland's biting pen constantly goaded his political enemies, and on one occasion the young editor, by sheer bravado, narrowly escaped the lynch rope. A feud developed between Wayland and a free-shooting town-sheriff, whose alleged corrupt actions were exposed in the *Cass News*. Wayland knew the value of having a six-shooter ready at all times in a comparatively frontier area. Once, so the story goes, he stood ready to shoot it out with the sheriff, after he had spit in the latter's face in a gesture of defiance.[7]

Four hectic years in Harrisonville sufficed for Wayland. To the relief of everyone concerned he returned to Indiana, where he repurchased his old printing and publishing business. But by 1882 he and his brood were again en route West, this time to Pueblo, Colorado, where more of his wife's kinfolk resided. The pattern of his economic ventures in Harrisonville was largely repeated. After an initial and unsuccessful two-year effort to publish a local weekly paper in partnership with two Hoosier friends, Lon Hoding and J. H. Tyson, he concentrated his efforts on his printing plant, which he called "Wayland's One Hoss Print Shop" because of its niggardly equipment.[8] The business expanded, however, and Wayland became the biggest job-printer in town. He also speculated in land; for what Henry George had seen some ten years earlier in California, the astute Wayland now observed in Colorado: property values were mounting steadily as the state developed and as its population increased. Within a few years Wayland owned some of the choicest property in Pueblo and was generally reputed to be an extremely shrewd judge of real estate values.

Wayland's boyhood struggles and business experiences had strongly impressed upon him the virtues of economic individual-

[7]*Ibid.*, p. 20; George D. Brewer, "The Wayland I Knew," *Appeal to Reason*, May 24, 1913; George A. England, "The Story of 'The Appeal,'" *Appeal to Reason*, Sept. 6, 1916.

[8]Wayland, *Leaves of Life*, pp. 21-22, 34-35.

ism. In a competitive world he had learned that a man must stand on his own feet if he is to survive. And he knew from experience that one can pull himself up by his own bootstraps. Apparently he had little or no acquaintance with radical social and economic doctrines. Yet suddenly, in Colorado, somewhere about 1890, Wayland's entire political and economic philosophy underwent a complete transformation: from a "hard-headed Republican" capitalist he became a militant socialist.

Wayland was converted to socialism by the missionary efforts of one of its legion of unsung apostles. The most widely accepted account is that an English-born Pueblo shoemaker, William Bradfield, guided him into the socialist camp. Significantly, he aroused Wayland's interest in socialism through a simply written pamphlet rather than through the works of the leading European Marxists. According to an autobiographical account, Wayland read and reread the pamphlet's elementary lesson in socialism with waxing enthusiasm. "I saw a new light and found what I never knew existed," he exclaimed.[9] Once Wayland had swallowed the bait, Bradfield kept him well supplied with socialist reading material. *Looking Backward*, which was in great vogue at this time, made a deep impression on him.

Wayland's turn to socialism coincided with a feverish burst of activity by the newly founded People's Party in Colorado. Populism was not socialism, but its strong criticism of plutocracy and monopoly amply satisfied the printer and publisher who was never to be a rigid doctrinaire. Also, Wayland greatly admired the aggressive and outspoken Aspen journalist and Populist leader, Davis H. Waite. The Socialist Labor Party in Pueblo, too weak to obtain the necessary names by petition to allow it to participate in elections, had thrown its support behind the Populists. Wayland, too, lent his assistance to the Populist cause during the hectic 1892 campaign. He had the approval of Bradfield, who, in typical Fabian fashion, was willing to work for socialism through the People's Party.[10]

The local Populist leaders were understandably suspicious when Wayland proffered his services. Knowing him as a real

---

9*Ibid.*, p. 24.
10Simons, *Metropolitan Magazine*, XXXII, 26.

estate speculator and as a Republican, they considered his offer of a $100 donation to the party as an ill-conceived effort at bribery. Refusing to be rebuffed, Wayland ultimately convinced them that he had undergone a genuine change of heart and mind. He became editor, without pay, of a small Pueblo Populist-labor paper, *The Colorado Worker*, which he immediately renamed *The Coming Crisis*. Under his skillful editing the paper's circulation pyramided from a few hundred non-paying, to nearly 4,000 paid subscribers.[11] In addition, the presses of the "One Hoss Print Shop" poured forth People's Party leaflets. Often these offended the sensibilities of the more solid citizens of the town, which was one of the state's conservative centers. Wayland distributed throughout Colorado hundreds of copies of *Seven Financial Conspiracies*, *Ten Men of Money Island*, and Gronlund's *Co-operative Commonwealth*. The first two were favorite Populist propaganda pamphlets.[12] During the campaign the power of propaganda impressed Wayland, and he mulled over the idea of founding a paper to preach the socialist gospel to the man in the street.[13]

While in Colorado Wayland tangled for the first time with Daniel DeLeon. The latter's editorial condemnation of the Populists as a bourgeois party of "small farmers" irked him. In an indignant letter to the *People*, he wrote:

> The 'small farmers' etc. are going to get there, and I want to say that the Socialist platform will be carried into effect by the same Populists. All the leaders and all the followers are as true and earnest socialists as you Eastern chaps, and by election returns stood by those principles far better at the polls. We are using the same literature, too, after we give the patient a few doses of the money question to get him in a condition to absorb it.[14]

Waite's surprising gubernatorial victory[15] was especially sweet to Wayland as he had wagered a considerable amount of money on the outcome. Shortly after the election he and his

---

[11]*Ibid.; People*, Dec. 4, 1892.

[12]*Social Democracy Red Book*, p. 90.

[13]Simons, *Metropolitan Magazine*, XXXII, 26.

[14]*People*, Dec. 4, 1892.

[15]Leon W. Fuller, "Colorado's Revolt Against Capitalism," *Mississippi Valley Historical Review*, XXI (1934), 349.

wife left Colorado to spend the winter at Jacksonville, Florida.
There the still-aroused Wayland bombarded the editor of the
Jacksonville *Times-Union* with letters and articles advocating
nationalization of the railroads, some of which were printed
along with the paper's editorial refutations.[16]

Wayland abbreviated his Jacksonville visit. The industrial
unrest of the time worried him, and his intuition told him,
correctly, that a depression was imminent. Making a hurried
trip back to Missouri and Colorado, he disposed of much of his
property below the prevailing market price and returned once
again to his native Indiana to await the coming cataclysm. He
brought back with him to the little town of Greensburg some
$80,000 in gold and government bonds.[17]

It was on the very eve of the panic of 1893 that Wayland
thought the time propitious for a nationally circulated weekly
newspaper devoted to propagandizing socialism. Accordingly,
he obtained as many subscription lists from reform and labor
papers as he was able to get. The initial issue of his new paper,
the *Coming Nation*, appeared on April 28, 1893. Ten copies
were sent to each person whose name appeared on the various
lists. The almost immediate success of the *Coming Nation* ex-
ceeded Wayland's wildest hopes. Within six months it had
14,000 paid subscribers and a weekly printing of 17,000 copies.
Its popularity was greatest in the Middle West and on the
Pacific Coast, with California leading in paid subscriptions
and Colorado following a close second.[18] Unlike other contemporary radical newspapers, which invariably operated in
the red, the *Coming Nation* made a tidy profit for its owner.[19]
Mystified editors of the orthodox press dispatched reporters
to Greensburg to discover the secret of the *Coming Nation*'s
success.[20]

The more discerning learned that the answer lay in Wayland's ability to gauge the intellectual temper of his readers.
He delighted in referring to himself as the "One Hoss Philos-

---

[16]*Coming Nation,* May 8, 1894.
[17]Wayland, *Leaves of Life,* p. 27.
[18]*Coming Nation,* Dec. 30, 1893.
[19]*Social Democracy Red Book,* p. 46; *People,* July 16, 1899.
[20]*Coming Nation,* Apr. 14, 1894.

opher"—a hang-over from the Pueblo printing shop—and used language that was homely, direct, and within the main tradition of American radicalism.[21] "You have a faculty of reaching the average man," Eugene V. Debs, an ardent Wayland admirer, wrote to the editor. Wayland excelled when speaking to those who lived on farms or in towns of less than 10,000 and who had "mental backgrounds built up from being taught in the public schools, reading weekly newspapers, attending Protestant services, discussing at the corner grocery, and belonging to one of the old parties."[22]

Wayland's capacity to win and hold readers came from two other related factors: a unique journalistic style, and lively and colorful editorial and literary fare. He was ever aware that articles running into a half-column or more usually went unread. Consequently he nearly always wrote in the form of short paragraphs, each carrying within it both a complete story and a socialist moral.[23] In the technique of composing such paragraphs, he had few peers. Writing effortlessly, Wayland was able to grind out in a morning's time an entire page of concise, pungent, didactic paragraphs, ranging over a multitude of subjects. His style, moreover, was highly personalized. Consistent use of the first person singular occasionally gave rise to reader complaints. Wayland gave these short shrift:

> So you don't like my way of writing, eh? Egotistical and scurrilous, eh? Very well, you needn't read me. That's your privilege. I shall write just as I feel. I'm not a hypocrite to use fine words to cover up my feelings. I prefer condemnation for what I am than praise for what I am not. Anything but a hypocrite who hides beneath an oily tongue the fangs of deception. Why should I write these lines and say 'we'? There is no 'we' about it. There may not be another man in the nation who coincides with all I write. Why should I use the first person plural because those who went before me have done so?[24]

The *Coming Nation*'s editorial offerings combined a generous mixture of utopian socialism, ill-digested scientific socialism,

---

[21]Commons, IV, 225.
[22]Simons, *Metropolitan Magazine*, XXXII, 25.
[23]Wayland to H. D. Lloyd, July 8, 1898. Lloyd Papers.
[24]*Coming Nation*, Jan. 20, 1894.

and radical Populism. According to the motto over the paper's masthead, it favored a "government of, by, and for the people, as outlined in Bellamy's *Looking Backward*, abolishing the possibility of poverty." Wayland urged readers to take to heart the lessons of the novel. He asserted that he, himself, constantly solved social problems "by the calculus given in this wonderful book by Bellamy."[25] Wayland gave voice to the general Populist clamor for free-silver coinage, not as an end in itself but as a means of winning new members to the People's Party. Likewise, he maintained an incessant socialist refrain for government ownership of the means of production and distribution. As short-term measures, the *Coming Nation* advocated government assistance to farmers and unemployed industrial workers. In the manner of the radical Populists, it fired loud salvos at the trusts and at the financial empire of Wall Street along with its foreign affiliations, particularly the Rothschild banking interests. Foreign royalty and nobility were continually lampooned and their extravagances, sometimes real and equally often imagined, were held up to ridicule. Frequent targets of Wayland's barbs were the President of the United States, justices of the Supreme Court, and members of Congress. The *Coming Nation* commiserated with victims of social injustice, though such sympathy was usually accompanied by sage words of advice. The downtrodden had no one but themselves to blame so long as they insisted on supporting the monstrous capitalistic system. The paper sought to demonstrate to the wage earner, from the point of view of his own welfare, the hollowness and insincerity of the leading issues on which the Republicans and Democrats battled. It railed against workers who voted for candidates of the traditional parties, and it scorned trade unionists who opposed committing their labor organizations to socialism.

The following sampling of Wayland's weekly editorial paragraphs in the *Coming Nation* reveal, to the extent that any such selection can, their general character, idiom, tone, and propagandistic quality:

---

[25]*Appeal to Reason*, Apr. 7, 1900.

When a hungry devil takes something to stifle hunger, that's stealing; when the rich compel the poor workman to pay $5 a ton for $1.75 coal, that's business.

Those who decry the People's Party for paternalism support parties that cost the nation a billion a year for being paternal to a few corporations.

If it was wrong for King George to rule America by open force a century ago, is it right for his successors to rule America today by the covert use of money among our law givers?

The Earl of Craven was injured by his pony, colliding with another at a race. It probably cost $500 to telegraph the account and set it up for all the press in the country that used it. And what of it? He is a worthless mortal; never did a day's useful labor in his life.

The surest way to destroy liberty and enthrone despotism is to define what is free speech and free press. Those who love power will soon put their definition upon it and suppress all who do not agree with them.

The Supreme Court the judges of which are railroad attorney republicans have granted injunctions to prevent Kansas counties from levying taxes against railroad property. It has reached a pretty pass when the people cannot collect taxes from wealthy corporations. It is well. Such things as these are needed to wake the people up to the drift affairs are taking in this country. The courts are the last resort of corporations, but the people can capture them—and will. Anarchists and corporations want no law.

I wouldn't give a snap for the union man who prates of unionism and votes for a system of wage slavery and competition—that is who votes the democratic or republican ticket. He is only a union man in name—he does not know the meaning of the substance. Get your eyes open, boys. The rich are pulling out the chestnuts with your votes.

So Coxey and Brown have been sent to prison by a Washington justice of the peace for stepping on the grass! And denied all appeal! And the grass around the King's council chamber is of more value than human liberty. That is cheaper than the ancients held human rights. That several hundred law-abiding, but poor, citizens, after hundreds of miles of travel to petition the King's compassion, should have no more notice taken of them, than to have their leaders arrested and imprisoned for stepping on a few blades of the royal lawn! And to this has American labor been reduced! This is the treatment the rulers deal out to the submissive serfs who go on a pilgrimage of petition. To such a farce has justice become . . . Russia has no case of more outrageous tyranny.

Poor, deluded citizens, don't you know that monopolies cannot be injured by any anti-trust laws made to govern them?

Behold the beauties of the 'protective system'! After thirty years of it, the protected workingman must pawn his Sunday suit to provide food for his hungry babies, and take sustenance for himself from a free soup kettle! Great is protection! Well protection protects, don't it? Of course it protects. It protects the anarchist of wealth, but not the workingman with a patch in his pants, who works ten to fourteen hours a day for 110 cents (or less) and carries a bit of tough meat and two cold potatoes in his pail for dinner.

Wayland considered the *Coming Nation* an elementary educational primer for socialism. Socialists, as he knew from personal experience, were made, not born. His contribution to making socialist converts was to print or reproduce articles and book excerpts which either directly or indirectly pointed the way to the co-operative commonwealth. A literary diet of Marx, Engels, and Kautsky, such as DeLeon served readers of the *People*, would more likely than not give the socialist neophyte an acute case of doctrinal indigestion. The end result would be discouragement with socialism itself. Among the widely assorted literary works reprinted either in whole or in part in the *Coming Nation* were Bellamy's *Looking Backward*, Gronlund's *Co-operative Commonwealth*, the Reverend F. M. Sprague's *Socialism from Genesis to Revelation*, Stephen Maybell's *Civilization Civilized*, Victor Hugo's *Address to the Rich and Poor*, Giuseppe Mazzini's *Duties of Man*, and Benjamin O. Flower's *Civilization's Inferno*. Essays by John Ruskin and Thomas Carlyle were found frequently on the *Coming Nation's* third page which was largely devoted to literary fare. Countless articles on all phases of contemporary social and economic problems were accepted and printed.

In defending the paper's general contents and the monotony of its constantly reiterated propaganda themes, Wayland maintained that he was reaching thousands "that *The People*, an abler paper than mine, could not touch."[26] His objective was to generate discontent to a high pitch. When men and women became sufficiently disgusted with the existing social order, he said, the *People* could "complete the work" and "indoctrinate them with scientific socialism."[27]

The *Coming Nation* afforded radical poets a publication medium for verse which, because of sentimentality, banality, or bathos, might otherwise have gone unprinted. Several bards, with souls over-brimming with social consciousness, wrote poems "specially for the *Coming Nation*" and it took a hard headed and discriminating editor, which Wayland in such cases was not, to reject these works of creative artistry. The following verses typify the poetry appearing in the *Coming Nation*:

"The Lay of the Unemployed" by Sumner Claflin

> Empty is the poor man's barrel,
> Every speck of flour is fled,
> Happy thought now softly whisper
> 'Lord, give us our daily bread.'
> Work shut down, the worker tramping,
> 'Vainly looking for a job,'
> Starving little children crying;
> Hear the poor wife sob.
> Hear the clink of golden millions
> Growing larger every day,
> Cleveland got his $50,000,
> But the devil is to pay!
> Homes are falling all around us,
> Merchants driven to the wall;
> Maidens sell their souls for mammon
> Do ye see the sparrow fall?
> Ask ye, 'Is there God in Israel?'
> Rather ask, 'Is manhood dead?'

26Wayland to Henry Kuhn, Apr. 28, 1894. SLP Papers.
27Wayland to J. C. Butterworth, Jan. 17, 1898. DeLeon Papers.

Man to man has been inhuman
Else why lack for daily bread?
Justice will not always slumber
When he wakes, ye rich beware!
If ye fail to solve these problems,
Blood and rapine you shall share.
For your souls have swelled in pride
Gold alone has been your trust,
Labor has been crucified
Manhood trampled in the dust.[28]

Wayland insisted time and again that the *Coming Nation* did
not represent the People's Party, the Socialist Labor Party,[29]
or any other political, social, or economic organization. Its
function was to educate for socialism; concentration on party
issues, he held, served only to distract readers from the true
goal of struggling humanity—the achievement of the co-operative commonwealth. Constant talk of parties and political
action had created "all the worshippers of the old parties today."
Forget party names, he advised. "Teach the principles of national co-operation. Time and suffering will do the rest."[30]

As between the People's Party and the Socialist Labor Party,
Wayland favored the former. While, like Bliss, he conceded
the superiority of the SLP program over that of the Populists,
he nevertheless preferred "to labor with the People's Party
as the best means of propagating the truth." He did not see
the incompatibility, so evident to DeLeon, between Populism and
socialism. He hoped the People's Party would serve as an in-
termediary resting place for the discontented before they finally
went over to the co-operative commonwealth. Consequently,
socialists would do well, he believed, to encourage Populism and
to work with the party to the end of infusing it with collectivist
principles. With sufficient indoctrination, most Populists would
see the light and embrace socialism. The socialist movement
would thus receive badly lacking mass support.

[28]*Coming Nation*, July 20, 1894. Claflin was a perennial Populist-Socialist
candidate in New Hampshire during the 1890's.
[29]Wayland to Henry Kuhn, Apr. 28, 1894. SLP Papers.
[30]*Coming Nation*, Jan. 20, 1894.

The criticism of the Socialist Labor Party leadership, which Wayland had expressed in Colorado, was carried over into the *Coming Nation*. "It makes me very tired," he wrote, "to hear a certain class of socialists inveigh against the Populist movement. They are bigots with a large B. If the pops would call themselves socialists, they would be all right! The uprising against the plutocrats by the 'small farmers' is the hope of liberty, and the leaders of the movement are as well read, as sincere and reliable, as those who boast of being socialists." In the same critical vein Wayland moralized: "Blind, indeed, must be the men who refuse to teach willing scholars when they furnish the school buildings. Such socialists do more harm than good."[31]

The *Coming Nation*'s increasing popularity, attested by its rising circulation, necessitated an increase in its staff. For the first seven or eight months, the staff consisted of Wayland, who handled editorial matters, his brother-in-law, Charlie Bevan, who managed the composing room, and a few part-time helpers. In January, 1894, Rousseau Hess of Akron, Ohio, came to Greensburg "to join the elect" and to become the paper's business manager. Several other persons were added to the staff, including A. S. Edwards, who became associate editor.[32]

Edwards was, like Thomas J. Morgan, an Englishman of Welsh extraction. He had come to the United States in 1867. A printer by trade, he had dabbled in the reform and labor press in Minneapolis.[33] The panic of 1893 found his personal finances seriously jeopardized, and he snapped up Wayland's offers of a job on the *Coming Nation* and of a personal loan which allowed him to bring his family and household goods to Greensburg. Edwards remained with Wayland until the latter decided to move on. Disagreement over financial affairs developed at this point and culminated in a suit by Edwards, who claimed $1,000 was due him from Wayland. For his part, Wayland not only vehemently denied Edwards' claim but also countered that the latter had never repaid the original loan.[34]

[31]*Ibid.*, Mar. 3, 1894.
[32]*Ibid.*, Apr. 14, 1894.
[33]*Social Democracy Red Book*, p. 111.
[34]Wayland to H. D. Lloyd, Nov. 23, 1895. Lloyd Papers. Rousseau Hess to Daniel DeLeon, Aug. 17, 1897. DeLeon Papers.

The two men thereafter became lifelong foes. Wayland noted with satisfaction the failure of Edwards' little paper, *Freeland*,[35] which the latter had sought to publish in competition with the *Coming Nation*.

The *Coming Nation* brought a certain notoriety which was unappreciated by the residents of Greensburg. Wayland and his family were avoided like the plague by the citizenry of the little Indiana community. Republicans might tolerate Democrats and vice versa, but icy stares and overt hostility greeted openly declared socialists. When, perchance, townspeople were obliged to have dealings with him, said Wayland, they discovered that a socialist was "a human being" and that "the one-hoss editor" had "*some* very good ideas."[36] He enjoyed twitting the people of Greensburg about the *Coming Nation*'s success. It was an effective, though not completely satisfactory, way of replying to the shabby treatment to which he and his family were subjected. Eight months after embarking on the publication of the paper, Wayland crowed: "It is slowly dawning on the citizens of Greensburg that the *Coming Nation* is not a wild fantasy which some fellow with more money than brains intends to blow himself in on but is a financial success that is astonishing. And it has not asked a cent of patronage from them either."[37]

In the long run the people of Greensburg won out, for the embittered Wayland decided to move his family and the presses of the *Coming Nation* to a different locale. But he was determined to go to a place where people had views congenial to his own. To this end, he proposed to underwrite a communitarian settlement whose inhabitants would actually practice socialism in their daily lives. Conceivably, in the back of his mind he had a blue print of the society envisaged in *Looking Backward*. While Wayland probably was not intimately acquainted with the histories of the Fourierist settlements of the 1840's and 1850's, he was aware that their record was largely one of failure. Yet when readers called this to his attention, he replied hotly: "You think the colony idea is impractical, do you? You think

35Edwards to H. D. Lloyd, Dec. 12, 1894. Lloyd Papers.
36*Coming Nation*, Feb. 17, 1894.
37*Ibid.*, Dec. 23, 1893.

it can't be successfully carried out because others have been more or less failures, eh? Well, I tell you that it can."[38]

The communitarian colony, of course, was largely an escapist solution for Wayland's personal problems. But he also shared with the communitarians of the forties the belief that a successful settlement would by example prove the correctness of socialistic co-operation in practice and serve as a beacon light to guide the society of the future toward the co-operative commonwealth. However, Wayland did not advocate resort to communitarianism as a general mode of social organization for the future, and in this respect he differed from the Owenites and the Fourierists. He explained the purpose of his proposed socialist community in answer to criticism from the left-wing Populist paper, *The Pittsburg Kansan*:

> Do you think that better conditions can ever come except by practical lessons? Are the masses so philosophic that they can realize any other kind of social system except by observation? . . . Hardly, the future perfect social state will be a growth from little beginnings. One practical success, widely advertised, showing that men can live and love and have peace and plenty, will do more toward bringing the Brotherhood of Man than a thousand speakers. I hereby invite you to visit our town two years from now and see what truth can do.[39]

Wayland outlined to his readers a plan that had the twofold merit of increasing the *Coming Nation*'s circulation and setting forth the basis for a socialist colony. He proposed that preparations for the establishment of the colony begin in earnest when the paper's paid subscription list reached 100,000. At such a time, Wayland estimated, net profits would amount to $23,000, a sum adequate to purchase a settlement site of 3,000 to 4,000 acres. Any person of good moral character who sent in two hundred subscriptions to the *Coming Nation* would automatically be a charter member of the colony as would any one who contributed a like amount of money in cash. All members and their wives would enjoy equality of rights and privileges. Wayland promised that the community would be situated on good soil and would be accessible to a railroad. An advance

---

[38]*Ibid.*, Dec. 2, 1893.
[39]*Ibid.*, Feb. 10, 1894.

party, he suggested, would erect houses and a plant to accommodate the *Coming Nation*'s equipment.

The *Coming Nation* would serve as the nucleus for the economic life of the colony. Income from the paper would be placed in a common fund, and all employees would draw their pay from it. Wayland expressed the belief that the presses of the *Coming Nation* would eventually employ a hundred or more persons in publishing and job printing. He boasted that he could attract other industrial establishments to the colony, to be operated on the same basis as the paper. Every member of the colony, however, would be a free agent and under no obligation to earn his livelihood through one of its co-operative enterprises.[40]

"Now go to work for subscribers, and show by your zeal that you are worthy of a fellowship in such a community," Wayland exhorted. The *Coming Nation*'s subscription list lurched and climbed but got nowhere near the 100,000 goal. The publisher, however, displayed a flexibility characteristic of his approach to socialism and settled for less. When the *Coming Nation* reached a circulation of 60,000 Wayland announced that he was proceeding with plans for founding a colony.[41]

Cheapness of land was Wayland's paramount consideration in choosing a site. He disclaimed any intention of purchasing property in the vicinity of Greensburg or in any other settled community where land values, by his own analysis, were inflated.[42] Rather, he searched out a sparsely inhabited area where land could be had almost for the asking. His quest ended in Tennessee. Rousseau Hess, his agent, selected a thousand acres of rocky and wooded land two miles north of Tennessee City and about fifty miles west of Nashville. Only in being close to a railroad—the Chattanooga, Nashville, and St. Louis—did the colony site answer the specifications which Wayland had outlined. Lack of decent bottom land was subsequently to induce the colonists to move a few miles away to Yellow Creek Valley.[43] Wayland later boasted that he had paid for the major

---

[40]*Ibid.*, Dec. 16, 1893.
[41]W. D. P. Bliss (ed.), *New Encyclopedia of Social Reform* (New York, 1908), p. 1079.
[42]*Coming Nation*, Feb. 3, 1894.
[43]*Ibid.*, Feb. 22, 1896.

portion of the land out of his own pocket—the rest having been donated to him.[44] He did not dig down very deeply since most of the land was obtained at about two dollars an acre. The last issue of the *Coming Nation* published from Greensburg was on July 21, 1894. Four days later the paper's presses and most of its personnel arrived in Tennessee, and the Ruskin Colony was born.

The colonists speedily organized the Ruskin Co-operative Association. Wayland, not surprisingly, was elected president. The Association was set up as a joint-stock company, with all but six of the male members of the community contributing $500 each for its use. In return, each received a share of stock. Each wife in the colony also was granted a share of stock in order to place her, in time, on an equal footing with her husband. Thus from the very onset the colony was organized capitalistically. Most of the actual capital of $17,050 was used to construct crude pine-board houses and a building to accommodate the *Coming Nation*'s presses.[45] Some of the colonists engaged in handicraft work; a few, with poor success, attempted to farm the inhospitable soil. But the main source of the colony's income was the *Coming Nation*, the *Ruskin Magazine Quarterly*, and the other products of Wayland's presses, including the publications of several labor organizations.[46]

If the ostracism of his Greensburg neighbors had irritated him, Wayland soon discovered that life in the little backwoods utopia did not measure up to expectations. Bickering between the colony's "co-operationists" and "individualists" disrupted the peace and harmony. Almost from the first, many of the colonists forgot about the alleged socialistic nature of Ruskin. Some purchased the produce of nearby farms and resold it at indecent profits to their fellow colonists. Dissension arose, too, over the fixing of a wage scale for the various members of the community.

The chief source of contention was the ownership and management of the *Coming Nation*. On this issue, two conflicting

[44]*Appeal to Reason,* June 17, 1899.

[45]William H. Muller, *Socialism in a Nutshell* (Ruskin, Tennessee, 1898), pp. 96-97; Bliss (ed.), *New Encyclopedia of Social Reform,* p. 1079.

[46]Eltweed Pomeroy, "A Sketch of the Socialist Colony in Tennessee," *American Fabian,* III (Apr., 1897), 2-3.

accounts have been left. According to Wayland, at the first meeting of the Ruskin Co-operative Association as a legal entity, he deeded to it title to the community's land and made out to it a bill of sale for the *Coming Nation*, its books, and its cash on hand. He claimed, too, that he received seven dollars a week as wages for editing the paper, a wholly inadequate amount since he was paying for all printing materials.[47] On the other hand, Wayland's enemies at Ruskin contended that he had never surrendered ownership of either the paper or its presses. They accused him, furthermore, of seeking to establish personal ownership over new presses which the Association had purchased for $5,000.[48]

Regardless of the accuracy of either account, Wayland decided at the end of July, 1895, after one of several stormy meetings of the Association, to leave the colony. His parting comment in the *Coming Nation* concealed the bitterness and rancor which he harbored against the majority of the Ruskinites. "With this issue [August 3, 1895] my association with the *Coming Nation*, child of my brain and heart, ceases. I will not worry you what has led up to this severance. As I have not been informed who will be my successor, I cannot, therefore, introduce him or her." Wayland made it clear, however, that this was by no means a swan song. He declared that as soon as he could find a suitable location he would create a new medium for his pen. "You will find my little banner in the thick of the fight for economic liberty of the masses and exhorting your hearty assistance."

The *Coming Nation*'s new editorial board, which published the paper until A. S. Edwards came from Greensburg to take over Wayland's former responsibilities, reassured readers that the latter's departure had not hurt the stability of the Ruskin community. On the contrary, they alleged, in the face of considerable internal dissension, the community was now "united and happy." "When it came to the point of tolerating in our midst the private ownership of the means of production or losing

---

[47] *Appeal to Reason,* June 17, 1899.
[48] *Coming Nation,* Aug. 3, 1895; Bliss (ed.), *New Encyclopedia of Social Reform,* p. 1079.

Brother Wayland, we did not hesitate! We felt bound to abide by our principles at all costs, and hence the severance."[49]

Disgusted with communitarian life, Wayland, accompanied by his brother-in-law, Charlie Bevan, and a small band of faithful followers from Ruskin, went to Kansas City, Missouri, where he began immediately to make plans for the publication of another socialist paper. The bite of the socialist propaganda bug had infected Wayland with a malady which he had no desire to cure, especially when such an illness could be so profitable financially. Often Wayland said that while he could make more money in real estate and other forms of economic enterprise, he could not be happy outside the publishing field. "Every person," he commented, "is striving for happiness at the point of least resistance, as they feel it . . . . I find a fuller expression of my being in Socialist propaganda than any other vocation I can conceive."[50]

Wayland was inclined toward calling his new four-page paper *Wayland's Weekly*. However, he wisely took the counsel of a friend, one T. E. Palmer, and decided upon *Appeal to Reason*, thereby associating himself spiritually, at least, with Tom Paine, the propaganda master of the 1776 revolution. The name proved an excellent choice, though it afforded critics the opportunity to refer to the paper by such puns as "The Squeal to Treason," "The Appeal to Unreason," and "The Repeal of Reason."[51]

The *Appeal to Reason* made its debut on August 31, 1895, with a printing of 50,000 copies, 4,700 of which were subscribed for by Dr. C. F. Taylor, the Philadelphia social reformer,[52] who had them sent to physicians throughout the country. Unlike the *Coming Nation*, the *Appeal* was not an instantaneous money-maker, and at the end of a year it was costing Wayland nearly a hundred dollars for each issue.[53] Its circulation hovered around 11,000, an anemic figure when compared to the 60,000 obtained by the *Coming Nation*.

49*Coming Nation*, Aug. 3, 1895.

50*Appeal to Reason*, Apr. 19, 1913.

51T. A. Hickey to Henry Kuhn, June (n. d.), 1899. SLP Papers.

52*Appeal to Reason*, Sept. 7, 1895.

53Wayland to H. D. Lloyd, Nov. 27, 1895. Lloyd Papers. George England, "The Story of the 'Appeal,'" *Appeal to Reason*, Aug. 30, 1913.

Wayland had poured a large part of his Pueblo fortune into the *Appeal* and had almost reached the point of halting publication. He decided on two last remedies. First, to reduce expenses, he moved the paper's offices to the little county seat of Girard, Kansas, a state which Laurence Gronlund thought "ripe for socialism" since many rank-and-file Populists were showing signs of restlessness with the People's Party's "concentration on the money question."[54] And, secondly, Wayland began to resort to high-pressure methods to obtain new subscribers.

Girard's citizenry was no more pleased to have the *Appeal* published in its community than had been the people of Greensburg when Wayland first began the *Coming Nation*. His children were again subjected to social ostracism. Wayland received frequent threats that the plant of the paper would be destroyed unless he ceased publishing the *Appeal*. But these threats never materialized, and only once, when President McKinley was assassinated, was there any real danger of physical violence. Gradually, hostility towards Wayland and his family died away, especially when the *Appeal to Reason* became one of Girard's principal economic assets and a cause for national distinction. In due time Wayland entered actively into civic affairs.[55]

In his drive to increase the *Appeal*'s subscription list, Wayland was greatly indebted to his imaginative circulation manager, E. W. Dodge, who had put in an unhappy stint at Ruskin. The latter had a positive genius for winning new subscribers, and he and Wayland made it a badge of distinction to be a subscription taker for the *Appeal*. In September, 1897, the paper began a column of circulation news entitled, "Patriots— Men and Women Who are Stirred by the Suffering of Humanity." Listed here were the names of new subscribers and the number of issues which each had ordered, for the price of the *Appeal* was reduced from fifty to twenty-five cents a year when four or more subscriptions were taken simultaneously. In 1898 this column of new subscribers was renamed "The Roll of Honor." The *Appeal* sponsored contests in which those sub-

[54]*San Antonio Labor,* Jan. 6, 1894.
[55]Fred Warren to Author, Mar. 8, 1947.

mitting the highest number of subscriptions might win prizes ranging from orchards and farms in Missouri and Arkansas— which some persons claimed were largely swamp and bog land[56] —to a seventeen-piece brass band "complete with a snare and bass drum."[57] Within a short period of time an "Appeal army" of subscription-takers was scouring the nation. While Wayland did not solicit money directly to help defray the expense of getting out the *Appeal*, he did not hesitate to ask for donations so copies of the paper could be sent to labor-union leaders and editors of the capitalistic papers, in order that they might acquaint themselves with the "fundamental truths" of socialism.[58] That the latter did not always appreciate these free subscriptions was revealed by the editorial comment appearing in the Dayton, Ohio *Daily Press*:

> The Kansas *Appeal to Reason* is a legitimate outgrowth of the treasonable Populism that has scourged that unhappy state for years. The sheet is edited in the interests of all incompetents and malcontents who hate the American government because it is not run on a paternalistic and pauper basis, and who have been contaminated by such APPEALS to unreason as abound in its seditious pages. Its editor proceeds with the rabid abuse of the American system upon the supposition that all the infamous lies of agitators and demagogues are divine truths and the degenerates who delight in ghoulish railings against our great republic are the only political economists, the only statesmen and the only philosophers.[59]

Wayland may not have converted many editors or labor leaders, but the *Appeal*'s circulation increased by leaps and bounds. Within a year it had risen to 36,000. Although it was given a temporary setback by the distraction of the Spanish-American War, the *Appeal* recovered rapidly, and by December 29, 1900, its regular paid subscription list came to 141,000. During the same year, when Eugene V. Debs was making his maiden run for the presidency, Wayland made the *Appeal to Reason* an all-out propaganda sheet for the newly organized Social Demo-

---

[56] John Lyons in conversation with Author at the Rand School, New York, Sept. 17, 1951.

[57] *Appeal to Reason*, Feb. 24, Sept. 15, 1900.

[58] *Ibid.*, May 13, 1899; July 14, 1900.

[59] Quoted in *Appeal to Reason*, May 13, 1899.

cratic Party. On November 3, just before the election, the total
issue of the paper reached 927,000, which according to Wayland
established a world record for any single newspaper edition up
to that time.[60]

The *Appeal to Reason* resembled the *Coming Nation* in general make-up and content.[61] Discussions of Marxist theory
again were kept at a minimum, while works and articles by
Edward Bellamy, Laurence Gronlund, Henry Demarest Lloyd,
Herbert Casson, Eugene V. Debs, and other more typical "American socialists" were prominently featured. Like the *Coming
Nation*, Wayland's new paper specialized in analogies, fables,
and parables. The most popular and most frequently reproduced of the latter was the famous "Parable of the Water Tank"
from Bellamy's *Equality*. Most of the news material came from
clippings from other reform or radical papers, and invariably
was concerned with public ownership of utilities, direct legislation, railroad regulation, trade unionism, and currency inflation. Wayland ran several weekly cracker-barrel columns
such as "Musings of a Mossback," "Echoes along the Way,"
"Thoughts for Your Uncle Sam," "Resistless Evolution," and
"Yeast." Readers had free rein to air opinions in a "letters to
the editor" column. Pictorial fare consisted chiefly of rough
but effective cartoons by Ryan Walker. To keep readers abreast
of the international socialist movement, never of real concern
to Wayland himself, a column of "World Socialist News" appeared weekly on the *Appeal*'s cluttered back page.

By 1900 the *Appeal to Reason* was by far the most widely
read socialist publication in the United States. The *Coming
Nation*, edited first by Edwards and later by Herbert Casson,
had faltered badly after Wayland gave up the helm, and such
socialist papers as the *People*, the *Social Democratic Herald*,
and the *Chicago Socialist* did not even come close to matching
the *Appeal*'s circulation. Wayland's foremost position in the
field was acknowledged by the *Railway Times*, official newspaper of Debs's American Railway Union, which stated: "As

---

[60]*Ibid.*, Nov. 10, 1900.

[61]Likewise, Wayland's new journal, *One-Hoss Philosophy: A Quarterly
Publication of Radical and Utopian Literature*, which sold for fifteen cents a
year, did not differ greatly from the *Ruskin Magazine Quarterly*.

an advocate of reform, Mr. Wayland has no superior and but few equals in the United States or elsewhere . . . . Whether Mr. Wayland writes of the past, the present or the future, he fascinates his readers, and his ringing words strengthen the weak, convert the doubting and inspire the halting to go forward and keep in step to the drum beats of reform."[62] Wayland and the *Appeal* received few such paeans of praise from non-socialists and from the more doctrinaire radicals.[63]

During the 1890's Wayland, like so many other undoctrinaire radicals, was an incurable optimist who saw the co-operative commonwealth emerging from behind every bend along the long and winding road to progress. Yet, paradoxically, he shared Samuel Clemens' low opinion of the human race and particularly of the very men and women supposedly destined to lead in the realization of a socialist society. Once, when the gentle and kindly Debs sat down to answer a letter from a "sufferer" of the existing system, Wayland berated him: "Debs, you're a fool. What is the sense in wasting your time on these human wrecks, hopeless victims who can never be of service to themselves or to society? They are only rubbish in the stream clogging the world's progress. Fight the system and let the victims go to the devil."[64]

Likewise, Wayland was scornful of the "voting kings," as he derisively labeled wage earners who habitually supported the Democratic and Republican parties. Referring to the ante bellum South, he sought by historical analogy to define the workingmen's relationship to the traditional parties:

> The poor white man in the South who never owned a slave, never expected to and who was not held as high as a slave, did just as hard fighting to preserve slavery as those who profited by the system . . . . the working people of the country are just as foolish, more so, for supporting the Democratic and Republican parties that favor the present system of wage slavery. But future generations will see it, and know it, and say it.[65]

[62]*Railway Times,* Oct. 1, 1895.

[63]W. J. Ghent, "The Appeal and Its Influence," *Survey,* XXVI (Apr. 1, 1911), 24.

[64]George D. Brewer, "The Wayland I Knew," *Appeal to Reason,* May 24, 1913.

[65]*Appeal to Reason,* Jan. 7, 1899.

Wayland was convinced that political action alone could bring about socialism in the United States. He was impatient with the "permeation" tactics advised by such Fabians as Bellamy and Bliss. While agreeing on the need for educating the American people in the principles of socialism, since he believed that this was his own mission in life, Wayland held that socialist gains at the polls accomplished infinitely more than the slow procedure of propaganda and education. Nothing succeeded like success, and he had not forgotten how Populism had swept all before it in Colorado. He was certain socialists could do the same once they were bound together in a militant, national political organization. "If you believe in socialism," he declared, "it is your duty to at once connect yourself with a socialist political organization, for by no other means can socialism be peacefully accomplished."[66]

Wayland's attachment to the People's Party became progressively weaker with time. By the end of 1895—that fateful year in the determination of Populist policy—he had all but given up on the party's being converted to a socialistic program and course of action. Because he advocated recourse to the ballot and membership in a socialist party, Wayland recommended until 1898 full support of the Socialist Labor Party. He offered readers this advice even though he was unenthused with the SLP's New York leadership.[67]

The *Appeal to Reason* never became an editorial vehicle for the Socialist Labor Party, nor did Wayland's attitude toward DeLeon change perceptibly after the latter's visit to Girard in the summer of 1896. In the *Appeal* Wayland took note of DeLeon's arrival and departure, but bestowed no effusive editorial praise on the SLP chief. His sole good-will gesture was to ask socialists to subscribe to the *People* and *Vorwaerts*.[68]

DeLeon was decidedly unimpressed by Wayland. He wrote to party secretary Henry Kuhn that Wayland seemed "to attract cranks," of whom some were "crookish." He conceded, however, that the editor was admired also by many of "the better sort." DeLeon, rarely one to admit ability in others, found

---

[66]*Ibid.*, Jan. 22, 1898.
[67]*Ibid.*, Aug. 15, Aug. 22, 1896.
[68]*Ibid.*, Sept. 5, 1896.

none in Wayland. "The incapacity of the man is indescribable. I suspect he is being played for a sucker by his wife's brother [Charlie Bevan]. This worthy looks like a peddler of wooden nutmegs. To him I ascribe all of the executive ability one is inclined to give Wayland credit for in view of his having set up the *Coming Nation* and now the *Appeal to Reason.*" Wayland, said DeLeon, "is a Salvation Army sentimentalist; his brother thinks he [Wayland] is a great writer; compound the two and you have it. This brother . . . and Wayland look like the very geniuses of famine."[69]

DeLeon's analysis of Wayland the man and Wayland the socialist who clearly did not know his Marx from his Bellamy, revealed, of course, their fundamental incompatibility. It came as no surprise to DeLeon, therefore, to learn that Wayland was among those involved in a rank-and-file revolt within the Socialist Labor Party in 1898 and 1899. During this period a war of editorial invective was carried on between the learned former Columbia professor in the *People* and the "One Hoss Philosopher" in the *Appeal.*[70]

When the Social Democratic Party was founded in 1898 to vie with the Socialist Labor Party for the socialist vote, Wayland only slowly bestowed upon it his blessing. Although the party included Debs and others whom Wayland admired, he could not forget that his old foe, A. S. Edwards, was editing the new party's official paper, the *Social Democratic Herald.* Not until the presidential campaign of 1900 did Wayland place the *Appeal* squarely behind the Social Democrats. But, as in the case with the SLP, he refused to convert it into an official party organ and Social Democratic Party news was surprisingly little publicized. When the Socialist Party of America was organized in 1901 Wayland finally appeared satisfied. To assist the party, he tried to form a "League of Independent American Voters" as a semi-secret auxiliary organization.[71]

Like all socialists, Wayland considered trade unionism "one of the chief emancipating factors" of the working class. Labor

[69]DeLeon to Kuhn, Aug. 29, 1896. DeLeon Papers.

[70]*People*, Mar. 13, 1898; May 28, July 16, 1899. *Appeal to Reason*, July 30, Aug. 6, 1898; June 24, July 1, July 8, 1899.

[71]*Cleveland Citizen*, Sept. 26, 1901.

unions, he wrote in the *Appeal*, were "logical necessary corollaries of capital combination—necessary like them in preparing the social state for the great change that is coming."[72] With regard to socialist trade-union tactics, Wayland favored the traditional policy of "boring from within," as opposed to DeLeon's dual unionism. He urged socialists to take an active part in union affairs with an end to socializing the labor movement in the United States.

If Wayland disagreed with DeLeon on dual unionism, he agreed with him on the general futility of strikes. He saw little to be gained by economic coercion on the part of the workers unless coercion were augmented by socialist political action. "Any union that does not make politics one of its means to an end is not worth the attention of any sensible worker," he declared. "The men who vote the same tickets as the capitalists are scabs no matter if they belong to every union in the land. The alleged labor papers that oppose the unions going into politics for themselves may not be in the pay of the capitalists, but they act just as I would if I had gotten pay from that source."[73]

Samuel Gompers, president of the American Federation of Labor, was the man Wayland had foremost in mind. In 1898, the year in which Gompers scored a crowning victory over the socialist opposition in the Federation, Wayland wrote: "That great fake, Gompers, who led so many workers to crimson strikes and purple failures, at so much salary out of their hides per annum . . . will forever deliver the working people tied into the hands of the capitalists so long as they follow him."[74]

Gompers was not the only noteworthy labor leader taken to task by the peppery editor. Terence Powderly, the deposed leader of the Knights of Labor, aroused Wayland's wrath when he announced his support of the Republican Party in the 1896 presidential election. Wayland branded him an "open enemy of organized and unorganized labor in the pay of the Hanna syndicate."[75] He considered P. M. Arthur, head of the Broth-

[72]*Appeal to Reason,* Jan. 27, 1900.
[73]*Ibid.,* Feb. 19, 1898.
[74]*Ibid.,* Feb. 26, 1898.
[75]*Ibid.,* Oct. 3, 1896.

erhood of Locomotive Engineers, "another shining example like Powderly and Gompers."[76]

Socialism was inevitable for the proletarian worker, Wayland maintained. But so was it also, he insisted, for the farmer, who would soon be strangled in the tentacles of corporate wealth which were being extended everywhere. The time was not far distant, he predicted, when the farmer would totally lack purchasing power for the technical equipment he had to have to enter a highly competitive market. More positively, many benefits would accrue to the farmer under a system involving the public ownership of land. In a socialist economy, Wayland argued, the farmer would work on a collectivist rather than an individualist basis, since the introduction of new and improved types of machinery made the individual method of production uneconomical and completely inadequate. Under socialism, large-scale operations would characterize all production. This would make possible the use of machinery which the individual farmer could not afford. A socialist economy, moreover, would allow for a greater degree of specialization since the individual farmer would not be compelled to raise staple crops for a world market.

Wayland assured the farmers, who constituted no small part of his reading public, that a socialist economy would not change the regular pattern of their lives except that it would eliminate many of their economic hardships. The farmer could continue to live on his own farm if he so desired, without the crushing burden of taxes and mortgages which ate away the greater part of his income. Even more important, socialism would end his sense of isolation by bringing to him access to schools, parks, museums, theaters, swimming pools, gymnasiums, libraries, etc.[77] Through socialism Wayland would have ended the farmer's terrible feeling of isolation, which was to be alleviated in time by the introduction of new types and methods of communication and transportation.[78]

---

[76]*Ibid.*, Oct. 10, 1896.

[77]*Ibid.*, Sept. 9, 1899.

[78]Cf. Arthur M. Schlesinger, "The City in American History," *Mississippi Valley Historical Review*, XXVII (1940), 65.

Wayland pictured farmers and wage earners alike engaged in a death struggle with the plutocracy. Although he did not approach the class-struggle thesis with the "scientific" rationality of the Marxists, he nevertheless was well aware of its existence. As in the *Coming Nation*, he emphasized in his own way the conflict between the "haves" and "have nots" in society. In 1899 he wrote in the *Appeal*:

> In the midst of plenty you are starving. In the midst of natural wealth and mechanized means waiting idly for the hand of labor many of you are deprived of employment, while those to whom work is given, must toil increasingly for a decreasing pittance. The more you produce the less you get. Why?

> Simply because that plenty of your own creation, those machines of your own make, and nature itself, the companion inheritance of men, have been appropriated by a class—the capitalist class.

> That class which you have enriched keeps you in poverty. That class, which you have raised to power, keeps you in subjection.

> Its maladministration of affairs, public and private, is stupendous; its corruption notorious; its despotism intolerable.

> You have given it the earth and everything on it. You are its tenants at will; its wage slaves when at work, and mere vagrants trespassing on it when out of work.[79]

Following the shooting of a group of striking miners by armed guards at Hazelton, Pennsylvania, in 1897, Wayland declared ironically: "the incident at Lattimer [Hazelton] should not cause the masses to hate the classes . . . . It is really too bad to see the hireling press of the robber monopolies worry about the attempt to make the classes hate the masses. In the next breath they will tell you that there are no such things as classes in the country."[80]

The *Appeal to Reason* bristled with evidence of the practical application of the class struggle in American life. The fruits of the capitalistic system were everywhere observable. Those

---

[79]*Appeal to Reason*, Feb. 4, 1899.
[80]*Ibid.*, Sept. 25, 1897.

who opposed socialism, said Wayland, should go among the mining centers of Pennsylvania or visit the mill towns of New England or make their way through the slums of the big industrial cities. "See the little ones; their forms slight and bent, their faces prematurely aged, and their features marked by that selfishness which alone preserves them in the merciless struggle for a mere existence. And do you think a just God will glorify you in upholding a system that dwarfs the minds and bodies and shortens the lives of His little ones?"[81]

Scarcely an issue of the *Appeal* passed without a reference to some social injustice. Not infrequently the sufferings of the poor were contrasted with the sybaritic existence of the rich who, more often than not, were accused of violating all accepted standards of decency and morality. The following are a few such references appearing in the paper:

> James Bryant of Grand Rapids, Michigan, 65 years old, unable to pay his rent and being ordered out into the street, blew his brains out with a shot-gun. Glorious system of private property in land where one man can order another to get off the ground.

> An 18 year old boy, a sweatshop victim in Baltimore, suicided the other day because he 'never had any pleasure to see light in life.'

> Benj. Smith, infirm and 86 years of age, with his blind wife of the same age, traveled on foot and begged their way from Whitehall, Ill. to Albany, N. Y. And all the way trains were running more than half their seats vacant every day!!! But we are civilized, and that is something to brag about.

> Want to buy some white slave men and women? Several hundred are offered for sale by the warden of the Indiana penitentiary on March 7. The state will furnish the clothing and the guards and let you have the slaves and if you kill them at work they will replace him or her with another without extra cost. This is the glorious system of civilization that we enjoy.

> Because in Marion, Ind., the butchers would not buy all their meat of Armour, he put in shops and retailed the best meats at 6 cents a pound and froze them out.

[81] *Ibid.*, Jan. 15, 1898.

Frick of Homestead infamy has given $100,000 for a picture. This is the way that the money that should have gone to the iron workers is spent. But then they vote that way and have no good reason to complain.

C. P. Huntington, the railroad millionaire, is dead. He had accumulated $100,000,000 that the people of this country had created and for which he had given no equivalent. He was a great man! He was a briber and a corruptionist of the worst type, but he aided in concentrating wealth and in that aided in producing pain in the minds of many people and that pain produced thought that will help change the system.

Anna Gould wanted to be a countess, so she bought an Italian imitation. She probably wanted to improve her plebeian blood. Her dearly beloved wanted her money only, and after he had squandered much of it, she called a halt . . . She married for love, don't you know!

Wayland's xenophobia, particularly his Anglophobia, was rooted in his experiences in Colorado, where British investments were heavy. It was carried over from the *Coming Nation* into the *Appeal*. So was his very special dislike for the crowned heads of Europe, notably Kaiser Wilhelm II, to whom Wayland always referred as "Crazy Bill of Germany." Wayland was in complete tune with the times, for criticism of Great Britain was a characteristic of virtually every contemporary radical movement in the United States. The general consensus was that Wall Street and British finance capital, welded together by the insidious House of Rothschild, were seeking to reduce American wage earners and farmers to the status of helots.[82] Wayland constantly warned that key industries in the United States were falling under British control and their profits siphoned across the seas to maintain a corrupt plutocracy and a lazy nobility. A typical Wayland paragraph calling attention to the menace of British economic penetration in the United States declared:

English capitalists are behind a trust with $5,000.000 to control the fish business of the Great Lakes. The great free American can not even go to the toilet without paying

[82]*Ibid.*, Jan. 25, 1896. Cf. *Railway Times*, Oct. 1, 1895; *Cleveland Citizen*, June 26, 1897.

an English combine tribute on the tissue paper. Great is such liberty.[83]

Likewise, Wayland expressed alarm over the diplomatic *rapprochement* taking place between the United States and the United Kingdom. It constituted a plot by American and British capitalists and their servants who held political power. When the United States and Great Britain became engaged in a diplomatic skirmish over the Venezuelan border in 1895, Wayland, unlike many jingoes in the United States, saw a peaceful solution. "It is all bluff, understood by the rulers of both nations." The British ruling class, he maintained, would not risk a war which might involve the confiscation of "every vestige of British title" in the United States.[84] A few years later, when members of Congress offered a prayer for the health of Queen Victoria on the occasion of her Diamond Jubilee, Wayland remonstrated: "British gold and cunning have reached the highest places of the nation and prayers for the throne are offered up in the highest tribunal of the state. And this is America! This is the greatest and freest nation on earth!"[85]

British policy in Ireland and the outbreak of the Boer War afforded Wayland excellent propaganda opportunities to twist the Lion's tail and to pick up new Irish subscribers. After the Spanish-American War, he suggested that "Uncle Sam had better try his hand at freeing the Irish as he did the Cubans and other Spanish subjects."[86] In condemning the Boer War and British imperialism in general, Wayland wrote, with far less concern for accuracy than for effect: "Fifty thousand dead English working people are rotting in the Transvaal. That is what the English working people contribute to help crush out the right of self-government in the Boer Republic. That is the reason English working people are slaves to capital and titles . . . . Fools kill each other that rich men may become richer."[87]

Wayland proclaimed that the inevitability of a co-operative commonwealth could not be halted by monarchy, international

[83]*Appeal to Reason,* Jan. 15, 1898.
[84]*Ibid.,* Nov. 9, 1895.
[85]*Ibid.,* June 11, 1898.
[86]*Ibid.,* Dec. 31, 1898.
[87]*Ibid.,* Aug. 18, 1900.

capitalism, or national plutocracy. "The world moves, human progress is not to pay tribute to monopoly or stop, and don't you forget it." He held that the abolition of chattel slavery was merely child's play compared to the task confronting socialists in their fight to end wage slavery. But ultimate victory could not be denied them. The socialist approach to society had been gaining more and more adherents during the past century.[88] The socialist order might not come "ready-made," but that it would come was beyond all question, since the gigantic combinations which were forming on all sides in the industrial world and which were reaching a state of perfection, were "essentially socialistic evolution." Likewise, concentration was already making itself evident in the realm of distribution. In an age in which the chain store had not as yet become a reality, Wayland noted that "a yell of terror" was going up from retailers that the "great department stores were crushing them out of business and monopolizing everything."[89] The new was coming as the old receded, said Wayland. "The little fellows are dying, the trusts rise over their graves, and public monopolies must and will rise over the prostrate forms of the giant trusts."[90] People will not be able to go back to competitive methods nor will they be able to "live under the trust system wherein all the necessities of life are owned by a few."[91]

Wayland's ideological position on socialism was such that he had little difficulty working up enthusiasm for such a "socialist" as William Randolph Hearst. Unlike DeLeon, he had no fixed standard by which to measure the sincerity of a man's belief in the tenets of socialism. Once, Wayland said that men like Mayor Samuel M. Jones of Toledo, John Peter Altgeld, and Hearst were socialists "in truth if not in name" because they were helping to educate the people in the principles of better government and hence were working for substantially the same ends as those who pinned the socialist label on themselves.[92] In March, 1899, Wayland wrote that Hearst's *New York Journal* was "hot stuff." It was not, he said, "in the employ of the

---

[88]*Ibid.*, Sept. 17, 1898.
[89]*Ibid.*, June 20, 1896.
[90]*Ibid.*, Mar. 25, 1899.
[91]*Ibid.*, May 13, 1899.
[92]*Ibid.*, Feb. 4, 1899.

exploiting class like some papers that pretend to assail the present system, yet make it so odious that the people will not affiliate with it. Some people protest too much," Wayland said, with reference to DeLeon with whom he was then feuding, "that they are the only simon pure friends of labor."[93] During the following year, however, when Hearst, Jones, and other "reformers" supported Bryan instead of Debs for the presidency, the mercurial temper of the *Appeal*'s editor turned fiercely upon them, and his denunciation of the Toledo mayor was matched only by his attacks on DeLeon.[94]

Wayland was flexible in his views on how the socialist society of the future was to be reached. He had no objections to the "one-step-at-a-time" method of the Fabians, which would work primarily through the local community. At the same time, however, he wished to see nationalization of the means of production and distribution carried out on a large scale in accordance with the program of the Marxists.[95] To make his views on socialist method even more confusing, he gave his approval to state socialism, which he considered as a means to the end. The motives of a capitalistic government in adopting a socialist program were of no concern to Wayland; the important thing was that it was a step in the direction of the co-operative commonwealth.[96] Of one thing he was certain: socialism was not to be attained through a co-operative colony. His Ruskin experience was an unforgettable lesson.

Through 1900 the *Appeal to Reason* was a one-man newspaper. Although Wayland had editorial assistants, the *Appeal* was almost entirely a projection of his own personality. This condition began to change, however, after Fred D. Warren, a vigorous and imaginative young journalist, joined the *Appeal* in June, 1901. Within a year's time he had taken over the direction of the paper from Wayland who, though not completely retired to the sidelines, was generally content to allow Warren to manage the *Appeal* as he saw fit. Save for a brief period between 1902 and 1904, when Warren left the *Appeal* tempora-

---

[93]*Ibid.*, Mar. 25, 1899.
[94]*Ibid.*, Nov. 24, 1900.
[95]*Ibid.*, May 13, 1899.
[96]*Ibid.*, June 9, 1900.

rily to resuscitate the defunct *Coming Nation*, this relationship existed until Wayland's tragic suicide shortly after the 1912 presidential election.[97]

Wayland never distinguished himself in socialist organizations or politics. He was a shy, introverted man who sought to fulfill his own mission in his own way. Like Debs, Wayland may have been somewhat short on socialist theory, but he was unquestionably long on ability to win over the doubting to the co-operative commonwealth. Frederic Heath's characterization of Wayland as "one of the greatest Socialist-makers this world of woe ever produced,"[98] has much merit.

---

[97]George D. Brewer, *The Fighting Editor or 'Warren and the Appeal'* (Girard, Kan., (1910), p. 29 ff.

[98]*Social Democracy Red Book*, p. 87.

VII. Socialism Faces Populism

TO UNDISCERNING conservatives of the 1890's Populism and socialism were one and the same bird irrespective of the coloration of their plumage. Their followers were regarded not merely as failures in life but, even worse, as immoral men who would displace with shocking arbitrariness those whom the Darwinian laws of natural selection had elevated to positions of leadership and authority in the world of enterprise.

To be sure, Populism and socialism, as radical movements, did have certain similarities.[1] Both represented strong currents of social protest against the concentration of economic power in a relatively few. Socialists and Populists could agree that existing special privilege was based on monopolistic control over the means of production and distribution. In the liberal tradition, each wished to destroy special privilege, since it prevented equality of rights and freedom of opportunity for all. And in method, both socialism and Populism would resort to the state, which alone could control in the public interest the predatory forces of industrial and finance capitalism.

Yet the end products sought by the socialists and the Populists differed markedly in spirit and in purpose. The Populists, mostly penurious agrarians from the South and Middle West, favored collectivist measures only insofar as they would eliminate the monopolist from control over economic and political life. Unlike the socialists, they wished to preserve rather than

---

[1] There is considerable literature on socialist-Populist relations. See Chester M. Destler, *American Radicalism, 1865-1901, Essays and Documents* ("Connecticut College Monograph," No. 3 [New London, 1946]), pp. 1-31, 162-74, 212-54; J. Martin Klotsche. "The 'United Front' Populists," *Wisconsin Magazine of History*, XX (1937), 375-89; Edward B. Mittelman, "Chicago Labor in Politics, 1877-1896," *Journal of Political Economy*, XXVIII (1920), 407-27; George H. Knoles, "Populism and Socialism, with Special Reference to the Election of 1892," *Pacific Historical Review*, XII (1943), 295-304; James Peterson, "The Trade Unions and the Populist Party," *Science and Society*, Vol. VIII, No. 2 (Spring, 1944), pp. 143-60; Anna Rochester. *The Populist Movement in the United States* (New York, 1933), pp. 120-24; Kerby, *Le Socialisme aux États Unis,* pp. 144-75.

to extirpate competitive capitalism as the best means of safe-guarding what remained of a society of small, independent, self-reliant producers. Thus, in advocating nationalization of the railroads and telephone and telegraph systems, the Populists did not necessarily assume that these collectivist measures were desirable ends in themselves: they believed that they would do away with exorbitant rates and discriminatory practices.[2]

The agrarians who rallied to the People's Party, then, wanted reform of capitalism rather than socialism. They would not sacrifice on the altar of socialist "regimentation" their position as independent producers. *The National Economist*, organ of the Farmers' Alliance and Industrial Union, expressed the sentiments of most Populists toward socialism: "Socialism would only replace one master by another; the monopolist by the community, substitute one slavery for another. All the systems of anarchy and socialism are based upon a supposed quality innate in man, which history from the earliest moment of his existence has disproved."[3] On another occasion the same paper said: "Without individual competition and rivalry what is there to emulate? The answer must inevitably be nothing."[4]

Despite the capitalistic character and orientation of the People's Party, its ranks included some who hoped to permeate it with socialist doctrines. These men were willing to use a reformist, albeit capitalistic, political party as a means of achieving socialism. They saw the logic of events gradually but radically transforming the People's Party from one that stood merely against the forces of greed into one that would espouse positively and frankly the co-operative commonwealth.[5]

The "permeation socialists," to coin a term, divided essentially into three groups. In the Eastern states, Nationalists, Christian Socialists, Fabians, and independent trade-union socialists constituted the largest part of the membership of an exceedingly weak People's Party organization. In the urban

---

[2] See William J. Peffer, *The Farmers' Side* (New York, 1891), pp. 172-73; A. Watkins, "Is Socialism an Element of Bryanism?", *Arena*, XXIV (1900), 231-32.

[3] *National Economist*, I (June 1, 1889), 166.

[4] *Ibid.* (Apr. 6, 1889), p. 1.

[5] See Henry D. Lloyd's Central Music Hall speech of Oct. 6, 1894, reproduced in Destler, *American Radicalism, 1865-1901*, pp. 212-21.

centers of the Middle West, notably in Chicago and Milwaukee, the effort to infuse socialism into the People's Party was coupled with an attempt to effect a farmer-labor alliance. In the agricultural regions of the Middle West, the permeation socialists were represented by a heterogeneous group of radicals who saw an opportunity to gain influence through Populist political action.   These were left-wing agrarians who subscribed to such papers as Wayland's *Coming Nation* and *Appeal to Reason*, Thomas Byron's *Farmer's Tribune*, H. W. Young's *Star and Kansan*, and George Howard Gibson's *Wealth-Makers*.

Negatively, and in many instances wistfully, the permeation socialists went along with the Populists largely because few of them could conscientiously support the Socialist Labor Party, let alone meet the requirements of its discipline. For them, moreover, little hope existed for a party consisting primarily of immigrants and obtaining an infinitesimal vote at each election.[6] Then as later, many socialists refused to "throw away their vote" for a cause that had absolutely no chance of success. A Republican Party which catered to the trusts and placed itself under the generalship of Marcus Alonzo Hanna was, of course, out of the question. A Democratic Party which took its cue from worthies like Senator David B. Hill of New York was scarcely better. Edward Bellamy, a talented coiner of aphorisms, said in comparing the merits of the traditional parties: "The capital of the Republican party consists in the virtues of its ancestry, and the capital of the Democratic party consists in the faults of its opponents."[7]

On the positive side, Populists were unreservedly against trusts, monopolies, and the insidious Wall Street "money power." They did not fear extension of governmental regulatory power over the economic life of the nation—providing they themselves were not too intimately regimented. Aside from DeLeon's Socialist Laborites, the Populists were the only organized party that dared to take a determined stand against the plutocracy. If some Populist leaders hesitated to support

[6]The Socialist Labor Party vote in 1888 was 2,068; in 1890 it was 13,331; in 1892 it increased to 21,157; in 1894 it went up to 33,133; and in 1896 it reached 33,564. Its high-water mark came in 1898, when it polled 82,204. *People*, Jan. 8, 1899.

[7]*Twentieth Century*, VIII (Mar. 31, 1892), 13.

social legislation beneficial to the urban working class, the party's 1892 Omaha platform pointed in the direction of progress. Finally, the Populists, who had nothing to lose, generally backed the demands of Eastern reformers for public ownership of municipal gasworks, power plants, streetcar lines, and waterworks.[8]

The Populist leadership, more inherently conservative than is often assumed, contemplated with ill-concealed hostility the efforts of the permeation socialists to convert the People's Party to a collectivist course of policy. At the 1892 Omaha convention it had been an unwilling witness of the successful attempts of Bellamyites and radical anti-monopolists to write into the party platform the sub-treasury plan, contemplating government-owned storehouses for farm staples, and planks calling for nationalization of railroads and telegraphs. While conservative and moderate Populists were willing to use government power as a corrective for economic abuses, they shied away from measures suggestive of state ownership. Fear of this collectivist tendency was evidenced in part by failure of the People's Party to extend appreciably its strength in the corn belt and Rocky Mountain silver-mining states in the presidential election of 1892. The rapid deterioration of the Farmers' Alliance and the drying up of contributions from silver-mine owners, financial angels of the party, offered further evidence of the distaste for a socialist-inclined program. Efforts of urban radicals to take charge of the Populist organization in Chicago and Milwaukee gave People's Party leaders the jitters, lest the party as a whole be associated in the public mind with socialism and anarchism, terms that spelled the kiss of death for any reform cause.[9]

After the election of 1892, the Populist leadership, which came almost entirely from the corn belt states, slowly arrived at the decision to retreat as far as possible from the radicalism of the Omaha platform. It would, instead, stake the party's fortunes on one issue, free silver—a course of policy criticized by Jesse H. Jones as "a lead on a false scent." It had noted that the popularity of the currency inflation issue, on which both

[8]*New Nation*, I (Aug. 20, 1891), 496.
[9]Destler, pp. 226-27.

Republicans and Democrats had committed themselves, had held the allegiance of voters to the traditional parties, notably in the Middle West.[10] The Populist leaders deduced from this that concentration on the money issue would wean away free-silver advocates from the Republicans and Democrats. Likewise, it would insure continued backing from silver-mine owners. Any discontent which the watering down of the Omaha platform might create among the radical anti-monopolists within the party, a large part of whom were from the South, would be more than compensated for by the prospect of drowning Wall Street's financial titans in a flood of free silver. A one-plank platform, furthermore, would have the merit of scotching allegations that the People's Party was a socialist wolf masquerading as a Populist lamb.

Immediately after the November, 1894, elections which saw "Silver Republicans" and "Silver Democrats" unseating Populist office holders throughout the West[11] and socialists and conservative Populists struggling for control of the People's Party in Illinois, the party's National Executive Committee issued a call for a special meeting in St. Louis on December 28 and 29. Its purpose, according to Committee chairman Herman E. Taubeneck, an Illinois agrarian, was to consider future party policies. Between 300 and 400 prominent Populists were invited; approximately 250 attended. While Taubeneck's invitation, by his own definition, was "broad enough to admit all who work and vote with the People's Party," some prominent left-wingers were intentionally ignored.[12] At the same time that Taubeneck sent out the call for the conclave, he issued a statement to the press indicating that the People's Party would junk much of the Omaha platform, take a stand against socialism, and commit itself solely to free-silver coinage at 16 to 1.[13]

---

[10]*Ibid.*, p. 227; John D. Hicks, *The Populist Revolt* (Minneapolis, 1931), pp. 301, 315; C. Vann Woodward, *Tom Watson, Agrarian Rebel* (New York, 1938), pp. 287-90; Russel B. Nye, *Middlewestern Progressive Politics: A Historical Study of Its Origins and Development, 1870-1950* (East Lansing, 1951), pp. 104-6.

[11]Hicks, *The Populist Revolt*, p. 333.

[12]Taubeneck to H. D. Lloyd, Dec. 10, 1894, and Geo. H. Gibson to Lloyd, Dec. 19, 1894. Lloyd Papers.

[13]*People*, Nov. 18, Dec. 9, 1894.

Taubeneck, General James Baird Weaver of Iowa, Senator William V. Allen of Nebraska, and Senator William A. Peffer[14] of Kansas, the People's Party high command, were heartened by the socialists' failure to capture control of the American Federation of Labor at its 1894 convention, which adjourned only ten days prior to the St. Louis meeting. They hoped that this was a straw in the wind and a portent for their own conference. But their initial optimism turned to consternation at St. Louis, where the conference got out of hand. Not only did the delegates refuse to scrap the Omaha platform for a new one which would place sole concentration on the free-silver issue, but they also adopted a resolution which called for public ownership of all monopolies "affecting the public interest."[15] Thus, instead of steering the People's Party to the right, as its leaders desired, the St. Louis meeting oriented it further to the left. Small wonder, then, that Taubeneck, Weaver, Allen, and Peffer thereafter removed such policy decisions from the control of the party rank and file.

In brief summary, this was the background against which the Socialists and Populists played a drama of alternate cooperation and bickering until the fateful presidential election of 1896. Socialist co-operation with the People's Party, however, did not include the Socialist Labor Party. Its leadership, if not always the rank and file, maintained an untarnished record of hostility toward the Populists.

The Socialist Labor Party's primary objection to Populism was its bourgeois character. This in itself was sufficient to preclude any possibility of close co-operation, let alone alliance. The People's Party, according to a resolution adopted at the 1893 SLP national convention, sought perpetuation of a class which was "doomed to dispossession and disappearance through the actions of economic forces evolved by the modern system of production."[16] Any temporary successes would have the effect of making the People's Party more conservative, of postponing the day of reckoning for the already harassed petty

[14]In 1891 Peffer had no great enthusiasm for free silver. See *The Farmer's Side,* p. 128.
[15]*Destler,* pp. 229-30.
[16]*People,* Aug. 13, 1893.

capitalist, and of retarding the formation of gigantic monopolies on which the future co-operative commonwealth would be based.[17] The *People* maintained that if such men as Bellamy really desired a co-operative ordering of society, they were, in reality, retarding it by supporting the Populists.[18] The paper welcomed the appearance of the People's Party on the American political scene as evidence of the desperation of the small-farmer class, but at the same time, it deprecated the waste of energy on the part of the truly radical Populist elements.[19] As the situation stood, said the *People*, "the greatest misfortune . . . that might occur would be the merging of the Eastern proletariat movement into that of the western farmers—a merging that will not fail to be advocated in the name of unity by mistaken men and designing politicians."[20]

During the 1892 presidential campaign, the Socialist Labor Party's National Executive Committee issued a manifesto stating the Marxist case against Populism. It read in part:

> The cyclone of concentrated capital which struck down the small industrial producers a generation ago has finally struck the small agricultural producers. The results are identical. The small farmer cannot hold his own. But he thinks he can. To accomplish this miracle he is beating about wildly, and demands mainly free coinage of silver . . . and sub-treasuries where he can pawn to Uncle Sam the products of his farm. In order . . . to do this he also must come into possession of the government; and to get there he sets himself up as the particular friend of freedom and of the working class . . . . But . . . the farmer would and does mob the man who should propose eight hours' work and higher wages for farm labor; ill paid as is industrial labor, farm labor is paid still worse; and it is a bit of effrontery that vies with that of Republicans and Democrats for the Small Farmers' party to ask the working men to aid it with their votes to make the small farmer comfortable, while they themselves shall remain in want, and sweating under hard toil.[21]

[17]*Ibid.*, June 7, 1891; Apr. 17, 1892.

[18]*Ibid.*, Nov. 6, 1892.

[19]*Ibid.*, Apr. 8, 1894.

[20]*Ibid.*, June 7, 1891. Here DeLeon was for once in agreement with Samuel Gompers. See Samuel Gompers, "Organized Labor in the Campaign," *North American Review*, CLV (1892), 93.

[21]*People,* Sept. 25, 1892.

Despite the official jeremiads against the "small farmers' party," SLP members, notably in the Mississippi Valley area, sometimes strayed off the reservation to work with and to vote for the People's Party. Such meanderings were deplored by the *People*. In a few cases where entire Socialist Laborite sections were involved, party disciplinary action was invoked.[22]

DeLeon saw only failure for permeation socialists. He compared the People's Party to an egg "that has been undergoing evolution." The "really radical or socialist element of the West," he said, had been led on with empty promises by the "reactionaries" in control of the party.[23] Eventually, however, the radical Populists would see the light, desert "the middle class movement" in disgust, and "unfurl the banner of international socialism."[24]

The increasing emphasis which the national Populist leadership placed upon the money issue brought telling editorial comment from the caustic DeLeon. "Silver bugs and gold bugs are capitalistic bugs," he said. "It matters not whether 16 of the first draw more blood than 1 of the latter. Both kinds are social vermin and should be exterminated."[25] In a debate with Thaddeus B. Wakeman, the New York People's Party leader, DeLeon argued that free coinage of silver meant a depreciated currency, which, while it might help the debt-ridden, *petit-bourgeois*, capitalistic farmer and land-owner, would be of no benefit to the wage earner, for whom money merely represented work done. With typically Marxist logic, he saw the property-owning farmer, once in possession of more money, seeking to reduce expenditures through purchase of new agricultural machinery. The result would be a widespread displacement of farm hands who would flee to the cities, "weigh down the unions, and still further reduce wages."[26]

Whereas the Socialist Labor Party criticized the Populist movement from its very inception, Bellamy's Nationalists, conversely, were sympathetic. Disastrous results of independent

---

[22]Klotsche, *Wisconsin Magazine of History*, XX, 385-87.
[23]*People*, Dec. 9, 1894.
[24]*Ibid.*, Mar. 3, 1895.
[25]*Ibid.*, May 26, 1895.
[26]*Ibid.*, June 5, 1892.

Nationalist political action in California in 1890[27] and in Rhode
Island in 1891[28] accentuated the need for co-operation or fusion
with a stronger political organization. When Bellamy founded
the *New Nation* in January, 1891, and in effect took over the
generalship of the Nationalist forces, he paid close attention
to the developments leading up to the formation of the People's
Party. In May, he advised Nationalist club members that the
party offered "the largest opportunity yet presented in the
history of our movement to commend it to the masses of the
country." He noted with particular approval the "religious
and patriotic feeling" displayed by the Populists and opined
that the Nationalists would be making a "fatal mistake" if they
failed "to take the utmost possible advantage" of co-operation
with the People's Party.[29]

Bellamy readily acknowledged that the predominantly agrarian program of the People's Party as of the summer of 1891
left much to be desired.[30] He believed Nationalists themselves
could remedy this condition by vigorous "missionary efforts"
in spreading a knowledge of their principles among the Populists. While conceding that the Populist leaders were "faint
hearted" and in some instances "unfaithful," he possessed great
confidence in the general party membership.[31] While Bellamy
consistently favored the People's Party in the *New Nation,* he
opposed conversion of the Nationalist clubs into Populist campaign organizations. "The clubs stand for more advanced principles than any party is likely at once to take up," he said, "and
it would be unwise policy for them as clubs to engage in any
line of work which would compromise the completeness of their
doctrine."[32]

Massachusetts, historically the cradle of social-reform movements, including Nationalism, was one of the few Eastern states
in which a People's Party was organized in 1891. The Nation-

---

[27]*New Nation,* I (Jan. 31, 1891), 18.

[28]*Ibid.* (Apr. 11, 1891), p. 165.

[29]*Ibid.* (May 30, 1891), pp. 277-78.

[30]*Ibid.* (June 13, 1891), p. 310. Many Nationalists attended the Populist
Cincinnati conference and propagandized for nationalization measures. *Ibid.*
(May 30, 1891), pp. 284-85. Five Nationalists helped to prepare the first na-
tional manifesto of the People's Party. Morgan, *Edward Bellamy,* p. 278.

[31]*New Nation,* I (May 30, 1891), 277.

[32]*Ibid.,* p. 278.

alists, while active in establishing the party in Massachusetts, did not initially exercise much influence in its councils. They shared the stage with Greenbackers, who formerly had been associated with the Union Labor Party, with Single Taxers, and with trade-union leaders from both the American Federation of Labor and the Knights of Labor. The first chairman of the party's central committee was George F. Washburn of Boston, a currency reformer.[33] Not until 1893, when Henry R. Legate, Bellamy's chief editorial assistant on the *New Nation*, became chairman of the state convention and Mason A. Green was appointed to head the resolutions committee, did the Nationalists take charge of the Bay State People's Party.[34]

The Massachusetts Populists, with the enthusiasm and optimism found only among political novices, entered a slate of candidates in the 1891 state elections. It was headed by Major Henry Winn of Malden, a graduate of Yale College and Harvard Law School, a former secretary to Charles Sumner, a follower of Henry George, and a veteran social reformer.[35] Their platform contained several planks which suggested Nationalist influence. These were concerned mainly with public ownership of utilities and nationalization of the trusts. The *Boston Post*, never friendly to the Nationalists or to the Populists, sourly commented that "the greater part of this strange assortment of ill-assorted ideas [in the platform] seems to have been adopted from Mr. Bellamy's conception of a millenium of paternalism. Indeed, if there is ever made a new party to fit the new platform, it must be the nationalists from whom its recruits will be drawn."[36]

Nicholas Paine Gilman, an advocate of profit-sharing and a loud critic of the Nationalists, had written that a party which held Mr. Bellamy as the "hero of a million homes" was not likely to do well at the polls in "a sensible American commonwealth like Massachusetts."[37] Gilman, who resided at West Newton, was an accurate though hardly remarkable prognosticator. The

---

[33]*Boston Post,* Aug. 25, 1891.

[34]*New Nation,* III (Sept. 9, 1893), 420.

[35]*Ibid.,* I (Sept. 12, 1891), 524.

[36]*Boston Post,* Aug. 26, 1891.

[37]N. P. Gilman, *Socialism and the American Spirit,* p. 201.

maiden political effort of the Massachusetts People's Party revealed that its tender young roots were planted in barren soil. Winn received only 1,772 votes, as compared to the 157,982 polled by the victorious Democratic candidate and 151,515 for his Republican opponent. Even the Prohibitionist Party with its 8,906 votes swamped the Populists.[38] Distressed with the poor showing, Bellamy took solace in "the determination of the electors to kill the Republican Party."[39]

The failure of the Populists to cut a wider swath in Massachusetts politics did not shake Bellamy's faith in the People's Party. He warmly approved the anti-monopoly platform adopted by the party's national convention which met in Omaha during the hot days of July, 1892. Pressure of work prevented him from attending the convention as a delegate from Massachusetts.[40] Nevertheless, the Nationalists were well represented.[41] During the convention Nationalist delegates met daily at the Windsor Hotel to discuss the proceedings. At one of these gatherings a committee of correspondence was created to keep Nationalists in different parts of the country in touch with the work of their fellow reformers.[42]

The influence of the Nationalists at Omaha alarmed conservatives among the Populists and occasioned almost hysterical reaction from some non-Populists. Unburdening his fears in the magazine, *Forum*, one of the latter group wrote:

> And when that furious and hysterical arraignment of the present times, the incoherent intermingling of Jeremiah and Bellamy, the platform was adopted, the cheers and yells which rose like a tornado from four thousand throats and raged without cessation for thirty-four minutes, during which women shrieked and wept, men embraced and kissed their neighbors, locked arms . . . leaped upon tables and

[38] Michael E. Hennessy, *Twenty-Five Years of Massachusetts Politics* (Boston, 1917), p. 18.

[39] *New Nation*, I (Nov. 7, 1891), 654.

[40] *Ibid.*, II (July 21, 1892), 416.

[41] George H. Knoles, *The Presidential Campaign and the Election of 1892* (Stanford University, 1942), p. 102.

[42] *New Nation*, III (Sept. 16, 1893), 428. The committee met in Chicago on Aug. 30, 1893, at the home of Mrs. Corinne Brown, who later became a loyal follower of Eugene V. Debs. Eltweed Pomeroy, leader of the direct-legislation movement, was among those present. Also see Fred E. Haynes, *Social Politics in the United States* (Boston and New York, 1924), p. 149.

chairs in the ecstasy of their delirium,—this dramatic and historical scene must have told . . . that there was something back of all this turmoil more than the failure of crops and the scarcity of ready cash. And over all the city that summer week brooded the spectres of Nationalism, Socialism, and general discontent.[43]

The 1,027,329 votes polled by the Populist presidential candidate, General James Baird Weaver, in the 1892 election made a not unimpressive beginning for a baby political party, and it led the oversanguine Bellamy to predict certain victory for the reform forces in 1896. Ignoring the highly unpopular legislation of the 51st and 52d Congresses, he ascribed Harrison's defeat by Cleveland to Populist inroads amongst traditional Republican voters. But he could not explain away the complete and stark failure of the Populists to make headway anywhere in the East. In Massachusetts, for example, Major Winn again had been the gubernatorial candidate of the People's Party and, though endorsed by the Knights of Labor and assisted in the campaign by the noted single-tax priest, Father Edward McGlynn, he had been able to garner only 1,977 votes. Winn had salvaged something for the Massachusetts Populists, however, by being elected mayor of Malden.[44]

Throughout 1893, Bellamy exhorted readers of the *New Nation* to rally behind the People's Party. But by the middle of that depression year he was beginning to have serious misgivings. Disturbed by the growing inclination of Populist leaders to relegate the party's anti-monopolistic platform to the background and to concentrate upon free silver, he sensed correctly that the very nature of the People's Party was changing. Bellamy had never manifested any degree of enthusiasm for free silver, although he appreciated the "spirit" of the demand for more currency.[45] In July, 1893, Bellamy wrote that the whole political struggle could not be narrowed down to the bimetallic issue.[46] Three months later he followed with another editorial

[43]Frank B. Tracy, "Menacing Socialism in the Western States," *Forum,* XV (1893), 332.

[44]*New Nation,* II (Dec. 10, 1892), 727.

[45]*Ibid.* (Apr. 16, 1892), pp. 242-43.

[46]*Ibid.,* III (July 22, 1893), 357-58.

caveat entitled: "An Abundant Currency Needful, but Nationalism the Only Way Out."[47]

The *New Nation* suspended publication in February, 1894, and simultaneously its publisher retired from the arena of active politics. In the passing of the *New Nation*, those Eastern Populists who opposed concentration on the silver issue lost their most effective organ of protest. In December Bellamy wrote to the meeting of Populist leaders in St. Louis a sharp letter arguing against allowing the free-silver issue to overshadow all others. Perhaps even more thoroughly alarmed than Bellamy was Henry R. Legate, who as early as 1890 had warned against the forcing of "a debased currency on the country" by the "Silver Kings." On the eve of the conference, Legate wrote frantically to Henry Demarest Lloyd, suggesting that they formulate a plan of strategy to head off the trimmers who advocated a one-plank platform. The state convention chairman of the Massachusetts Populists announced his intention of attending the conference, as he felt that the entire reform cause was at the crossroads. He volunteered to express Lloyd's views before the delegates, should the Chicago reformer be unable to attend.[48]

When the Reverend W. D. P. Bliss was not organizing one group, he was joining another. He was one of the first non-Marxian socialists to jump aboard the Populist bandwagon. "Christian Socialists as Christian Socialists," he acknowledged, "do not go into politics. Our work is to educate the conscience to the need of pure Nationalist and municipalist action." Yet Bliss declared unequivocally that the "political movement is the way out."[49] He saw no reason for radical Christianity to abstain from politics. "If politics and prayers do not go together," he wrote, "something is wrong with both our politics and our praying."[50]

Bliss, too, preferred the Populists to the Socialist Labor Party. His objections to the latter typified the attitude of

47*Ibid.* (Oct. 14, 1893), pp. 457-58. For other expressions on the silver issue, see *ibid.* (Sept. 2, 1893), pp. 409-10; *ibid.* (Dec. 9, 1893), p. 524.

48Legate to Lloyd, Dec. 19, 1894. Lloyd Papers.

49*Dawn*, II (July-Aug., 1890), 163.

50*Ibid.*, III (Jan. 29, 1891), 2.

most middle-class radicals who had been caught up in the "great awakening" of socialism during the early 1890's. While personally "cordial" to the Socialist Labor Party and finding its program superior to those of the Populists and other reform groups, Bliss decried its leadership and its tactics. He found the *People* "needlessly vindictive and censorious," and DeLeon and his associates "utterly incompetent to advance the cause of reasonable socialism" in the United States.[51]

The inadequacy of the People's Party from the standpoint of socialism first became apparent to Bliss at the Populist convention in St. Louis in February, 1892. Attending as a spectator, he noted that the delegates were at best only mildly interested in far-reaching social reform measures. Consequently, at this juncture he saw little hope in the agrarian radicals. "We say this with great reluctance," Bliss wrote in the *Dawn*, "for more than ever do we see the necessity of a political reformation."[52] Yet his disappointment with the Populists at St. Louis did not prevent him from supporting the People's Party in the 1892 presidential election. While lacking in appeal to "the deep moral religious feeling of the American people"—a point upon which Bliss and Bellamy obviously did not see eye to eye —it was still preferable to other parties in the field. Through the *Dawn*, he urged all believers in social Christianity to support the People's Party even though it would undoubtedly go down to defeat.[53]

For nearly three years after Grover Cleveland's victory in the 1892 election, which Bliss attributed to "a desire for a new ordering of society, Nevada silver, and Tammany Rum," the Christian Socialist leader retired to the political sidelines. His initial enthusiasm had waned to the extent of refusing to give the People's Party unqualified endorsement in the 1894 Congressional elections.[54] He suspected, too, the growing Populist infatuation with the currency issue. He deplored the party's completely agrarian orientation and advocated a national Populist referendum to reveal more accurately what the "mechanic

[51]*American Fabian,* I (Feb., 1895), 5, 8; *ibid.* (Dec., 1895), p. 6.

[52]*Dawn,* III (Apr., 1891), 6.

[53]*Ibid.,* IV (Nov., 1892), 2.

[54]*Ibid.,* VI (Nov., 1894), 162.

of the East" desired.[55]   Yet Bliss could not abandon entirely the fight for social justice.   When the hosts of plutocracy massed behind William McKinley and the Republican Party in 1896, the ebullient Boston clergyman returned to the political battle.

The ubiquitous Laurence Gronlund also urged close co-operation between socialists and agrarian radicals during the early nineties.   Gronlund, who had retreated from his fundamentally Marxist position of the 1880's toward a more congenial Fabian socialism, supported the Populists because they had the only "reform," "moral," and "American" party.[56]   But he insisted that the People's Party was doomed to failure and oblivion unless its leaders abandoned their politically myopic policy of ignoring the industrial wage earner. The Omaha platform, as it stood, was inadequate.   To satisfy the minimum demands of proletarian workers, the Populists, he said, would have to add planks calling for the outright nationalization of the railroads, state employment for the unemployed, and government banking.[57]

In 1894, Gronlund was among those who were admonishing Populist policy makers against committing the party solely to the free-silver issue.   In November he wrote: "In the future we must try to curb that vicious horse, capitalism, by the mouth, the bit, and no longer by the tail, and ropes of sand will not hold it down.   And if Greenbackers [the free-silver men] will not voluntarily do this, why then they must be relegated to the rear."[58]   Formation of a new political organization, "a Plebeian Party," said Gronlund, might be the only way out for those whose interests the Populist leadership persistently disregarded.[59]

The People's Party in New York, unlike that of Massachusetts, was primarily a working-class party.[60]   The impetus for its formation came from trade unionists who for the most part

[55]*Direct Legislation Record,* I (July, 1894), 38.
[56]*Twentieth Century,* XIII (Nov. 22, 1894), 7.
[57]*Ibid.* (Nov. 8, 1894), p. 5.
[58]*Ibid.* (Nov. 22, 1894), p. 7.
[59]*People,* Dec. 16, 1894.
[60]*Twentieth Century,* XIII (Nov. 1, 1894), 10.

were affiliated with the crumbling Knights of Labor.[61]   However, some American Federation of Labor men, including National Treasurer John B. Lennon, joined the party.[62]   Among its middle-class supporters were Thaddeus B. Wakeman and William J. Ghent, who had been active in Nationalist and reform activities in New York City, and Charles Somerby and Daniel O'Loughlin, editors of *The Commonwealth* and *Twentieth Century* magazines, respectively.

The Populists in both New York City and New York state ran candidates on outspokenly socialistic platforms. The platform drafted for the 1894 state election reaffirmed the resolutions of the Omaha convention. But it went further in that it contained the following statement, which committed the New York party organization to socialism: "and that industrial co-operation [i.e., socialism] should eventually supersede both the wage system and the monopolies, in the interests of the People, as they may approve."[63] The same platform incorporated several specific recommendations which Eastern radical leaders undoubtedly wished the national party program had adopted. These included various "labor" demands, such as adoption of the eight-hour day by all industries, obligatory arbitration of all industrial disputes, modification of labor conspiracy laws to permit collective bargaining, public construction of projects to provide work for the unemployed, sickness and old-age insurance, and outlawing of "Pinkertons" and other paid agents of law enforcement.[64]

If the People's Party made a dismal showing in the Massachusetts electoral contests, it fared no better in New York. In New York City in 1892 it failed to make a dent in the labor vote, even though Henry Hicks, its mayoralty candidate, and several others who ran on the Populist ticket, were trade-union officials. While Tammany's sachems were usually anti-labor

[61]*National Economist,* VII (May 14, 1892), 130.

[62]*Twentieth Century,* XIII (Nov. 1, 1894), 10; *Commonwealth,* I (Oct. 6, 1894), 17-19.

[63]*Commonwealth,* I (Sept. 22, 1894), 2.

[64]*Ibid.,* pp. 1-3.

in industrial disputes,[65] the wigwam, nevertheless, maintained the support of the working class. Without the labor vote the Populists could hardly make a respectable showing, let alone contemplate success. In the 1893 New York City municipal election, the People's Party, with 2,229 votes, trailed miserably behind both the Prohibitionists and the Socialist Laborites.[66] If this was the best that the party could do in a year of economic panic, it could hold only the slimmest of prospects for the future.

The following year, the Populists entered a full slate of candidates in the elections for state officers. Their gubernatorial candidate, Charles B. Matthews of Buffalo, enjoyed some public reputation for his courageous fight, as manager of the Buffalo Refining Company, against the Standard Oil Company.[67] While he ran on a platform committing the New York People's Party to the co-operative commonwealth, Matthews was not a socialist by any stretch of the imagination. In the election, the party picked up a little strength in the upstate counties, but failure of the New York City Labor Clubs to enter actively into the campaign resulted in a shrinkage in the already small Populist vote in the Metropolitan area.[68] In disgust, Charles Somerby wrote in the *Commonwealth*: "Organized labor was, as usual, disappointing . . . . [it] did not 'vote as it strikes,' though urged to do so by some of its prominent officers."[69] The 1895 state elections found the Populist organization completely demoralized in New York. Its vote dropped to barely 5,000, a total insufficient to give it official standing in the state.[70]

---

[65] The attitude of the *Tammany Times* toward Eugene V. Debs during the Pullman Strike is indicative. It directly accused Debs of inciting violence. "He found he had to 'do something' or lose his prestige as a leader, so he took the flimsy pretext offered by the local labor trouble at Pullman and made war upon the railroads, and indirectly upon thousands of people who had no connection with and no interests in the Pullman troubles. . . . Debs will be taught a costly lesson, and one that every man who becomes a menace to society ought to be taught. He has sown the wind. Let him reap the whirlwind and have a care lest he perish before it." *Tammany Times*, III (July 14, 1893), 6.

[66] *Twentieth Century*, XI (Nov. 16, 1893), 16.

[67] *Commonwealth*, I (Sept. 15, 1894), 3.

[68] C. B. Matthews to H. D. Lloyd, Nov. 22, 1894. Lloyd Papers.

[69] *Commonwealth*, I (Nov. 10, 1894), 3.

[70] DeLeon, *Reform or Revolution*, p. 22.

The extreme debility of the Populists in Massachusetts and New York characterized the People's Party throughout the East. It had not developed more than a semblance of a party organization largely because of the failure of Populist leaders, mainly well-meaning but ineffectual intellectuals and skidding trade-union officials, to catch the imagination of any sizable segment of the population. Nor could the politically amateurish Eastern Populists, despite their advocacy of urban and labor reforms, escape the odor of hay and the tarnish of silver that clung to the national party. The Eastern wage earner, even if economically unsophisticated, was usually intelligent enough to realize that free-silver coinage would have the immediate effect of raising prices more rapidly than wages. In the last analysis, the Eastern social reformer, wage earner, and politically important immigrant voted not for the feeble and untried Populists, even when sympathetic to them, but rather for the Democrats who traditionally had given lip service, and as often as not actual service, to their demands. On the immediate left, the Marxists had no need for the Populists since the Socialist Labor Party was already in the field.

In some areas in the Middle West, a real urgency existed for a coalition between agrarian Populists on the one hand and progressive labor leaders and independent socialists on the other. In Illinois and Wisconsin, for instance, farmers, on the whole, were far less hard hit by the depression of the early nineties than their brethren in the tier of states extending from Minnesota to Kansas. The People's Party in Illinois and Wisconsin, consequently, lacked widespread support even among agricultural producers.[71] Contending for political power on their own, the agrarian radicals in these states had no chance of success. Only by making tremendous inroads into the Democratic and Republican voting blocs in the big cities like Chicago and Milwaukee could the Populists become a political factor to be reckoned with. The logic of the situation called for an entente, if not an outright alliance, with the urban socialist and labor elements.

The panic of 1893 made such an alliance mandatory for the Populists, since Chicago labor, restive and disgruntled with

---

[71] Destler, pp. 166-67.

the old parties, veered toward independent political action. To forestall such an eventuality and to channelize labor's voting strength into the People's Party, Populist leaders began to make friendly gestures toward pure-and-simple trade unionists and the various reform and radical groups which were closely associated with the labor movement.[72]

The possibility of a coalition with the agrarian Populists was not lost upon the urban-labor, reform, and radical groups—the socialists being notable among the latter. Henry Demarest Lloyd, Thomas Morgan, Jesse Cox, and others saw the not unattractive opportunity of dovetailing the Omaha platform's limited collectivism with the socialists' more comprehensive demands.[73] Negotiations between urban-labor and radical leaders and Populist chieftains were held just prior to the People's Party state convention in May, 1894. An agreement was reached endorsing the Omaha platform and recommending favorable consideration of the American Federation of Labor political platform, which then contained the highly controversial Article 10 demanding government ownership of the means of production and distribution.[74]

The Populist state convention sanctioned these efforts at coalition and adopted all of the proposals suggested, with the exception of Article 10, on which it gagged. In rejecting Article 10, first in the resolutions committee and then on the convention floor by the top-heavy vote of 76 to 16, the agrarian Populists, backed by conservative Chicago labor leaders, served notice that they would not allow their party to become an instrumentality for the espousal and achievement of the co-operative commonwealth.[75]

Thoroughly humiliated, the socialists and their allies among the radical trade unionists considered withholding support from the People's Party. Their position of authority within the important Cook County Populist organization, however, made them reluctant to resort to such a tactic. Yet even in Cook

[72]*Ibid.*, p. 168. My account of the socialist-Populist relations in Illinois depends heavily on the exhaustive studies of Professor Destler.

[73]*Ibid.*, p. 198.

[74]*Ibid.*, p. 169.

[75]*Ibid.*, p. 170; Klotsche, *Wisconsin Magazine of History*, XX, 380.

County they had formidable opposition from conservative trade unionists, who for either doctrinal or opportunistic reasons, wanted no part of socialism.

The internal schism within the Cook County Populist group erupted into the open late in the summer when two sets of candidates, both claiming official aegis of the People's Party, were presented for the November statewide elections. The official organization, headed by Lloyd and Morgan, sponsored candidates sympathetic to socialism. A rump People's Party, controlled by conservative, and in some instances corrupt, trade-union leaders, also offered a slate of anti-socialist candidates. The latter remained in the campaign until nearly election time, when they finally withdrew.[76]

The campaign proved hard fought, bitter, and inglorious for the Morgan-Lloyd forces. The rump Populist group muddied the political waters, obfuscated the issues, and confused the voters. Henry George, speaking before a Chicago audience, vehemently attacked the socialist-Populist coalition, thereby causing the defection of a sizable single-tax group. An even more crowning blow was the refusal of the annual convention of the Illinois Federation of Labor in October to support Article 10. This repudiation of socialism helped to cement the working-class vote to the Democratic Party.[77] Finally, the results of the voting were far from gratifying. If the revolution was at hand, as Lloyd had asserted in a Chicago Music Hall speech of October 6, most voters were conspicuously unaware of the fact. In Cook County the labor-Populist alliance made an undistinguished showing. Not a single candidate was elected to office.

To all intents and purposes, the election was the coalition's final effort. On November 26, Morgan saw the Cook County People's Party organization "captured" by the "old line Pops on horseback." The socialists, Morgan wrote to Lloyd, withdrew from the meetings in "silent dignity" and now considered themselves outside the fold. Morgan ascribed the defeat of his group to "the same old scramble for offices." He announced

[76]Willis J. Abbot, "The Chicago Populist Campaign," *Arena,* XI (1895), 333; Destler, pp. 183-89.

[77]Destler, pp. 200-2.

his determination to form a new political organization that would rest on the bedrock of socialism.[78]

Likewise, Clarence Darrow, even before the opposition faction had gained control of the local Populist organization, was beset with misgivings. He looked askance upon the socialist attempt to infiltrate the People's Party in the face of strong resistance. After the November election he turned his back on the party. His friend, Lloyd, however, held on tenaciously, hoping against hope that a socialist-Populist alliance might become a permanent reality.[79] Yet even he came close to conceding the impossibility of a coalition, especially when the Populist leadership began an all out drive for free silver. By April, 1895, the situation had reached the point where Chicago Populist newspapers were charging Lloyd and other "communists" with being involved in an infamous conspiracy to destroy the People's Party.[80] After much soul-searching, Lloyd decided to make his last stand at the 1896 national convention of the Populists.[81]

Little need be added to the account of Chicago socialist-Populist relations to make it hold true for Milwaukee. Socialist influence in Milwaukee labor circles, particularly the Federated Trades Council, bulked large due mainly to the persistent efforts of two able German socialist editors, Paul Grottkau and Victor Berger. The labor movement, moreover, was a power to be reckoned with in Milwaukee politics, as was manifested by the coalition of old-line parties for the purpose of defeating the Union Labor Party candidate in the 1888 mayoralty election.[82]

Milwaukee had a People's Party. Characteristic of Populist organizations in most urban centers, its ranks included those reformist elements who were lumped together by conservative newspapers under the generic term, "cranks"—Nationalists, Single Taxers, non-Marxist socialists, Direct Legislationists, and advocates of unorthodox currency policies. Likewise, the Milwaukee People's Party membership included many of the

---

[78]Morgan to Lloyd, Nov. 27, 1894. Lloyd Papers. Mittelman, *Journal of Political Economy,* XXVIII, 425.

[79]Darrow to Lloyd (n. d.), and Lloyd to Darrow, Nov. 23, 1894. Lloyd Papers.

[80]Destler, p. 253.

[81]Lloyd to Thomas J. Morgan, Sept. 13, 1895. Lloyd Papers.

[82]Still, *Milwaukee, The History of a City,* p. 279.

Knights of Labor, most prominent among whom was Robert Schilling. Schilling held the reins of party leadership and thoroughly distrusted the socialists.[83]

After two years of relatively harmonious co-operation,[84] the inevitable clash between Populists and socialists developed at the People's Party state convention in Milwaukee in July, 1894. On this occasion the Schilling group gave way to the socialist–trade-unionist faction led by Victor Berger, and the convention consequently drew up a platform which contained the entire American Federation of Labor political program. In the ensuing elections, the People's Party polled nearly 26,000 votes, of which over 9,000 came from Milwaukee County.[85]

The socialists had scored an undeniable triumph at the 1894 convention and were quite willing to continue the coalition, provided the People's Party did not retreat from its collectivist platform. While the entente was an uneasy one, it lasted until the 1896 presidential election, when it collapsed on the free-silver issue. Thereafter, the Populists, usually, in collaboration with the Democrats, opposed the socialists at every turn.

In Chicago and Milwaukee the socialist efforts to use the People's Party for their own purposes met with a sharp rebuff. They paralleled and, in fact, were closely associated with the socialist failure in 1894 to commit the American Federation of Labor to support of the controversial Article 10. The socialist challenge also had the effect of creating an alliance of expediency between right-wing Populist agrarians and conservative trade unionists to forestall "boring from within" tactics. In short, there was demonstrated the basic incompatibility between the advocates of the co-operative commonwealth on the one hand and the wage- and job-conscious trade-unionists and individualistic farmers on the other.

In Kansas, the very heartland of Populism, J. A. Wayland headed a group of socialists who were eager to work for the

---

[83]*Ibid.*, p. 295.

[84]*Ibid.*, pp. 301-3; Klotsche, *Wisconsin Magazine of History*, XX, 382; Marvin Wachman, *History of the Social Democratic Party of Milwaukee, 1897-1910* ("Illinois Studies in the Social Sciences," Vol. XXVIII [Urbana, 1945]), p. 13.

[85]Klotsche, *Wisconsin Magazine of History*, XX, 383; Wachman, pp. 13-14.

co-operative commonwealth through the People's Party. When socialists and Populists failed to harmonize their efforts, declared Wayland, it meant only one thing, "lack of able leadership."[86] He himself had had cordial relations with the Populists in Colorado in 1893. The following year in Greensburg he sponsored the formation of a Decatur County People's Party organization.[87] Wayland, however, saw no panacea in free silver. He felt that the insufficiency of the 16-to-1 issue, once evident, would turn those seeking "a permanent cure" to socialism.[88] As early as January, 1894, he had cautioned the Populists against banking their entire fortunes on the currency issue alone.[89]

By the end of 1895, that fateful year in socialist-Populist relations, Wayland had lost faith in the People's Party and by April, 1896, his break was complete save for one tenuous proviso: the nomination of Eugene V. Debs by the Populists in 1896.[90] At best, this was a remote possibility, and mere hope for it did not blind Wayland to the increasing Populist emphasis on the silver issue or to the bitter attacks on socialism currently being made by Tom Watson, Ignatius Donnelly, and other Populist spokesmen. Wayland answered these attacks in kind.[91] Furthermore, to the consternation of local People's Party leaders, he dispatched street-corner speakers to Kansas City nightly to solicit the support of local Populists for the Socialist Labor Party.[92] The latter's platform found its way into nearly every issue of the *Appeal to Reason*, and Populist news, once prominently featured, received little coverage.

---

[86]*Coming Nation,* Apr. 14, 1894.

[87]*Ibid.,* Mar. 31, 1894.

[88]*Ibid.,* Jan. 6, 1894.

[89]*Ibid.,* Jan. 20, 1894.

[90]*Appeal to Reason,* Jan. 18, Mar. 14, and July 18, 1896. Debs was also supported for the Populist presidential candidacy by several other reform papers including *The Socialist* of San Francisco; *Cleveland Citizen; Pittsburg Kansan; Cooperative Age* of Minneapolis; *Kansas City Labor Record; Dakota Ruralist; East and West* of Penn Yan, New York; *Grander Age* of Mississippi; *Labor Advocate* of Birmingham, Alabama; *Coming Events* of Indiana; and *Wealth-Makers* of Nebraska. See *Railway Times,* Feb. 1, 1896.

[91]*Appeal to Reason,* Apr. 11, 1896.

[92]Wayland to Henry Kuhn, May 30, 1896. SLP Papers.

Wayland's increasing pessimism as to what the People's Party would do at its 1896 national convention in St. Louis[93] was shared by other independent socialists, especially after Populist national chairman Taubeneck publicly advised his party to abandon "the path that leads to socialism."[94] The Ruskin Colony's paper, the *Coming Nation*, which for over a year had been quietly telling its readers of the danger of the Populists going silver mad, now opened up with loud editorial criticism. While "many strange things" happened in the progress of reform, it said, the strangest would be to see the radicals who met at Omaha "squat before the free silver men" at St. Louis. Though the paper considered this unlikely,[95] it did observe that "influential" Nebraska Populists had gone "into hysterics over Bryan"[96] and that reformers had been "coquetting with the plotters of the two old parties for free silver." The *Coming Nation* speculated that Taubeneck was working not in the interests of the "party born" at Omaha, but of one that was "yet unborn."[97]

Henry Demarest Lloyd had few illusions regarding the opportunistic "Glaubenichts" Taubeneck. He believed the latter had been "flim-flammed" on the silver issue by slick politicians of the People's Party in Washington.[98] Taubeneck's open declaration of war on the collectivists within the People's Party stirred Lloyd to write to Richard T. Ely, suggesting that the two of them, in collaboration with Edward Bellamy, Edward W. Bemis, and other anti-monopolists, put together a pamphlet to "spike his [Taubeneck's] guns." The pamphlet would be distributed to Populist and reform papers for reprinting.[99] Free silver, said Lloyd, was a fake, the "cow-bird of the reform movement."[100] It "was a step—but a step backwards." He wrote to Dr. Bayard Holmes, the Populist mayoralty candidate in Chicago in 1895, that the People's Party managers who fav-

[93]*Appeal to Reason,* July 18, 1896.
[94]*Coming Nation,* May 23, 1896.
[95]*Ibid.,* Apr. 25, 1896.
[96]*Ibid.,* May 2, 1896.
[97]*Ibid.,* May 16, 1896.
[98]Lloyd to R. I. Grimes, July 10, 1896. Lloyd Papers.
[99]Lloyd to Ely, Apr. 6, 1896. Lloyd Papers.
[100]Lloyd to A. B. Adair, Oct. 10, 1896. Lloyd Papers.

ored the "free silver backfire" were precisely the same ones who "specially and bitterly and traitorously" opposed the real issues confronting the general public.[101]

With the approach of the People's Party convention in St. Louis, Lloyd shared the misgivings of Henry Legate, who saw the Populists veering toward "inevitable disruption." Nor was he heartened by Legate's news that fifteen of the twenty Massachusetts delegates favored trimming the Omaha platform. Only after a long period of deliberation did Lloyd agree with Legate that socialists had to fight for their principles at the convention. Not to make a stand might be interpreted as an act of cowardice. To bolt the convention would be still worse for, as Legate pointed out, responsibility for a certain People's Party defeat could be shifted over to the socialists. Let the Populists take their drubbing, Legate advised, and then be ready to gather up the pieces of their organization.[102] Lloyd disagreed with this last proposition. A new, vigorous, radical party, he said, ought not to arise out of ruin, confusion, and defeat.[103]

The Populist convention which opened in St. Louis on July 22 completely justified the fears of the radical collectivists within the People's Party. Lloyd called it "the most discouraging experience" in his life.[104] The party leaders, bedazzled with the prospect of success, were determined on fusion with the Democrats who, at their Chicago convention a few weeks before, had succumbed to free silver and nominated as their presidential standard-bearer William Jennings Bryan, the young Nebraska congressman of "Cross of Gold" speech fame.[105] Lloyd, a delegate at St. Louis, was infuriated by the iron-handed methods by which the party leaders controlled the convention. His anger spilled out in an account of the convention written for the British Fabian publication, *The Progressive Review*:

> The People's Party—the party of radical revolt, and industrial and political emancipation—in its National Convention was gagged, clique-ridden, and machine ruled. Members

[101]Lloyd to Holmes, July 13, 1896. Lloyd Papers.

[102]Legate to Lloyd, May 13, 1896. Lloyd Papers.

[103]Lloyd to Holmes, July 13, 1896. Lloyd Papers.

[104]Lloyd to A. B. Adair, Oct. 10, 1896. Lloyd Papers.

[105]Strong elements opposed fusion. See Hicks, pp. 357-79; Woodward, *Tom Watson, Agrarian Rebel*, pp. 293-94.

who were opposed to the plans they knew to be afoot to deliver the People's Party to the Democracy, were privately informed with cynical frankness by the presiding officer, that he would never allow them to catch his eye on the floor. The Committee on Resolutions was packed, and summarily squelched any attempt to get into the platform anything that would endanger the leaders' plans for fusion. When the platform was reported to the convention, the previous question was at once moved and declared carried, and the party went into the campaign on a declaration of principles, of which the delegates who adopted it knew only so much as they had been able to catch, as it was read rapidly amid the tumult and disorder of the convention of fifteen hundred, surrounded by a noisy audience of thousands of onlookers.[106]

Despite Senator William V. Allen's dictatorial rule, Lloyd and a small group of socialists had devised a strategy to swing the convention away from free silver and fusion. The Chicago reformer believed, not incorrectly, that the strongest element at St. Louis would be the radical anti-monopolists who might be won away from the fusion-bent convention leaders by a frank appeal for public ownership of all monopolies.[107] He was no less sure that he could count on the support of the Southern delegates and those of the Colored Alliance, both of whom desperately opposed what they knew would be a suicidal fusion with the Democratic Party.[108] Lloyd observed that the representatives of the Silver Convention, which was meeting concurrently in St. Louis, were largely ignored by the rank and file of the delegates,[109] whom he considered, all in all, a "splendid body of men."[110]

Lloyd's plan to swing the convention never passed beyond the conceptual stage. He did not deliver a prepared speech against free silver and fusion because he had received a telegram from Eugene V. Debs stating flatly that he would not be a candidate

[106]Anon. (Henry Demarest Lloyd), "The Presidential Campaign in America," *Progressive Review* (London), I (1896), 120-21.
[107]Henry Demarest Lloyd, "The Populists at St. Louis," *Review of Reviews*, XIV (1896), 303.
[108]*Ibid.*, p. 300.
[109]*Ibid.*, p. 303.
[110]Lloyd to A. B. Adair, Oct. 10, 1896. Lloyd Papers.

for the presidency.[111] Despite Debs's reiterated disavowals of presidential ambitions,[112] Lloyd and his coterie hoped that he would accept the Populist presidential nomination if it were offered to him. It was on this proposition, which conceivably had been buttressed previously by some more positive commitment from Debs, that they devised their strategy. Nor was their plan necessarily destined to failure, for many of the antimonopolist, middle-of-the-road Populists sported cards bearing Debs's portrait and the following inscription:

<blockquote>
No fusion! No trimmers! No traitors!
In the Middle of the Road
People's Party Candidate for President
Eugene V. Debs
'From Prison to the White House.'
</blockquote>

Debs's leaders, according to one report, had secured 412 written pledges out of a total of 1,300 delegates.[113] Although his name eventually was placed in nomination, there was no active campaigning in his behalf. The party bosses, by trickery, bulldozing, and betrayal, seduced the convention into accepting Bryan. Debs received only eight votes.

Heartsick, angry, and frustrated, Lloyd returned to Chicago. The People's Party had been lost, surrendered to its leaders—men who had "never been well grounded in reform principles nor really desirous of effecting fundamental social and industrial changes."[114] Initially he found it difficult to understand

---

[111]Telegram in Lloyd Papers.

[112]In 1895, Debs wrote from Woodstock Jail regarding reports that he might be nominated at the 1896 Populist convention: "I wish no political nomination in '96, nor at any other time. I want nothing from the people—I simply want them to do something for themselves. I care nothing about empty honors. Besides I don't know that there is any particular glory in being president of a nation of slaves and cowards." *Railway Times,* July 15, 1895. In February, 1896 Debs again denied that he was interested in the nomination. "I don't desire, nor can I conceive of any conditions under which I could agree to accept any such nomination. I'm a labor organizer, not a politician, and I don't mix. and if a man who is identified with the labor movement as I have been would accept a nomination, he would be under suspicion of seeking political office. To make it still stronger, I would not accept the nomination if I knew I could get the office, because a successful politician is nothing more than a bundle of compromises." *Appeal to Reason,* Feb. 1, 1896.

[113]*Social Democracy Red Book,* p. 54.

[114]Lloyd to James H. Ferriss, Aug. 1, 1896. Lloyd Papers.

how the delegates, mostly poor and honest men, could have been led so credulously, so easily, and so completely into the maw of Democracy.[115] But after due reflection he came to the unhappy conclusion that such a course had been foreordained by an almost prurient desire for political power. "The solution of the paradoxical action of the convention as to Democracy and money," he wrote, "was the craving for a union of reform forces which burned with all the fires of hope and fear in the breasts of the delegates, and overcame all their academic differences of economic doctrine and all their political prejudices." Lloyd confessed that he could realize why the delegates accepted silver and fusion when he saw men like Bellamy, George, and Bliss "taking the same attitude and for precisely the same reason that the real issue" was " 'between man and money' in Bellamy's phrase." They could not "afford to side with money against men."[116]

The Socialist Labor and Democratic Party conventions were held simultaneously during the second week of July. If, as one may safely assume, the Democrats were completely indifferent to the deliberations of the Socialist Labor convention in New York, the reverse was true of DeLeon and his cohorts, who followed, as intimately as news sources permitted, the course of events at Chicago. They hailed capture of the Democratic convention by free-silver forces as the beginning of "a new era in the development of capitalism and capitalistic politics." While hesitating to predict the outcome of the forthcoming November elections, Lucien Sanial asserted that the political success of the debtor capitalists now in control of the Democracy "would only hasten its economic downfall by precipitating a monetary, financial, industrial, and commercial crisis of unprecedented magnitude."[117] The SLP national executive committee accurately foresaw not only the end of efforts to infuse the People's Party with socialism but also extinction of the party itself as a political entity. Such a development would be highly beneficial to the Socialist Labor Party. Once fusion with the Democrats began,

[115]Caro Lloyd, *Henry Demarest Lloyd* (New York, 1912), II, 263.

[116]Lloyd, *Review of Reviews,* XIV, 303.

[117]*Proceedings of the 9th Annual Convention of the Socialist Labor Party,* p. 60.

the People's Party would cease to obstruct the growth of genuine socialism in the Western states, "where the allurements held out by Populist politicians served to give them quite a large following from among the working class." Henceforth men would have less difficulty in discovering political loyalties.[118]

The Socialist Labor leadership saw in the disharmony among the Populists after the St. Louis convention an excellent opportunity to step up its own organizational and propaganda drive that had begun the year before in the Western states. Its first gesture was a clumsy and ponderous "manifesto" addressed to "the thinking and socialistic members and friends of the Populist Party." The small farmers in particular were told they could not maintain their middle-class status through the People's Party, which was destined to collapse before the onslaught of all powerful industrial and finance capitalism. The handwriting on the wall should also be clear to middle-class liberals. They would do well to desert the reform forces for those of revolution which promised to remove the class struggle itself and to usher in the co-operative commonwealth.[119]

DeLeon himself went on an organizational tour of the West, where he found "an unquestionable revulsion against Bryanism in people with Socialist 'instincts.' "[120] His letters, which went winging Eastward to party secretary Henry Kuhn, though laden with complaints regarding the poor organization of the Socialist Labor Party, were at the same time highly optimistic for the future.

After the People's Party convention had cast the die for Popocracy, three distinct courses were open to socialists not affiliated with the Socialist Labor Party. As a gesture of protest they could throw their support to the SLP. They could make the best of the unsavory Populist-Democratic alliance and attempt to help defeat the Republicans. Or they could withdraw from political affairs and concentrate their efforts on socialist education and propaganda.

Although Henry Demarest Lloyd wavered as late as October 10, he finally decided to take the first course. He could not

---

[118]*Ibid.*, p. 10.
[119]Manifesto, 1896. SLP Papers.
[120]DeLeon to Henry Kuhn, Aug. 29, 1896. DeLeon Papers.

accept William Jennings Bryan as "the Knight of the Disin-
herited." On election day, he cast his ballot for Charles H.
Matchett and Matthew Maguire, the Socialist Labor Party candidates. Lloyd revealed dolefully that he would be obliged to
continue supporting the Socialist Labor Party until some other
was formed "under more representative American leadership"
to advocate the same principles.[121]

J. A. Wayland also repudiated the Populist-Democratic
fusion. He urged socialists to stand by their convictions "turning neither to the right nor the left."[122] "If you want socialism,
vote for it," he told his readers. A sizable vote for the Socialist
Labor Party, now on the ballot in twenty-seven states, would
place it on a firm footing and attract converts. Trust could no
longer be placed in the People's Party with its "office itching"
leaders. It had "run its course, performed its mission, and
helped prepare the way for a party of scientific principles . . .
the socialist party." Nor could any real reform be expected
from the Democratic Party, which had "proven itself the willing
servant of its principal men—the well-to-do classes who live
by interest, rent, and profit."[123] Wayland admitted a personal
liking for Bryan. "But Bryan is only one man," he said. "The
men who put him in power will be the administration, and they
are the same corrupt and ignorant politicians—barring a few
millionaires—who have helped and aided in the passing of the
infamous laws of the past thirty years."[124]

A victory for Bryan would actually retard, rather than advance, the cause of socialism in the United States, said Wayland.
The small amount of relief that might come from his election
would "cause the people to rub their hands, dive deeper into
'business' and cease to take further interest in public affairs."[125]
Approximately a month before the elections Wayland penned
the following analysis:

> To me it appears that socialists have no choice between
> Bryan and McKinley. A certain amount of wealth concen-

---

[121]Lloyd to Wharton Barker (n. d.). Lloyd Papers.
[122]*Appeal to Reason*, Aug. 22, 1896.
[123]*Ibid.*, Aug. 15, 1896.
[124]*Ibid.*, Sept. 5, 1896.
[125]*Ibid.*, Aug. 8, 1896.

tration and consequent oppression MUST come to the
middle class people of the nation before they will demand
or allow a radical change. Anything that tends to lighten
the load they are carrying prolongs the suffering . . . . If
the election of McKinley would make times harder, make
the trusts more despotic and exacting, scoop more property
into the possession of the greater capitalists, then McKin-
leyism will hasten the final disruption of society more than
Bryan's election which is trying to put a check on corporate
wealth rapacity without attempting to change the character
of the government.[126]

Edward Bellamy had little to say during the campaign, and
if he voted for Bryan, it was certainly without relish. Laurence
Gronlund, deprecating the free-silver issue on the one hand and
the class struggle on the other, supported McKinley.[127] The
Reverend W. D. P. Bliss waded into the political battle with his
usual gusto. As an American Fabian first, a Christian Socialist
second, and a Populist third, Bliss backed Bryan unstintingly.
Bliss pictured Bryan as a knight in silver mail who had come
out of the West to slay the plutocratic dragon—piecemeal. Although Bryan never admitted or acknowledged a belief in
socialism, Bliss had no difficulty in decorating the escutcheon
of his champion with a socialist coat of arms. "Mr. Bryan is an
evolutionary socialist," said Bliss. "He believes in taking and
in talking about one step at a time—that step toward socialism.
Everywhere he denounces trusts; everywhere he exalts government above money. And circumstances will compel him to go
further than he now thinks wise . . . . He must act and he can but
act on socialist lines."[128] Socialists who refused to support
Bryan were like ostriches with heads in the sand, said Bliss.
Bryan and Populism were part of the evolutionary trend toward
the co-operative commonwealth. The money issue, he confessed,
might not be wise, but he did not look on it as the cowbird of
the reform movement, as did Lloyd. It had been in the main
current of American radicalism for the past thirty years. Be-

---

[126]*Ibid.,* Oct. 3, 1896.
[127]T. J. Dean to Henry Kuhn, Jan. 18, 1897. SLP Papers.
[128]W. D. P. Bliss, "Why Socialists Should Vote for Bryan," *American
Fabian,* II (Oct., 1896), 10.

fore socialism could be tried, silver first had to be given the chance to prove its worth.[129]

Populists needlessly befogged the whole currency issue by charges of a conspiracy against silver, said Bliss. For socialists, the real issue was that they should support silver because it "incalculably more than gold means the issue and control of the medium of exchange by, and in the hands of, the nation rather than in the hands of private banks." Bliss did not go so far as to claim that the remonetization of silver would per se put control of money completely in the hands of the government, but he asserted that it would lend to that result.[130]

Bliss, in his own fashion, gave the campaign the aspect of a class struggle. Behind McKinley, he said, were marshalled "the bankers, the manufacturers, the railroad magnates, the established press, the colleges, the overwhelming majority of the clergy, the unthinking clerk class, the satellites of money in every form." Against them were the farmers, the urban laborers, and the more thoughtful members of the professional class. These were the people of the nation. And the people would win, said the righteous and confident Bliss, because their cause was just.[131]

As spokesman for whatever organized American Fabian socialism may have existed in 1896, Bliss found himself in doctrinal hot water with the London Fabian Society. Edward Pease, secretary of the London Fabians, wrote an open letter to the *American Fabian* criticizing Bliss's espousal of free silver. He argued that unlimited coinage of silver at 16 to 1 would bring about an inflationary condition that would spell disaster for the urban laboring class because of the lag between wages and prices. Somewhat pontifically he asked whether Bliss's "decision to support the silver-mine owners against gold bankers"

---

[129]*Ibid.* Not all of Bliss's Christian Socialist friends were so enthusiastic for Bryan as was he. The Reverend J. E. Scott, editor of the San Francisco Christian Socialist journal, *The Socialist,* refused to support the Populists and Democrats and sharply criticized their emphasis on currency reform. See *Socialist* II, (Aug. 15, 1896), 1-2; *ibid.* (Aug. 29, 1896), p. 2; *ibid.* (Sept. 26, 1896), p. 1.

[130]Bliss, "Why Socialists Should Vote for Bryan," *American Fabian,* II (Oct., 1896), 2.

[131]*Ibid.,* p. 6.

was based "on any very exhaustive study of one of the most difficult of the practical questions of the day." If such was the case, British socialists, who were gold monometallists, would appreciate seeing any of the published results of such an investigation. And lastly, Pease added: "If your financial experts, your bankers and merchants favor gold, we should need strong reason to regard them as wrong."[132]

Hurt by this blunt questioning of his intellectual integrity, Bliss, who was a moderate on the currency issue, felt compelled to write an elaborate defense of free silver in the *American Fabian*. In replying to Pease, he could not restrain himself from swinging a few well-directed blows at his English critics. "Here in America at least," he said, "facts have compelled us to discriminate and not to declare that all money except gold in a lump is bad." He answered Pease's statement that bankers and merchants favored gold with the dry retort: "This seems to us a rather remarkable Fabian statement" and advice "not expected" from the Fabian Society of London.[133]

In New York the editors of the Fabian journals, the *Commonwealth* and *Twentieth Century*, differed sharply in their attitudes toward the People's Party following the St. Louis convention. Charles Somerby of the *Commonwealth* was never completely satisfied with the People's Party, but he shared with Bellamy the hope that it would become a vehicle for socialism. After the Populist presidential convention, he adopted a policy that was to be pursued by most non-Marxist socialists after the elections. "Real reformers," he said, "will now unite on straight socialistic lines for educational work, through the circulation of standard socialist literature." As things stood, Somerby insisted, the political party could not achieve socialism nor would it be able to do so until a socialist communal psychology was attained through educational efforts.[134]

Daniel O'Loughlin, the free-thinking Irishman who edited *Twentieth Century*, had been smitten by 16 to 1. Consequently, when the Democrats at Chicago went on record in its favor,

---

[132]*Ibid.*, p. 7.

[133]*Ibid.*, pp. 9-10.

[134]Somerby to Lloyd, Sept. 16, 1896. Lloyd Papers. *Commonwealth*, III (Aug. 8, 1896), 3-4.

O'Loughlin, along with the New York People's Party chairman, Thaddeus B. Wakeman, was ready to have the Populists join in their attempt to bring about the annihilation of the plutocracy. "What can the Populist convention do in case it refuses to endorse the Chicago platform?" O'Loughlin asked. "The Populists have forced 16 to 1 upon the Democracy."[135] O'Loughlin did not believe that the Populists should give up their own political virginity. With respect to the Democrats, he said, they should assume the role of a "coy maiden" toward an ardent suitor.[136]

The *Coming Nation* agreed with Somerby's stand. It endorsed none of the candidates in the election. Ordinarily, its editors noted, the paper had supported the People's Party, but the "subtle dissimulation" of the party's leaders and its abandonment of a program standing for the "abolition of industrial slavery" for one based on the money issue alone left no alternative. "Our course is clear and well defined now as that of the managers of the People's Party has become devious and wicked," said an editorial in the issue of August 15. "The *Coming Nation* will no longer favor socialism within the People's Party or any other party. We have made the discovery that socialism is bigger than any political party yet has capacity to hold." Henceforth, according to the editors, the paper would continue to espouse socialism, co-operate with the socialist press, and assail "a system that sanctifies property and crucifies man."

After Bryan's defeat his supporters among the socialists sought to pour balm over their wounds. There was general agreement that the great mistake of the campaign had been the emphasis on the currency question. Words of bitterness and pessimism intermixed with expressions of hope for the future. Bliss wrote belligerently that the "sense of wrong" was deepening among the masses who already were "lining up for a struggle against monopoly as determined and momentous as any that history has known."[137] However, his general optimism was not curdled by the election result. He was pleased with the closeness of the race. "I do not think," he wrote to Henry Demarest

---

[135]*Twentieth Century*, XVII (July 16, 1896), 3; *ibid.* (Sept. 10, 1896), p. 17.
[136]*Ibid.* (July 16, 1896), p. 5.
[137]*American Fabian*, II (Dec., 1896), 4.

Lloyd, "a *narrow* defeat will discourage reform so much as a narrow victory might cause reaction."[138]   Herbert N. Casson, the Lynn Labor Church minister and political gadfly, who had also backed the Democratic-Populist coalition, declared: "We have only had the first inning of the game and the score stands 5 to 6 with the wind in our favor. Let the triumphant trusts remember that the just demands of the Chicago platform may be slight and trivial compared to the demands that shall be enforced by the people in 1900."[139]   O'Loughlin, too, still had hope. "The People's Party," he declared, had proven the "most compact and perfect organization of any political combination in this country" during the campaign. It held the key to the future.[140]   O'Loughlin's main animus was directed against those socialists who refused to follow the suicidal path of free silver, Populism, and fusion. "The Socialists—not the broadminded, party-free, but the members of the SLP have again demonstrated how pig-headed and fanatical they can be when they want to," he wrote in the *Twentieth Century*. "Between Mark Hanna on the one hand and William J. Bryan on the other to throw away . . . votes on Matchett! How preposterous! . . . But it was no use arguing with them. They are convinced they have an absolute monopoly of the truth and of the right way of acting."[141]

Henry Demarest Lloyd was satisfied that the "free silver fake" had received its death blow in the election. But he was frankly discouraged with the prospects which the future offered. Shortly after McKinley's victory he observed:

> At this moment the most distracted and helpless body of political radicalism in the world is, perhaps, that which in the United States has no place to lay its head. There has been no more striking development in the evolution of public opinion anywhere of late years than the growth of Socialism in the United States. But this Socialism is unrepresented. It hoped to effectuate itself through the People's Party, but the betrayal of that promising movement to the Democrats and free silver has put an end to

---

[138]Bliss to Lloyd, Nov. 5, 1896. Lloyd Papers.
[139]*Railway Times,* Dec. 15, 1896.
[140]*Twentieth Century,* XVII (Nov. 5, 1896), 3.
[141]*Ibid.* (Nov. 19, 1896), p. 12.

those hopes. Our Socialist Labour Party, of German Marxians, has never taken hold of the Americans and never will, for the Americans, whatever their political mistakes, are not so stupid as to make a class movement of an agitation to abolish class. The most uncertain element in American political arithmetic today, is in what form this unrepresented Socialism of the United States will precipitate itself, and what channels it will make for itself when it begins to move.[142]

The perplexed Lloyd wrote to several friends in the reform movement asking their opinions on the course of policy that ought to be charted out for the months that lay ahead. He himself favored the immediate convening of a meeting of reform leaders. Jesse Cox, the Chicago independent socialist, in reply favored organization of a non-political "progressive economic movement."[143] Richard T. Ely said he was considering writing a program around which all reformers could gather. He counseled against any attempt to co-operate with the Socialist Laborites, whom he described as "too stiff necked a generation."[144] Edward Bellamy cautioned against an immediate conference of reformers. Better wait a few months to see how things stand, he advised. Bellamy expressed satisfaction with the disintegration of the People's Party since it had "fallen into evil hands." He also agreed with Bliss that the campaign had helped spread discontent and would have the effect of preparing people for "radical doctrines." If and when any reform conference did convene, said Bellamy, it ought to come out unqualifiedly for "full nationalization of the productive and distributive machinery."[145]

Out of the welter of confusion which Lloyd observed in the disorganized ranks of the unaffiliated socialists and radicals, three groups were to emerge. One, as has already been suggested, was to renounce political-party activity in favor of a campaign of education, agitation, and organization. It was to attempt to shift the emphasis of the radical attack away from the demand for socialization of the means of production to that

---

142Anon. (Henry Demarest Lloyd), "The Progressive Movement Abroad," *Progressive Review* (London), I (1897), 361.
143Cox to Lloyd, Nov. 27, 1896. Lloyd Papers.
144Ely to Lloyd, Nov. 17, 1896. Lloyd Papers.
145Bellamy to Lloyd, Dec. 5, 1896. Lloyd Papers.

for direct legislation. Another group was to seek its ends through the organization of a socialist political party which would act independently of all existing political groups. The collapse of the People's Party had left a vacuum which needed to be filled by another radical political organization. Many agreed with Lloyd that the Socialist Labor Party was inadequate to take over such a task. The third group was to rekindle briefly the embers of community socialism. However, the old idea of establishing isolated socialist colonies was to give way to the grander conception of converting an entire state into a co-operative commonwealth.

VIII. Non-Partisan Socialism

WITH BUT a few exceptions Fabian and Christian Socialists had supported Bryan in the 1896 election. Eager to place the forces of reform in power, they had been willing to subordinate their broad socialist principles to the narrow issue of free silver. Bryan's defeat wrecked their immediate aspirations. It also had two other distinct and more permanent effects. First, many "one-step-at-a-timers," refusing to acknowledge that they had been hoodwinked by free silver, became completely disillusioned with the feasibility of achieving reform and social change through means of a political party, socialist or otherwise. Secondly, they were impelled increasingly toward reform of the existing political machinery and away from the more meaningful social and economic questions. In brief, they assumed a role like that of the civil-service reforming Don Quixotes of the two decades after the Civil War. Tilting at the windmills of corrupt politics and political organizations, they closed their eyes to the economic interests which were making American government the shield for special privilege.

Most middle-class socialists credited the Republican triumph in 1896 to the party's financially well-oiled, smooth-running political machine which dispensed money lavishly and in places where it would do the most good. The *American Fabian*, however, attributed McKinley's victory to a politically and socially uninformed middle class which threw in its lot with the plutocracy.[1] As long as middle-class ignorance persisted and gullible workingmen were hoaxed into voting for candidates of their capitalistic overlords by the empty promises of full dinner pails, the cause of economic and social reform could make little, if any, progress. It followed that the chief task of those interested in the public weal was to educate the electorate in the principles of social, economic, and political reform. "The *American Fabian* feels that it has a work before it no less important than

---

[1] *American Fabian*, II (Dec., 1896), 4.

that performed by the *Liberator* in the hands of William Lloyd Garrison," wrote Bliss in December, 1896. "The war for the new emancipation has only begun."[2]

However much they might wish to keep themselves and the citizenry free from the contaminating and corrosive influences of party politics and unscrupulous politicians, Fabians like Bliss realized the impracticality of concentrating solely on educational efforts. Politics had irresistibly attracted American reformers for generations and there was no turning back the clock of history. Fabians, therefore, had to find at the same time a means of satisfying normal political appetites and a way of directing people away from their baneful allegiance to party organizations.

The Fabians quite ingeniously sought to meet this problem by espousing "non-partisan" politics and direct legislation. Nonpartisanship permitted the voter to choose the better candidates of all parties without committing himself to the support of any. Through direct legislation, party machines and bosses—the scourges of honest representative government—might be overcome or at least circumvented. Deficiencies of the existing political system could be resolved by the electorate's determination to assert a sovereignty arrogated by ward heelers and party bosses.

A clear-cut statement of this course of policy came, even before the 1896 election, from the Reverend Joseph E. Scott, a Presbyterian Christian Socialist minister of San Francisco. Writing in a February, 1895, issue of his militant little paper, the *Socialist*, Scott held the existing political parties to be a noxious outgrowth of capitalism and monopoly, and government by parties to be the rule of their leaders and bosses. Was it even necessary to have parties, which inherently consolidated power and privilege in the hands of a few? Not at all, answered Scott, if the electorate really desired democratic government. The only requisite parties were groups for or against measures affecting all. When measures were decided upon by the people speaking in their collective capacity, parties as such would disintegrate. Direct legislation—i.e., the initiative, referendum, and imperative mandate—would be the method by which the people would

---

[2] *Ibid.*, p. 5.

make known its will. "The man who says the people cannot be trusted to make their own laws and execute them," said Scott, "is in favor of monarchy."[3]

Although the movement for direct legislation assumed sizable proportions after 1896, agitation for its adoption was by no means a by-product of the election of that year. Benjamin Urner, a former Greenbacker from Elizabeth, New Jersey, was probably the first public figure to advocate its use. Urner's espousal of the initiative and referendum came in 1882, after he received a drubbing in a local congressional election.[4] In the late eighties and early nineties the Nationalists included direct legislation among their political objectives.[5] Ten years after Urner first urged the adoption of the initiative and referendum, Joseph R. Buchanan, who shifted almost casually from one reform group to another, succeeded in persuading the platform committee of the People's Party at the Omaha convention to include direct legislation among the Populist political demands.

The guiding spirit behind the direct-legislation movement, however, was Eltweed Pomeroy, a veteran reformer and non-Marxist, non-party socialist from Newark. Pomeroy, intensely religious, a wealthy manufacturer of mucilage, and a practitioner of profit-sharing, was regarded by Edward Bellamy as "one of his most able coadjutors."[6] He was chiefly responsible for issuing a call for a meeting in July, 1896, to organize a National Direct Legislation League. The meeting was held in St. Louis the day before the People's Party convention opened. Once it became a going concern, the Direct Legislation League filtered countless columns of propaganda into reform journals.[7]

Critics of direct legislation, and there were many among those socialists who favored organization of a political party,[8] pointed out the inconsistency between the contentions of the direct legislationists and the complaints of men such as Bliss that the elec-

---

[3]*Socialist,* I (Feb. 22, 1896), 1-2.

[4]*Direct Legislation Record,* I (May, 1894), 2; Bliss (ed.), *New Encyclopedia of Social Reform,* pp. 384-87.

[5]*Nationalist,* II (Dec. 1889), 11-17; *New Nation,* I (Jan. 31, 1891), 15-16; III (Jan. 21, 1893), 32-33.

[6]Henry D. Lloyd to John H. Gray, July 8, 1893. Lloyd Papers.

[7]*Direct Legislation Record,* III (Sept., 1896), 25-28.

[8]See Chapter X, below.

torate was politically and socially uninformed. What assurance was there that voters would display greater wisdom with the initiative and referendum than they had shown in casting their votes for McKinley? And could it be denied that the electorate on many occasions had been misled by the demagogic appeals of agitators and by the distorted news and slanted editorials of the capitalist-owned press?

Henry Demarest Lloyd, for one, did not go overboard on direct legislation. He had read that the 1896 International Socialist Congress had warned against overemphasizing the questionable virtues of the initiative and referendum.[9] And he valued the opinion of Sidney Webb who thought that the masses were far better prepared to pass judgment on results rather than to make proposals. To ask people to attend to the exacting duties of direct legislation, Lloyd wrote to Pomeroy, would be "to overload an animal" whose back was "already nearly broken." So long as capitalism and monopoly prevailed, he argued, the plutocracy could control the initiative and referendum as easily as it manipulated existing political parties.[10]

The 1896 campaign, in addition to discouraging Fabians from party political activity, dissipated their interest in political socialism. If the electorate showed itself unready to accept the mild reforms of the Populists, how could it be won over to socialism? Was it not necessary to work even more slowly than hitherto contemplated? Thus, social reform within the capitalistic system and along gradualist lines suggested by Richard T. Ely and Frank Parsons,[11] rather than government ownership of the means of production and distribution, became increasingly the main goal of the Fabians. The spirit of revolt of the early nineties, while never really threatening actualization, was replaced by a cautious, premeditated opportunism.

Illustrative of this general Fabian retrenchment was the Reverend Joseph E. Scott's decision to change the name of his monthly journal from *The Socialist* to *The Social Economist*.

---

[9]*Fabian News*, VI (Apr., 1896), 9; *ibid.* (Dec., 1896), pp. 9-10.

[10]Lloyd to Pomeroy, Dec. 28, 1896. Lloyd Papers.

[11]See Sidney Fine, "Richard T. Ely, Forerunner of Progressivism, 1880-1901," *Mississippi Valley Historical Review*, XXXVII (1951), 599-624; Arthur Mann, "Frank Parsons: The Professor as Crusader," *ibid.* (1950), 471-90.

In the magazine's first issue Scott had defended the choice of name, asserting he had no intention of proceeding under "false colors." A few months later he wrote that "there is still a large amount of unreasonable prejudice in the minds of the people, both intelligent and unintelligent people, regarding the word 'socialist.' 'Social' is all right with them, but the ending 'ist' seems to transform the word into something terrible. What is the matter with the word 'Socialist'?" By the spring of 1897, he suddenly discovered something was wrong with the "ist" at the end of the term "social." In rechristening his magazine the *Social Economist*, Scott explained that he was doing so to avoid the "partisan restrictions" wrongly attached to "socialism."[12]

At the same time that Eugene V. Debs was professing to see a new light in Marxism, Bliss, Herbert N. Casson, and Pomeroy were giving it an increasingly wide berth. They were more convinced than ever that the gradualist methods of the British Fabians were the only ones by which socialism could be brought about in the United States. They denied vehemently the applicability of the class-struggle thesis to American conditions. Not by mere coincidence did the leaders of Debs's Social Democratic Party, which was organized in 1898, direct their heaviest ideological attacks against the social reforming "permeation socialists" rather than against Daniel DeLeon and the Socialist Laborites.

The first Fabian bugle call for retreat was sounded almost immediately after the 1896 election in the *Coming Nation* by Casson, who was equally adept at preaching from the pulpit or writing editorials for William Randolph Hearst. Surveying the wreckage of the political battlefield, Casson saw no chance for success in the near future for the hopelessly undermanned socialist forces. Instead of seeking to regroup the countless weak reform cliques into one new political party, he suggested that socialists would accomplish more by concentrating their efforts entirely on education and organization. When one American in five hundred was even remotely aware of what socialism in-

[12]*Socialist*, I (July 13, 1895), 3; *ibid.* (Oct. 26, 1895), p. 1; *Social Economist*, II (Apr. 17, 1897), 4.

volved, he asked, what possible chance of success had a socialist party? A series of defeats in politics, certain to result, would have the effect of making socialists a laughing stock before the general public and nullify gains made by patient propagandizing.

Casson saw no salvation in the Socialist Labor Party. Still smarting from his expulsion from that hard-shelled group, Casson said that he, for one, had no desire to repeat his experiences with the DeLeonites. The Socialist Laborite program, admirable in print, was meaningless in the light of the party's "low, despotic methods." Those who emerged to the fore of any party organization, he wrote self-righteously, were not the "thoughtful heroic teachers and pioneers" but the "crafty wire pullers and bosses."

Socialists in 1896, Casson advised, could take a leaf from the history books and profit from the experiences of the Abolitionists. Parties dedicated to abolition, pure-and-simple, had been miserable failures even though their members were in agreement on fundamental propositions. A small radical party could never accomplish much because as it grew larger, it inevitably split and then disintegrated. Since 1789 some forty parties had come and gone in the American republic, leaving little heritage. Such a fate awaited a new socialist party, particularly one dedicated to the principles of the class struggle.

For thinking socialists, then, the task at hand was to educate, agitate, and remold public opinion. To organize a party meant certain antagonism from other political groups. "Why should we raise the war cry and call every Socialist out from among the Populists and Free Silver men and howl at him as a 'traitor' if he is too clear-headed to obey?" inquired Casson. Henry George, Hazen S. Pingree, and William Jennings Bryan were all good men; each had value and should be used accordingly. "An evolutionary socialist," he maintained, "should be above partyism."[13]

Casson elaborated further on this general non-partisan approach to socialism in the *American Fabian*. American socialists, he said, could not follow the same tactics as their European

---

[13]*Coming Nation*, Nov. 28, 1896. Also see *American Fabian*, II (Jan., 1897), 6.

comrades because of structural differences in political and social institutions. Reforms could be achieved in the United States, albeit slowly, through both national and local governments. Therefore, it behooved all socialists to grasp every opportunity offered them by capitalists and workers alike to obtain socialistic legislation and thereby prove in practice the desirability of the public ownership principle as a solution for the industrial problem.[14]

Prestonia Mann, a wealthy and articulate New York feminist who inherited from Bliss the editorship of the *American Fabian*, gave enthusiastic endorsement to this general policy.[15] The British Fabian Society, she declared, owed "most of its strength to its steadfastness in standing by its determination not to be beguiled into becoming a political party." It had kept clear of "passion and prejudice, the suspicion, corruption, and partizanship" which characterized all political organizations and, instead, had maintained its "high purpose as a guild of teachers devoted to spreading the principles of the cause they herald."[16] She asserted that American Fabians had no choice other than to follow the British example. Their very last course of action under any circumstances would be to associate themselves with the "barbarous" Socialist Labor Party, "a foreign product—alien to our character and institutions" and preaching a doctrine of "destructionism."[17]

During the spring of 1897 frequent articles espousing non-partisan politics and admonishing against the pitfalls of independent socialist political action appeared in the *American Fabian*, the *Coming Nation*, the *Social Economist*, and *Commonwealth*. Typical was one published in the *American Fabian* just a scant two months before the meeting in Chicago that was to eventuate in the organization of the Social Democracy of America. Such a party, according to the author, a San Francisco Presbyterian clergyman, Jean Dupuy, would only help

---

[14]*American Fabian*, IV (Jan., 1898), 1.

[15]Miss Mann's summer home in the Adirondacks was a favorite gathering place for Fabians. See *Twentieth Century*, XVII (Nov. 26, 1896), 15; Leonard Abbott, "A Latter Day Brook Farm," *International Socialist Review*, I (1901), 700-3.

[16]*American Fabian*, II (Jan., 1897), 6.

[17]Mann to Henry D. Lloyd, Dec. 30, 1896. Lloyd Papers.

further to array the "'proletariat' against the 'bourgeoisie'—to use two stock phrases of the social democrats." A far better alternative was in co-operation with non-socialist political groups. This opportunistic policy would allow Fabians to engage in politics and at the same time "permeate" non-socialist parties with their doctrines. There would be no necessity of compromising principles and Fabians could prove themselves "practical and useful citizens." Dupuy insisted that the Fabians disassociate themselves from other socialists lest they be stigmatized by the popular prejudices connected with the latter. "It is a fact, for instance, that a great many Socialists in this country and in Europe have discredited ethics, attacked religion, and hinted, to say the least, at revolution," Dupuy wrote with an almost charming naïveté. "Now if we, as American Fabians, do not wish to be understood as endorsing these views," he asserted, "then we ought to say so."[18]

Fabian leaders felt that, as a religion required believers before a church could be established, so socialism first had to win the minds of the American people before its principles could be carried out into the realm of political action. "It is *thought* that rules the world," said Charles Somerby, "and if we can attack this citadel by literary and educational influence, we shall undermine the basis on which existing society rests." Socialism was even more than an intellectual principle, it was a faith; its challenging truths had to be made known to all. Greater need existed to develop a socialist climate of opinion than to "patch up laws." Contemplating the problem as both a publisher and a Fabian, Somerby believed the amount of socialist literature in circulation, rather than the returns of the ballot box, was the correct way to estimate the extent of progress being made toward the realization of the co-operative commonwealth.[19]

Literally every spokesman for American Fabianism after 1896, like their Nationalist predecessors, attacked the class-struggle thesis. According to one, it was the only subject on which they, as a group, were intolerant. "Appeals to the prejudices of the workers—hatred of the rich, jealousy of those in

18*American Fabian*, III (Apr., 1897), 6-7.
19*Commonwealth*, IV (Oct. 30, 1897), 4; V (Oct. 8, 1898), 4.

comfortable circumstances—emphasizing 'class consciousness' and the 'class struggle,'" said Somerby, merely hindered the progress of socialism in the United States.[20] The Fabians denied that society was being cleaved into two sharply delineated, warring classes. And they contemptuously refused to admit, even for the sake of argument, that the class struggle was a factor in social development. Existing social and economic conditions in the United States convinced them that the Marxist analysis did not apply. Nor did it hold good for Great Britain. Whatever might be the case in continental Europe, "this sort of socialism has not the ghost of a chance with the Anglo-Saxon temperament," said the *American Fabian*.[21] The class-struggle idea, too, was repugnant to the strong religious overtone which characterized the American Fabian movement. Ministers of the gospel, like Bliss and Casson, contested the validity of a doctrine which denied that all men were joined together by a bond of brotherhood.

While Somerby called on "evolutionary" socialists to concentrate their efforts on educating the "so-called middle classes" rather than the proletariat, he and his fellow Fabians would have resented deeply any inference that they were not concerned with the welfare of the working class. Morrison I. Swift declared indignantly that American Fabians rejected "as harmful, vicious and Americanly unhistoric, the attempt to divide the working from middle class." The battle for social justice could not be won if it was to be fought out "on lines of hate," he said. "The hate and class hostility method wins only a small handful of adherents. The end of that method is the reign of Robespierres, Marats, and Napoleons. In this country we want none of it."[22]

Nonetheless, the Fabians were always acutely conscious of their middle-class status. As one of the more cynical Fabians observed, the great trouble with "parlor socialists" was that they were a "trifle insipid, too clean, cultured, and courteous."[23] It was almost unthinkable that they would be willing to subor-

---

[20]*Ibid.*, VI (Aug. 5-29, 1899), 2.
[21]*American Fabian*, V (Jan., 1899), 9.
[22]*Social Economist*, II (May 29, 1897), 2.
[23]*Twentieth Century*, XVII (Nov. 26, 1896), 14.

dinate their own interests to, or identify them with, those of the
"mean," "vulgar," and "low" proletarians. "To expect useful,
industrious people to become class conscious proletarians," wrote
the Reverend Scott, "is to expect them to become . . . what they
are not . . . a very peculiar part of genus homo."[24]

Fabians believed strongly that they, rather than proletarian
workers, should direct the American people toward the co-operative commonwealth. The only strength of the poor lay in
its number. The proletariat in general, wrote one Fabian, was
"no match for the greater intelligence of the middle class and
the combined intelligence and wealth power of the capitalistic
class."[25] Dr. John Miller, a regular contributor to the *Social
Economist*, was even more emphatic on this score. "As soon as
the knights of offensive breaths and malodorous toilets are
taught their place is to follow and not to lead," said Miller,
"socialism will begin to grow to influential proportions."[26]

The logical man to get out and do something for Fabian
socialism in the United States was the Reverend William Dwight
Porter Bliss. Shortly after he arrived in San Francisco late in
the summer of 1897 on a lecture tour under the auspices of the
Episcopal Christian Social Union, Bliss proposed to Scott,
Swift, and other Bay-area reformers another of his grandiose
schemes. This was a plan to unite the nation's social reformers
—not necessarily socialists—into a single national federation.
As was typical of all of Bliss's organizational efforts, the initial
response was encouraging, and on September 3 he met with a
small group of men and women to launch the Union Reform
League. Those who organized the League were mostly Christian
Socialists, but its membership soon came to include persons of
a surprisingly conservative stripe. Paul Tyner of Denver, who
chanced to be visiting in San Francisco, was elected national
president, Scott became secretary, and Bliss assumed the congenial and familiar role of national organizer.[27] On September 9
the first public meeting of the League was held at Pythian
Castle; and, according to a report which Scott unburdened on

---

[24]*Social Economist,* II (May 8, 1897), 4.
[25]*American Fabian,* V (May, 1899), 2.
[26]*Social Economist,* II (Apr. 10, 1897), 4.
[27]*Ibid.* (Sept. 11, 1897), p. 1.

the League, many persons were turned away at the door because of lack of seating space.[28] Soon, Union Reform League branches were flourishing in San Francisco, Oakland, East Oakland, Ventura, and Alameda.[29]

Though the League was organized as a national society, it made concessions to the local California scene. Singled out for attack was the Southern Pacific Railroad, principal stalking horse for more than one generation of California reformers. The real government of the state, Bliss wrote in the *San Francisco Call*, was not "the band of quarreling, disorganized politicians who wrangle occasionally at Sacramento, but the very quiet, highly organized, shrewdly managed . . . Southern Pacific Railroad." Though Bliss, in good Fabian fashion, refrained from criticizing the Southern Pacific leaders as individuals, he declared that the Union Reform League was formed expressly "to proclaim a revolution" against the insidious, invisible government which they controlled.[30]

While emphasizing that the League was not a church movement, the founders nevertheless maintained it was essentially religious in nature. "This league of ours is a protest against the popular confusion of religion with sectarianism; it is a protest against the claims of any church, of all churches, to a monopoly of religion," Tyner asserted. Referring to the Marxists, he declared that the League was also a protest against "any similar claim to exclusive possession of righteousness on the part of those outside the churches."[31] Scott agreed with Tyner. He said, however, that while the League rejected the idea that man is motivated by material desires, it nevertheless believed that "man's first need is bread."[32]

The League imposed no limitations of any kind on its membership.[33] It supported no single political party and held that none could solve society's ills. This policy required no justification, said Bliss. "Any party that appeals to the interests of

[28]*Ibid.* (Sept. 18, 1897), p. 3.

[29]*Ibid.* (Sept.-Nov., 1897), *passim.*

[30]Article is reproduced in *American Fabian,* III (Oct., 1897), 3.

[31]*Social Economist,* II (Sept. 11, 1897), 5.

[32]*Ibid.* (Sept. 18, 1897), p. 4.

[33]*Coming Light,* I (1897), 60.

any one class or of the whole people will, as soon as it becomes large enough to be worth buying, be sold out by its leaders. Millionaires can afford to spend millions in purchasing immunity from socialistic legislation, millions in defeating the people's will." The League's duty was beyond the arm of wealth and the purchase of votes.[34]

To the consternation of California conservatives, Bliss revealed that the League's symbol would be a red flag. This announcement, coming at approximately the same time that San Francisco papers were garbling one of his many speeches to make it appear that he condoned the activities of the Haymarket anarchists, brought a hurried explanation from the clergyman. The red banner would not stand for "anarchy and destruction," he said, but rather would be representative of "society, of fraternity, of that common humanity which makes of one blood all nations upon the earth."[35]   But this explanation proved unsatisfactory, and Bliss decided to superimpose upon the red flag a white cross, the "symbol of peace, of love, of Christ, of sacrifice."[36]

The platform of the Union Reform League was written into its constitution. Except that it did not advocate government ownership of all of the means of production and distribution, its immediate demands were substantially the same as those of the Socialist Labor Party. The League asked for direct legislation and proportional representation; employment of the unemployed by the federal, state, and local governments; nationalization and municipalization of all public services; rapid increase in the taxation of land and the imposition of income and inheritance taxes; government issuance of currency without interference by banks; establishment of postal savings banks; constitutional limitation of the use of the injunction; woman suffrage; civil service for all local, state, and federal workers; prohibition of child labor and closer regulation of the hours and conditions of woman labor; compulsory accident insurance; unemployment compensation legislation; and enactment of social security laws.

[34]*Social Economist,* II (Sept. 11, 1897), 7.
[35]*American Fabian,* III (Oct., 1897), 5.
[36]Dombrowski, *Early Days of Christian Socialism in America,* p. 106.

The League's chief function was to propagandize for social reform. It was not to engage in political activity on its own except in those places where its membership included at least one-quarter of the voting population—a highly remote possibility. If two-thirds of the League's members, either locally or nationally, endorsed a candidate in any election, the latter would receive the League's official stamp of approval.[37]

When the League became firmly implanted in the San Francisco Bay area, Bliss left for the southern part of the state, both to fulfill lecture engagements for the Christian Social Union and to continue his organizational activities. In Los Angeles, where social reformers were almost as common as fruit flies, he encountered many old Christian Socialist friends. On January 19, 1898, the philanthropic Dr. John R. Haynes invited the ministers of the greater Los Angeles area to a banquet in Bliss's honor at the Hotel Van Nuys. Bliss used the opportunity to deliver a speech outlining the program and objectives of the League. He made such an excellent impression that one enthusiastic reformer offered $500 to be used toward the construction of a building to house the League's Los Angeles headquarters.[38] Bliss found the general atmosphere around Los Angeles so congenial to his work that he took up residence in Alhambra, a suburb of the city. Thus, while San Francisco was the League's birthplace, Los Angeles soon became its nerve center. When new national officers were chosen, Bliss succeeded Tyner as president, William H. Knight of Los Angeles replaced Scott as secretary, and Frederick D. Jones, also of Los Angeles, was selected to be treasurer.

To carry out the League's educational program, Bliss arranged with several well-known young economists and reformers, including John R. Commons, Charles Spahr, and Frank Parsons, to prepare tracts on various social, economic, and political problems. He planned with Tyner, who had become editor of the *Arena*, to publish the tracts in that magazine and later to distribute them in pamphlet form to URL members.[39]

[37]*Social Economist*, II (Sept. 4, 1897), 5.

[38]*Coming Light*, II (1898), 224-25.

[39]W. D. P. Bliss, "Union Reform League Activities," *Arena*, XXII (1899), 112-13.

Bliss desired to give the Union Reform League a national scope although its activities were concentrated in California. To this end, he offered a free copy of his *Encyclopedia of Social Reform* to any person enrolling twelve new League members. Also, he arranged for nearly two dozen nationally prominent reformers to be appointed vice-presidents of the organization. Then, in January, 1899, Bliss informed Henry Demarest Lloyd of his "unanimous election" as the League's new national president—an honor which the Chicago reformer apparently declined.[40]

To Bliss's disappointment, the League did not develop on a nation-wide scale. It had vitality only in California and in Ohio, where Samuel M. Jones, mayor of Toledo, was demonstrating that politics could be conducted on a non-partisan basis. A curious Union Reform Party was organized in Ohio in May, 1898, through a coalition of former members of the People's, Liberty, Socialist Labor, Silver Republican, and Negro Protective parties. The Union Reformers, it would seem, had but one concrete political objective—direct legislation.[41]

All in all, Bliss had chosen an unfortunate time to launch the League. By 1898 interest in social and economic reform was reaching a low point for the decade. The prosperity promised by the Republicans in 1896 was beginning to make itself evident. The agrarian revolt was in its death throes as farmers unloaded bumper crops of wheat in a world market almost free of competition because of poor harvests in Russia, Asia, and Argentina. In the political field the editor of the *Journal of the Knights of Labor* noted that "General Apathy" seemed to be "in supreme command." He observed that "indifference has been manifested in . . . the past generation; but old campaigners declare that conditions like those now prevailing are without parallel."[42]

Bliss, a tried fighter for lost causes, did not surrender easily. The approach of presidential elections invariably lifted his spirits and galvanized him into action, and he was anxious that

---

40Bliss to Lloyd, Jan. 10, 1899. Lloyd Papers.

41*New Times*, III (1898), 43; *Direct Legislation Record*, VI (Mar., 1899), 12-13.

42*Journal of the Knights of Labor*, XIX (Nov., 1898), 4.

reformers be united in 1900. The Republicans would begin the campaign, he lamented, with the backing of organizers of the trusts, presidents and directors of every bank, officers and large stockholders of every railroad, employers in every protected industry, and managers and beneficiaries of every corporation operated under, or in the hope of, special privilege. In addition, McKinley and Hanna could count on the votes of countless retainers of plutocracy, such as most of the clergymen, editors, college professors, lawyers, doctors, small merchants, salesmen, and the poorest workingmen.[43] In contrast to the solidified Republican ranks, Bliss saw the opposition replete with weakness, discouragement, poverty, and division. Only by unity among the different reform and socialist groups was it possible to whip the alliance of the plutocracy and the Republican Party.[44]

Bliss favored a popular front of all socialist and reform groups behind the Democratic Party, which was recuperating from its "free silver" malady. He suggested that, should the Democratic leadership refuse to accept the recommendations of the reformers, a new radical party could be built around the Union Reform League.[45] This was a fine political pipe dream, but Bliss proposed it in dead earnestness. His political calculations did not include consideration of the old Socialist Labor Party or of the new, up-and-coming Social Democratic Party, which had won local but impressive electoral victories in his home state of Massachusetts. The unwillingness of Bliss in particular, and the Fabians in general, to work with and through a promising and essentially revisionist socialist political party, indicated a lack of political courage characteristic of the whole middle-class socialist movement.

Bliss's desire for a conference of reformers coincided with the plan of Eltweed Pomeroy, the Reverend B. Fay Mills, a Boston Christian Socialist, and several other Eastern radicals for the summoning of such a meeting.[46] In the spring of 1899 he

---

[43] W. D. P. Bliss, "Unite or Perish," *Arena,* XXII (1899), 78-79.

[44] *Ibid.,* pp. 81-82.

[45] *Ibid.,* pp. 88-89.

[46] Eltweed Pomeroy, "The National Social and Political Conference," *The Challenge,* II (June 1901), 15; *Direct Legislation Record,* VI (July, 1899), 33-35.

joined them in issuing a call for a six-day National Social and Political Conference to open on July 28 in Buffalo, New York. Its purpose was to consider the state of the nation's political and economic affairs and to plot a course for social reformers in the future. No person attending the conference was to be bound in any way by its recommendations.

The Buffalo meeting brought together Fabian Socialists, Single Taxers, Free Silverites, Free Traders, Direct Legislationists, Prohibitionists, Woman's Rights Advocates, Republicans, Democrats, Populists, Social Democrats, Imperialists, and anti-Imperialists. Among those present were John R. Commons, Edward W. Bemis, Thomas E. Will, and Duren H. Ward, young academicians whose social and economic criticisms had recently cost them their teaching positions.[47]

The *Buffalo Express* did its best to discredit the conference from the very onset. It described the delegates in DeLeonish terms as a "lot of freaks," though harmless ones, and summed up the opening session in the following manner:

> A ragout of reformers with an ollapodrida of reform reveled yesterday in a series of speeches ranging from a hocus-pocus money talk to a lamentation over the town of Philamundelphia famed even among direct legislationists as the home of Lou of the vaudeville trust.[48]

Social reformers in a group are characteristically noisy, contentious, and ineffective. The debates and speeches at the Buffalo convention were frequently laden with the type of verbal TNT that makes men of good will desire to bash in the skulls of their opponents. Free silver, which only three years before had split the reform ranks, was almost completely ignored. The merits of socialism, on the other hand, were vigorously debated, with the chief attack coming from Bolton Hall, a prominent single-tax exponent. But the most bitterly contested issue was imperialism. Black-bearded George Herron, displaying to advantage his magnificent oratorical ability, chided the McKinley administration for betraying the Filipinos by its failure to give them independence. A vocal minority,

---

47 *Arena*, XXII (1899), 285-86. A list of the personnel of the Buffalo Conference appears in the *Direct Legislation Record*, VI (July, 1899), 49-56.
48 *Buffalo Express*, June 29, 1899.

headed by the rather eccentric, red-bearded William J. Ghent of New York and the Reverend Robert Ely of Cambridge, Massachusetts, replied angrily and pugnaciously to Herron. Ghent scored the convention for lack of patriotism in failing to applaud more warmly the name of Admiral George Dewey, the recent victor at Manila.[49] And he defended the effort of American military commanders to suppress the "barbaric" Aguinaldo insurrection. N. O. Nelson, the presiding officer, stalked out of the convention hall in high dudgeon following the adoption of an anti-imperialist resolution.[50]

The question of political action also engendered a hot debate. Although considerable sentiment was expressed for formation of a reform party, the delegates ultimately followed the advice of Herbert N. Casson, who implored them not to contaminate themselves in the dirty game of politics.[51] After spokesmen for the Republican, Democratic, Populist, Silver Republican, Social Democratic, Prohibition, and Union Reform parties had delivered speeches outlining the reasons why their respective organizations merited support, the convention adopted Joseph R. Buchanan's resolution to back any political party which pledged itself to adopt the convention's recommendations.[52]

The conference's most constructive act was the reorganization of the Union Reform League into the Social Reform Union. Like the League, the Social Reform Union was dedicated to uniting the nation's reform groups into a federated body while at the same time allowing each to pursue its separate line of work. It also undertook an extensive educational campaign designed to inform the citizenry on matters of social, political, and economic importance. The Union Reform League's program was streamlined into five major planks designed to appeal to the country's principal reform organizations. These called for direct legislation and proportional representation, an ample

---

[49]*Ibid.*, June 30, 1899.

[50]*Ibid.*, July 2, 1899.

[51]The *Social Democratic Herald* of Sept. 2, 1899, interpreted the refusal of the conference to come out for the Social Democratic Party as a clear indication that the reformers planned to support the Democrats. It went on to ask how they could support a party controlled by Richard Croker, Roswell Flower, David Lamont, Roger Q. Mills, Perry and Oliver H. P. Belmont.

[52]*Social Forum*, I (1899), 88.

supply of circulating currency, public ownership of public utilities, taxation of land values, and antimilitarism.[53]

Bliss and his friends envisioned the Social Reform Union as a "great Chautauqua movement of social reform," as Samuel M. Jones phrased it. They aimed at education, not political action. "While our organization is not political," said Bliss, "the right politics will be sure to come. Politicians that are afraid of education we shall do well to avoid. Let ideas lead to politics; not politics distort ideas."[54]

A correspondence school, the College of Social Sciences, was the most ambitious of the Union's activities. Initially endowed with $15,000, it was located in Boston, headed by Professor Will, and staffed by Frank Parsons, Duren H. Ward, and the Rev. J. W. Caldwell. Will, Parsons, and Ward had been appointed by a Populist regime to the Kansas State Agricultural College— Will as President—and later had been dismissed for political reasons by the college's new Republican-dominated Board of Regents.[55]   Caldwell was the founder of LeClaire Academy. Edward W. Bemis and John R. Commons, who felt the absence of academic freedom at the University of Chicago and Syracuse University, respectively, assisted in the preparation of the new college's curriculum, as did Willis J. Abbot, nephew of the renowned clergyman, Lyman Abbot.[56]

The leaders of the Social Reform Union took pains to assure the public that their new educational institution was "not designed in any sense to be a 'socialist' college" or to conduct "socialist propaganda." They acknowledged that some of its faculty had taken an "advanced" position on much of the socialist program, but maintained that the College of Social Sciences was essentially a protest against the narrowness of established educational institutions with repect to social issues.[57] The College espoused absolute freedom of inquiry and instruc-

---

[53] Bulletin of the Social Reform Union, No. 1 (Sept. 15, 1899), p. 1.

[54] Ibid., No. 2 (Oct. 1, 1899), p. 2.

[55] Social Forum, I (1899), 66.

[56] Bulletin of the Social Reform Union, No. 1 (Sept. 15, 1899), p. 7. For discussions of the "academic freedom" issue, see Commons, Myself, pp. 57-58; Charles A. Towne, "The New Ostracism," Arena, XVIII (1897), 433-51; American Fabian, I (May-June, 1895), 6; ibid., III (Sept., 1897), 4.

[57] Arena, XXII (1899), 480.

tion.[58] Among its correspondence courses were: History—"The Nineteenth Century: The Greatest Movements of the Greatest Age"; Literature—"Social Ideals in Literature, or Utopias from Plato to Howells"; Economics—"The Principles of Economics: How Nations are Fed"; Economics—"The Evolution of Industrial Monopolies and Trusts"; Finance—"American Monetary History"; Ethics—"The Origin, Evolution, and Consummation of Morality"; and Civics—"The Science of Citizenship."[59]

Internal dissensions, characteristic of the most outwardly harmonious academic institutions, were quick to crop up in the College of Social Sciences and helped to bring it to an early demise. Chief complainer was Edward W. Bemis, who saw the institution evolving into a liberal arts college if and when sufficient endowments could be obtained. He looked askance upon its organizational committee, or its board of trustees, as it were. The committee included Edwin D. Mead, editor of the *New England Magazine*, and Charles F. Washburn, former Massachusetts People's Party chairman, from Boston; George H. Shibley a bimetallic-currency advocate from Chicago; Willis J. Abbot, a journalist currently operating out of New York; Dr. C. F. Taylor, a Philadelphia social reformer and editor of *Medical World*; and John W. Breidenthal and C. B. Hoffman, former members of the Board of Regents of the Kansas State Agricultural College.

Bemis considered the appointment of Breidenthal and Hoffman particularly unwise because of their primary interest in People's Party politics and their general lack of intellectual stature. He believed Washburn a distinct liability because of his association with a retail credit clothing store and his affiliation with the Boston People's Church, which he conceived to represent "a sort of Buffalo Bill of religion" and to be "synonymous with pulpit buffoonery and extreme advertising." Washburn, he claimed, was virtually unknown among the intelligentsia of Boston and would be of no assistance in obtaining funds for the College. Bemis objected to Abbot's desire to use the College's courses to spread social-reform propaganda. "There is an essential vital difference between a College and a

---

[58]*Social Forum*, II (1900), 164.
[59]*Bulletin of the Social Reform Union*, No. 1 (Sept. 15, 1899), p. 8.

propaganda movement" and any attempt to intermix the two would be fatal to the former, he wrote to Carl Vrooman. Finally, Bemis charged the organization committee with making grandiose claims and engaging in patently fraudulent advertising. He insisted that before making any pretense of offering a liberal education, it was necessary to raise money and then to establish a real university, preferably in Chicago.[60]

Because of its broader organizational base, the Social Reform Union attracted more members than Bliss's previous ventures —the League of Christian Socialists, the American Fabian League, and the Union Reform League. The five hundred odd members of the Social Reform Union were spread among only eight states: California, New York, Illinois, Ohio, Missouri, Massachusetts, Pennsylvania, and Kansas.[61]

Yet, by no stretch of the imagination was the Social Reform Union either well knit or aggressively active; and, as national organizer, Bliss chafed under the lack of funds which compelled him to limit his activities to Alhambra, where he published the semi-monthly bulletin.[62] Bliss realized that if the Union was to maintain its national character, it would have to move its headquarters from the Far West. Consequently, in the autumn of 1899 he welcomed the decision of the National Executive Committee to transfer the central office to Chicago, where the National Christian Citizenship League,[63] which had been established in 1894 largely to propagate Herron's ideas of social Christianity, was working in the Union's behalf.

The presidential election of 1900 exemplified the divergent political views of the Social Reform Union leaders. Herron, it will be recalled, returned to the United States from the Middle

---

[60] Bemis to Vrooman, July 25, 1899; Bemis to Henry D. Lloyd, July 26, 1899; Lloyd to Richard T. Ely, July 19, 1899. Lloyd Papers.

[61] *Bulletin of the Social Reform Union,* No. 1 (Sept. 15, 1899), pp. 5-6.

[62] *Ibid.,* No. 4 (Nov. 1, 1899), pp. 4-5.

[63] The *Social Forum,* official journal of the NCCL, was the successor to the *Kingdom,* which suspended publication in 1899. It went even a little further than the paper of Gates and Herron in that it openly espoused socialism. Hopkins, *Rise of the Social Gospel in American Protestantism,* p. 197. John W. Leonard and Frederick G. Strickland were Editor and Associate Editor, respectively. *Social Forum,* I (June, 1899), 1. During 1900 the *Social Forum* carried the Social Reform Union studies by Edward W. Bemis, Frank Parsons, Reverend W. T. Brown, Louis F. Post, T. E. Will, George Fred Williams, R. A. Dague, Samuel M. Jones, and others.

East to join in the exciting campaign for Debs and Harriman and the Social Democratic Party. Jones and Bliss, on the other hand, supported the reformist Democratic Party.[64] McKinley's election, naturally, pleased no one.

During the spring of 1901 the Social Reform Union, now deserted by its more radical followers, held a referendum as to its future course of policy. Only a small part of the membership expressed an opinion with the vote standing at 41 to 19 in favor of forming a new social reform political party. Bliss, unhappy with this result, sought to salvage from it what he could. It reflected, he said, the insufficiency of any of the existing parties insofar as the Union's membership was concerned. But more indicative—and on this point there could be no dispute—was the very small vote of all of those who were circularized. This revealed that few were interested in starting a new party, Bliss maintained with a display of sophistry that was out of character. Any fears that the peripatetic Christian Socialist clergyman may have had on this score, proved groundless, since the Social Reform Union itself was due for extinction in the near future.[65]

The Social Reform Union ceased to be a going concern after the second National Social and Political Conference met in Detroit in June, 1901. Bliss did not attend, nor did many of the other reformers who had gathered in Buffalo. Herron, thoroughly disgusted with the timidity of reformers in general, and the Social Reform Union in particular, for refusing to back the Social Democratic Party, publicly scorned the conference. He saw no good coming from it.[66]

The conference opened in Detroit under far from ideal conditions. The city and the nation sweltered under one of the worst heat waves in years. The local press was filled with the names of persons who had collapsed from heat prostration. That the delegates remained away from many of the sessions was understandable.

H. Gaylord Wilshire, a former Nationalist and now publisher of a new socialist weekly, *The Challenge*, and A. M. Simons, the

[64]*Social Democratic Herald,* Sept. 22, 1900; *Worker,* June 9, 1900.
[65]*The Social Unity,* I (June, 1901), 81.
[66]*Worker,* June 23, 1901.

young editor of the *International Socialist Review*, represented
the Social Democratic Party and were among the most active
delegates.   Wilshire, egotistical, handsome, genial, and ambitious, was found insufferable by Debs and not a few other
socialists.[67]   But the wealthy Los Angeles resident possessed
an undeniable ability to win press notices.   In April, 1891, for
instance, he invited Professors William Graham Sumner and
Arthur T. Hadley of Yale to hear him lecture before the Trades
Council of New Haven on the topic: "Is the Yale College laissez-
faire theory of political economy false?" Neither Sumner nor
Hadley appeared, permitting Wilshire to boast that they were
afraid to accept his challenge.[68]   Wilshire's chief stock in trade
was his standing offer of $10,000 to William Jennings Bryan
to debate with him on the question of public ownership of the
trusts.   Wilshire, whose banker father was closely associated
with the Standard Oil Company, fancied himself an expert on
this particular topic, the motto of the *Challenge* being "Let
the Nation Own the Trusts."   Bryan ignored the offer of the
"millionaire socialist," but the Californian never allowed the
issue to drop.   Wherever he went he repeated his offer and thus
obtained for himself and his magazine much publicity in the
non-socialist press.   Simons, on the other hand, was one of the
few creative thinkers then active in the socialist movement. He
was probably the first person to write a history of the United
States within the framework of Marxian analysis.   At this time
he represented the Social Democratic Party's left wing.

Representatives of virtually every political shading and reformers for nearly every political cause had an opportunity to
speak their piece before the convention.   As at the Buffalo
and Chicago meetings, the debate eventually got around to
politics.   Joseph Parker, a middle-of-the-road Populist from
Kentucky, and Mayor Jones debated the relative merits of organizing a new party of political reform as against non-partisanship
in politics.[69]   Simons, who listened to the debate with complete
cynicism, later wrote that there had been hopes of forming at

[67] E. V. Debs to Frederic Heath, Jan. 3, 1903. Personal Papers of Frederic
Heath, Milwaukee, Wis. For a more complete account of Wilshire, see Ralph
Hancock, *Fabulous Boulevard* (New York, 1949), pp. 85-112.

[68] *People,* Apr. 26, 1891.

[69] *Detroit Journal,* July 1, 1901.

Detroit a "Fabian, anti-class struggle, initiative and referendum-first, confused and non-descript 'socialist' party."[70] Simons and Wilshire, as might be expected, pleaded with the convention to support the Social Democratic Party. The best they could obtain was the convention's approval of a resolution to send a delegation of observers to the Social Democratic unity convention which was to meet in Indianapolis later in the month.[71] At the same time, the convention voted not to pledge itself to endorse any political organization.

By shrewd parliamentary maneuvering, Wilshire and Simons nearly succeeded in placing the convention on record in favor of a series of resolutions which would have committed it to socialism and the Social Democratic Party. The first resolution, which stated that the worker should have the product of his labor, was easily adopted, 45 to 6. The second resolution, voted on favorably 43 to 9, asserted that the only guarantee of such a condition lay in the ownership of land and machinery by the producer himself. The third resolution proposed by the socialists stated that, since large scale industrial production was most economical and desirable, the people should own all land and machinery. The vote went 38 to 6 in support of the resolution. Having pushed the convention to this point, Simons and Wilshire drew out and successfully cashed their trump cards. A resolution that the government—national, state, and local— should own all land and machinery was passed 35 to 20. Another, that the convention should support a political party seeking these ends, was approved 27 to 20.[72]

But their success was short lived. Willis J. Abbot, a staunch supporter of William Jennings Bryan and leader of the "moderates" at the conference, was not present when the socialists were "wedge-driving" through their resolutions. When Abbot returned to the convention hall, just after the delegates had adopted the final two resolutions, he made a violent protest on the floor. After much wrangling the convention reversed its

---

[70]A. M. Simons, "The Detroit Conference," *International Socialist Review*, II (1901), 113.

[71]*Ibid.*, p. 114.

[72]*The Challenge,* II (July 17, 1901), 11.

position and, by the close vote of 35 to 30, decided to table the five resolutions.[73]

During the latter years of the 1890's several Fabian papers and magazines, including the *Coming Nation*, the *American Fabian*, the *Social Economist*, and the *Coming Light*, followed on the heels of one another in suspending publication, thereby reflecting the low ebb in the tide of social reform. The few that remained, such as Somerby's *Commonwealth*, were hard pressed to keep going from issue to issue. To help fill the vacuum caused by the cessation of so many Fabian organs, Rice H. Eaton and T. C. Easterling, two reformers from Kearney, Nebraska, began publication in April, 1900, of *The Socialist Review*, subsequently renamed *The Bellamy Review*, lest anyone mistake its Fabian bent. Within a few months Easterling withdrew from editorial direction of the paper and was replaced by Herbert N. Casson and his poetess-wife, the former Lydia K. Commander. Casson was now residing in New York where he was on the editorial staff of the *New York Journal*. With the exception of Bliss's short-lived *Social Unity*, the *Bellamy Review* was the last of the Fabian periodicals to be published before 1902.

The *Bellamy Review*'s editorial policy, by its own statement of principles, combined Mayor Samuel Jones's "Golden Rule" philosophy and the Christian Science precepts of Mary Baker Eddy. It proposed to substitute unity and universal brotherhood for strife and fear, to elevate men's thoughts to the highest ethical plane, to make them think of "palaces and mansions instead of hovels, poor houses, and jails," and of health and good instead of sickness and evil. In short, it aimed at "gently turning society upside down" so the laborer would obtain his just rewards while "the pampered drone" would be stripped of "his suit of purple and fine linen" which he wore without right.[74]

The *Bellamy Review*'s contents represented the fare of most contemporary socialist and reform journals. Appearing in its pages were the usual "news of the movement," "notes of socialist progress," reviews of books on social reform and economic problems, and articles dealing with socialist theory and practice.

---

[73]*Ibid.*, p. 11; *Detroit Free Press*, July 4, 1901.
[74]*Socialist Review*, I (1900), 1.

Besides the facile writing Casson, those contributing articles
of a more substantial nature were Morrison I. Swift, Samuel
Jones, and John Preston.

Swift, a Johns Hopkins Ph.D. in philosophy, who for over a
decade had hovered on the peripheries of anarchism and organized socialism on the one hand and religious unorthodoxy on the
other, argued forcefully against independent socialist political
action. This founder of a short-lived "Society of American Socialists," which was centered in San Francisco, began to doubt
the efficacy of socialist politics after failing to organize a "Public Ownership Party" in 1896.[75] Bryan's defeat in the national
election of that year conclusively clinched the argument.

Swift held that socialists could best engage in politics by
working outside the confines of institutionalized political parties. He proposed that as soon as a sufficiently large number
of persons became thoroughly indoctrinated with socialist principles, their leaders should meet shortly before election time,
organize a temporary political body, and nominate candidates.
If these candidates were elected, the political organization which
sponsored them would wither away upon their assumption of
office, like the Marxian state.[76]

Anarchistic rather than socialistic, this approach was quite
properly condemned by those socialists who were more appreciative of the organizational problems of American party politics. Among those subscribing heartily to it, however, was the
idealistic Samuel Jones. The Toledo mayor believed that political conventions had no more right to nominate candidates for
office than monarchs had to dispense them on the electorate.
Such a power lay within the sovereignty of the people. Jones
saw no hope in political progress until resort to party organization was abandoned, until others followed his lead. "I believe
in the absolute unity of the entire race," he wrote, "not in any
select crowd, whether party, sect, or whatever it be called."[77]
Jones maintained that he had no alternative other than to be
a socialist because he loved his fellow men. But he contended
that only socialist propaganda could bring men together under

---

[75]*Socialist,* II (Nov. 21, 1896), 3.

[76]*Bellamy Review,* I (1901), 366.

[77]*Socialist Review,* I (1900), 160-61.

the brotherhood of man. "I know," he exclaimed, "there are party Socialists and party Republicans who will have no trouble in 'riddling' my arguments. To them I simply desire to say that I do not seek to impose my mode of politics or religion or life on them or on anyone. I merely want to be a free soul and be true to the highest and best that is in me."[78]

John Preston, the last editor of the defunct *American Fabian*, called for a greater sense of realism among American middle-class radicals. The socialist millennium, "dawning" for the past twenty years, was still not visible on the horizon, nor was the world saturated with unrest and longing for change. Most non-socialists still were unwilling to concede that "selfishness and oppression" characterized the existing social order. The 1900 presidential election, with its overwhelming triumph for McKinley, bore testimony, in fact, to a general satisfaction with the status quo. The thoughtful Preston advised his fellow Fabians: "Look facts squarely in the face. Don't distress yourself with the idea that doing so may take away your 'enthusiasm.' You will probably do better work without enthusiasm than you have ever done with it."[79]

The editorials which Casson wrote for the *Bellamy Review* sounded thoroughly familiar to those who had read his articles in various socialist publications since 1896. He did not ask Fabians to hold back from practical politics, as such would be a crime against generations of patriots who had struggled to make the suffrage possible. But Fabians ought not to lose their reason in the hysteria of political campaigns. To think was better than to vote, and ultimately ideas became transformed into action.[80] As for the Marxists and their loose talk of immediate political revolution and assumption of power by the proletariat, Casson remarked:

> There are some wild agitators, who have cayenne pepper in their heads instead of brains, who want to establish socialism in a day. Their idea of social reform is to have a red flag on every saloon and a guillotine on every street corner. To offer such fanatics a plan that might take

---

[78]*Bellamy Review,* I (1900), 217.

[79]*Ibid.,* I (1901), 344-45.

[80]*Socialist Review,* I (1900), 155.

twenty years to do its work would be like offering a cigarette to an opium fiend.[81]

Another short-lived, contemporaneous Fabian review was *Social Unity*, edited by the indefatigable Bliss. The Christian Socialist clergyman was able to get out only a few issues of the little paper in 1901 before being obliged to suspend its publication, but its opposition to the class-struggle thesis and to party socialism was clearly discernible. By this time Bliss had become convinced of the inadvisability of Fabians' seeking to permeate the Democratic Party. Instead of being courageously for the people, he maintained, it was rather a party of "magnificent negations," anti-imperialist, anti-trust, and anti-gold.[82] But Bliss found little better the Social Democratic Party to which George Herron had attached himself. The factional strife then existing within the Social Democratic ranks illustrated the evils attendant on the party system in general and on a class party in particular.[83]

The literature of American Fabian socialism was enriched by the publication of Edward Bellamy's *Equality*, a sequel to *Looking Backward*, in 1897, and Laurence Gronlund's *The New Economy* in 1898. Ironically, both Bellamy and Gronlund died the year after their works were published.

In completing *Equality*, Bellamy wrote desperately against time, for tuberculosis was steadily sapping his waning strength. The book's publication was a triumph of his indomitable will. Its reception by the general public, however, was disappointing. The popular success of *Looking Backward* was not repeated, partially because the element of novelty of the utopian novel had worn off, but mainly because *Equality*, in spite of its flimsy utopian facade, was a work that did not admit of casual and uncritical reading. In *Equality* were found Bellamy's most mature thinking and his most cogent analysis of American institutions. Much of the same pointed, incisive criticism which characterized Thorstein Veblen's *Theory of the Leisure Class* appeared in a more direct and readable form in *Equality*.

[81]*Ibid.* pp. 103-4.
[82]*Social Unity*, I (Jan., 1901), 4.
[83]*Ibid.*, pp. 7-8.

Bellamy wrote in *Equality* that the beginnings of the revolution currently transforming the United States into a co-operative commonwealth first became evident in 1873. In that year of economic panic Americans first became generally aware of the "irrepressible conflict" between democracy and plutocracy, the former standing for equal rights for all and the latter for their suppression in the interests of special privilege. For approximately a quarter of a century plutocracy prevailed, in large measure because it controlled the nation politically under a thinly veiled dictatorship. The puny forces of organized workers were overpowered either by resort to state militia or by lockouts, blacklists, and other similar anti-labor devices. Agrarians were kept in rein and in bondage by the plutocracy's control of credit and mortgages. Fear of unemployment cowed the masses, always one step removed from the grim specter of famine.[84]

Living in oriental pomp and luxury and ever seeking to ape the European aristocracy, the masters of American industrial capitalism practiced a hypocritical and ostentatious form of public charity and philanthropy in an attempt to maintain the status quo and their own position of dominance. They also utilized the services of a host of minions who sought to influence public opinion. But such efforts were in vain. Beginning with the agrarian unrest in the 1890's the forces in opposition to the plutocracy, united by a growing lack of economic opportunity, gradually took charge of the nation. The rule of the aristocracy of wealth was replaced by a new, fraternal, socialistic order, one that brought general economic security and opportunity, a purified political democracy, and a more ethical way of life.[85]

The way to the co-operative commonwealth was by no means a primrose path. The plutocracy had erected stout defenses, and its retainers who were chiefly responsible for forming public opinion,—namely, the journalists, the academicians, and the clergy—fought a last-ditch battle before capitulating.

Bellamy did not make a blanket indictment of the press, for he conceded that a few papers were controlled by men of independence and high principle. Nevertheless, he argued cogently

[84]Bellamy, *Equality,* pp. 9-13, 70-91, 307-11.
[85]*Ibid.,* pp. 153-95.

that American journalism was the handmaiden of the nation's capitalistic interests. The large metropolitan newspaper, he pointed out, was itself a big business enterprise, requiring a considerable amount of investment capital, and hence was inevitably owned by men of wealth. Furthermore, urban dailies, dependent upon corporate enterprise for advertising, could not afford to espouse policies opposed by the capitalist class. The distorted picture which the reading public received resulted in large measure from the monopolization of facilities for gathering and disseminating news. In reality, Bellamy claimed, the press in America exercised a censorship "almost as effective as that prevailing at the same time in Russia or Turkey."[86]

Harnessed by "golden chains" to the chariot of the plutocracy were the institutions of higher learning in the United States. Relying on the benefactions of the rich, in some instances for their very existence, colleges and universities were obliged to muzzle those professors who dared to find fault with the status quo. Academic freedom prevailed, if at all, only in those subjects which were completely remote from the present, such as the dead languages. And lastly, since colleges and universities had to depend on the small well-to-do class for their enrollments, they were not likely to allow themselves to become instruments for social and economic progress.[87]

Compared to the clergy, the journalists and academicians got off lightly, for Bellamy's criticism of American Protestant churches and churchmen was not marked by restraint. In a torrent of Social Gospel criticism, the pastor's son scored the various denominations for obsequiousness to the wealthy, for lack of concern for the economically less privileged, for preoccupation with arid theologies and false finalities, and for a pessimistic outlook on the possibilities of man in the here and now. He conceded that many among the clergy were not guilty of these sins, but the majority of the churchmen of the late nineteenth century were men "who thought the cornerstone of Christianity was the right of property and the supreme crime was the wrongful expropriation of property.[88]

[86]*Ibid.*, p. 335.
[87]*Ibid.*, pp. 335-36, 401.
[88]*Ibid.*, pp. 114, 258-68, 340-47.

If Edward Bellamy had written *Equality* while fighting a losing battle against the white plague, Laurence Gronlund had waged a desperate struggle against poverty while writing *The New Economy*—by his own analysis his "most mature work." During the height of the Nationalist movement, he had given up the security of a position as statistician in the office of Commissioner of Labor Carroll D. Wright, to evangelize the socialist gospel from lecture podium and street-corner soapbox throughout the length and breadth of the United States.[89] While lecturing suited Gronlund temperamentally, particularly when addressing groups of college students among whom he hoped to organize a national socialist fraternity, it failed woefully to give him sufficient income on which to live. Often an empty wallet obliged the shabbily dressed Dane to sleep in parks or under steps, and on more than one evening he had to go without dinner.[90] In October, 1898, the year in which *The New Economy* was published, Gronlund wrote pathetically to Henry Demarest Lloyd:

> The next three months will be a serious time for me. I think a man has a right to commit suicide
> 1) When he is troubled with an incurable disease—that is not the case with me.
> 2) When he cannot procure the means of living and thus can be of no further use. That unfortunately is the prospect with which I am threatened.[91]

Through the help of Lloyd and a group of Chicago friends, Gronlund was carried over this crisis,[92] and shortly thereafter he obtained employment as an editorial writer on the *New York Journal*. But he was not to enjoy for long the relative degree of comfort and well-being that his new job could afford him. On October 15, 1899, almost a year to the week after he had written his despairing note to Lloyd, Gronlund died suddenly at the age of fifty-five.[93]

[89]L. Gronlund, "Une Tournée Missionaire Socialiste à travers Les États-Unis," *Revue d'Économie Politique*, X (1896), 687.

[90]*Social Democracy Red Book,* p. 101.

[91]Gronlund to Lloyd, Oct. 20, 1898. Lloyd Papers.

[92]Lloyd to Dwight H. Perkins, Nov. 1, 1898. Lloyd Papers.

[93]*New York Times,* Oct. 17, 1899.

In *The New Economy* Gronlund reaffirmed his faith in socialism, though he preferred to call himself a "collectivist." He
hailed it as the working out of evolutionary tendencies and as
a manifestation of Divine will. Sooner or later all humanity
must reach the co-operative commonwealth irrespective of
whether it be a resting place on the road of progress or the
final goal toward which all history pointed.[94]

In the United States, said Gronlund, "the Power behind evolution" had destined the floriation of gigantic trusts. The trust
was indeed the "clincher of the resistless logic of events." It
was the womb in which socialism had been conceived and out of
which it was to be born. And the birth would be without pain,
for to place the well-unified trust organizations under government ownership would be a comparatively simple procedure.
A socialist economy could be ushered in peacefully and without
great derangements. The trust was, in truth, a blessing in dis-
guise, and it was to the interest of those concerned with the
welfare of struggling humanity to encourage rather than to
discourage large-scale industrial combination.[95]

Another factor conducive to the coming socialist order was
the absence among the American people of sharp class-distinc-
tions which existed in other countries. This condition had been
one of the primary reasons for the nation's great development
in the past, and American socialists of the present would do
well to recognize its value and uniqueness. Socialism rested
fundamentally on the brotherhood of all men, not just a single
class. To channelize American socialism into a class movement
would be the greatest imaginable misfortune to the country and
the cause. "God preserve us here from such a doctrine," said
Gronlund. "We should have friends of our cause among all
classes."[96]

Pause and take stock, Gronlund urged his fellow socialists
in the United States. The 1896 presidential election had proved
conclusively that the nation was completely unprepared for a
radical change. A whole generation of men and women had
to be educated in the principles of socialism before the co-op-

[94]Laurence Gronlund, *The New Economy,* pp. 18, 37.
[95]*Ibid.,* pp. 15-35.
[96]*Ibid.,* pp. 10-11, 63.

erative commonwealth could possibly become an actuality. While hitherto reformers had taken for their motto "Agitation, Organization, and Education," it was now necessary to change to "Educate, Educate, Educate." The armies of reform were at hand and ready for action, but they were unprepared—a "dangerous condition" which the late campaign had made painfully clear. An educated leadership was sorely needed, and it was the task of the coming generation to create one. What the individual could do, and ought to do, was "first to educate himself and others; next, organize for education; and lastly and mainly, learn to discern and follow the direction in which the finger of the World Will points."[97]

If Fabian socialists were to follow Gronlund's advice, no marriage, either official or unofficial, could unite them with their brethren who were at this very time laying the foundations for the Socialist Party of America, which, after many near miscarriages, was born in 1901. In England, the Fabian Society, after no little end of temporizing, finally came to the support of the Independent Labor Party. In the United States, however, the Social Reform Union, the closest American counterpart of the British Fabian Society, did not endorse the Socialist Party. The more radical and politically minded members of the Social Reform Union allowed their memberships to lapse, and it was not long before the Union itself dissolved. For those who did not follow George D. Herron into the socialist camp, there was a new outlet in "muckraking," which was becoming both popular and fashionable during the early years of the twentieth century. But, surprisingly enough, the Fabian reformers of the 1890's played relatively minor roles in the muckraking era and some, like Casson, went over into the camp of the enemy. Many had given up in despair, while others had fallen by the wayside on the long and hard road to social and political regeneration.

How, then, shall the Fabians be evaluated? Here one must bear in mind, of course, that the Fabians, accepting the "inevitability of gradualness," projected their goals into the distant future. But now that the future may be said to be at hand, one can hardly assert that their objectives have been appreciably

97 *Ibid.*, pp. 11, 343-44, 363-64.

realized. In terms of concrete achievements, they rate a low
score, and in popularizing socialism amongst the middle class—
the Bellamy movement excluded—they did not enjoy any widespread success. One would be hard pressed also to show how and
where the Fabians succeeded in permeating the older parties
with their doctrines. In one area they did leave their impress
—in publicizing direct legislation. But even here it must be
remembered that they were only one of many groups seeking the
political reforms that were widely adopted during the progressive era.

IX. The Communitarians' Last Stand

In SENTENCING Eugene V. Debs to a jail term of six months for defying a court injunction during the tempestuous 1894 Pullman Strike, Federal Circuit Court Judge William A. Woods helped to further the transformation of a wage-conscious labor leader into a class-conscious socialist. In the homelike atmosphere of the little McHenry County jail in Woodstock, Illinois, Debs crowded the reading of several socialist books and pamphlets into a busy and highly organized daily routine. His constant stream of visitors included many socialists, among them Victor Berger, Thomas J. Morgan, and Keir Hardie, the last having recently arrived from England for an extended lecture tour. During the evening hours between eight and ten, Debs habitually discussed socialism and social and economic reform with six other American Railway Union officials who were with him at Woodstock serving three-months sentences.[1]

Debs was impressed by the relevancy of the general Marxist critique of contemporary economic life and particularly by its contention that the economically dominant class always controlled a nation's political and judicial machinery. The cogency and reality of this analysis had been revealed to him in the crushing of the Pullman Strike through a court injunction secured by the General Managers' Association. In Judge Woods, a friend of the railroads, and in his colleague, Judge Peter Grosscup, a pronounced foe of labor unions, the Association possessed a pair of obedient servants willing and eager to accom-

---

[1] In general, the most satisfactory and scholarly biography of Debs is Ray Ginger's *The Bending Cross, A Biography of Eugene Victor Debs* (New Brunswick, 1949). Also see McAlister Coleman, *Eugene V. Debs: A Man Unafraid* (New York, 1930); Floy Ruth Painter, *That Man Debs and His Life Work* (Bloomington, Ind., 1929); H. T. Schnittkind, *The Story of Eugene V. Debs* (Boston, 1929); David Karsner, *Debs, His Authorized Life and Letters* (New York, 1919); H. M. Morais and William Cahn, *Gene Debs: The Story of a Fighting American* (New York, 1948); August Claessens, *Eugene Victor Debs: A Tribute* (Pamphlet; New York, 1946).

plish its ends.[2] What chance, then, had ordinary trade unionism, when the cards of the prevailing economic system were so thoroughly stacked against it?[3]

Before Debs entered Woodstock he was not a socialist, and, popular legend to the contrary, it may be seriously doubted whether he was one when he left. Woodstock gave him no sudden revelations; it was rather a conditioning experience. During his incarceration, it was true, Debs talked in airy generalities to reporters. He called the co-operative commonwealth "the hope of the world"[4] and spoke glibly of the need of emancipating labor from the "grinding, degrading, pauperizing conspiracy" against it. But he also urged workers to "eschew all ISMS" in their common struggle against the plutocracy.[5] Not once did Debs do more than acknowledge a sympathy for the ultimate goals of socialism.

After leaving Woodstock, Debs looked to the People's Party as the best means of combating and crushing the power of organized wealth. But the Democratic-Populist coalition, which he had ardently supported, failed in the supreme test in 1896. What next? Loyal but despairing members of the disintegrating American Railway Union importuned their leader for words of council and a sign of hope. On New Year's Day, 1897, he answered with a declaration of faith in socialism.

In making what was probably the most momentous decision of his life, Debs acknowledged the enormity of his error in having backed Bryan and the Populists in the hope that their victory "would blunt the fangs of the money power." But socialism, happily, provided a means of correcting that mistake. The socialists had shown the "toiling masses" the way out of the existing political and economic labyrinth. He, for one, was going to take it, not only as an escape route from the degradation and oppression of the present but also as a highway to happiness for the future. No person who loved humanity and opposed

[2]See Almont Lindsay, *The Pullman Strike: The Story of a Unique Experiment and of a Great Labor Upheaval* (Chicago, 1942) ; Ginger, *The Bending Cross,* pp. 108-51.

[3]*Social Democrat,* Nov. 4, Nov. 18, 1897.

[4]*Railway Times,* July 15, 1895.

[5]*Ibid.,* Mar. 15, 1895.

the "degeneracy of the race" could be other than a socialist. The capitalistic system had become completely cannibalistic, and the time had come to regenerate society. The eve of universal change was at hand. Bluntly, the issue was socialism versus capitalism.[6]

While the general press greeted Debs's espousal of socialism with derisive "I-told-you-so's" or with questioning of his sanity, socialists were jubilant. Debs undeniably commanded respect and support from thousands of American workers. His conversion to the cause, consequently, was an event of prime importance. Victor Berger learned the news at the Milwaukee Passavant Hospital, where he was recovering from an operation. Frederick Heath, who brought him the tidings, recalled that Berger "almost leaped out of his bed in joy." The two men at once composed a letter of congratulations to Debs. They also broached the possibility of forming a new socialist party.[7]

Daniel DeLeon, usually quick to pass editorial judgment, reserved opinion as to the sincerity of Debs's new faith. Despite Debs's support of the Populists in 1896, DeLeon retained a warm regard for the union leader of whom he had written in 1894: "Of all the trade union leaders in America none is so justly popular as Eugene V. Debs."[8] Earlier in the same year DeLeon had predicted in the *People* that Debs would probably flounder for a while but that eventually he would join the socialist ranks.[9] Now that his prediction had been substantiated, the curious DeLeon waited to see just what kind of a socialist Debs would be. DeLeon's chief Chicago lieutenant advised that Debs bore close watching in view of his flirtations with the Brotherhood of the Co-operative Commonwealth.[10]

Next to the Kaweah Colony in California, the Ruskin Co-operative Association, and the Social Gospel radicals who established the Christian Commonwealth Colony in Georgia, the Brotherhood of the Co-operative Commonwealth was the most

---

[6]*Ibid.,* Jan. 1, 1897.

[7]Address by Frederic Heath before the Wisconsin Socialist Party State Convention in Milwaukee, June, 1940. Mr. Heath gave the author a copy of his address.

[8]*People,* Dec. 16, 1894.

[9]*Ibid.,* Aug. 12, 1894.

[10]Barney Berlyn to DeLeon, Jan. 1, 1897. DeLeon Papers.

widely known of the various communitarian groups, fellowship leagues, and co-operative societies that flickered in and out of existence during the 1890's.[11] The Brotherhood, brainchild of an obscure Thomaston, Maine, reformer, Norman Wallace Lermond, was founded in the autumn of 1895 on the basis of a three-point program. Its modest aim was to educate Americans in the principles of socialism. Its ambitious long-range goal was to unite all co-operationists in the United States into "one vast fraternal organization." Its immediate and most important objective was to colonize en masse a sparsely inhabited Western state with persons desiring to live in socialist communities. Once established, the colonists would be in a position to capture control of the state's government and lay the foundation for a socialist commonwealth.

For approximately a year the Brotherhood of the Co-operative Commonwealth was confined to three puny chapters in Maine—a hardly impressive beginning for an organization that aimed at revolutionizing the entire institutional life of the nation. But Lermond was a letter-writing dynamo, and he bombarded reformers throughout the country with appeals for assistance. He received enough sympathetic replies to encourage him to go on. Frank Parsons, impressed by his proposed educational plan, pledged his aid. Imogene C. Fales, the Bensonhurst, New York, reformer who was a charter member of innumerable humanitarian and socialist movements in the 1880's and 1890's, agreed to serve with Lermond as co-organizer.[12] Henry Demarest Lloyd, whose financial generosity helped to sustain many a weak reform organization, was invited to assume the presidency of the Brotherhood, if and when it became a national body.

Constantly on the alert for occasions to publicize the aims of the Brotherhood, Lermond sensed such an opportunity at the National Co-operative Congress scheduled to be held in St. Louis simultaneously with the 1896 national convention of the People's Party.[13] Both Lermond and Mrs. Fales were Populist delegates

---

[11]Kerby, *Le Socialisme aux États Unis,* pp. 69-89; Caro Lloyd, *Henry Demarest Lloyd,* I, 45-46, 52-53; Reverend Alexander Kent, "Co-operative Communities in the U. S.," *Bulletin of the Department of Labor,* Vol. VI, No. 35 (July, 1901), pp. 604-12, 617-18. For Marxist criticism, see *People,* Aug. 6, 1893; Jan. 6, 1895.

[12]Lermond to Lloyd, Mar. 31, 1896. Lloyd Papers.

[13]*Coming Nation,* May 16, 1896.

and hence would be on hand. Reformers from all parts of the country would be present. Here was an occasion not to be missed. Lermond wrote to the reform press that the national organization of the Brotherhood would be proposed at the Congress.[14]

Lermond accomplished absolutely nothing at St. Louis because the National Co-operative Congress itself proved a dismal failure. The protracted sessions of the People's Party convention and the complete domination of "the political craze" reduced those attending the Congress to less than a hundred.[15] Even Lermond, conceivably with good reason, found it impossible to tear himself away from the Populist convention to sit in on the Congress, of which he was a sponsor. The garrulity of those who did attend did not make for any considerable concrete achievement. In disgust, the St. Louis communitarian, Alcander Longley, reported: "So much of the time was taken up in speech making, some of which was not relative to the subject, that no opportunity was afforded for the reports, proposals, and discussions which some of the members desired."[16] The Congress' sole accomplishment was the organization of the American Co-operative Union headed by Alonzo Wardell of Topeka, Kansas, as president and the energetic Mrs. Fales as secretary.[17] The Union, like Lermond's proposed plan, aimed at uniting all of the co-operationists in the United States into one huge federated body. It was only a few months, however, before Wardell and Mrs. Fales were in violent disagreement as to how this should be accomplished,[18] and by the spring of 1897 the American Co-operative Union had disappeared into the limbo of ambitious but lost reform causes.

Immediately after the St. Louis Co-operative Congress, the *Coming Nation* became a quasi-official paper for the Brotherhood of the Co-operative Commonwealth. This development resulted in columns of free and much needed publicity for Lermond. In early September, a national Brotherhood organization

---

[14]*Ibid.*, June 27, 1896.

[15]*Ibid.*, Aug. 1, 1896.

[16]*Altruist*, XXVIII (Aug., 1896), 29.

[17]*Coming Nation*, Aug. 1, 1896.

[18]Fales to Henry D. Lloyd, Jan. 21, 1896. Lloyd Papers.

was finally consummated through the medium of a referendum conducted by the Ruskin Colony paper. "Elected" to the Brotherhood's offices were: Henry Demarest Lloyd, president; Norman Wallace Lermond, secretary; B. Franklin Hunter, treasurer; Frank Parsons, dean; Morrison I. Swift, national organizer; A. S. Edwards, editor-in-chief; and J. E. Dean, master workman.[19] All of those elected accepted their positions, save Lloyd and Hunter. Lloyd doubted the soundness of the colonization scheme. He did, however, contribute ten dollars to help the Brotherhood achieve a favorable financial balance of $3.44 as of October 17, 1896.[20] Rebuffed by Lloyd, the Brotherhood turned to the Reverend Myron Reed, the Denver Christian Socialist, who agreed to take the presidency.

McKinley's crushing victory in the 1896 presidential election sent many discouraged, poverty-stricken "little" men staggering into the Brotherhood. Blacklisted union members also turned hopefully to the new organization. By June of the next year the Brotherhood had 125 branches and a membership of over 2,000.[21] In February, the *Coming Nation* had announced that 107 members had pledged nearly $45,000 to be used for colonizing a Western state, preferably Washington.[22]

This was the organization in which Debs, the tyro, made his debut into socialism. In the same month that he had announced his adherence to the cause of the co-operative commonwealth, he succeeded Swift as the Brotherhood's national organizer. Surely this was not what his socialist friends had hoped of him. With good reason they feared that failure of the utopian-tinged Brotherhood might chill his new found ardor for socialism.[23] Berger and Heath in Milwaukee and Seymour Stedman in Chicago attempted to convince him that he was on the wrong road to socialism and that the correct approach was by way of socialist political action.

Berger was especially anxious to wean Debs away from the Brotherhood since he was at the very time sounding out Lloyd

---

[19]Lermond to Lloyd, Sept. 21, 1896. Lloyd Papers.

[20]Lermond to Lloyd, July 16, 1896. Lloyd Papers. *Coming Nation*, Oct. 17, 1896.

[21]*Coming Nation*, June 26, 1897.

[22]*Ibid.*, Feb. 6, 1897.

[23]Berger to Lloyd, Jan. (n. d.), 1897. Lloyd Papers.

and others regarding the formation of a new socialist political
party.[24]   Aggressive, vindictive, and outspoken, Berger was one
of the shrewdest socialists in the Middle West.   Born in Austria-
Hungary in 1860 and educated at the Universities of Vienna
and Budapest, he had migrated to the United States in 1878.
Despite his excellent education, he found employment difficult
to obtain.   Before settling permanently in Milwaukee in 1881,
he had polished metals, mended boilers, sold leather goods, and
punched cattle.   In Milwaukee Berger taught school and took
an active interest in German Turner affairs.   In 1892, he assumed the editorship of the *Milwaukee Arbeiter-Zeitung*, the
oldest established socialist daily in the United States.   He
changed its name to the *Wisconsin Vorwaerts*.   The new editor
was largely responsible for reinvigorating the city's languishing
socialist movement.[25]

Berger had been willing to co-operate with the People's Party
in Wisconsin because he considered himself above all things a
political realist.   Yet he was not willing to tolerate or to accept
willy-nilly those disgruntled Populists who, after the 1896 election debacle, suddenly decided that they were socialists without
having the slightest realization of what socialism involved.   If
these self-professed socialists were to be of use in the achievement of the co-operative commonwealth, they had to be grounded
in socialist fundamentals.[26]

Socialist fundamentals did not necessarily preclude the adap-
tation of Marxist theory to meet concrete situations.   And in this
regard Berger developed a working position that foreshadowed
the revisionist critique of Eduard Bernstein, the contemporary
German socialist theoretician.   If socialism were to gain a mass
following in the United States, Berger held, it would have to
cater pragmatically to the everyday needs of the American
people.   The co-operative commonwealth on the far distant horizon offered a glorious millennial hope, but the average American

[24]Berger to Lloyd, Jan. 11, 1897. Lloyd Papers.
[25]*Social Democracy Red Book*, p. 107; Commons (ed.), *History of Labor
in the United States*, IV, 225-26; Fine, *Labor and Farmer Parties in the
United States, 1828-1928*, p. 192; Wachman, *History of the Social Democratic
Party of Milwaukee, 1897-1910*, p. 10; Still, *Milwaukee, The History of a City*,
p. 303; Hillquit, *Loose Leaves from a Busy Life*, p. 53.
[26]Commons, IV, 226.

was interested primarily in a socialist program for current action. Hence, Berger maintained, socialists ought to pitch their appeal, especially on the local, urban level, on concrete everyday problems demanding immediate solution. Particularly did they need to win trade-union support.

Berger's enormous influence over his fellow Milwaukee socialists was reflected in the platform on which socialist candidates ran in the 1898 municipal election. It demanded an end to the sale or gift of franchises for public utilities and services; greater taxation of large corporations; city employment, where possible, of the unemployed; appointment by the city of public defenders to conduct legal cases for the economically underprivileged; extension of free medical care to the poor, through municipally paid physicians; erection of at least three additional public baths; condemnation of all slum areas; free schools and adequate educational facilities for all; at least one municipally arranged, free symphony concert a month; half-holidays on all election days; abolition of the contract system for public work; and employment, wherever possible, of union labor on jobs given out by contract.[27]

Berger had been a lone wolf in socialist politics. The *Volkszeitung*–Rosenberg-Busche split in the Socialist Labor Party in 1889 found him on the side of the Lasalleans. For many years his estimates of other socialists were largely predicated on their stand in this particular controversy. However, he apparently did not join the impotent Social Democratic Federation which the dissident Rosenberg-Busche faction organized in 1896 in the hope of capitalizing on the intensifying conflict within the Socalist Labor Party on trade-union tactics.[28]

One of Berger's most important converts to socialism was Frederic Heath, reporter and art editor for the *Milwaukee Sentinel*. Here was a *rara avis* for the Milwaukee socialist movement, for not only was Heath a native-born American but also he could trace his ancestry to seventeenth-century New England. He had come gradually into socialism via membership in the Liberal Club and the Milwaukee Ethical Club, two or-

[27]*Social Democrat*, Feb. 10, 1898.
[28]Kerby, p. 58.

ganizations devoted to discussion of contemporary social, economic, and intellectual problems. He had also served an apprenticeship in the People's Party before Berger proudly exhibited him at a local *Sozialistische Verein* meeting as the "first Milwaukee Yankee Socialist."[29]

Seymour Stedman, a Chicago attorney, was another ally of Berger. A native New Englander, Stedman, like Heath, claimed ancestry far back into the American past. In 1881, the year in which Berger came to Milwaukee, Stedman settled in Chicago where he found employment first in an iron foundry and then with Western Union. Dissatisfied, he decided to study law and was admitted to the Illinois bar in 1891. Interest in politics, a hallmark for many a young lawyer, brought him first into the Democratic Party and then into the Populist Party, which, on two different occasions, sponsored his candidacy for city attorney and state attorney. Stedman opposed the Populist-Democratic fusion but supported Bryan in 1896. The collapse of the fusionists found him scurrying into the socialist camp. His background indicated that he was not to be a rigid doctrinaire.[30]

Berger, Heath, and Stedman failed to shake Debs's faith in the colonization scheme of the Brotherhood of the Co-operative Commonwealth. The plan's magnetism lay in the possibility of its providing a refuge for the unemployed, discouraged, and blacklisted American Railway Union men[31] whose welfare was closer to Debs's heart than political socialism. He was sufficiently realistic, however, to know that the Brotherhood's leaders were well intentioned but ineffectual. In its existing organizational form, the Brotherhood could not offer the immediate relief which the railroad men needed. Therefore Debs decided to part company with the Brotherhood, but to use its colonization scheme for the benefit of the suffering Railway Union workers. If he had been unable to lead them to victory as industrial unionists, he would at least seek to guide them to the

---

[29] Address by Frederic Heath before the Wisconsin Socialist Party State Convention, June, 1940; *Social Democracy Red Book,* p. 113; Heath, "How I Became a Socialist," *Comrade,* II (1903), 154-55.

[30] *Social Democracy Red Book,* pp. 116-17.

[31] Ginger, pp. 178-80.

co-operative commonwealth. Accordingly, he issued a call to
the union's membership to meet in special convention at Chicago
on June 15, 1897.

In a letter to the *New York Journal* before the convention,
Debs acknowledged the bankruptcy of the American Railway
Union as a labor organization. It had, however, a new mission.
The union's old structure would serve as a framework for a
national association of men and women seeking to bring about
a new co-operative social order. Such an organization, because
of its very nature, would be open to all men and women regardless of race, color, or previous servitude. Debs reported "some
of the foremost men in the reform movement" had agreed to co-
operate in any plan adopted by the convention to colonize a
Western state.[32]

Prior to the conclave Debs significantly made no mention of
a socialist political party, except acknowledging that one would
eventually be formed to secure government control of the state
to be earmarked for colonization. The example of a socialist
commonwealth operating successfully in one state would induce
people in others to throw off the yoke of capitalistic government.[33] "Unduly excited persons who fear this to be an exodus
of 'bums' and 'beats' may possess souls in patience," said Debs.
And he added parenthetically that those persons who went into
paroxysms of fear at the "mere mention of the Ragged Army
of the Republic" were invariably the very ones responsible for
its existence.[34]

When the American Railway Union meeting opened in Chicago, it was evident that the delegates would follow Debs in
whatever direction he saw fit to lead them. Despite the union's
dire straits, he still commanded an intense personal devotion.
Heath, Berger, and Stedman realized that a crisis was at hand.
If Debs could not be steered away at least partially from the
colonization project, the immediate future might be dark indeed
for socialist political action independent of the Socialist Labor
Party. Their feelings were shared by Charles R. Martin of
Tiffin, Ohio, a former dignitary in the Knights of Labor, a

---

[32]*New York Journal,* Apr. 17, 1897.
[33]*Ibid.*
[34]*Railway Times,* June 1, 1897.

recent accession to the socialist ranks, and a delegate to the convention. The four men consequently teamed up in a last-ditch effort to commit to political socialism whatever new organization might come out of the convention. It called for great personal sacrifice from Heath and Berger, who commuted daily to the convention from Milwaukee. According to Heath's recollection forty-three years later:

> Each afternoon Victor and I took a train to Chicago, spent the evening in the old McCoy Hotel in South Clark Street, planning with Debs the moves next day in the convention. When the two of us left the hotel about midnight we had some four hours to kill before the earliest Milwaukee train. We tried to catch a few winks of sleep in the depot, but a watchful policeman kept interfering. The next night after leaving the hotel we wandered into the entrance of the Y. M. C. A. in Lasalle Street, dark as a pocket, and tried to sleep on the stairs. But after an hour or more we were both rudely awakened by blows on the soles of our shoes. The night watchman was giving us the hotfoot. We did not argue the matter but resumed our wanderings.[35]

The highlight of the opening session was Debs's hour-long address delivered in his own inimitable style. Pacing nervously up and down the speakers' platform, gesturing frequently, and in a voice vibrant with intensity, he told the delegates that they were not assembled as representatives of organized labor. Rather, they were the vanguard of a great new humanitarian movement which aimed to better the condition of men and women whose only "capital" consisted of "their brains and their hands." The convention's purpose was not to denounce the rich, but rather to lay the foundation for a new social and socialized order.

Debs asserted pointedly that the abolition of the wage system was not to be achieved overnight. Alluding to DeLeon and his followers, he said he had no quarrel with those who desired the immediate effectuation of a socialist order. He was sure that both they and he were working for the same goal. But while it was "well enough to extoll the beauties of the ideal system," declared Debs, immediate action was necessary because millions were suffering under the weight of capitalistic oppres-

---

[35]Address by Frederic Heath before the Wisconsin Socialist Party State Convention, June, 1940.

sion. The action, dictated by "common sense," was the establishment of a co-operative commonwealth in a Western state.

Debs professed not to know whether the entire industrial question could be settled peacefully, but he thought that it could. In any event, a colonization effort was going to be made. If, by chance, in defiance of the Constitution, federal troops were sent to prevent it, they would not only be kept busy in their march across the country but upon reaching the state line of the socialist commonwealth would be confronted by "300,000 patriots ready to receive them."[36]

Debs was followed on the rostrum by Frank Parsons who spoke for the Brotherhood of the Co-operative Commonwealth, which obviously was being short-circuited. Parsons acknowledged the handwriting on the wall insofar as the Brotherhood's role at the convention was concerned. He intimated, however, that the Brotherhood would continue on in spite of Debs's impending desertion. Parsons explained to the railroad men that neither he nor the other officers contemplated the American Railway Union merging voluntarily with the Brotherhood. But neither could it be expected, he said, for the Brotherhood to throw in its lot with a "labor union." Eventually, perhaps, the two organizations might join forces, but only on the condition that the resulting association would not be limited to the "laboring classes so-called." The Fabian Parsons maintained that any organization which combined the memberships of the Brotherhood and the American Railway Union would have to be "broad enough to include the doctors, lawyers, ministers, artisans, laboring men, and the unemployed—everybody who believes in co-operation and is willing to do his or her share of the world's work."[37]

Once it became apparent that the Brotherhood of the Co-operative Commonwealth was not destined to be a factor at the convention, the delegates began to act on plans outlined by Debs to convert the American Railway Union into "The Social Democracy of America." By the end of the third day the affairs of the old American Railway Union were closed, and the new

[36]*Railway Times,* June 15, 1897; *Chicago Times-Herald,* June 22, 1897.
[37]*Coming Nation,* July 3, 1897.

Social Democracy had adopted a Declaration of Principles, a political program, and an economic program. The colonization plan, of course, was provided for in the economic program, but Victor Berger's fine Viennese hand was evident in the political program.[38]

The Declaration of Principles closely resembled that of the now defunct Nationalist movement. It emphasized the discrepancy between the political equality and the economic inequality of the American people. It considered the former useless under an economic system "essentially destructive of life, liberty, and happiness." The direct opposition of the despotic system of economics and the democratic system of politics, said the Declaration, could be traced to the existence of a class which "corrupts the government, alienates public property, public franchises, and public functions, and holds this, the mightiest of nations, in abject dependence." This same class helped to divorce workers from ownership of the means of production, appropriated a disproportionate share of their labor, and slowly wore down members of the middle class to a proletarian status.

Concluding with an appeal to the people of the United States to overthrow the existing unjust economic system, the Declaration called upon "all honest citizens to unite under the banner of the Social Democracy of America, so that we may be ready to conquer capitalism by making use of our political liberty and by taking possession of the public power, so that we may put an end to the present barbarous struggle, by the abolition of capitalism, the restoration of land and of all the means of production, transportation, and distribution, to the people as a collective body."

---

[38]After Debs's defection the Brotherhood limped along though seriously weakened by the desertion of many members to the Social Democracy. Out of its plan to colonize a state with thousands of co-operationists, it was able to establish but one small colony, "Equality," in Edison, Washington, which lasted approximately a year. Lermond lost control of the Brotherhood in 1898. He later claimed he never favored establishing a single colony but that his views had not prevailed in a referendum vote on the issue by the membership. Countering this contention are letters to Lloyd which by no means indicate his opposition. Lermond to Lloyd, Aug. 31 and Nov. 26, 1897. Lloyd Papers. By the end of 1898 Lermond was again busy founding an "Industrial Brotherhood" which sought to organize all industry on a co-operative basis. *Appeal to Reason,* Apr. 14, 1900. The Industrial Brotherhood published a little paper, *Humanity,* in 1900 and 1901. In spite of Lermond's plans, the Brotherhood quickly passed out of existence.

With a view to the immediate relief of the suffering, the Social Democracy pledged itself to seek employment for those without jobs. "For such purpose," said the Declaration, "one of the states of the Union, to be hereafter determined, shall be selected for the concentration of our supporters and the introduction of co-operative industry and then gradually extending the sphere of our operations until the National Co-operative Commonwealth shall be established."

The program of immediate demands adopted by the convention represented a combination of revisionist socialism and left-wing Populism. Its most radical plank called for public ownership of all industries controlled by monopolies, trusts, and combines. The program asked for government ownership of all transportation and communication facilities as well as of all mines, oil wells, and mineral deposits. It demanded reduction of working hours in industry; inauguration of a public-works program for the employment of the unemployed; inventions free to all and inventors compensated by the state; establishment of a postal savings bank; and adoption of the initiative, referendum, imperative mandate, and proportional representation.[39]

After the organization of the Social Democracy of America had been completed, the doors of Uhlich Hall were thrown open to representatives from the Brotherhood of the Co-operative Commonwealth, the Socialist Labor Party, and local social- and monetary-reform organizations. Among the new delegates were Mary Harris Jones, the "Mother Jones" of labor movement fame, and Lucy Parsons, widow of the Haymarket Affair anarchist, Albert R. Parsons.[40]

It was on this same day that Debs dispatched to John D. Rockefeller a letter soliciting financial support for the Social Democracy colonization venture.[41] The letter had a twofold purpose. Debs, unquestionably sincere, actually hoped that the Standard Oil potentate might assist the Social Democracy, as he conceded him to be a "Christian gentleman." A refusal by Rockefeller would not detract from the letter's propaganda value. Yet, at best, the letter was a clumsy gesture, and it af-

[39]*Social Democrat,* July 1, 1897.
[40]*Chicago Times-Herald,* June 20, 1897.
[41]*Chicago Tribune,* June 20, 1897; Ginger, p. 201.

forded the Socialist Labor Party papers a sitting-duck target at which to blast editorial shots against the Social Democracy.

Control of the Social Democracy organization remained firmly in the hands of the old officials of the American Railway Union. Debs and five former fellow prisoners at Woodstock were elected to its executive offices. Each was voted a salary of $100 a month. Debs was chosen chairman; James Hogan, vice-chairman; Sylvester Keliher, secretary and treasurer; and William E. Burns and Roy M. Goodwin, organizers.[42] When Henry Demarest Lloyd learned that the men of the Union had applied a stranglehold upon the "offices, power, and revenue" of the Social Democracy, he was thankful that he had had no part in its founding. He expressed the belief to Isaac Hourwich, the New York lawyer and labor economist, that Debs had sought to prevent this development since "the merest instinct of self preservation dictated that he should do so" but that "his hungry followers—poor fellows, they have suffered greatly—could not be restrained." Lloyd predicted that the Social Democracy would wreck itself on the reefs of "pure and simple selfishness."[43]

When the convention adjourned, most of the delegates who marched out singing the "Marseillaise" were unsure of the Social Democracy's future course of action. A considerable number of them contemplated formation of a new socialist party and believed the organization's task primarily political. The Social Democracy constitution provided not only for a national organization but also for state and local branches which ostensibly would serve as the core for political activity in the future. Furthermore, a resolution was adopted during the waning hours of the convention which stated:

> No member of this organization shall accept an office, elective or appointive, from any political party [i. e., non-Social Democracy political organization] until he first severs his connections with this body; and no local or state branch shall go into politics through fusion or otherwise, without the consent of the National Executive Board, except in states already under the control of the order.[44]

---

[42]Social Democrat, July 1, 1897; Chicago Times-Herald, June 22, 1897.
[43]Lloyd to Hourwich, July 21, 1897. Lloyd Papers.
[44]Social Democrat, Aug. 2, 1897.

The slim majority by which this Debs-endorsed resolution was carried indicated that many of the delegates were far more interested in colonization than in socialist politics.[45] Among the Social Democracy officers, Burns, Goodwin, and Hogan were outspokenly opposed to straight political action. Throughout the ensuing year the difference in viewpoint between the political and colonization elements plagued the Social Democracy and eventually led to its dissolution.

Debs did not clarify his own position until some two weeks after the convention. Interviewed in Berger's Milwaukee bailiwick, he stated unequivocally that the Social Democracy's primary purpose was political. The Social Democracy, he declared, was a party, "a political party as much so as the Republican or Populist parties." The colonization scheme was very much misunderstood and overemphasized, even by his own friends. According to Debs, it was an incidental part of the organization's program and designed solely to relieve those persons currently in distress. "Were the colonization plan to prove a failure," Debs continued, "it would not stop the Social Democracy movement."[46]

Answering inquiries from readers as to the ideological status of the Social Democracy, *The Social Democrat*—the *Railway Times* with a new name—stated editorially: "The Social Democracy is a political organization which recognizes the class struggle and is based on the principles of International Socialism."[47] The paper lashed out against those Fabians who condemned political action as a means of fostering socialism. The promoters of the Social Democracy, it said, did "not believe that they have the power to interfere with any process of social evolution . . . but they feel we have arrived at a point in the evolutionary process where the unconscious, blind forces which are forcing the human race in its forward march may be assisted by those who have a knowledge of the conditions of the problem and by directing otherwise uncontrollable elements, the final consummation may be not only assured, but brought that much

---

[45]*Chicago Times-Herald,* June 22, 1897.
[46]*Social Democrat,* July 15, 1897.
[47]*Ibid.,* Aug. 12, 1897.

nearer—the period of struggle may be both eased and considerably shortened."[48]

The *Social Democrat* also sought to mollify trade unionists, after Debs, in an interview during the convention, had expressed the opinion that strikes were useless since organized workers invariably had to capitulate to the corporations and trusts.[49] In an editorial entitled, "Trades Unionism and Social Democracy," editor Louis W. Rogers asserted that the Social Democracy objectives harmonized with the goals of organized workers. It aimed, furthermore, to do what trade unionism could never do, namely, "guarantee to every worker not a part, but all the product of his toil." The trade union, said Rogers, was an "economic class movement." The Social Democracy was a "political movement to abolish class and place all men on economic equality." The two movements could and should work side by side.[50]

Even before the Social Democracy became a going concern, a barrage of criticism greeted it from both the political right and the political left. Throughout the course of the convention news articles and editorials in the two principal Chicago newspapers, the *Tribune* and the *Times-Herald*, contained slurring references, distorted analyses, and outright mendacities. Ignoring almost completely the political program, the papers directed their fire at the colonization project and at Debs himself, whom the *Times-Herald* denounced as "the uncrowned king of the new industrial utopia." It was uselsss, said the *Times-Herald*, "to expect any peaceable solution of any phase of the labor problem from this erratic agitator." Debs's "peculiar temperament," it continued, made him unfit "to lead the unemployed into an industrial paradise, even though the plan of the co-operative colony were practical." The entire colonization plan was said to be premised on "the right of the poor of Chicago to help themselves to the possessions of the rich."[51]

The *Tribune*, not a paper to be outdone by a rival daily, predicted that the people of the West would never willingly sur-

---

[48]*Ibid.*, July 15, 1897.

[49]*Chicago Tribune*, June 20, 1897.

[50]*Social Democrat*, Aug. 19, 1897. Cf. for similarity of viewpoint W. S. Carter, "Trade Unionism and Socialism," *American Federationist*, IV (1897), 132.

[51]*Chicago Times-Herald*, June 22, 1897.

render their state governments to the "economical mountebank Debs" and his band of "city loafers" who preferred the "gregarious life" of the saloon to the hard work of the farm. In the state of Washington, favored by the Social Democracy for colonization, everything of value was already pre-empted, the *Tribune* maintained. Consequently, it would be only a matter of time before the commonwealers in desperation would be begging for money to get back home. Kansas, then under People's Party control, would be a far better state for Debs's colonizers, said the *Tribune*, since it was already populated by hundreds of unbalanced men who screamed for 16 to 1.[52]

Thunder came also from the left. Even before the convention met, Henry Kuhn, national secretary of the Socialist Labor Party, told the *New York Journal* that the colonization plan, if attempted, would result in "flat failure." J. J. Pallas, corresponding secretary of the New York Central Labor Union, believed that the colonization idea "smacked too much of the millennium."[53] Isaac Hourwich denounced colonization in a letter to Henry Demarest Lloyd, who in turn suggested that true socialists had no alternative at the moment than to "keep on laying our eggs in the sand, and waiting for the sun of some future spring to hatch them out."[54]

In Chicago the local Socialist Labor Party, harking to the *Communist Manifesto* for authority, warned the national membership against the "Duodecimo Edition of the New Jerusalem Known as the Debs Plan."[55] These words of caution did not deter some of its own members from attending the convention and seeking to bore from within. Rebuffed in these efforts, they addressed to the *Times-Herald* an open letter criticizing the colonization plan and contending that only the Socialist Labor Party could speak for American socialism.[56]

Daniel DeLeon, high lama of the Socialist Labor Party, reacted less frenetically than did some of his followers. When Debs first proposed the colonization project, DeLeon rapped

[52]*Chicago Tribune,* June 19, 1897.
[53]*New York Journal,* Apr. 18, 1897.
[54]Lloyd to Hourwich, July 21, 1897. Lloyd Papers.
[55]*People,* June 13, 1897.
[56]*Chicago Times-Herald,* June 22, 1897.

him across the knuckles rather gently. The attack of the socialists, he said, should not be centered on the state of Washington,
nor on any other Western commonwealth, but rather on Washington, D. C. If socialist colonization was needed, it was in
Congress and in the White House. Debs's plan, he declared,
started "at the wrong end like all schemes do."[57] Even when
the Social Democracy became an accomplished fact, DeLeon did
not unleash upon Debs the stream of vituperation usually heaped
upon the socialist deviationist or heretic. Apparently, he still
had hopes of winning Debs into the Socialist Labor Party.
"With warm esteem for the good intentions of Mr. Debs, but
fully appreciative of the harm that more failures will do," he
wrote, "we earnestly warn the proletariat of America once more
not to embark on this chimera; not to yield, out of love for the
good intentions of Mr. Debs, greater respect for his judgment
than it deserves; to hew to the line of the principle of the class
struggle."[58]

Attacks on the Social Democracy by the capitalistic press were
largely ignored by its leaders. Those from Socialist Laborites
posed a more serious problem, since the Social Democracy and
the SLP were now rivals for the political allegiance of the
country's limited number of socialists. Initially, the *Social
Democrat* announced its intention of turning a deaf ear on the
criticisms of SLP spokesmen. "We have no desire to waste
our energy fighting socialists. We prefer to train our guns
upon the enemy."[59] However, the *Social Democrat* was not adverse to taking editorial pot shots at the Socialist Laborites in
general and at DeLeon in particular. In one of its first snipings
it declared: "When a man who claims to be a socialist attempts
to 'read out of the party' those of the socialist faith who don't
follow his peculiar ideas, his socialism is one of the tyrannical
kind and is no improvement on the old political tyrannies."[60]

Despite DeLeon's increasingly sharp strictures against the
"Debs Party" and its impossible colonization scheme, the Social
Democracy won the backing of hundreds of political come-

---

[57]*People*, Apr. 25, 1897.
[58]*Ibid.*, June 27, 1897.
[59]*Social Democrat*, Sept. 2, 1897.
[60]*Ibid.*, Aug. 2, 1897.

outers, particularly in the Middle West. Here was a socialist organization of American origin and consequently free from the stigma of foreignness attached to the SLP. It offered, too, a convenient haven for the Social Democratic Federation which, in convention during November, 1896, had gone on record as favoring an organization that would unite all socialists opposed to the Socialist Labor Party.[61] Not surprisingly, the first bursts of Social Democracy activity were in Illinois, Wisconsin, Missouri, and Ohio—states where dissatisfaction with the SLP was strong.

Debs himself started the organizational drive at Milwaukee, where on July 9 he spoke before the first formal meeting of the Social Democracy Branch No. 1, headed by Victor Berger. On the same evening he addressed the Milwaukee Fabian Society, which forthwith became another branch of the Social Democracy.[62] When Debs left Milwaukee after a week's visit, Roy Goodwin and John Lloyd, former American Railway Union men, moved in to join Berger and Heath in rallying the city's reform elements behind the Social Democracy.

Chicago was also a beehive of Social Democratic activity with Stedman and Jesse Cox taking the initiative in founding Social Democracy branches, of which some twenty were flourishing by mid-August.[63] The Social Democracy leaders in Chicago failed to scrutinize prospective members with care, and as early as September the National Executive Board was obliged to suspend Chicago Social Democracy Branch No. 2 because it had been captured by DeLeonites.[64] In St. Louis, Social Democracy vice-chairman William E. Burns helped to establish two large branches. But more important for the movement was the support accorded it by the powerful *St. Louis Brauer-Zeitung*, which spoke for the socialist-dominated brewery workers' union.[65] Cleveland, headquarters of the Social Democratic Fed-

[61]*Ibid.*, July 15, 1897; Ray S. Baker, "The Debs Co-operative Commonwealth," *Outlook*, LVI (July 3, 1897), 540; Kerby, pp. 57-58.

[62]*Social Democrat*, July 15, 1897. According to the organization's constitution, a branch consisted of not less than five nor more than five hundred members.

[63]*Social Democrat*, Aug. 12, 1897.

[64]*Ibid.*, Sept. 23, 1897.

[65]*People*, Aug. 29, 1897.

eration, was another Social Democracy stronghold. The Federation's German-language newspaper, *Der Volkanswalt*, joined Berger's *Wisconsin Vorwaerts* as an official Social Democracy foreign-language publication.[66] Two other German socialist Lassallean newspapers which early threw their support behind the new movement were the *San Francisco Tageblatt* and the *Philadelphia Tageblatt*.[67]

Many who joined the Social Democracy were former Socialist Labor Party members who had been read out of the party because of minor or major deviations from the official line proscribed by DeLeon and his little New York group. The most heinous sin for a Socialist Laborite at this particular time was opposition to dual unionism, which the party leadership encouraged through the Socialist Trade and Labor Alliance after DeLeon's conspicuous failure to infiltrate and capture control of the Knights of Labor.

Among DeLeon's most vocal critics, it will be recalled, was a group of New York East Side Jewish intellectuals and labor leaders. Faced with expulsion from the SLP, they had left it in 1897. On April 22 of that year they began publication of the *Jewish Daily Forward* as an independent socialist newspaper. As was true of nearly all new socialist foreign-language newspapers, the *Forward* was beset in its early years with seemingly insurmountable financial difficulties. These were gradually overcome, and the paper developed into the "World's Largest Jewish Daily." It maintained high literary and journalistic standards, and its annual profits were distributed to educational and charitable institutions as well as to funds for the relief of striking workers. Under Abraham Cahan, who had been its first editor and returned to the post after a four-year period during which Michael Zametkin and others held it, the *Forward* surged ahead, vigorously opposing both the reactionary right and the revolutionary left. It espoused a gradual approach to socialism and emphasized the need for spiritual freedom and individual dignity as well as economic security.

---

[66]*Social Democrat,* Aug. 12, 1897.

[67]*People,* Aug. 29, 1897.

The die thus had been cast on the East Side. The executive committee of the Socialist Labor Party of Greater New York celebrated the Fourth of July holiday with its own loud report which ceremoniously expelled the already resigned *Forward* writers and the members of four party assembly districts who had stood by them. Immediately, the dissident Jewish radicals made plans to affiliate with the Social Democracy, though the latter admittedly left much to be desired from their point of view. The union was consummated at a convention held between July 31 and August 2. Fifty-eight delegates, claiming to represent 1200 old SLP members and 10,000 trade unionists, agreed to throw in their lot with the new Debs movement. In justifying this action they issued a manifesto which said among other things: "All parties which have existed heretofore have either failed to support the principles of a revolutionary class struggle, or where they have supported this principle, they were organized into a small isolated sect which was never united with the great mass of the militant proletariat."[68]

In addition to Zametkin and Cahan, other prominent East Side Jewish leaders who went over to the Social Democracy were Isaac Hourwich; Meyer London, a future United States congressman; Morris Winchevsky, a noted poet; Max Pine, an organizer in the needle trades industries; and Louis F. Miller, founder of the *Wahrheit*.[69] All foreign born, they constituted an unusually able body of men. They provided the Social Democracy with adherents who, unlike the converts from Populism, were well grounded in socialist theory. While the Jewish Social Democracy branches were not the only ones in New York, they served as the nucleus for the Gotham movement.

DeLeon's choicest invective spewed forth on this development. It proved a case of the pot calling the kettle black. The Curaçao-born editor delighted in directing attention to the fact that many of the bolters from the Socialist Labor Party were comparatively recently arrived immigrants. "The moral, physical, and intellectual riffraff from Russia in this city, . . . unable to use the Socialist Labor Party for their own crooked purposes,

---

[68]*Social Democrat,* Aug. 12, 1897.

[69]Fine, p. 192. For an excellent account of the Jewish labor movement in New York, see Melech Epstein, *Jewish Labor in U. S. A.* (New York, 1950).

hope to find asylum in the Debs party," he wrote in the *People*.[70] Socialist Laborites had nothing to fear from a party made up of "freaks and crooks and schemers—the flotsam and jetsam of society." In Boston, the barbed-tongued DeLeon convulsed a Socialist Labor Party audience with laughter when he declared:

> Two streams—pure imagination and unqualified falsifica- tions—met. Each deceived the other with its pretenses. It was the case of 'dupers duping dupers.' Out of the copula- tion of these two duping forces was born that queer produc- tion that eventually, if not sooner, will find its place in the museum of political curiosities as the 'Social Democracy of America and Patagonia.'[71]

DeLeon's vilification brought angry threats of libel suits and demands that he prove his various charges in a "court of honor."[72] Shrugging them off with contumely,[73] DeLeon knew, as did his opponents, that he could convert either, if he so de- sired, into excellent propaganda occasions.

The Social Democracy idea attracted a host of converts on its own merits, but it was Debs's magnetic personality that unques- tionably won the movement most of its adherents. Due to a severe case of sunstroke suffered while speaking bareheaded at a meeting of striking West Virginia coal miners, he was unable to fill several lecture engagements during the summer of 1897. But in those places where he was able to go, the kindly and amiable socialist neophyte gained friends from all walks of life for the Social Democracy. Debs was not, nor was he ever to become, a great or an original socialist thinker, but he was ex- traordinarily effective on the lecture platform, where the shining sincerity of his speeches and the glowing honesty of his person- ality more than compensated for the lack of knowledge of the more delicate points of Marxist theory. His soul was filled with a longing for social justice, and he communicated this feel- ing to the audiences who gathered to hear him extol the new Social Democracy. During a tour of the East, the Middle West, and the South between October, 1897 and March, 1898, he ad-

---

[70]*People*, Aug. 8. 1897.

[71]*Ibid.*, Dec. 19, 1897.

[72]*Social Democrat*, Jan. 13, 1898.

[73]*People*, Jan. 23, 1898.

dressed men and women from all classes of society, ranging from Yale students, sons of the rich and comfortable, to miserably paid textile workers and sharecroppers in Georgia. Rarely was a city or town without a Social Democracy branch after a Debs visit.

If the "scientific" socialists of New York and other large urban centers looked askance upon the Social Democracy colonization scheme, the less doctrinaire audiences which Debs addressed were smitten by its potentialities. Nearly everywhere he went in the South and in the Middle West, men and women came up to him after his lectures to inquire of the progress of the three-man Social Democracy colonization commission which had been appointed early in August.

After Henry Demarest Lloyd and Laurence Gronlund had begged off serving on the commission, each for reasons of ill health, the Social Democracy National Executive Board agreed on Richard T. Hinton of Washington, D. C., as chairman of the colonization project; Cyrus Field Willard as secretary; and W. P. Borland as treasurer.[74]

"British-born and Chartist-bred," Hinton was a veteran of the social-reform movement. He had been an intimate friend and a biographer of John Brown, and during the Civil War he had organized a corps of Boston newspaper reporters to fight in the ranks of the Union Army. After the defeat of the "slavocracy," he followed Wendell Phillips' example and took up the cudgels against "wage slavery" as a crusading journalist and editor.[75] It was at this time that Hinton became associated with the socialist movement, and he served as corresponding secretary of the Washington, D. C., American section of the International.[76] He was active in the 1886 New York mayoralty campaign and served as assistant editor to Serge Schevitsch on the *Leader*. Edward Aveling wrote of him: "No man or woman is more clear than he as to the bearing of all the various struggles here and there, now and then, upon the one great struggle between the working class and the possessing."[77] Yet

[74]*Social Democrat*, Aug. 19, 1897.
[75]*Ibid.*, June 23, 1896.
[76]Commons (ed.), *History of Labour in the United States*, II, 211.
[77]Edward and Eleanor Aveling, *The Working Class Movement in America*, p. 197.

Hinton's socialist orthodoxy was not sufficiently straight-laced for DeLeon, with the result that he was expelled from the Socialist Labor Party in 1893, allegedly for seeking to get labor to vote Republican.[78]

Willard, encountered previously as a devotee of Theosophy and as a co-founder of the Boston Nationalist Club, had moved to Chicago, where he was employed as a labor reporter. During the Pullman Strike he was one of the few Chicago journalists who attempted to present events in a light favorable to the workers.[79] Borland was an anarchist of the Kropotkin school and a railway employee. Barely making a living for his wife and four children,[80] he welcomed colonization as a means of economic amelioration. In addition to his work on the colonization commission, after September 20 Borland served as editor of the *Social Democrat*. Since Willard also wrote a weekly column of colonization news, the paper's editorial slant was distinctly favorable to colonization.[81]

The commission's labors were hampered from the very onset, as the colonization plan had to be financed by voluntary contributions from individuals or from local branches of the organization.[82] Such a method of fund-raising was soon found inadequate, and early in September the Social Democracy National Executive Board called on each branch to contribute at least $20 to the fund.[83] The enthusiasm which the colonization plan evoked among the rank and file of the Social Democracy membership was hardly reflected in the contributions to the fund, which amounted to only $2,421 in June, 1898.[84]

Even had contributions been heavier, it may be doubted whether the commissioners would have achieved constructive results. Hinton, Borland, and Willard proved completely incompetent. Disregarding the expressed plan of the Social Democracy's founders to colonize a sparsely inhabited Western

[78]*People*, July 30, 1893.

[79]*Social Democrat*, June 23, 1897.

[80]Borland to Joseph A. Labadie, May 24 and May 26, 1896. Labadie Papers.

[81]Ella Reeve Bloor wrote a children's column for the *Social Democrat*. See her autobiography, *We Are Many* (New York, 1940), p. 53.

[82]*Social Democrat*, Aug. 19, 1897.

[83]*Ibid.*, Sept. 23, 1897.

[84]*Ibid.*, June 16, 1898.

state and ignoring their own announcement to the membership of their intention to do so,[85] they began almost immediately to investigate land sites near Crossville, in Cumberland County, Tennessee.[86] These were some twenty-five miles distant from the short-lived New Rugby Colony founded in 1880 by the famed English Christian Socialist, Judge Thomas Hughes. Hinton and Willard, moreover, had the temerity to approach the Nashville City Council with a plan to build a small railroad to link the Nashville and Knoxville with the Cincinnati Southern systems. Construction of the line would be undertaken by the Social Democracy, and its financing would be by the Nashville municipality.[87] Nothing developed from this scheme. Yet apparently neither it nor DeLeon's revelation of the poor quality of the land in the Crossville area[88] weakened the confidence of the Social Democracy National Executive Board in the good judgment of its three commissioners. On the contrary, on December 9 the Board gave them permission to open negotiations for the purchase of a large tract of undeveloped Tennessee land.[89]

Negotiations dragged on through the winter and into the early spring. They collapsed suddenly in May when Hinton and Willard, not surprisingly, were unable to find a reputable financial concern to underwrite the purchase. But the commissioners were not left high and dry since they had in their possession an offer of some 560 acres of "gold mining" land at Ute Pass, Colorado, from one H. C. Childs, a mining engineer and "veteran socialist." Hinton and Willard had seen the property during a visit to Idaho and Colorado the previous autumn.[90] But at that time they had been more impressed with the Tennessee site and had pigeon-holed Childs's offer.

Time was pressing in on the commissioners. The Social Democracy's second national convention was in the offing, and they could delay no longer, lest they appear before it with a

85*Official Circular No. 1 of the Colonization Commission, SDA* (n. p., n. d.).
86*Social Democrat*, June 16, 1898.
87*Ibid.*, Oct. 7, 1897.
88*People*, Nov. 7, 1897.
89*Social Democrat*, Dec. 23, 1897; June 16, 1898.
90*Ibid.*, Oct. 21, 1897.

record of travel expenses and nothing else. Willard entrained for Colorado to close a deal. He agreed to pay Childs $3,000 in sixty days, $2,000 more in ninety days, and the balance in five per cent twenty-year bonds. The bonds were to be issued by a Social Democracy adjunct, the Co-operative Commonwealth Company, organized early in May as a corporation under the laws of Kansas.[91] According to the contract which Willard arranged, the company would be permitted to issue mortgage bonds up to the value of $200,000.[92]

Such was the condition of the colonization venture in the early summer of 1898. When the commission made its report to the Social Democracy convention, from the $2,421 collected it had spent $2,388 chasing rainbows in Tennessee and seeking pots of gold in Colorado.[93] Those socialists who had had mild doubts in 1897 as to the colonization scheme were now completely convinced that the venture would have to be scrapped if the Social Democracy was to continue.

Because the political socialists realized that the colonization plan was the magnet which attracted many men and women into the Social Democracy, they had hesitated to attack it too openly or violently. A few socialist papers like the *Philadelphia Tageblatt* did take a firm stand against colonization from the very start. The *Tageblatt* predicted the colonization venture would end in failure, though with the salutary aftermath of funneling socialism once and for all into politics.[94] Berger's *Vorwaerts* carefully avoided more than lukewarm approval of colonization. It was an excellent means of agitation among workingmen, Berger conceded, but he doubted that the latter would be better off in Utah or Washington than in New York or Chicago.[95] In New York, too, colonization was contemplated as utopian and unfeasible. Isaac Hourwich expressed the general sentiment of the New York Social Democracy in a letter to Henry Demarest Lloyd. He said that people could not "be kept enthusiastic in forty-four states over the prospect of estab-

[91]*Ibid.*, May 12, 1898.
[92]*Ibid.*, June 2, 1898.
[93]*Ibid.*, June 16, 1898.
[94]Cited in the *Coming Nation,* July 10, 1897.
[95]*Ibid.* See Wachman, p. 17.

lishing a model commonwealth in the 45th on easy monthly payments."[96] When Hinton came to New York in 1897 to persuade another Socialist Laborite excommunicant, Charles Sotheran, and other socialists in the city to support the colony program, he met with a decidedly frosty reception. He left New York discouraged and disappointed.[97] Boston was still another hotbed of opposition to colonization. In a letter to the *Social Democrat*, one of the few of its kind to be printed in the correspondence column, the policy committee of the Boston Social Democracy branch urged that all colonization plans be shelved until the organization was sufficiently well established to assure their success. It deplored the emphasis that colonization was receiving at the expense of the more important political program.[98]

The leaders of the Social Democracy had agreed at the 1897 convention that politics should be by-passed completely for at least a year. They had decided also to postpone formulation of a national political program until after the 1898 convention.[99] As a consequence, Social Democracy candidates were not entered in any of the 1897 autumn elections. When queried as to which party deserved the support of Social Democracy members, Debs answered unhesitatingly the Socialist Labor Party, since it was the only "anti-capitalist party in the field." To those of the Social Democracy who were embittered because of real or fancied persecutions by the Socialist Laborite leadership, Debs had a message of Christian charity. "Show that you are a true socialist by returning good for evil," he advised. At stake were principles, not personalities.[100]

In a few localities Social Democracy members chafed under the no-politics ban. Berger and Heath were especially anxious to test the political strength of the Social Democracy in Wisconsin. In Massachusetts, too, Social Democracy leaders were distinctly disposed toward political activity. Finally in January, 1898, the Social Democracy National Executive Board

---

[96]Hourwich to Lloyd, June 23, 1897. Lloyd Papers.

[97]Alice H. Sotheran, *Horace Greeley and Other Pioneers of American Socialism* (New York, 1915), pp. xxxv-xxxvi.

[98]*Social Democrat,* Oct. 14, 1897.

[99]*Ibid.,* Feb. 3, 1898.

[100]*Ibid.,* Oct. 21, 1897.

gave the Wisconsin Social Democrats permission to participate
in the Milwaukee and Sheboygan municipal elections.   Berger
believed he could count on the support of the Milwaukee Federated Trades Council and thereby assure the Social Democracy
a creditable showing at the polls.[101]   He was to be deceived, as
the leaders of the Council worked secretly for the Democratic-
Populist candidates.[102]

The Milwaukee Social Democracy campaigned vigorously,
though entertaining little hope of defeating either the Republicans or the Democratic-Populist coalition.   Just before the election Debs and Stedman came from Chicago to address several
rallies, for the reputation of the Social Democracy as a political
organization was at stake.   Paul Grottkau, then residing in San
Francisco, was brought back to Milwaukee by the Social
Democracy and several labor unions to lend his influence.[103]
This was Grottkau's last contribution to the cause of socialism
in the United States, for death was to take him four months
later.   The energetic socialist campaign brought forth canards
in both the Democratic-Populist and Socialist Labor papers
that Republicans were secretly subsidizing the Social Democracy.[104]

The election took place on April 5.   Herbert Meister, the
Social Democracy mayoralty candidate, received 2,444 votes as
against the 26,219 polled by the Democratic-Populist standard
bearer, the notoriously corrupt David G. Rose, and against the
18,207 for the Republican, William Geuder, whose nomination
by the Republicans was made with traditional concern for the
German-American vote.[105]   The Social Democracy vote was
insignificant save in those wards heavily populated by Germans.[106]   Berger and his supporters derived one satisfaction
from the campaign, however, and that was the fact that the
Socialist Laborites were able to muster only 423 votes for their
candidate.   In nearby Sheboygan, moreover, the Social Democ-

[101]*Ibid.*, Feb. 3, 1898.
[102]Wachman, p. 24.
[103]Still, p. 304.
[104]*Social Democrat*, Apr. 14, Apr. 21, 1898.
[105]*Ibid.*, Apr. 14, 1898; Still, p. 306
[106]Wachman, p. 24.

racy was successful in electing two aldermen, Fred Haack and August Mohr.[107]

Unimpressive as this showing was, the *Social Democrat* nevertheless heralded the Wisconsin elections as an illustrious beginning in the political struggle for social and economic emancipation. It made the dubious claim that the major parties in Milwaukee had been obliged to adopt public-ownership planks in their platforms because of the Social Democracy's strong stand on the issue. And it boasted that henceforth the Social Democracy would be a powerful third force in any election in which it chose to participate.[108]

The entrance of the Social Democracy into Wisconsin politics accentuated the differences between its political and colonization factions. Not only a question of tactics was involved; underlying that was a more basic one of ideology. In general, those favoring concentration on politics were revisionist socialists of the Berger stripe who accepted most of the Marxist postulates, including that of the class struggle. Conversely, those who would make the colonization plan at least co-ordinate with political action were not infrequently former Populists who were poorly grounded in, or in many instances unequivocally rejected, Marxist theory. Still fundamentally individualistic in heart and head, they could not bring themselves to accept the class struggle. That class conflict existed was readily acknowledged, but they believed it developed from abuses inherent in an impersonal system rather than from malevolent intent of one group of individuals to oppress another. What was necessary was correction of these abuses through socialization of the means of production and distribution. While the colonizationists favored establishment of a co-operative commonwealth and to this extent parted company from the orthodox Populists, nevertheless their general social psychology and social philosophy were more akin to those of the Populists than to the socialists. In its own way, the divergence between colonizationists and political actionists was a carry-over of the ideological cleavage which had separated the Populists and socialists prior to 1896.

---

[107] *Social Democrat,* Apr. 14, 1898.
[108] *Ibid.*

Solution of the colonization–political-action controversy, which had been brewing for nearly a year, was imperative if the Social Democracy was to be a cohesive instrument for either aim. By the spring of 1898 the colonizationists had become completely and adamantly opposed to subordinating their program to politics. From a project for relief of the unemployed, colonization became the sole goal for a sizable portion of the Social Democracy membership. Furthermore, the Social Democracy leaders themselves were in violent disagreement, and the close fellowship that had existed among the American Railway Union directors during their imprisonment at Woodstock was strained irreparably and tragically on the question of Social Democracy objectives. Keliher, a strong trade unionist, opposed colonization, whereas Burns, Hogan, and Goodwin, all of whom were far more attached emotionally to Populism than to socialism, favored it. Debs was the enigma. He had openly espoused socialist politics, yet sentimentally he was not unfavorably inclined toward colonization. It had been his first socialist love, and he could not rudely brush it aside without considering himself something of an ideological cad.

The second national Social Democracy convention was scheduled for June 7 in Chicago, and both sides prepared for the showdown. The colonizationists were particularly active in Chicago where, on the very eve of the gathering, several new Social Democracy branches were organized by Burns, Hogan, and Lloyd to insure greater representation for their faction. The political socialists not only condemned these as "dummy" branches but also warned of anarchist influence in them. Their criticisms in the latter respect had a certain plausibility and some authenticity, since Johann Most, writing in the *Freiheit*, had strongly urged anarchists to join the Social Democracy.[109]

Excitement charged the air in Uhlich Hall almost from the very minute the convention opened. Those who came as spectators to witness a battle royal were not to be disappointed. The lists had been drawn long before. Most of the political actionists came from New York, Wisconsin, and Massachusetts; their opponents were from Chicago and the Western corn belt and mining areas, the old Populist strongholds. Spearheading the

---

[109]*Social Democracy Red Book,* p. 59.

political faction were Keliher, Berger, Hourwich, G. A. Hoehn, Margaret Haile, and James F. Carey. The colonizers were led by Willard, Hogan, Burns, J. S. Ingalls, and John F. Lloyd.

Immediately the stage was set for the struggle for control. After the disposition of routine business, both Debs and Burns gave short welcoming speeches in which each announced his disinclination to seek re-election as chairman and vice-chairman, respectively. The leadership of the Social Democracy therewith was thrown open to which ever of the two groups could gain the majority of the delegates, and the crucial question at once developed as to whether the new Chicago branches were entitled to representation.

Keliher threw the fat into the fire by demanding that the eleven delegates from the new Chicago Social Democracy organizations be excluded on the ground that the branches which they claimed to represent had not been granted charters by the National Executive Board. He charged Willard with establishing the branches for the express and sole purpose of packing the convention. And he warned, too, that several of them were led by well-known anarchists. Debs supported Keliher, though with restraint. A benign man, he sought to avoid controversy with friends who had been loyal to him during the troubled days of the past.

Keliher's charges were protested vigorously by Hogan, Goodwin, and J. S. Ingalls. Obviously none of them cared to acknowledge the presence of Emma Goldman, who came as a delegate of one of the new Chicago branches. At the last moment the colonizers had decided against presenting her credentials, and she sat in the gallery as a spectator.[110] When the discussion threatened to get out of hand, the convention chairman in desperation referred the matter to the credentials committee. Since the colonization faction controlled the committee, it reported favorably on the admission of the Chicago delegates.[111] But the report's only effect was to rekindle the argument, during the course of which Margaret Haile declared flatly that the Massachusetts delegation would never submit to the dictates of the

[110]*Chicago Times-Herald*, June 8, 1898.
[111]*Chicago Tribune*, June 8, 1898.

credentials committee.[112]   Mrs. Haile, a former newspaper reporter and Socialist Laborite, was a fiery and forceful speaker, and her implied threat of a bolt occasioned a momentary effort at compromise.

Sensing victory, the colonization faction refused to compromise. The convention rejected a proposal whereby the eleven delegates in question might sit on the convention floor but not vote. At this point the National Executive Board, which was also controlled by the colonizationists, took matters into its own hands. Over the strenuous objections of Keliher and the milder protests of Debs,[113] it issued charters to the eleven disputed Chicago branches. This gave them an unquestionable status of legality. The next day their delegates took seats on the floor, and to all intents and purposes the colonization faction had now captured the convention.

By comparison with the events of the first day, those of the second day were quite tranquil. They were featured by jockeying and maneuvering for control of the important rules and platform committees. The colonizationists succeeded in placing two of their number on the three-man rules committee. The political group, however, managed to put Berger and Mrs. Haile on the platform committee. John F. Lloyd, an alleged Chicago anarchist,[114] represented the colonizers as the third committee member. Throughout the remainder of the day and the following morning, the delegates carried on a desultory debate, as each side mobilized for the showdown battle certain to ensue when the platform committee reported to the convention.

Debs, generally considered sympathetic to the political socialists, gave them little cause for rejoicing. In a speech delivered late on the third day of the protracted gathering, he both criticized the class-struggle thesis and reaffirmed his belief in colonization. The "broad spirit of American socialists," said the curiously vacillating Debs, could not countenance such a narrow ideological doctrine as the class struggle.[115]   As to the colonization project, he declared:

---

[112]*Chicago Times-Herald,* June 8, 1898.
[113]*Chicago Daily Dispatch,* June 8, 1898.
[114]B. Berlyn to DeLeon, Jan. 6, 1897. DeLeon Papers.
[115]*Social Democrat,* June 16, 1898.

Give me 10,000 men, aye 10,000 in a western state with access to the sources of production, and we will change the economic conditions, and we will convince the people of that state, win their hearts and their intelligence. We will lay hold upon the reins of government and plant the flag of Socialism upon the State House. The state government in this offers us an advantage that is not found in any European country. We can take possession of one state, and not wait until we get the whole United States. We must get one state at a time. In a movement such as this there is always some friction. We are in the birth throes of a new movement, the most responsible movement the world ever saw, and it demands the most careful consideration of honest men and women.[116]

When the convention dragged on into its fourth day, the Massachusetts and New York delegates complained that the colonizationists were seeking to prolong the sessions so that those from the East would have to depart before decisive action could be taken on the Social Democracy platform.[117] The business of the morning session lent credibility to these accusations, for the time was taken up almost entirely by Hogan's charges of Keliher's incompetence and dishonesty. The principal claim was that Keliher had paid an "exorbitant price" for Social Democracy membership cards! But the basis of Hogan's real animus toward Keliher was revealed when he alleged that the former treasurer[118] had failed to pay him his salary when he was a Social Democracy organizer. Though he was unwilling to criticize Debs directly, Hogan indicated that he was disturbed by Debs's defense of Keliher in Social Democracy councils. "As to Mr. Debs," said Hogan, "all I will say of him is that he has been shamefully lenient."[119] Keliher listened to Hogan's charges in tight-lipped silence. He refused to answer his accuser on the convention floor but offered to refute the claims if and when they were placed in writing.[120]

---

116 *Ibid.*

117 *Social Democracy Red Book,* p. 67.

118 In April, 1898, a shake-up of Social Democracy officers took place. Hogan resigned as vice-chairman and became treasurer; Burns succeeded him as vice-chairman; Keliher, who had been secretary and treasurer, retained the former office. *Social Democrat,* Apr. 14, 1898.

119 *Chicago Journal,* June 10, 1898.

120 *Chicago Inter-Ocean,* June 12, 1898.

A report from the colonization commission followed Hogan's outburst. Willard reviewed the commission's activities over the past year and suggested the purchase of the Ute Pass property in Colorado. He did not explain where the Social Democracy was to obtain the money for this undertaking—that was a matter for the convention to decide. The commission's financial report showed a sickly balance of thirty-three dollars. Under the circumstances, the financing of a colonization project obviously would have to fall on the Social Democracy treasury which was hardly in a robust condition. The convention accepted Willard's report but postponed action on it.[121]

The beginning of the final showdown came at the start of the afternoon session when the platform committee submitted two reports. Berger and Mrs. Haile presented the majority report which called for political action only. Lloyd's minority report advocated both politics and colonization. The debate raged through the afternoon and evening sessions and into the early hours of Saturday morning. The last speech was Lloyd's two-hour summation of the colonization argument. He told the sleepy delegates that the Social Democracy needed a platform and methods that "would conform to American conditions and lines of thought." The point at issue was whether old German or new American socialist methods should prevail.[122]

When Lloyd finally concluded the delegates demanded a vote on the platform. A roll call disclosed 52 votes for the minority report and 37 for the majority—a clear and undeniable victory for the colonizationists. In the midst of the pandemonium which followed, Hourwich stood on a chair and called for all opponents of the minority report to convene at once in Parlor A of the Revere House. By strange coincidence this was the same room in which the Haymarket Affair jury had come to its fateful decision to hang the anarchists. An exodus of delegates from the convention hall began immediately, and as dawn was breaking on June 11 the political socialists were busily at work organizing a new Social Democratic Party.[123] Debs, convenient-

[121]*Social Democrat,* June 16, 1898.
[122]*Ibid.*
[123]*Chicago Tribune,* June 12, 1898.

ly ill at the hotel and thus unable to attend the disruptive session, sent a message of support to the political faction.

Having captured the Social Democracy, the colonizationists met the next morning to wind up the convention. They adopted a new constitution which placed political action and colonization on co-ordinate levels.[124] Hogan, an ex-People's Party leader in Utah, was elected the new chairman and Borland, an anarchist, became secretary and treasurer. On Sunday, the Social Democracy issued a manifesto which sought to clarify its position with respect to other socialist groups. "While fully aware of the international character of the socialist movement and while in the fullest accord with Socialist organizations in other lands," said the proclamation, "we are Americans, and we shall adopt methods consonant with American habits of thought and of action, and with the genius of American institutions." The Social Democracy was willing to achieve its political aims through the agency of another party organization, whether it espoused socialism or not. "We are not wedded to party names," it declared, "and we care not by whom or in what name good may be done . . . . In short, we propose to use for the noblest of purposes the same sagacity politicians employ for evil ends." In those states where no party advocated practical steps toward socialism, the Social Democracy would sponsor its own candidates.[125]

The manifesto brought from the political socialists the retort that the Social Democracy would disintegrate through fusion with other groups. Through the *Social Democrat*'s editorial columns, the harassed Willard replied that the Social Democracy neither intended fusion nor would countenance any measures leading in that direction. "But does that demand an abandonment of common sense?" he asked. "Are we to rush into political action here, there, and everywhere without regard to votes, means, or any of the conditions which control reasonable beings? Shall we 'engage in conflicts for spoils only' or seek to disturb an 'honest effort' toward Socialism simply because it doesn't emanate from us or use the exact phrase of our cult?" The Social Democracy did not intend to create a political machine for

---

[124]*Social Democrat*, June 16, 1898.
[125]*Ibid.*

manipulative purposes. Rather it sought to teach socialism by the example of its "civic actions and propaganda."[126]

The split in the Social Democracy, which Berger's Milwaukee friend, Elizabeth H. Thomas, described as "the best debated, instructive, and orderly" she had ever had occasion to witness,[127] delighted Daniel DeLeon. He wrote that a "smashup was inevitable" in the Social Democracy, and that when it came "the spirit of the SLP stalked through the convention and scattered it like a potter's vessel." As for Lloyd's claim that the colonizationists represented an "American" variety of socialism, DeLeon remarked acidly: "But what Americans! . . . the types of the worst thoughts and most backward ideas that this country has ever produced." He cited a Southern colonizationist delegate who allegedly declared: "We Americans don't believe in CLASS-consciousness; we believe in RACE-consciousness." The best description the irascible editor could muster for the political-actionist bolters on this occasion was "a rabble rout of queers."[128]

The *Chicago Tribune* also hooted over the Social Democracy debacle. It centered its editorial spleen on Debs, who never ceased to be anything for the paper other than the villain of the Pullman Strike. The *Tribune* held that while the bulk of the Social Democracy members was willing to follow Debs on colonization, it would not tolerate another "side show" party of which the nation already had too many. When the controversy within the Social Democracy finally resolved itself, the *Tribune* predicted that Debs would "resume his old trade of fomenting labor disturbances." In the meanwhile the "world's greatest," if not always its most accurate, newspaper bruited a wholly unfounded story that Debs was leaving for Europe.[129]

Control of the *Social Democrat* remained in the hands of the rump Social Democracy. Borland, Willard, and their friends used the paper to criticize the bolters, justify their own position, and hammer away at the "European" origins, theories, and methods of their opponents. Hogan's charges against Keliher were aired, and other bits of the organization's dirty linen were

[126]*Ibid.,* June 30, 1898.
[127]Elizabeth H. Thomas to C. Vann Woodward, Dec. 12, 1938. Letter is in possession of Professor Woodward of The Johns Hopkins University.
[128]*People,* June 19, 1898.
[129]*Chicago Tribune,* June 10, 1898.

hung out on the line for public scrutiny.[130] Blithely ignoring Debs's defection, the editors claimed that all of the old American Railway Union officials except Keliher had remained loyal to the Social Democracy. Berger and Stedman were accused of conspiring to capture the Social Democracy for the purpose of converting it into another class-conscious, unnecessary, and undesirable Socialist Labor Party.[131] In nearly every issue of the paper the class-struggle thesis was attacked as inconsonant with American ideals and institutions. "We preach no class war. It is unscientific," wrote Willard. Class consciousness was "self-consciousness, another term of selfishness."[132] A decidedly nativist strain, not unlike that found in the contemporary Populist papers, crept into the columns of the *Social Democrat* when it sought to contrast the "American" nature of the Social Democracy with the European character of the bolters. On one occasion the paper remarked cryptically: "Delegates Winchevsky, Hourwich, Barondess, Levin, Kuhn, Hunger, Moerschell, and Berger were among the bolters. Comment is superfluous."[133] In another issue it featured prominently a letter from a reader who found it no surprise that "Canadian-born" Mrs. Haile and Mrs. Kinkaid, "a Jewess from Russia," should have played leading roles in the political faction.[134]

Hard pressed for a leader of stature and renown, Borland, Willard, and other Social Democracy stalwarts sought to place Laurence Gronlund into the breach. Gronlund had been in Chicago at the time of the convention to arrange for the publication of *The New Economy* and had attended the Social Democracy sessions. He was sympathetic to the colonizationist faction partly because of its repudiation of the class-struggle thesis and partly because he thought the experiment well worth trying. It was the genius of the federal system that such experiments were possible, said Gronlund, and therefore it ill behooved socialists to pass up the opportunity of socializing a state. Just before the convention's adjournment, Gronlund

---

[130]*Social Democrat,* June 23, 1898.
[131]*Ibid.,* June 16, 1898.
[132]*Ibid.,* June 23, 1898.
[133]*Ibid.,* June 16, 1898.
[134]*Ibid.,* July 7, 1898.

told the colonizationists that he was with them "heart and soul" and would be glad at any time to assist their movement.[135] Borland and Willard quickly and gratefully accepted this offer, and for three consecutive weeks the *Social Democrat* featured articles by the "foremost writer on Socialism now living in America."

But the most able leaders of the Social Democracy had bolted, and it was not destined to survive for long. Four weeks after the convention's stormy, disruptive session the *Social Democrat* ceased publication because of lack of funds.[136] Moreover, the strength of the Social Democracy was soon found to be almost completely local and based on flimsy foundations. Outside of Chicago the Social Democracy branches were throwing in their lot with the new Social Democratic Party.

Willard and Hinton, however, were determined to go ahead with their colonization scheme, even if on a greatly reduced scale. In August, Willard and J. S. Ingalls purchased a tract of land at the entrance to Henderson Bay in the state of Washington. Shortly afterward a colony of 110 co-operationists was founded. As with Lermond's Equality settlement, this was a far cry from the ambitious plan to colonize an entire state. Nor was the Social Democracy colony any more successful than that of the Brotherhood of the Co-operative Commonwealth.

With the passing of the hybrid Social Democracy went the last real vestige of utopianism in the American socialist political movement. The collapse of the Social Democracy left the way open for the organization of a Social Democratic Party modeled to a great extent after that of the same name in Germany and the Independent Labour Party in Great Britain. After 1898, American socialism began to achieve maturity, though by no means liberation from doctrinal controversy.

---

[135] *Ibid.*, June 16, 1898. See Laurence Gronlund, "Socializing a State," *Progressive Thought*, No. 13 (Oct. 1900), pp. 15-22.

[136] *Social Democracy Red Book*, p. 68.

X. American Socialism Comes of Age

THE THREE years between June, 1898, and July, 1901, constituted a "Sturm und Drang" period in the history of American socialism. From the time of the Social Democratic Party's formation in 1898 until its transmutation into the Socialist Party of America in 1901, the organization created by the Social Democracy bolters suffered from most of the usual, and some of the unusual, growing pains which have characterized the early days of nearly every left-wing political movement. Conflicts over ideology and tactics, bitter personal attacks and recriminations, demands for co-operation with other leftist and reform groups, and internal schisms kept the Social Democratic Party in a state of constant turmoil.

The split in the Social Democracy was ideologically salutary. Like a strong wind, it cleared the air of utopianism and cut adrift from the socialist standard many who at best possessed a vague and romantic notion of what modern socialism, even in its most conservative form, involved. In the pre-Civil War period, the colonization plan might have had considerable merit. After all, the determined Brigham Young and his band of faithful followers had demonstrated its practicability on Utah's barren salt flats. But that was a long time ago, before the rise of an all conquering industrial capitalism which spread its power and influence into the most inaccessible recesses of the nation and bowled over its opponents like so many tenpins. The very character and nature of the new economic order made a repetition of the Mormons' success literally impossible.

None of the rebels who trooped wearily out of the Social Democracy convention in Uhlich Hall and over to the Revere House in the early hours of June 11 had been associated with the leadership of the old organization. Although Keliher's sympathies were with the bolters, he refused to leave the Social Democracy until accorded an opportunity to refute Hogan's charges.[1] Once assembled at the Revere House,[2] the bolters were too exhausted to do more than confer with the ailing Debs and agree on organizing a new Social Democratic Party.

Fortified with a few hours of badly needed sleep, they met later in the day at Jane Addams' Hull House, the doors of which were always open to social and economic reformers and political radicals. Debs, still ill, was unable to attend but sent word that he would do all that he could "to help along the new organization" as soon as his health would permit.[3] The delegates at once issued to the press a statement condemning the colonizationists. They also drew up a constitution for a new Social Democratic Party, formulated a political program, and elected officers. Jesse Cox, the veteran Chicago socialist, was named acting chairman; William Mailly, a young Tennessee coal miner with intellectual proclivities, was chosen acting secretary; and A. S. Edwards, recently resigned as editor of the *Coming Nation* and currently on a covered-wagon socialist propaganda tour,[4] was elected acting national organizer. An executive committee, consisting of Cox, Stedman, Berger, Debs, and Heath, was also elected.[5] A few weeks after the end of the convention Theodore Debs replaced Mailly as secretary, and Edwards relinquished his position as national organizer to devote all of his time to editing the party's official weekly newspaper, the *Social Democratic Herald*.[6]

Berger, the principal architect of the new party's platform, relied on time-tested materials. The preamble called for complete government ownership of the means of production and

[1]*Chicago Tribune*, June 12, 1898; *Chicago Journal*, June 11, 1898.

[2]Those who met at the Revere House included Jesse Cox, Seymour Stedman, and George Koop of Illinois; Anna F. Smith of California; Theodore Debs and Hugo Miller of Indiana; James F. Carey and Margaret Haile of Massachusetts; G. A. Hoehn, "Mother" Mary H. Jones, and C. F. Meier of Missouri; F. G. R. Gordon of New Hampshire; Samuel Levine of New Jersey; Joseph Barondess, William Butscher, Louis E. Miller, I. Phillips, and Morris Winchevsky of New York; W. J. Carberry and Charles R. Martin of Ohio; A. S. Edwards and William Mailly of Tennessee; and Victor Berger, Frederic Heath, John Doerfler, Jacob Hunger, Charles Kuhn, Oscar Loebel, and George Moerschel of Wisconsin. *Social Democratic Herald*, July 9, 1898.

[3]*Chicago Journal*, June 11, 1898.

[4]Edwards to H. D. Lloyd, Feb. 7, 1898. Lloyd Papers.

[5]*Chicago Tribune*, June 12, 1898.

[6]*Social Democracy Red Book*, p. 67.

distribution and asserted categorically that independent political action and trade unionism were the chief emancipating factors of the working class. The platform itself reflected the three-fold plan of its framers to steer the organization along straight political lines, to repudiate the Socialist Labor Party's policy of dual unionism, and to win the support of agrarian radicals.

In adopting a set of immediate political and economic demands the founders of the Social Democratic Party showed a strong doctrinal kinship with the "revisionism" of Eduard Bernstein, the German socialist theoretician. Bernstein's critical essays in the Stuttgart socialist publication, *Die Neue Zeit*, in 1897 and 1898, and his treatise, *Die Voraussetzungen des Sozialismus und die Aufgaben der Sozialdemokratie*, published the following year, had precipitated a fierce controversy among European Marxists on the question of reformist versus revolutionary tactics. The new party's political demands were substantially the same as those appearing in the Social Democracy platform. The only noteworthy additions were, first, the extension of equal civil, political, and legal rights to women, and, second, the abolition of war as an instrument of national policy and its replacement by international arbitration.

The farmers' demands were a frank acknowledgment that orthodox Marxist theory had little application to, or attraction for, American agricultural producers. A number of things were asked for: 1. An end to the sale of public lands by the federal and state governments, and the utilization of such lands either for public improvements or for lease to farmers in parcels not exceeding 640 acres—the state to have power to make regulations for cultivation and improvement; and all forests and waterways to be placed under the control of the nation. 2. Construction of grain elevators, magazines, and cold-storage buildings by the nation, to be used by the farmers at cost. 3. Consolidation of all postal, railroad, telephone, and telegraph services, and extension of telephone service to all farmers at cost. 4. Uniform rates for the transportation of agricultural products on all railroads. 5. Extension of public credit to county and town governments for improvement of soil, roads, irrigation, and drainage.

The labor section of the platform, repudiating the Socialist Labor Party's dual-unionism policy, called for close and amicable relations with the existing national and local trade-union organizations. The platform advocated adoption of the eight-hour daily workday and a four-hour Saturday workday and affirmed the historic necessity of the strike and the boycott. The attitude of the Social Democrats toward organized labor stood in apposition to that of the 1896 International Socialist and Trades Union Congress in London toward political action. Both deemed it imperative for the working class to use its political power for the purpose of advancing its own interests, and each maintained that differences of opinion within the labor movement should not be a deterrent to co-operation or to separate organization.[7]

The sections of the platform dealing with labor and with immediate political and economic issues found general approval among the party membership, but the farmers' demands at once became a source of controversy. The *Social Democratic Herald* was a polemical battleground for protagonists and antagonists of the demands. The latter, usually hailing from Eastern industrial states where the farmer's economic and political importance was dwindling into insignificance, argued that the demands catered to bourgeois interests for the sake of obtaining votes. On the other hand, the party's Middle Western wing, guided by Berger and Stedman and still possessing a strong spiritual kinship with Populism, contended that the party would be extraordinarily "unscientific" if it ignored the special conditions existing among farmers which Marxist theory utterly failed to take into account. They maintained, furthermore, that socialization would have to become completely pervasive in the industrial realm before it could be considered for, let alone introduced into, agriculture.[8] If economic concentration was the *leitmotif* of American industrialism, such was not as yet true of agriculture. The Middle Western Social Democrats were all too conscious of the fact that the average farmer bristled

---

[7]G. A. Hoehn, "True Socialism: Marxism and Pseudo Marxism," *American Federationist*, V (Oct., 1898), 153.

[8]Victor Berger to H. D. Lloyd, Jan. 11, 1897. Lloyd Papers. *Social Democratic Herald*, June 9, 1898.

at the mere suggestion of land nationalization and collective husbandry.[9] Anxious to capture and hold the farmer's support, they were willing to offer meliorative rather than revolutionary measures. Such immediate assistance, they argued, would be of little consequence in the long run.

The conflict raged unabated for over a year. Finally, a conference of party leaders in Chicago on July 6, 1899, decided to submit the question to the general party membership. The balloting strongly favored deletion of the demands from the platform.[10] The mandate was obeyed, but the issue was to continue to be a very live one.

The Social Democratic Party's first year was not one to lend encouragement for the future. Many socialists, discouraged by the split in the Social Democracy, adopted a cautious "wait and see" attitude. Dues from party members trickled in slowly, if at all, and at one time the SDP treasury contained all of two dollars.[11] J. A. Wayland, whose editorial assistance was needed desperately, was aloof and gave the party little publicity in the *Appeal to Reason*. The *Social Democratic Herald* was published from week to week under the most trying circumstances. For purposes of economy, its format was reduced from six to four columns. In November, Edwards closed the *Herald*'s bare and shabby Chicago office and moved its few pieces of equipment to the little nearby town of Bellesville, where the paper could be printed more cheaply.[12] It remained there until the following June.

Disharmony prevailed within the party organization. Massachusetts rumbled with not completely unjustified complaints of the predominance of Chicago and Milwaukee men in the party's top councils. Also from the Bay State came innuendos to the effect that the party's National Executive Board was seeking to prevent the Eastern branches from being represented proportionally at the next national convention. Debs replied angrily to this allegation: "If other states had done as little as Massachusetts for the national party since it was organized a year ago,

[9]*Social Democratic Herald*, Aug. 12, 1899.
[10]*Workers' Call* (Chicago), July 15, 1899.
[11]MacAlister Coleman, *Eugene V. Debs: A Man Unafraid*, p. 200.
[12]*Social Democratic Herald*, Nov. 26, 1898.

we would not have a sign of a national party in existence . . . .
Massachusetts should also be in when the coin is needed . . . .
They have met every appeal for finance . . . with a deaf ear."[13]

One notable highlight brightened this somber picture. If
Massachusetts was not contributing adequately to the treasury,
as Debs maintained, it nevertheless was placing the Social Democratic Party before the attention of the American people. In
the autumn elections of 1898 the shoe-manufacturing town of
Haverhill amazed everyone by electing to the state legislature
two Social Democratic trade unionists, James F. Carey and
Louis M. Scates.[14] The more prominent of the two was Carey,
a thirty-one-year-old shoe-worker and president of the city
council. He had come into the socialist movement via a Bellamy Nationalist club and had been elected an alderman on the
Socialist Labor Party ticket in 1897.[15] His association with
the DeLeonites, however, was a brief one, as may be recalled,
for he had invited expulsion by the SLP moguls by voting, as
alderman, for an appropriation for a new armory.[16] Scates
was thirty-six years old and also a shoemaker by trade. He
had been dismissed from his last job as a conductor on the Law-
rence and Haverhill Railroad for leading a strike.[17]

These electoral victories received scant attention. But when,
approximately a month later, the same town elected as mayor
another young Social Democrat, John C. Chase, a twenty-eight-
year-old co-operative grocery store clerk and a former textile
worker,[18] many who hitherto had ignored the Social Democratic
Party began to give it some notice. Paul Tyner, editor of the
Arena and president of the Union Reform League, wrote hopefully that Chase's election would be the first of a spiraling series
of political successes which would seep socialism into the United
States at the local level.[19] J. A. Wayland declared in the *Appeal*

---

[13]*Ibid.*, Aug. 5, 1899.

[14]*Ibid.*, Nov. 12, 1898.

[15]*Social Democracy Red Book,* p. 107; *People,* Dec. 12, 1897.

[16]*Proceedings of the 10th National Convention of the Socialist Labor
Party,* p. 45.

[17]*Social Democracy Red Book,* p. 116.

[18]*Social Democratic Herald,* Dec. 10, 1898. Also see *Social Democracy Red
Book,* p. 108; J. C. Chase, "How I Became a Socialist," *Comrade,* II (1903),
109-10.

[19]*Arena,* XXI (1899), 125.

to Reason: "The mere casting of these 2500 votes has done more to direct attention to Socialism than could have been done with any other means."[20]

The successes in Haverhill were exploited fully by the party press, which glossed over the poor showing of the Wisconsin and Missouri branches the same autumn and the virtual lack of Social Democratic activity in Illinois.[21] "Education, organization and the ballot will take them all," crowed the jubilant *Herald*.[22] The paper followed closely the vicissitudes of Chase's administration and carried long reports of the activities of Carey and Scates in the state legislature, where they were presenting bills for an eight-hour workday and for social security legislation. The party officials took great pride in the Haverhill victories and derived no little end of satisfaction from them, since these, together with the almost immediate collapse of the old Social Democracy, seemingly confirmed their wisdom in withdrawing from the June convention.

In the fall of 1899 the Massachusetts Social Democrats repeated their impressive showings. Chase was returned to office in a bitterly contested campaign in which the Boston and Maine Railroad allegedly contributed $25,000 to the opposition.[23] Charles Coulter was elected Social Democratic mayor of the shoe-manufacturing town of Brockton. He carried every ward and had a plurality of over 1,560.[24] Carey was sent back to the state legislature with an increased plurality and was joined there by Frederic O. MacCartney, a former Unitarian minister who won on the Social Democratic ticket from Rockland.[25] In Newburyport, George Hussey and Elizabeth G. Porter, Social Democratic candidates, were elected to the city council and

[20]*Appeal to Reason*, Dec. 24, 1898. For DeLeon's reaction see *People*, Dec. 18, 1898.

[21]Wachman, *History of the Social Democratic Party in Milwaukee, 1897-1900*, pp. 23-24. Eltweed Pomeroy, the social reformer and direct-legislation exponent, campaigned in the Wisconsin election in behalf of the Populists. *Social Democratic Herald*, Dec. 3, 1898. Also see *Social Democracy Red Book*, p. 69.

[22]*Social Democratic Herald*, Dec. 17, 1898.

[23]*Appeal to Reason*, Dec. 16, 1899.

[24]*Social Democratic Herald*, Dec. 16, 1899.

[25]*Ibid.*, Nov. 11, 1899.

school board, respectively.[26] The only casualty was Scates, who was beaten by a Republican-Democratic coalition. Everywhere in Massachusetts the Social Democratic vote was up. Even the party's gubernatorial candidate, Winfield P. Porter, a former Newburyport YMCA executive, whose interest in socialism was first awakened by *Looking Backward*, made a creditable showing.

The absence of electoral victories save in Massachusetts caused some less doctrinaire Social Democrats to consider the advantages that might accrue through political co-operation with the Populists, independent labor parties, or even with the "reformed" Democrats. The *Social Democratic Herald* was on guard against this temptation and warned constantly of the evils of coalition and fusion. If socialists wanted the co-operative commonwealth, it said, they could obtain it only through a socialist party, the Social Democratic Party. Aside from DeLeon's completely impossible Socialist Labor Party, every other organized political group was dedicated to advancing the interests of the capitalistic class. So-called reformers only served to impede the fulfillment of socialism by useless efforts to patch up the capitalistic system.

Oddly enough, the first noteworthy attempt by party members to work with non-Social Democrats came not from the graduates from the Populist ranks in the Middle West but in New York City. There, at the conclusion of the famous Brooklyn Trolley Strike in the late summer of 1899, a group of labor organizations which had supported the strike, including the socialist-oriented Central Labor Federation and the Central Labor Union, made plans to form an "Independent Labor Party" to contest in the coming municipal election. They invited and received the co-operation of the Social Democratic Party of Greater New York.

The Independent Labor Party program was largely Social Democratic in origin, and for a short time relations between the Social Democrats and the new party were harmonious. The old socialism versus trade-unionism issue cropped up, however, and friction began to generate when some trade-union leaders balked at accepting the party's program. The controversy broke

---

[26]*Ibid.*, Dec. 23, 1899.

into the open late in September when the Independent Labor Party officials, over the protests of the Social Democrats, agreed to seat at a party conference several outspoken supporters of William Jennings Bryan. The socialist delegates withdrew immediately. Shortly thereafter, the Social Democratic Committee of Greater New York decided to sever all connections with the Independent Labor Party.[27]

The Social Democratic Party chieftains, watching the course of events from the Middle West, were highly disturbed by the somewhat bizarre antics of the New Yorkers. At about the same time that the New York Social Democratic Committee was withdrawing support from the Independent Labor Party, which Morris Winchevsky characterized as "a child of the SLP born out of wedlock," the SDP National Executive Board condemned all deviations from straight socialist politics. Speaking for the Board, Debs said: "The incident of our branches of Greater New York 'fusing' with the Independent Labor Party of that city was a mistake, to put it mildly, and I am glad our comrades awakened to the fact and corrected the error by withdrawing from the alliance before experiencing the harmful effects which must have followed. How our comrades in the East, who have among them some of the brightest lights in the party, could have been led into a situation in which they have everything to lose and nothing to gain, is not easy for me to understand, and I confess to having been greatly surprised when I heard of it."[28]

Social Democratic spokesmen feared less the Socialist Laborites on their left and the Republicans and Democrats on their right than reformers of the Bryan stripe and "non-partisan socialists" like Samuel Jones and Herbert Casson. With the Socialist Labor Party there existed an ideological affinity but a complete divergence on the matter of tactics. With the Republicans and Bourbon Democrats there was no common ground whatsoever. Reformers, however, could easily obfuscate the real issues while apparently—and, in their own light, sincerely—acting in the interests of the working class. By clamoring for political reform through such devices as direct legislation, for economic amelioration through public ownership of municipal

[27]*Ibid.,* Oct. 7, 1899.
[28]*Ibid.,* Oct. 21, 1899.

utilities, and for better working conditions for labor through remedial legislation, the reformers could turn wage earners aside from their basic aims and cause long and unnecessary delays in the attainment of socialism. Their promise to bring about socialism without a socialist party tended also to confuse some middle-class liberals who might otherwise throw in their lot with the Social Democratic Party. In their de-emphasis of political activity, in fact, lay their greatest danger.

Social Democratic editorialists strove constantly to impress upon their readers that socialism was a matter of principles and not of personalities. When Social Democrats were chided for failing to support and thus helping to defeat John P. Altgeld in the 1899 Chicago municipal elections, the *Herald* explained that while the party approved of Altgeld as an individual, it could not endorse him because he was not running as a socialist.[29] Debs took much the same position when Samuel Jones sought the governorship of Ohio on the Union Reform Party ticket during the same year.[30] Closer to home, Jones's off-brand socialism was censured by Max Hayes, the socialist editor of the Cleveland Central Labor Union's weekly paper, the *Cleveland Citizen*. "If Jones were not a rich man, his self-glorification and political gymnastics would be laughed at," wrote Hayes. "It may be taken for granted that no Socialist will be attracted by the Jones fad."[31]

The editors hoisted caution flags warning those showing interest in the Fabian policy of achieving immediate reform and eventual socialism through the Democratic Party. Debs argued persuasively that the displacement of the Republicans by the Democrats would involve simply a change of masters for the working class.[32] Imogene Fales, now a Social Democratic Party organizer in New York, also placed unwary socialist mariners on guard against sirens seeking to lure them toward treacherous Democratic reform reefs. The Democratic Party, she declared, was in control of the same unscrupulous men who had knifed Bryan in the back during the 1896 campaign. That some in-

---

[29]*Ibid.*, Apr. 15, 1899.
[30]*Ibid.*, July 1, 1899; Ginger, *The Bending Cross*, pp. 201-2.
[31]*Cleveland Citizen*, Aug. 26, 1899.
[32]*Social Democratic Herald*, July 1, 1899.

dividual Democrats espoused public ownership of utilities and
abolition of the trusts could not conceal their party's true reactionary character.[33]   To discredit efforts of certain Fabians
to portray Bryan as a socialist at heart, the Social Democratic
Party papers and Wayland's *Appeal to Reason* frequently reproduced the following letter from the Commoner to F. G. R.
Gordon dated May 11, 1897:

> You ask me whether I am in favor of socialism and define
> it to mean 'collective ownership of all the means of pro-
> duction and distribution' and desire an answer 'yes' or 'no.'
> I answer 'no.'

Debs and other party leaders frankly acknowledged as a vote-
getter the plank in the Social Democratic platform calling for
adoption of the initiative and referendum.   To A. M. Simons,
the young Chicago writer, direct legislation was "good sucker
bait,"[34] though not a lure on which confirmed socialists would
bite.   The *Social Democratic Herald* insisted that nothing was
wrong with the representative principle.   It was, rather, a good
thing, becoming dangerous "only when applied to working by
proxy on the part of the rich and eating in the same way on the
part of the poor."[35]   Victor Berger considered direct legislation
a "fad" but a nevertheless potent weapon for capitalistic parties
to use as a *"last resort"* for appealing "to the grand *stupidity*
of the *masses"* before using "sheer force."[36]

The more that non-partisan socialists seized on direct legislation as a general all-around panacea and advocated it as a means
of bringing about socialism without a socialist party, the more
hostile and truculent became the attitude of the Social Democrats.   A fierce, all-out, concerted assault on direct legislation
took shape on the eve of the 1899 National Social and Political
Conference in Buffalo.

Anticipating the conference's emphasis on the initiative and
referendum, the *Herald* on July 1 opened the attack with a
prominent front-page article entitled, "The Referendum Not
an Unmixed Blessing."   Since direct legislation was essentially

[33]*Ibid.,* Sept. 9, 1899.
[34]*Direct Legislation Record,* III (1900), 62.
[35]*Social Democratic Herald,* June 3, 1899.
[36]Berger to H. D. Lloyd, Jan. 11, 1897. Lloyd Papers.

democratic in principle, the difficulty of attacking it was baldly acknowledged. Not to expose its fallacies, however, would be reprehensible. One major argument against it was that an uneducated electorate, certain to exist under capitalism, could easily be misled into making both unwise and socially dangerous decisions. Had Debs's fate been left at the bar of public opinion during the Pullman Strike of 1894, for example, he "would have been hanged for the crime of trying to help humanity." Equally dangerous was the tendency inherent in direct legislation to destroy political parties. It might also be employed as an instrument of tyranny, as was demonstrated when Napoleon used the plebiscite to have himself crowned Emperor of France. In a telling shot directed against those middle-class reformers who categorized themselves as Fabian socialists, it was noted that the British Fabian society had put trade unions on guard against overhasty transference of power through direct legislation.

Subsequent issues of the *Herald* featured several elaborations on these criticisms of direct legislation. In one, Mrs. Fales wrote:

> This is a battle we are fighting, and we must have all the shrewdness and strategic keenness of a general commanding his forces. We must watch not only the movements of the enemy, the upholders of the competitive system, who will employ all the means at their command for our destruction, but also those who, actuated by the best motives, are unintentionally playing into the enemy's hands. This is defensive and offensive warfare. The time has come for the employment of both methods. Let us stand by our guns.[37]

The acerbity of the Social Democrats' onslaught against the reformers was strikingly counterbalanced by their circumspect attitude toward the American Federation of Labor. In a series of articles in the *American Federationist*, G. A. Hoehn not only praised the policies and tactics of the AF of L president, Samuel Gompers, but sought to show that they were intrinsically in accord with those of bona fide Marxists.[38] While the party heads were anxious to see the Federation go on record in favor

---

[37] *Social Democratic Herald,* Aug. 19, 1899.

[38] See in particular G. A. Hoehn, "True Socialism, Marxism and Pseudo Marxism," *American Federationist,* V (1898), 175-77.

of socialism, they were by no means ready to denounce it if it did not. Nor did they ask Federation support of the Social Democratic Party as such. The *Social Democratic Herald* expressed disappointment rather than bitterness when the AF of L national convention in Kansas City in December, 1898, overwhelmingly defeated a Social-Democratic-endorsed resolution in favor of government ownership of the means of production and distribution.[39]

That James Carey and two other Social Democrats at Kansas City opposed Gompers' re-election as Federation president gravely disturbed Seymour Stedman, who attended the convention with Victor Berger. Even though socialists disliked Gompers for personal reasons, he wrote in the *Herald*, unsuccessful opposition to his re-election undoubtedly undermined their position at the convention. Stedman claimed that the party could have obtained Gompers' support. He said that the latter had told Victor Berger that he would vote for the Social Democratic candidates and advise his friends to do likewise.[40]

Some exception was taken to what appeared to be an overeager and unwarranted effort to appease Gompers,[41] who, as usual, had delivered an anti-socialist tirade at the convention. But the issue quickly faded from the pages of the *Herald*. During the remainder of the year and through 1900 the paper treated relations between the party and the Federation as gingerly and perfunctorily as possible.

Early in 1899 a small group of Texas socialists, still redolent with the sweet-grass aroma of Populism, organized the "Socialist Party of America." But like the Texan Republic, the little Texas socialist party with the impressively big name was to have only a brief period of independence. In June, 1899, Debs was lecturing in San Antonio. He met with W. E. Farmer and other members of the party's executive board and charmed them

---

[39]The vote was 1,971 to 493. *Report of the Proceedings of the 18th Annual Convention of the American Federation of Labor* (1898), p. 110.

[40]*Social Democratic Herald*, Dec. 31, 1898. John F. Tobin in a speech to the AF of L convention also declared that Gompers had assured him that he would vote for the Social Democratic Party. *Report of the Proceedings of the 18th Annual Convention of the American Federation of Labor*, p. 107.

[41]*Social Democratic Herald*, Jan. 14, 1899.

into combining their organization with the Social Democratic Party.[42]

For the expansive Texas socialists, at least, this graceful surrender of independence was an event of regrettable but primary magnitude. But of greater significance to the socialist movement as a whole was the rebellion on the very verge of eruption within the Socialist Labor Party. Back of the revolt were dissatisfaction with the policy of dual unionism in the trade-union field and discontent with the leadership of DeLeon, Hugo Vogt, Lucien Sanial, Henry Kuhn, and a small group of adherents in New York. These were substantially the same issues which had occasioned a minor crisis in the SLP in 1897.

By December, 1898, the opposition within the Socialist Labor Party had begun to crystallize around the daily *New Yorker Volkszeitung*, edited by the scholarly and highly capable Hermann Schlüter. Although the paper was recognized as an official organ, its relationship to the party was somewhat involved. Like its weekly supplement, *Vorwaerts*, and the party's national organ, the *People*, the *Volkszeitung* was put out by the Socialist Co-operative Publishing Company and was thus legally independent of the party. But the party exercised a considerable amount of control since it appointed the company's directors and the paper's editors.[43] Notwithstanding these factors, the *Volkszeitung*'s editorial writers had an opportunity, if they wished to use it, to question the party line laid down by DeLeon.

Although the *Volkszeitung* had published a few pin pricks against the party leadership during 1898, it did not challenge DeLeon's basic policies until December 14, when an editorial was printed expressing regret at the abandonment of the old socialist trade-union policy of "boring from within." Gompers and his supporters within the American Federation of Labor, said the *Volkszeitung*, were formerly not so comfortable:

> at the time . . . there were more socialist pikes in that [AF of L] pond; at a time—namely, when a part of these had

---

[42]*Ibid.*, June 3, June 17, 1899; *Cleveland Citizen*, Sept. 2, 1899; *Social Democracy Red Book*, p. 71. The relationship of the Texas socialists to Populism is discussed in Roscoe Martin, *The People's Party in Texas* ("Bureau of Research in the Social Sciences Study," No. 4 [Austin, 1933]), p. 79.

[43]*Appeal to Reason*, June 24, 1899; Fine, *Labor and Farmer Parties in the United States*, p. 170.

not yet chosen to lead, outside of the American Federation, a separate existence of doubtful success, instead of, as formerly, tirelessly, unflaggingly, step by step boring their way forward from within. At that time the corruptionists of the labor movement always felt quite uncomfortable at the opening of every annual convention, because they were in the dark as to the strength which the socialists might turn up, as to the weapons of attack these might be equipped with, and as to how far these would succeed in making breaches in the ranks of the shaky. This sense of uneasiness has now wholly vanished.[44]

Five days later an editorial in similar vein referred to the poor showing made by the socialists at the AF of L convention at Kansas City as indicative of the harm caused by the disruptive activities of the SLP-sponsored Socialist Trade and Labor Alliance. It argued that the latter's attacks on non-socialist unions allowed Gompers and other "corrupt opponents of socialism at the convention" to rally the politically "indifferent" delegates against Carey's resolution calling for the Federation's endorsement of government ownership of the means of production and distribution.[45]

With even something more than his characteristic vigor, DeLeon struck back in the *People* at the *Volkszeitung* naggers. He accused Schlüter and the paper's other writers of being under the influence of "bourgeois doctrines" and of deviating from the true Marxist line.[46] The furor in the socialist world created by the publication of Bernstein's revisionist critique played neatly into DeLeon's hands, for he immediately associated the *Volkszeitung* group with the principles of "the German fakir, Edward Bernstein."[47] He also trumped up a controversy with the *Volkszeitung* on the question of taxation. He took issue with the latter's "middle-class" contention that the wage earner, in his capacity of consumer, ultimately shouldered the full brunt of paying all direct and indirect taxes levied by a capitalistic government.[48] For presuming to support the *Volkszeitung*

[44]*New Yorker Volkszeitung,* Dec. 14, 1898.

[45]*Ibid.,* Dec. 19, 1898.

[46]*People,* Dec. 25, 1898; Jan. 1, Jan. 8, 1899.

[47]*Ibid.,* July 23, 1899.

[48]The entire taxation controversy is aired in a special English-language edition of the *New Yorker Volkszeitung,* Apr. 29, 1899.

on this particular issue, one Benjamin Feigenbaum was immortalized in this choice bit of DeLeon defamation:

> The *Volkszeitung*'s position was preposterous, and the paper . . . selected the right man to defend it—a man named Feigenbaum, a semi-lunatic, a freak, with more kinks in his head than the average well-balanced man could ever begin to think of, and more mental dishonesty in his make-up than could be traced with a thousand x-rays.[49]

Finally, DeLeon succeeded in having the directors of the Socialist Co-operative Publishing Company reprimand the *Volkszeitung*'s editors for "coming to definite conclusions" on the entire dual-unionism question.[50]

DeLeon's counterblasts and the censure of the *Volkszeitung* editors—which the latter refused to publish—by no means ended the issue. On the contrary, they merely exacerbated it. On March 23 the entire membership of the Socialist Co-operative Publishing Company met and, to DeLeon's mortification, voted by a two-to-one majority to uphold the *Volkszeitung* editors on the trade-union question. In effect, this vote removed the reprimand administered by the company's directors, several of whom thereupon resigned.[51]

On the basis of the *Volkszeitung*'s heresy, the party's National Executive Committee, over the protest of one member, Henry Stahl, appealed to Socialist Laborites throughout the country for support.[52] Using the same tactics employed two years earlier against the Jewish recalcitrants, they proposed to the national membership a referendum which, if adopted, would sever all connections between the party and the Socialist Co-operative Publishing Company and, at the same time, turn over to the party heads the property and mailing lists of the *People* and *Vorwaerts*, which the company had in its possession.[53]

As DeLeon and his friends had anticipated, the result of the referendum, according to their own count, was in their favor.

---

[49]*Proceedings of the 10th National Convention of the Socialist Labor Party*, p. 18.

[50]*People*, Jan. 8, 1899.

[51]*Ibid.*, Aug. 20, 1899. For a defense of DeLeon's position, see Kuhn and Johnson, *The Socialist Labor Party During Four Decades*, pp. 28-45.

[52]*People*, May 1, 1899.

[53]*Ibid.*, June 11, 1899.

But they had not given sufficient thought to the views of the
members of the Cleveland section, which constituted the party's
Board of Appeals. Acting on a petition from the publishing
company, that section ruled that the National Executive Committee had no power to order a referendum. Thus the situation
was more confused than ever.[54]

The *Volkszeitung* affair touched off a nation-wide uprising in
the Socialist Labor Party. Although the paper's subscribers
were mostly Germans living in the New York metropolitan area,
the news of the attack on the party leadership inspired other
elements of the SLP to revolt against DeLeon. In New York
itself, the name of Morris Hillquit, a rising East Side lawyer,
began to be associated increasingly with the anti-DeLeonite
forces. Max S. Hayes of Cleveland joined in the rebellion. In
Chicago, A. M. Simons repudiated the party's National Executive Committee, as did Eugene Dietzgen, who wrote a stinging
pamphlet entitled, "Lèse Majesty and Treason to the 'Fakirs' of
the Socialist Labor Party." From Philadelphia came word
that J. Mahlon Barnes, the AF of L trade-union leader, had
deserted DeLeon. In San Francisco, G. B. Benham assumed
command of the insurgents. Job Harriman in Los Angeles
joined in condemning the party leaders. Charles H. Matchett,
the SLP candidate for president in 1896, denounced DeLeon
and his cabal. And in the midst of this general uprising, J. A.
Wayland and the harried DeLeon intensified an exchange of
editorial insults and invective that had begun early in the previous year.[55] Throughout the country in the summer of 1899
the SLP reeled like a pugilist battered, bleeding, and groggy
from an unceasing barrage of blows. With grim satisfaction,
Debs wrote: "The carbuncle at New York has come to a head
and the pus is flowing freely. Purification is bound to follow,
but in the meantime the olfactory nerves will be put to the
severest test."[56]

The Rosenberg-*Volkszeitung* controversy just ten years previous had shown that the Socialist Labor Party was so organized

[54]*Proceedings of the 10th National Convention of the Socialist Labor
Party,* p. 21.
[55]See *Appeal to Reason,* July 30, 1898; June 24, July 1, July 8, 1899. Also
see *People,* Mar. 13, 1898; May 28, July 16, 1899.
[56]*Social Democratic Herald,* Sept. 2, 1899.

that whoever dominated the General Committee of its Greater New York section could control the party. The General Committee was responsible for the appointment of the party's National Executive Committee. The latter, in turn, determined the national policies of the organization. When a meeting of the General Committee was called on the night of July 8 at the Labor Lyceum on East Fourth Street, both the pro- and anti-DeLeon factions turned out in force. Trouble began almost at once when the party chief questioned the qualifications of several of those present, since this was the first meeting after the semi-annual election of new delegates. The nomination of a temporary chairman resulted in several fist fights in various parts of the hall. The meeting ended in a general melee.[57]

Leaders of the insurgent faction—dubbed the "kangaroos" by DeLeon—claimed that their supporters were in the majority. Accordingly, they decided to take matters into their own hands. Acting in the name of the General Committee, they called another meeting for the night of July 10. The DeLeonites boycotted the meeting, holding it to be unauthorized. But the insurgents, of course, ignored this contention. With a minimum of debate, they deposed DeLeon and his henchmen from the party leadership. DeLeon was replaced by Henry L. Slobodin, an East Side attorney, and a new seven-man National Executive Committee was appointed.[58]

Following the meeting, a band of insurgents marched over to party headquarters at 184 Williams Street to take over the meeting rooms and the offices of the *People*, which were housed in the same building. DeLeon and his loyal followers, armed with clubs and improvised weapons, were on hand to greet them. A riot ensued and the hated "capitalistic" police were called in to end the fracas among the comrades. The DeLeonites, many with bashed and bloody heads, remained unbowed and in control of party headquarters.[59] They had triumphed in the battle of Williams Street even though on the next day they were

[57]*Proceedings of the 10th National Convention of the Socialist Labor Party,* p. 23.

[58]Members of the Committee were Morris Hillquit, Henry Stahl, Richard Bock, S. Berlin, Julius Halpern, Franz Seubert, and Robert Woodruff.

[59]*Proceedings of the 10th National Convention of the Socialist Labor Party,* pp. 24-25; *People,* July 16, 1899.

obliged to stage a strategic retreat to a new headquarters at 61 Beekman Street.

Two Socialist Labor Parties, both claiming the loyalty of tried and true Marxists, presented themselves for public acceptance. Each had its own national officers and headquarters and each published a paper called the *People*. This condition existed for several weeks. It came to an impasse when both groups sought to register candidates in the 1899 autumn elections in New York. The matter was brought before the Secretary of State, who ruled in favor of the DeLeon faction, which thereby retained possession of the party name and its arm-and-hammer trademark.[60] This decision was a severe blow to the anti-DeLeonites since it prevented them from participating in the elections under the name, seal, and official auspices of the Socialist Labor Party. Though the "kangaroos" were obliged to stand by while the despised DeLeon ran for State Assemblyman in the 16th district, they were not completely inactive. They circulated handbills urging his defeat. One such handbill read:

Socialists Don't Vote
Daniel DeLeon
aided by TAMMANY Police Board
Stole the Name and Emblem of
The Socialist Labor Party.
He is a Union Wrecker
an Enemy of
Organized Labor.
Socialists, Don't Vote
for This Adventurer.

Another handbill cited DeLeon's record:

1884 a paid spellbinder for the Democratic Party.
1886 a Single Taxer
1888 a Nationalist
1889 a Socialist (?)
1899 a nominee through the favor of a Tammany Police Board aided by Republicans.

[60]*People,* Oct. 22, 1899.

What next?

A foreigner himself, he hates and denounces every foreign born citizen.

No socialist, no honest workingman, can vote for this man.

Remember, the Socialist Labor Party has no ticket in the field this year.

Sixteenth Assembly District, SLP[61]

The dissident Socialist Laborites, for their part, secured an injunction which prevented the DeLeon faction from using *The People* as the name of its party paper.[62] Under this title they continued to publish the paper, which was placed under the direction of N. I. Stone, who agreed to edit it until the services of a professional socialist journalist could be obtained. In October, 1899, Algernon Lee, a young Minneapolis newspaperman, succeeded Stone. DeLeon's paper appeared thereafter under the name of *The Weekly People*.

With the DeLeon coterie in control of the regular party organization and in possession of the party name, the "kangaroo" group faced the alternative of forming a new party or uniting with the Social Democrats. The former course was not seriously contemplated. With the DeLeon Socialist Laborites and the Social Democrats already in the field, little room existed for still a third socialist party. On the other hand, union with the Social Democrats was eminently practical from the point of view of both ideology and tactics. Little ideological difference existed with the Social Democrats, who had dropped the agricultural demands from their platform. A union of forces could give American socialists, for the first time, a relatively strong and well-organized national party. Some objection was raised against outright fusion on the Social Democrats' own terms. Also, some opposition was voiced to uniting with Victor Berger and several of the New York Jewish socialists who had left the SLP in 1897.[63] These were not considered serious enough, however, to stand in the way of unification.

[61] Handbills in Archives of the Rand School of Social Science, New York City. Also see *Proceedings of the 10th National Convention of the Socialist Labor Party*, p. 29.

[62] *Weekly People*, June 23, 1900.

[63] *People*, Nov. 19, Nov. 26, 1899.

The Social Democrats were far from being in accord on union with the Socialist Labor Party insurgents. Many of the native born among them were convinced that the addition of the Socialist Laborites, most of whom were immigrants of relatively recent vintage, would weaken rather than strengthen their party. Berger, who had nursed a grudge against the *Volkszeitung* group ever since the deposition of the Rosenberg-Busche faction in 1889, was maliciously delighted at its present discomfiture and under no circumstances wished to relieve it. Debs, on the contrary, favored an amalgamation of the socialist groups. Believing that there were "hundreds of perfectly straight 'Kangaroo' socialists" who wanted to come into the Social Democratic Party, he resented Berger's vindictiveness.[64]

In the main, sympathy for union came from party members in Massachusetts, New York, and Missouri. But even in Massachusetts and New York unanimity of opinion was badly lacking. In Massachusetts, where Carey, himself a former Socialist Laborite, was enthusiastic for union, Margaret Haile eyed with suspicion the professed good intentions of Hillquit and his associates.[65] The Jewish Social Democrats of New York, mindful that many of the same Socialist Laborites now suggesting union, only two years earlier had stood by DeLeon in his dispute with the *Forward* group, adamantly opposed any plan for unification.[66]

The most stubborn resistance came from Social Democratic leaders in Wisconsin and Illinois. For over a year they had labored to build up the party. In complete control of the national party organization, it was quite understandable that they had little inclination to share it with men whom they did not trust. A union of forces would serve to strengthen appreciably the party's Eastern wing. A real danger existed that the party's center of gravity would shift from Chicago to New York, a development which would seriously jeopardize their own hegemony in party councils.

---

[64]Debs to Frederic Heath, Dec. 26, 1899. Letter in possession of Mr. Heath of Milwaukee, Wis.

[65]*People,* Dec. 3, 1899.

[66]*Ibid.,* Mar. 18, 1900.

Debs was the only member of the Social Democratic Party's National Executive Board who was eager for union. Yet, ironically, he was the first of the party chieftains to air his doubts as to its desirability. His opposition was premised on personal rather than doctrinal or even organizational grounds. His indignation had been aroused by a letter in the *People*, now ostensibly purified of all taint of DeLeonism, alleging that he (Debs) was a Populist at heart and a dictatorial leader like DeLeon.[67] The letter was written by one Leon A. Malkiel, who was not associated with the *People*. That the letter had been published irked Debs, who for over a year had endured a constant stream of DeLeon's calumny. Clearly, if the dissident Socialist Laborites allowed such attacks to be made in their official paper, they were not yet free of their former leader's poisonous influence.

Under the stimulus of Malkiel's letter and to what must have been the immense satisfaction of his associates on the National Executive Board, Debs dispatched to the *Social Democratic Herald* a scorching letter accusing the new editors of the *People* of adopting DeLeon's journalistic methods. Disregarding the fact that the criticism had not been made by any member of the *People*'s staff, Debs stated that while he favored a union of socialists, the time seemed inopportune for such action. He did not preclude the possibility of fusion. But before any union could be contemplated, "the serpents of defamation" had to be eliminated from the Socialist Laborite ranks and the *People* would have to "clean its skirts." Though Debs did not even address his letter to the editors of the *People*, he peremptorily demanded from them an apology for printing Malkiel's letter.[68]

Debs did not receive an apology; for his charges, weighed by almost any standard of judgment, were not merited by the facts of the case. From the time that DeLeon's foes had taken over the *People*, its articles concerning the Social Democratic Party had been laudatory with one sole exception—an editorial which charged Berger, not without some degree of truth, with being a "would-be boss."[69] In a carefully written editorial reply to

67 *Ibid.*, Dec. 24, 1899.
68 *Social Democratic Herald*, Jan. 20, 1900.
69 *People*, Nov. 26, 1899.

Debs, Lee stated that he would not impose censorship on the paper for anyone. He, too, expressed the belief that the time might not be propitious for unification and suggested caustically that it never would be until the Social Democrats ceased indulging in hero worship.[70]

The interchange between Debs and Lee, while illustrating the suspicions held by both groups, failed to alter appreciably the course of events. Probably a majority of the Social Democrats and nearly all of the "kangaroo" Socialist Laborites desired unity. The latter were resolved to take steps toward that end at a conference scheduled to open in Rochester, New York, on January 27, 1900.

Fifty-nine delegates from all parts of the United States attended the Rochester convention. Unquestionably, the most impressive figure present was Morris Hillquit who, as a youth of fifteen named Moses Hilkowitz, had come to the United States in 1886 from his native Latvian city of Riga. He had hardly landed before he was helping to organize the United Hebrew Trades of New York. He also joined the Socialist Labor Party and became a regular contributor to one of its Yiddish-language publications, the *Arbeiter-Zeitung*. During his spare time, Hillquit taught English in Americanization classes for newly arrived immigrants and also managed to attend New York University Law School, from which he received a degree in 1893. Between that year and 1899 he devoted nearly all of his time to his law practice and very little to the Socialist Labor Party.[71] But when the uprising against DeLeon developed in 1899 he suddenly emerged as one of the chief leaders of the opposition and was elected to the new SLP National Executive Committee.

The Rochester conclave was distinguished among socialist gatherings by the high degree of harmony among the delegates. It had little difficulty in agreeing on a fully "class-conscious" program. As was anticipated, it passed a strongly worded resolution repudiating dual unionism. All party members were

---

[70]*Ibid.*, Jan. 28, 1900.

[71]Hillquit's autobiography, *Leaves of Life,* relates many interesting aspects of his early career in the United States. For a DeLeon appraisal of Hillquit, see *Proceedings of the 10th National Convention of the Socialist Labor Party,* p. 22.

urged to join an organization of the trades to which they belonged.   Once the platform had been agreed upon, the delegates
prepared to take up the most important matter on the agenda,
that of effecting a union with the Social Democratic Party.[72]

Even before discussion of the issue began, the road to unity
was beset with a formidable stumbling block.   The National
Executive Board of the Social Democratic Party, sensing correctly that the conference would make a gesture for union, was
anxious to maintain the upper hand in any bargaining that
might occur in the future.   If union was to result, the Social
Democratic leaders wished it on their terms.   Accordingly, they
sent the convention the following telegram:

> The National Executive Board of the Social Democratic
> Party sends fraternal greetings.   The Board has learned of
> the divisions which have arisen within the ranks of the
> Socialist Labor Party, and, recognizing the desirability of
> concerted action by all class-conscious Socialists in this
> country, hereby extends a hearty invitation to your conven-
> tion, as well as to all the members of your party, to join
> the Social Democratic Party in the struggle to emancipate
> humanity from class rule and the slavery of capitalism by
> the establishment of the Cooperative Commonwealth. With
> an earnest desire for the success of the cause, we remain,
> fraternally yours, etc.[73]

Many of the SLP members at Rochester were unduly over-
sensitive and resented what they considered a condescending
tone in the telegram.   Hillquit declared that while unity "had
become a matter of necessity," the attitude of the Social Democratic leaders had made its fulfillment doubtful.   "They proceed
on the unwarranted assumption," he stated in what was little
less than braggadocio, "that our party is in a state of anarchy,
without a name, organization, or cohesion."   The Social Democratic Party, he said, would have to meet the Rochester convention "half-way."   The Socialist Laborites would not come
begging for admission.   Hillquit alluded unpleasantly to the
possibility of instigating internal strife among the Social Demo-

---

[72]*Report of the National Executive Committee to the National Convention
of the Socialist Labor Party, Rochester, Jan. 27, 1900,* pp. 2-7; *People,* Feb.
4, 1900.

[73]*Social Democratic Herald,* Feb. 3, 1900.

crats. Should the National Executive Board refuse to nego-
tiate on an honorable basis, he said, the Socialist Laborites
might appeal to the party rank and file which, he claimed, had
shown itself to be favorably disposed toward union.[74]

Following a short debate, the convention voted to wire a reply
to the telegram. After thanking the Board for its felicitous
greetings, the message went on: "If it is a call for friendly and
harmonious action by both parties, we welcome it and heartily
reciprocate the invitation." As important as the message itself
was the following sentence which was deleted from the original
draft at the insistence of Hillquit and some of the other cooler-
headed members of the convention: "If it is an invitation for
us to disband and join the Social Democratic Party collectively
or individually, we hope for the honor and good sense of the
membership of your party that your Board does not bear the
approval of the rank and file of your party in addressing such
a highly peculiar request to the National Convention of another
self-respecting Socialist party."[75]

The convention framed a series of resolutions setting forth
its own position on the problem of socialist unity. They declared that union with the Social Democrats was highly desirable but only possible if both sides gave up their "petty
ambitions" and sought to work out an equitable agreement. To
effect the union, the convention appointed a committee of nine
to act as a "Permanent Committee of Socialist Union" until
such was accomplished.[76] Its members were authorized to attend
the Social Democratic National Convention, scheduled to open
on March 6 in Indianapolis, and to present the unity resolutions
to it. They were also to seek the creation of a similar committee
within the Social Democratic Party. All agreements arrived
at by consultation between the representative groups were to
be submitted to a general vote of both organizations.[77]

---

[74]*People,* Feb. 4, 1900.

[75]*Ibid.*

[76]Members of the Unity Committee included J. Mahlon Barnes of Philadelphia; G. B. Benham of San Francisco; C. E. Fenner of Worcester, Massachusetts; Max S. Hayes of Cleveland; Job Harriman of Los Angeles; Morris
Hillquit and N. I. Stone of New York City; F. J. Sieverman of Rochester;
and W. E. White of New Haven. *Ibid.,* Apr. 1, 1900.

[77]*Ibid.,* Feb. 4, 1900.

Before adjourning, the conference nominated candidates for the Presidency and Vice-Presidency, although adverse court decisions in New York and Massachusetts precluded the use of the name "Socialist Labor Party." The advisability of choosing candidates had been questioned because of the plans for negotiating with the Social Democrats. It was decided, however, that since the meetings had not yet begun and since there was no guarantee that they ever would occur, the naming of candidates should not be put off. Accordingly, the convention nominated Job Harriman for the Presidency and Max Hayes for the Vice-Presidency.[78] Harriman, an Indiana-born socialist, had once been in the ministry of the Christian Church but was currently practicing law in Los Angeles. In 1898 he had run for governor of California on the SLP ticket and had polled 5,600 votes.[79]

The reasonableness of the Rochester convention's unity resolutions placed the Social Democratic Party's National Executive Board in a quandary. For over a month, the *Social Democratic Herald* made no mention of them. This was no accident, as the resolutions made it difficult to justify opposition to union. Nor was Hillquit's implied threat to stir up dissension in the party by a direct appeal to the general membership lost on the Board members who recognized that such a tactic might meet with considerable success. Yet Berger, Heath, Cox, and Stedman were determined not to allow the party reins to slip from their hands and see the fruits of a year's organizational efforts snatched away. If no real issue separated the two socialist groups, they were not unprepared to create one. The best they could do in this regard was to insist on retention of the party name as an absolute prerequisite to any negotiations. Since some of the Socialist Laborites had expressed dissatisfaction with the name,[80] it was hoped that this flimsy pretext might be converted into a formidable barrier to any hasty consolidation.

The Social Democratic Party national convention in Indianapolis in early March was, in general, as acrimonious as the

---

[78]*Ibid.*, Feb. 11, 1900.

[79]*Workers' Call*, Feb. 17, 1900. Also see *Appeal to Reason*, Nov. 3, 1900; Job Harriman, "How I Became a Socialist," *Comrade*, I (1902), 170-71.

[80]As early as December, 1898, the name issue arose in speculations over a possible SLP-SDP union. *Social Democratic Herald*, Dec. 10, Dec. 13, 1898.

Rochester gathering had been harmonious. Almost immediately after the convention was organized, Meyer London, one of the principal proponents of the policy of collaboration with the Independent Labor Party, found himself hard pressed to answer a bitter attack by his fellow New York delegate, I. Phillips.[81] The Phillips-London tiff had hardly subsided when A. S. Edwards, editor of the *Social Democratic Herald*, heard himself accused of attempting to gag the party membership by refusing to print letters expressing opinions contrary to his own. The unhappy little Welshman had the satisfaction of having the convention vote its confidence in him though not until he had been subjected to some brutal criticism from several Eastern representatives.[82] Next a resolution by James Carey opposing the use of trade unions as socialist political adjuncts was countered by a plea from Frederic Heath who was depending heavily on Milwaukee labor organizations to support his mayoralty candidacy in the coming municipal elections.[83] Carey's resolution was tabled for the sake of expediency, if for no other purpose, after the excitable Victor Berger shouted that it was "intended as a slap in the face of the Milwaukee comrades."[84] Then an attempt to restore the farmers' demands into the party platform created still another furor. It was beaten back after a hot discussion in which the Wisconsin-Illinois faction permitted the somewhat bewildered W. E. Farmer to bear the brunt of Carey's forceful attack.[85] And finally, an effort by the Los Angeles Social Democrats to delete all mention of the class-struggle concept from the party platform was howled down in a thundering chorus of "nays."[86]

The tensions within the Social Democratic Party were not lost on Morris Hillquit, Max Hayes, Job Harriman, and G. B. Benham, who attended the convention as representatives of the Socialist Labor Party committee on unity. On the motion of Debs, who was rumored to be out of sympathy with his fellow

[81]*People,* Mar. 18, 1900.
[82]*Ibid.*
[83]Still, *Milwaukee, The History of a City,* p. 304.
[84]*People,* Mar. 18, 1900; *Indianapolis Journal,* Mar. 7, 1900.
[85]*People,* Mar. 18, 1900.
[86]*Ibid; Indianapolis Journal,* Mar. 8, 1900.

members on the Executive Board,[87] they were given seats on the
convention floor. Hillquit was invited to sit on the speakers'
platform, as was Benham, editor of the San Francisco paper,
Class Struggle.

The Socialist Laborite delegates were correctly silent during
the interparty squabbles, but when discussions on unity arose,
they were not reticent to speak their piece. Harriman stated
flatly that personalities rather than issues were keeping apart
the two socialist groups. He found both parties in fundamental
ideological agreement now that the Socialist Laborites had
repudiated dual unionism and the Social Democrats had junked
the farmers' demands. Indiscreet and unscrupulous men doubtless existed in both parties, said Harriman, in an all too thinly
veiled reference to the Social Democratic officers, but their
machinations could be throttled effectively in a vigilant, unified
socialist organization. Hillquit also urged union and indicated
a willingness to accept the name "Social Democratic" if it could
be demonstrated that its use would be conducive to the success
of the socialist movement. Hillquit cautioned against the party
name becoming a fetish and asked the delegates to keep an open
mind on the problem. "In this point as in any point," he said,
"our interests are identical."[88]

The convention, it would seem, gave a sympathetic hearing
to the visiting delegates, and a motion was presented for the
appointment of a committee to discuss unity with them. After
some last-ditch maneuvering by the opponents of unity, a committee of fourteen was delegated to study the problem and
report its findings back to the convention. This committee, in
turn, appointed a four-man subcommittee to treat with Hayes,
Hillquit, Harriman, and Benham.

Following a lengthy discussion with the delegates from the
Rochester convention, the subcommittee submitted its report to
the larger group which debated the matter still further. Finally,
the committee issued two reports, one signed by a majority of
nine, the other signed by a minority of five. Each agreed that
the convention should appoint a working committee on unity.
But different opinions were given on the question of a party

[87]*Indianapolis Journal,* Mar. 7, 1900.
[88]*People,* Mar. 18, 1900.

name. The majority report demanded that the party stand by
the name "Social Democratic" regardless of consequences. The
minority report was more tractable. While it recommended the
adoption of the party name, it did not consider the matter of
sufficient importance to impede unity.[89]

The issue was debated all over again on the convention floor.
Berger said that capitulation on the party name would be tantamount to surrender to the Socialist Laborites. He maintained
that it would hurt the party's respectability before the American
people and especially before organized labor. Meyer London,
Seymour Stedman, F. G. R. Gordon, William Mailly, and Margaret Haile sided with Berger. Squire Putney, on the other
hand, pointed out that the Socialist Labor Party was willing to
unite without making demands of any kind. Carey, G. A.
Hoehn, John Chase, and E. V. Putnam joined him in debating
for the minority report.

Ultimately, Hillquit's opinion was solicited. The little New
York lawyer stated flatly that he and his companions would
leave the convention if the majority report was adopted. The
delegation had come uninstructed, he said, but it desired to work
on the basis of equality. Under no circumstances would it
submit to the majority's "command" report. Hayes spoke also.
"We wish to meet on terms of equality, not to seek great advantages nor to be benevolently assimilated," he said.

The admonitions of Hillquit and Hayes, even if made in bluff,
as was undoubtedly the case, had a sobering effect on the convention. Those who opposed unity were hardly willing to take
the responsibility for causing the SLP delegates to leave. Frederic O. MacCartney and Stedman, originally supporters of the
majority report, swung over to that of the minority. Debs, too,
spoke in behalf of the minority report, and once his views were
known, the issue was no longer in doubt. The majority report
was rejected. A unity committee of nine was appointed consisting of Victor Berger, Frederic Heath, James F. Carey, John
C. Chase, Seymour Stedman, Margaret Haile, G. A. Hoehn,
William Butscher, and William Lonergan.[90] Of this group,
Berger, Heath, Stedman, and Mrs. Haile all opposed union.

[89]*Ibid.*
[90]*Ibid.*

The convention's last problem was the selection of candidates for the Presidency and Vice-Presidency. Debs dismayed the delegates by refusing to allow his name to be placed in nomination. He pleaded poor health and the necessity of continuing his lecture work to earn enough money to liquidate the $30,000 debt which the American Railway Union had incurred for legal fees during and after the Pullman Strike.[91] Besides, in the previous autumn he had stated publicly that he would not run for political office, and he did not want to bring upon himself the charge of hypocrisy.[92] Debs's Wisconsin and Illinois friends professed to be alarmed by his reluctance to run. But they hoped to capitalize on the situation since the Rochester delegation was anxious for Debs to head a unified socialist ticket. If Debs's name could be withheld from the convention floor, concessions might be forthcoming from the Socialist Laborite delegates. Debs, of course, could always change his mind at the last minute.

With Debs apparently out of the running, Carey and Mailly nominated the SLP candidates, Harriman and Hayes. For a few brief minutes it appeared that they might be selected by acclamation. If this happened, the Wisconsin and Illinois Social Democrats would have been miserably tricked by their own strategy. But they did not allow it to occur. Berger, Stedman, Heath, and London in quick succession pointed out that the SDP constitution prohibited the nomination of any non-party member. Stedman then suggested the nomination of MacCartney, the Unitarian minister recently elected to the Massachusetts legislature, but he declined. Harriman and Benham personally appealed to Debs to reconsider, but he was adamant in his refusal.[93] Only a hurried motion to adjourn prevented the convention from falling into complete confusion.

While the DeLeonites in Indianapolis were publishing a report that the "kangaroos" had captured the convention, Hayes, Hillquit, Benham, and Harriman were conferring behind closed doors in the Occidental Hotel with Berger, A. S. Edwards, and other Social Democratic leaders. Paradoxically, the visiting

[91]*New York Times,* Mar. 10, 1900.
[92]Ginger, p. 209.
[93]*Indianapolis Journal,* Mar. 9, 1900.

delegation was distressed by the turn of events, even though the
convention was supporting its candidates. The outcome of
the conference was Debs's decision to retract his refusal to
become the party's presidential candidate.[94]

The convention delegates were visibly and boisterously pleased
when Debs's availability was made known during the evening
session. The impasse had been broken. The nominations of
Debs for President and Harriman for Vice-President were
rushed through by acclamation. That Harriman was not a
member of the Social Democratic Party was prudently ignored.

Debs, as always, rose to the occasion with a magnificent acceptance speech. He told the delegates that he had been determined not to become the party's candidate. "But now," said
Debs, "with your united voices ringing in my ears, with your
impassioned appeals burning and glowing in my breast and
your eyes searching the depths of my soul, I am brought to
realize that in your voice is a supreme command of duty." It
would be treason not to accept the mandate of the convention.
Debs also expressed complete satisfaction with the selection of
Harriman as his running mate.[95]

The great majority of delegates left Indianapolis firmly convinced that a unified socialist party was on the verge of formation. Good feeling was everywhere prevalent, with the ebullient Texas delegation boasting that their state would be the
first to be won for socialism.[96] After the convention closed,
the four Socialist Laborite delegates and the nine members of
the Social Democratic Party's unity committee met to make
arrangements for a conference in New York on March 25. But
political deals made in smoke-filled hotel rooms frequently hit
snags, and unity proved easier to discuss than to achieve.

---

[94]*People*, Mar. 18, 1900.
[95]*Indianapolis Journal*, Mar. 10, 1900.
[96]*Appeal to Reason*, Mar. 24, 1900.

XI. Socialist Unity Achieved

FROM its very inception, the world-wide socialist movement, notably in its Marxist variants, has suffered acutely from the inability of its advocates to reach areas of agreement, let alone to work harmoniously with one another. This condition is inherent in the nature of socialism, providing as it does not only a political method but also a social faith which demands from its adherents a dedicated way of life and a religious devotion. In fact, the histories of Christianity and socialism share certain definite similarities. Both are militantly missionary. Both are teleological. Just as the Church has been torn by dissensions over dogma, so has the socialist movement been split over matters of doctrine. Just as Christian heretics were burned at the stake in the later Middle Ages, so have socialist deviationists been pilloried, harassed, excommunicated, and even liquidated by those claiming doctrinal infallibility.[1]

In considering the disunity in the socialist ranks, the personal factor must not be minimized. Socialism, in demanding a radically different form of societal organization, is a revolutionary creed. And rarely does one find a large area of agreement on means and ends among any group of revolutionaries, especially when the original creed tends inevitably to proliferate in response to new social and economic pressures and changes. Desire for power, suspicion, vituperation, and jealousy have rivaled ideological factors in the socialist movement. In the United States during 1900 and 1901 personal factors were more important than doctrine in determining the course of events leading up to the formation of the Socialist Party of America.

Seymour Stedman, Frederic Heath, and Margaret Haile, three members of the Social Democratic Party's Committee on Socialist Unity, had serious misgivings as to the desirability of union with the Socialist Laborites when the conference with

---

[1] Norman Thomas discusses this problem in *A Socialist's Faith* (New York, 1951), pp. 5, 23.

the latter's committee opened at the Labor Lyceum in New York City on Sunday, March 25, 1900. (Victor Berger, another Social Democratic member who shared their feelings, did not attend the talks). They were concerned, and understandably so, lest they and the others who had brought the Social Democratic Party into existence be rudely separated from its direction. They were discomfited to be meeting in the very lair of the Socialist Laborites. The atmosphere of Union Square, reeking of class-conscious radicalism and resounding with learned and unlearned disquisitions by soapbox orators on what Marx did and did not mean, made them vaguely uneasy. In all probability they possessed that inherent distrust which most people from the "provinces" hold of New Yorkers who, in many ways, are the greatest provincials of all. Actually, only two SLP unity committee delegates, Morris Hillquit and N. I. Stone, and one Social Democratic Party representative, William Butscher, came from New York.

The meetings of the joint committees were launched on Sunday afternoon with a minimum of preliminary sparring. G. A. Hoehn, editor of the St. Louis paper, *Brauer-Zeitung*, at once brought up the question of the party name. He urged the adoption of the name of his own Social Democratic Party, primarily on the basis of its recent electoral victories. Another Social Democrat, James F. Carey, expressed no fondness for the name but thought its adoption necessary in view of the coming campaign.[2] On the other hand, several Socialist Laborites felt that a new name would help to dissolve old prejudices and would signify a unity of forces.

After the Socialist Labor Party committee members had expressed their views on the name question, Heath demanded that the meeting go into executive session, thereby barring the public and the press from the proceedings. When this was done, he dramatically accused Hillquit, Hayes, Harriman, and Benham of reneging on promises made at the Occidental Hotel conference in Indianapolis. He claimed that, as a gesture of unity,

---

[2] As early as October, 1898, opposition developed in Massachusetts to the name "Social Democratic Party" because of a peculiar state electoral law which made it necessary for the party to register on the ballots as the "Democratic Social Party." *Social Democratic Herald*, Oct. 22, 1898.

they had pledged themselves to support unqualifiedly the name "Social Democratic Party" at the present meeting.

The four Socialist Laborites denied breaking any promises, contending that at no time had they agreed unreservedly to advocate the Social Democratic Party name. When the majority of the conferees showed no inclination to accept Heath's argument, he stalked angrily out of the meeting and did not return until three days later, when it was on the point of adjourning. His absence placed the cause of the Wisconsin-Illinois socialist group squarely on Seymour Stedman and Margaret Haile.

Heath's precipitous action disrupted the conference for the day. On the following morning the two unity committees assembled once again. The Social Democratic delegates, after conferring prior to the meeting, decided against taking an intransigent stand on the name issue. This course was in the interest of socialist unity, explained Mayor John C. Chase of Haverhill. The conference approved N. I. Stone's suggestion that the names "United Socialist Party" and "Social Democratic Party" be presented to a referendum vote of each organization.

Selection of a site for national party headquarters brought about another conflict and another defeat for the Wisconsin-Illinois faction. Stedman proposed that the headquarters be located in Chicago. Mrs. Haile also spoke in behalf of the Middle Western metropolis. But Chase opposed both New York and Chicago on the ground that they were the seats of the old parties. Hillquit expressed similar sentiments although he believed that the campaign headquarters ought to be in Chicago because of its proximity to Debs's home in Terre Haute. Harriman suggested Springfield, Massachusetts. In the end, Chicago, New York, New Haven, and Springfield were put up for balloting. Chicago and New Haven were eliminated quickly. After a futile attempt by Stedman to bring Chicago back into the running, the conference voted to locate the party's national headquarters in Springfield, a city never particularly renowned as a socialist stronghold. The choice was clearly one of sheer expediency.

On the matters of the subsidization of the party press and the selection of a National Executive Committee, Stedman found himself again outvoted. Though the conferees agreed that the *Social Democratic Herald* should continue as the official party paper, they refused to subsidize it out of the party's funds for more than six months after union had been effected. Stedman warned that the *Herald* could not exist under such conditions, since every party member was entitled to receive a copy. The Chicago lawyer unavailingly opposed the creation of a ten-man provisional National Executive Committee to consist of four members each from Massachusetts and New York and two from Connecticut. Such a committee clearly eliminated the Wisconsin-Illinois branches from all control of the party.

Before adjourning, the conference endorsed Debs and Harriman as the socialist presidential and vice-presidential candidates, adopted the Social Democratic platform in toto, selected Chicago as campaign headquarters, and appointed Eugene Dietzgen as the party's representative at the International Socialist Congress in Paris. The conference's actions were to be submitted to a referendum vote of each party. If a majority of all the votes cast favored union, it would be considered accomplished.[3]

On the night of the conference's adjournment, a rally was held at Cooper Union to celebrate socialist unity. Prominent members of the Greater New York sections of both the Social Democratic and Socialist Labor parties sat together on the stage to signify and to symbolize the new harmony within the socialist ranks. To an audience which overflowed onto the stage and into the street outside, *Literary Digest* art editor Leonard Abbott, the opening speaker, asserted that the union of socialist forces opened "a new political era in the United States." He compared the Socialist Laborite–Social Democratic union with that of the Lassalleans and the Eisenachers in Germany. G. A. Hoehn, who also addressed the meeting, praised the "good sense" and "friendly spirit" shown by both parties at the conference. Other speakers included Carey, Harriman, Hayes, Benham, Charles Matchett, E. V. Brewster, and Ben Hanford.[4]

Heath, Stedman, and Mrs. Haile, significantly, did not attend the rally. Their worst fears had been realized at New York

[3] Accounts of the conference may be found in *People*, Apr. 1, 1900; *Social Democratic Herald*, Apr. 7, 1900; *New York Times*, Mar. 27, 1900; *Jewish Daily Forward*, Mar. 26-28, 1900.

[4] *People*, Apr. 8, 1900.

where the conference, showing a complete unwillingness even to compromise, had brutally euchered the Wisconsin and Illinois socialists out of the party leadership. They were manifestly bitter at this brazen development and particularly were they infuriated at the Massachusetts and Missouri delegates of their own party who had worked hand in glove with the Socialist Laborites. When Heath and Stedman detrained at Chicago, they wasted no time in reporting to their friends in the party on the disastrous events in New York.

The Social Democratic Party's National Executive Board, of which Heath and Stedman were members, vehemently opposed surrendering its organization on the conference's terms. When Berger learned of the New York happenings from Heath, his wrath exploded in the pages of his newspaper, *Wahrheit*. He excoriated Carey as a "ward politician" and Harriman as a "Tammany politician of the seventeenth degree." Berger, himself half-Jewish, referred to Morris Hillquit as "a rabbinical candidate," "a Moses Hilkowitz from Warsaw," and "a Polish apple Jew." His abuse of his fellow German socialist, G. A. Hoehn, would have done credit to Daniel DeLeon.[5]

Determined to save the party from both its internal and external enemies, the National Executive Board issued a manifesto completely repudiating the New York conference and at the same time calling for a referendum of its own on the question of unity.[6] Based on a "minority report" submitted by Heath, Stedman, and Mrs. Haile, the manifesto contained two principal accusations. It repeated the charges of duplicity which Heath had brought up at the conference with respect to the alleged agreement to support the name "Social Democratic Party." And it complained, with justice, that the conference had ridden roughshod over the recommendation made at the Social Democratic convention, that each party vote separately and as a unit on the referendum for unity. The Board held that the following question in the conference's proposed referendum violated the will of the Social Democratic Party as specifically expressed at Indianapolis: "In case the party name voted by you fails to obtain the concurrent majority of both parties, shall the

[5] *Ibid.*, May 6, 1900.
[6] *Social Democratic Herald*, Apr. 7, 1900.

name receiving the majority of the total vote of both parties be adopted?"

What allegedly had transpired at the meeting of the Socialist Laborite and Social Democratic leaders at the Occidental Hotel in Indianapolis was revealed in the manifesto and in two sworn affidavits signed by A. S. Edwards and F. G. R. Gordon. According to these accounts, Gordon called the parley to ascertain what settlement could be worked out in view of Debs's refusal to accept the nomination. Hillquit, Harriman, Hayes, and Benham were all present, though Hayes was obliged to leave before the meeting's conclusion. The visiting delegates were asked point-blank if they would support the name "Social Democratic Party" in the event Harriman and Hayes were nominated as the party's candidates. They replied in the affirmative. Berger then inquired if they would still support the name if Debs were the candidate. He said he might be able to persuade Debs to change his mind but that it was necessary to be clear on the name question. Edwards' report declared that Hillquit and Harriman agreed without reservation but that Benham refused to commit himself. The Socialist Laborites' breach of faith came at New York, the manifesto said, where all of them, Hayes excepted, voted for the submission of two party names.

The manifesto suggested a referendum vote such as was proposed at New York might be rigged easily, inasmuch as the secretary of the SLP group had been evasive in furnishing details as to the party membership. In view of this possibility and the dissimulation on the part of the Socialist Laborite delegates, the National Executive Board asserted that it felt compelled to act in order to save the party from utter disintegration. "Political unity, formed upon diplomacy, tainted with bad faith and double dealing, can never stand," said the Board. The great question for the membership of the party to decide then was, "Is union between the Social Democratic Party and the Socialist Labor Party faction desirable?"

A joint reply to the manifesto came quickly from Hillquit and Harriman, who branded it an attempt to wreck socialist unity "on the petty schemes and jealousies of individual ambitions."[7]

[7]*People*, Apr. 15, 1900.

They claimed with some disingenuousness that the agreements reached at New York had been adopted unanimously and that even Heath had appeared to be satisfied. Answering the charges of Gordon and Edwards, they denied categorically that they had assured the Social Democratic conferees of unreserved support of the party name. With reference to Berger's question, Hillquit and Harriman said that the Milwaukee leader had first asked how it would appear if they were willing to support the party name providing Harriman and Hayes were nominated, but not if Debs were the candidate. Berger had then asked them the following question: "Will you therefore permit me to say to him [Debs] that your position on the question of name would not be changed if he accepted the nomination?" Hillquit and Harriman said that they had answered in the affirmative, but that Benham had refused to commit himself.

Hillquit and Harriman added that although Berger might have been unaware of the fact—actually a correct surmisal which they were later to revise—Debs had already agreed to accept the nomination while the conference at the hotel was taking place. Such being the case, if any commitments were made at the meeting, they could not be held binding, inasmuch as the talks were being made under false pretenses on the one side and false assumptions on the other. Once the SLP delegates realized this, they had not seen fit to attend another get-together scheduled for two hours later.

Hillquit and Harriman denied that the New York conference had violated any promise by its referendum proposal and noted that neither party was necessarily bound by it. They stated that the National Executive Board appeared to fear the decision of the members of its own party. The New York conferees, on the other hand, were prepared to leave the issue up to the intelligence of the country's socialists. Hillquit and Harriman also said that they considered unworthy of reply the insinuations that the Socialist Labor group's membership rolls might be padded.

Each side thus presented its case. More than a little sincerity was lacking in both. The reply of Hillquit and Harriman to Berger's question as to whether they would support the name of the Social Democratic Party if Debs were nominated, indicated that they would. Yet certainly, insofar as Debs was concerned, the party-name issue was a case of much ado about nothing. Sufficient reason existed, moreover, to suspect the good intentions of those who called the meeting. Hillquit believed that it was no coincidence that just as the conferees were leaving the hotel room they were met at the door by Frederic O. Mac-Cartney, Elizabeth H. Thomas, and Margaret Haile, who jubilantly informed them that Debs would be a candidate. Might not Berger have known of this all of the time when he was seeking to wring concessions from the unsuspecting SLP delegates?[8] Such a view placed the conference in the worst possible light, but in the jockeying for power that was taking place, it was quite understandably entertained. Finally the creditability of Edwards and Gordon, on whose affidavits the manifesto had been based, must be taken into account. Edwards' position as party editor was jeopardized by the prospect of removing financial support from the *Social Democratic Herald*. Therefore he had a personal stake in opposing the agreements reached at the Unity Conference. Gordon had been a radical gadfly in the past (and he was eventually to become a lobbyist for the National Association of Manufacturers). A former Socialist Laborite himself, he had developed a passionate loathing for his former fellow party members.

Almost at once the official organs of both parties began to present charges and countercharges. An editorial in the *Herald* defended the constitutionality of the manifesto and held that its issuance was absolutely necessary to inform the party membership of the SLP maneuvers. In the same issue, Jesse Cox, announcing his resignation as chairman of the National Executive Board, acknowledged frankly that he had opposed union at Indianapolis and wanted no part in any action toward that end.[9] A letter from Debs was featured prominently to dispel any doubts as to his support of the manifesto. He expressed full confidence in Berger and denied unequivocally that the latter had been aware of his decision to accept the nomination. Debs stated that he was opposed to unity until the Social Democratic Party was "rescued from the maelstrom" which threatened "to

[8]*Ibid.*, May 1, 1900

[9]*Social Democratic Herald*, Apr. 21, 1900.

engulf it." Fulfillment of the resolutions made by the New York conference, said the disarmingly honest Debs, "would simply mean the swallowing up of the Social Democratic Party and its domination." He admitted that his judgment was based largely on "intuition" and even advocated a Social Democrat–Socialist Labor common front on candidates in the elections. What Debs objected to most was the "spirit" of the Socialist Laborites, and on this point he declared:

> For years the Socialist Labor Party organ [*The People*] has drilled it into their members that the Social Democratic Party consisted of a lot of freaks, frauds, and fakirs. . . . The Socialist Labor Party was trained in the bitter school of bigotry and intolerance. It must preserve an air frigidly scientific. Emotion and sentiment must be banished. Hard and stern are the party methods and it must be strictly confined to the working class. Tolerance is a crime. . . . It has taken years to cultivate and intensify this spirit that has dwarfed Socialism in America, and it CANNOT BE OVERCOME IN A DAY nor by resolutions passed in a conference. Diametrically opposed to this is the spirit of the Social Democratic Party. . . . Better far to keep them in separate parties until the logic of events has ripened them for union . . . my judgment is that this consummation will not be deferred long after the national election.[10]

Berger, who hardly personified sweetness, light, and tolerance, expressed similar sentiments. In a caustic letter to the *Herald*, he insisted that no essential difference separated the DeLeon and anti-DeLeon Socialist Labor Party factions. He charged that the latter, instead of joining the Social Democratic Party, was attempting to destroy it by starting a "new sect with the old spirit under a new name." Berger also blasted the Socialist Laborites for vilifying all reformers who disagreed with them, a rather curious indictment to come from him, since the *Herald* itself concentrated most of its fire on the Populists and Bryanite Democrats. Referring directly to the New York East Side radicals, Berger scored those socialists who orated volubly in Marxian parlance without ever quite understanding what they were talking about.[11]

---

[10]*Ibid.*

[11]*Ibid.*, Apr. 28, 1900.

The *Herald* published numerous letters discussing the pros and cons of the manifesto. Not surprisingly, the pros outnumbered the cons. It was applauded by New Englanders F. G. R. Gordon, Margaret Haile, and Frederic O. MacCartney, all of whom appeared to share a common dislike for Carey and the other Haverhill Social Democrats. In New York City, seven of the seventeen SDP branches supported the National Executive Board. Meyer London and Max Pine were largely instrumental in holding six East Side and Brooklyn Jewish branches behind the Board. A German branch in Brooklyn also remained firm in its allegiance. Some of the *Jewish Daily Forward* writers had undergone a change of heart since attending the unity rally at Cooper Union and they, too, repudiated union.[12] The Illinois and Wisconsin branches were conspicuously loyal. The Milwaukee SDP Central Committee approved a resolution asserting that union would be tantamount to suicide, and Frederic Heath wrote that "Save the Party" should henceforth be the Social Democratic watchword.[13]

Contrariwise, a large segment of the party was openly critical of the manifesto. The most violent attack on the National Executive Board came from members in Haverhill, St. Louis, New York, and San Francisco. All of these cities were totally unrepresented in the party's national councils. Terming the manifesto illegal, the Haverhill *Social Democrat* advised all party members to vote for unity in the National Executive Board referendum. American socialists, the paper said, were tired of "bossism" whether by DeLeon or by others.[14] The St. Louis SDP Central Committee condemned the National Executive Board for betraying the interests of the party, and E. Val Putnam of the same city called the manifesto a "disgraceful blunder."[15] In New York City, William Butscher, I. Phillips, and Joseph Barondess censured the Wisconsin-Illinois cabal.[16] J. F. Franz of the Cincinnati *Brauer-Zeitung* repudiated the National Executive Board's action, while Charles R. Martin of Tiffin, Ohio,

[12]*Ibid.*
[13]*Ibid.*, May 12, 1900.
[14]*People*, May 1, 1900.
[15]*Ibid.*, May 15, 1900; *Social Democratic Herald*, Apr. 21, 1900.
[16]*People*, Apr. 15, May 20, 1900.

said the manifesto was "damnable" and "sure to react."[17]   Two
SDP branches in Cleveland, having achieved unity with the Socialist Laborites, lodged a strong protest.[18]   In San Francisco,
Benham's *Class Struggle* said: "On the matter of pledges, we
insist that it is both unjust and unfair to hold the joint conference on unity responsible for any pledges made at any private
conferences held without authority or sanction of the convention."[19]   From Debs's home town of Terre Haute, James Oneal
praised the reply of Harriman and Hillquit to the manifesto's
charges and urged the party membership to override the National Executive Board by voting for the union.[20]   In Texas,
the state convention of the Social Democratic Party decided to
sever temporarily all ties with the national organization.[21]

On the surface, at least, the dissident Socialist Laborites professed to take an unruffled view of the entire affair.   Unity
with the Social Democrats, the *People* maintained, would be accomplished irrespective of temporary obstacles.   The Socialist Labor Party was going ahead with the unity referendum proposed
at the New York conference, without reference to the National
Executive Board's attitude.[22]   A. M. Simons of Chicago termed
the whole controversy farcical.   He urged Socialist Laborites to
vote for the name "Social Democratic Party."   If the National
Executive Board members insisted on behaving like children,
said Simons, they should be treated as such and be given their
playthings.[23]

Job Harriman further muddied the waters by taking issue
with his running mate.   Answering Debs's letter to the *Herald*
supporting the manifesto, Harriman denied that the Social Democrats would surrender anything essential by uniting with the
Socialist Laborites.   Not only would they possess the party leader (Debs) and the official party newspaper, he pointed out, but
also they would undoubtedly retain the party name.   He con-

[17]*Ibid.*, Apr. 15, Apr. 22, 1900.
[18]*Social Democratic Herald,* Apr. 28, 1900.
[19]*Class Struggle,* May 5, 1900.
[20]*People,* Apr. 22, 1900.
[21]*Ibid.,* July 16, 1900.
[22]*Ibid.,* Apr. 15, 1900.
[23]*Ibid.*

curred with Debs on the unimportance of the name issue but held that it was not the Socialist Laborites who had reneged on their promises at the New York conference. The Social Democratic representatives, Harriman said, had consented to the submission of two party names. Again, Harriman differed with Debs on the matter of co-operation between the two socialist groups in the coming campaign. He favored union, not fusion, and immediately rather than after the campaign. A socialist common front in the election fight, he held, would tend to eliminate all differences of opinion between the members of the two organizations.[24]

The voting on the National Executive Board's unity referendum failed to provide much solace for the party leaders. While the Board's position against unity was upheld, the margin was extremely close, with 1,453 ballots against union and 1,249 for it. Only in Wisconsin and Illinois was sentiment against unity strong. In New York, Massachusetts, Ohio, California, New Jersey, Pennsylvania, Connecticut, and Missouri the tide went against the party leaders.[25]

Thus in the spring of 1900 a completely muddled situation existed among the socialists. The Social Democrats were badly divided among themselves and the official party was saddled with an unwanted Vice-Presidential candidate. The Socialist Laborite dissidents, while more cohesively united, were without a real party organization. Though generally favorably inclined toward Debs, they could not stomach his closest advisers. Amidst a steady outpouring of charges and recriminations, the Socialist Laborite and Social Democratic unity committees made one last attempt to escape from the impasse. They scheduled another conference in New York on May 20.[26]

The second conference simply aggravated the already strained relations between the national Social Democratic organization on the one hand and the rapidly developing coalition of party rebels and Socialist Laborites on the other. Although Heath did not attend the meetings, the presence of Victor Berger com-

[24]*Ibid.*, May 1, 1900
[25]*Social Democratic Herald,* May 26, 1900; *People,* May 27, 1900.
[26]*Social Democratic Herald,* May 19, 1900; *People,* May 20, 1900.

pensated for his absence. G. B. Benham, who had left for California, was also absent.

The deep chasm between the two committees was apparent from the very beginning of their parleys. When John Chase, the presiding officer, explained that the conference had been called because of the failure of the Social Democratic Party to carry out the referendum proposals of the first unity gathering, Stedman immediately disputed the meeting's very legality. He claimed that his party was automatically freed of the necessity of fulfilling the first unity conference's recommendations inasmuch as the National Executive Board's referendum had repudiated union. The current discussions, hence, were informal and not really concerned with the problem of unity at all. He suggested, however, that the delegates advance their common cause by coming to an agreement on political co-operation.[27]

Stedman's arguments, supported by Mrs. Haile and Berger, were challenged by Carey and Hillquit, who maintained that the conference's purpose was most assuredly to carry out the union of the two socialist groups. Hillquit termed Stedman's proposition an insult. Anything less than union was out of the question. He said that the referendum vote agreed upon at the first unity conference was still the basis for socialist union.[28]

When Carey, Chase, Lonergan, and Butscher of the Social Democratic committee sided with Hillquit, it brought withdrawal from the conference by Stedman, Berger, and Mrs. Haile. Before leaving, they conferred with Debs, who was in New York, and received his approval of their stand. The remaining conferees thereupon proceeded to make plans for carrying out the referendum. Since the National Executive Board had refused to arrange for the referendum, the four remaining members of the Social Democratic unity committee decided to appeal over its head to the party's rank and file. William Butscher of Brooklyn was appointed acting secretary to receive the votes cast.[29]

Before concluding, the conference issued a public statement answering the National Executive Board's manifesto. It de-

---

[27]*People*, May 27, 1900.
[28]*Ibid.*
[29]*Ibid.*

clared flatly that the barrier to socialist unity lay in the desire of the Board's members to retain their power. Subsidiary
to this was the Board's insistence on keeping the party seat in
Chicago and on maintaining control of the party newspaper.
Stedman, Berger, Heath, and Mrs. Haile were dissimulative in
professing a desire for unity while covertly sabotaging genuine
efforts to achieve it. The Social Democratic leadership was
guilty of treason to socialism in by-passing the expressed will
of the National Party Convention, which was clearly for amalgamation with the Socialist Laborites. And, finally, the Board's
referendum proposal was a shameless attempt to conceal the true
issue from the party membership.[30]

From the other side of the fence, Margaret Haile, reporting
the conference proceedings for the *Herald*, placed responsibility
for the existing dilemma on the Socialist Laborites who, she
said, had betrayed their insidious desire to capture the Social
Democratic Party by refusing to co-operate in the coming campaign. She exposed an alleged plot at the conference to get rid
of Debs as the party standard bearer. Specifically, she quoted
N. I. Stone as stating: "Now is our chance to throw down Debs
once and for all." Mrs. Haile implored the party membership
to ignore the committee's referendum.[31]

In carrying out the unity referendum among the Social Democrats, Butscher was substantially hampered by his lack of the
party's mailing list. Nor was the National Executive Board sufficiently charitable to provide him with a copy. He was obliged,
consequently, to solicit votes through appeals in the socialist
press. To add to his troubles, the SDP officials were urging
party members to abstain from voting in the referendum.
Under these circumstances, the total vote cast could not be expected to be large. When the results were finally announced
late in July, 1,094 favored unity as against only 13 opposing it.
The name "Social Democratic Party" was endorsed, Debs and
Harriman were confirmed as the party's candidates, and William
Lonergan of Connecticut, S. M. Jones and John C. Chase of
Massachusetts, and William Butscher and I. Phillips of New
York were elected to the National Executive Committee of the

[30]*Ibid.*, June 10, 1900.
[31]*Social Democratic Herald,* June 2, 1900.

combined parties. The referendum returns also opposed subsidizing the *Social Democratic Herald.*[32]

The Socialist Laborites also voted overwhelmingly for unity in their referendum by a count of 2,518 to 28. On the party name question, they gave unqualified approval to "Social Democratic Party," with 2,227 votes for it and 326 for "United Socialist Party." Elected as Socialist Laborite members of the National Executive Committee were C. F. Fenner and M. Kaplan of Massachusetts, W. E. White of Connecticut, and Henry Slobodin and Morris Hillquit of New York. Strangely enough, whereas the Social Democrats had voted against subsidization of the *Social Democratic Herald,* the Socialist Laborites favored it.[33]

The summer of 1900 found the nation confronted with only one Socialist Labor Party but with two Social Democratic parties, one with headquarters in Chicago and the other in Springfield. Both parties supported the same Presidential and Vice-Presidential candidates and had the same platform. Each party, however, acted almost as though the other did not exist. In Texas and Iowa, the state Social Democratic organizations had declared their independence of both national parties.[34] The Social Democratic rank and file could well be excused for being confused.

The chief gainers from the Social Democratic schism were the non-partisan socialists. While the *Social Forum*'s editors were advocates of socialist political action, they were constrained to admit that the impasse among the Social Democrats lent weight to the arguments of the Fabians. "Such contentions between men banded together to secure social justice," said a *Social Forum* editorial, "seem to corroborate, if they do not entirely prove, the contention of Mayor Jones of Toledo, that the only way to secure any important degree of progress toward better conditions is in the non-partisan way."[35]

The Chicago faction did not accept the situation in particularly good humor. Although the presidential campaign be-

[32]*People,* July 22, 1900.
[33]*Ibid.,* July 15, 1900.
[34]Wm. Butscher to P. J. Cooney, Sept. 10, 1900. Socialist Party Collection, Duke University. (Cited hereafter as Socialist Party Papers).
[35]*Social Forum,* II (May, 1900), 200.

gan in June and was featured each week in the pages of the *Herald*, Harriman's name was conspicuously omitted from all discussions. Following the second unity conference, George H. Strobell, a leading direct-legislation advocate from Newark, had suggested dropping Harriman from the party ticket in favor of W. E. Farmer of Texas. While this bit of gratuitous advice was rejected, it was not until September that the *Herald* finally acknowledged Harriman's role in the campaign. Meanwhile the paper's editorials spoke gloweringly or were downright abusive of the Springfield faction.

On the other hand, from its Springfield headquarters the National Executive Committee continued to take a more rosy view of things than the immediate situation warranted. It maintained that, despite the divergency in the socialist ranks, unity would be attained ultimately. In a manifesto to its followers, the apparently imperturbed Committee asserted that it would treat "unaffiliated Socialists or Socialist organizations as a necessary transient phenomenon in the development of our party." Stating that "differences of opinion on minor questions of policy and tactics" would have to be tolerated in the interests of socialist unity, the Committee confidently believed that a "cool, common sense policy" would "pave the way to a grand reunion of all true Socialists."[36]

Transpiring events gave some justification to the Springfield faction's optimism. In spite of the differences between the Chicago and Springfield organizations, Social Democrats and former Socialist Laborites were co-operating throughout the country and demonstrating a willingness to work for the election of Debs and Harriman and for state and local candidates. Social Democrats and former Socialist Laborites ran together on unity tickets in several states, including New York, Massachusetts, New Jersey, Connecticut, Pennsylvania, Ohio, Illinois, Missouri, Washington, and California. Debs was "gratified to note" that the socialists were working "in union and harmony" and had no doubt that the election returns would vindicate the "wisdom of our comrades in deciding upon a policy of united action."[37] The climax of socialist unity in the campaign came

[36]*People*, July 29, 1900.
[37]*Workers' Call*, Sept. 22, 1900.

in New York on October 30, when Debs, Harriman, Hayes, and Ben Hanford, the Social Democratic candidate for governor of New York, spoke before a Cooper Union audience that packed the hall within a few minutes after the doors were opened.[38]

Debs himself led the way in the efforts to conciliate the opposing socialist groups. Out of personal loyalty to Berger, he had gone along with his fellow National Executive Board members, but his heart was not in their cause. In June, at the very height of the feud, Debs asked for socialist unity in the campaign, noting that SDP and SLP groups were already co-operating "without organic union." Let everyone work on the basis of the status quo, he said, and when the time was ripe for unity, nothing could stop it.[39] When Butscher notified Debs that he had been approved as the Springfield faction's candidate, the latter expressed his appreciation of the honor. "Let us all dismiss minor considerations and unite in every state and territory . . . in one mighty effort to hasten the end of capitalism and the inauguration of the Co-operative Commonwealth," Debs wrote.[40] Butscher was delighted with Debs's letter and informed Harriman that it would undoubtedly strengthen the Springfield faction's position and cause "many weak-kneed" Social Democrats to give up their allegiance to the National Executive Board.[41]

Heath and Berger were furious at Debs's action and expressed themselves forcefully on the point in a telegram to him. Debs's answer to Heath was withering and magnificent. One might even conjecture that Debs wrote it with one eye cocked toward the record of history:

> Returning from Danville, I find your telegram asking if I accepted to Butscher and announcing that your boys are wild. I am sorry to hear this, and all I have to say is that they will simply have to get tame again. There are fools and fanatics on our side as well as the other who would sacrifice the ticket and sink the movement to gratify their miserable 2 x 4 spite and resentment. It has been said that war is hell and the same is true of the man who is the candidate of such dwarfish creatures. You know under what

---

[38]*People,* Nov. 4, 1900.
[39]*Social Democratic Herald,* June 30, 1900.
[40]*Ibid.,* Aug. 11, 1900.
[41]Butscher to Harriman, Aug. 7, 1900. Socialist Party Papers.

circumstances I accepted the nomination. Besides a thousand other objections I had to it, it knocked me out of at least $2000 financially and from that day to this hell has been popping around my ears in token of grateful appreciation of my sacrifice.

I have made up my mind to do as I please, that is to say, as I think right and if the wild men who nominated me do not like it all they have to do is to nominate somebody else to dance on with hob nail shoes.

I have accepted the ratification of my nomination by the Springfield party. I did it in the interest of the Socialist movement compared with which all parties so far developed in this country amount to less than nothing. Had I done otherwise, I would have been as small and contemptible and as unworthy of the position I occupy as those in the other party our people are making so much fuss about.[42]

Butscher and other Springfield officials never did appreciate Debs's strong desire for unity. Unfortunately, Debs's public utterances and his letters to the party press concealed this fact. Before the campaign got underway they had decided not to ask him to speak under their auspices and instead to use Harriman as their principal "drawing card."[43] But the socialist audiences, Butscher soon learned, wanted to hear the Social Democratic presidential candidate, rather than his running mate. Ultimately, the Springfield-sponsored Massachusetts and New York state committees invited the party standard bearer to address rallies during the campaign. In Butscher's mind, however, the invitations were not disassociated from party strategy, for he believed that they would compel Debs to "show his hand." If he did not accept them, he would incur the opposition of the "entire Socialist movement in the Eastern states." This, Butscher opined, he dared not do.[44] Debs, as noted, did speak in the Eastern states during the campaign, though he did not do so for the motive suggested by Butscher. As his letter to Heath indicated, he towered above petty party bickering.

Throughout the campaign Butscher and his Chicago-Milwaukee Social Democratic counterparts were engaged in political

[42]Debs to Heath, Aug. 6, 1900. Letter in possession of Mr. Heath of Milwaukee, Wis.

[43]Butscher to A. M. Simons, Aug. 13, 1900. Socialist Party Papers.

[44]Butscher to T. J. Morgan, Sept. 17, 1900. Socialist Party Papers.

warfare, doing most of their infighting by correspondence and editorial sniping. Again in the realm of party strategy, Butscher believed that the visit to Chicago by Haverhill Mayor John Chase would be "an eyesore for the National Executive Board" and would "do much to cast the impression that organic union" was accomplished. Butscher dropped hints or stated outright that the National Executive Board was on the verge of bankruptcy, that subscriptions to the *Social Democratic Herald* ought to be discouraged, and that the paper itself would undoubtedly suspend publication after the election. He also advised that, if possible, "our boys ought to get hold of" the New York *Jewish Daily Forward*, which strongly supported the Chicago faction.[45]

While the campaign of 1900 was not one of the most memorable in American history, neither was it so listless as many other presidential contests both before and since. It was undeniably a letdown from the election of 1896. Most of the farmers who had vented their wrath at the polls in 1896 had shed their rebellious mood as they began to enjoy the fruits of the famed "McKinley prosperity." The Democrats, anxious to regain respectability after a brief inebriation on free silver and Populism, campaigned against imperialism and trusts and for the party's traditional low tariff policy. What was left of the People's Party staggered toward the political graveyard reserved for unsuccessful third parties.

For those socialists who supported Debs and Harriman, the 1900 campaign proved both exciting and educational. Despite the division in the ranks, which was generally considered a temporary phenomenon, they were confident of making a good showing and a real beginning in American political life. The socialist movement, to a large extent, had been delivered from De-Leonism and freed from utopianism. It had a vigorous, intelligent, and incorruptible leader in Debs and an ever-widening group of supporters from among the native-born. Though the great bulk of the working class was still to be reached, Debs and Harriman had the backing of the Western Federation of Miners, the International Typographical Union, the New York

45Butscher to Morgan, Sept. 20, 1900; Butscher to A. W. Ricker, Aug. 21, 1900; Butscher to E. Val Putnam, Aug. 20, 1900; Butscher to P. J. Cooney, Sept. 10, 1900; Butscher to Gerber, Sept. 5, 1900. Socialist Party Papers.

Central Labor Federation, the St. Louis Trades and Labor Council, the Milwaukee Federated Trades Council, and several other local labor organizations. Most of the orthodox press committed what Thomas J. Morgan called the "crime of silence" in refusing to give the socialists reportorial coverage. But the socialists had several well-read papers of their own, including the *Social Democratic Herald*, the *People*, the *Workers' Call*, the *Class Struggle*, and the *Appeal to Reason*. Most important of all, they had hope for the future. The co-operative commonwealth might not eventuate from the election of 1900, but that it was coming within a decade or so was a certainty. Debs expressed the millennial hope of socialists in the concluding remarks of a speech on September 29 at the Chicago Music Hall, where he and George D. Herron formally opened the 1900 Social Democratic campaign. "I look into the future with absolute confidence," he said. "When I strain my vision the slightest, I can see the first struggling rays of the rising sun of the co-operative commonwealth; it will look down on a nation in which man and woman . . . will enjoy . . . a land without a master, a land without a slave."

The Social Democratic Party's basic propaganda position during the campaign was outlined by Debs in the same address. He declared that the one "vital issue" sprang from private ownership of the means of production and distribution and involved the "whole question of political equality, economic freedom, and social progress." The Republican and Democratic parties, in contradistinction to the Social Democratic, had "studiously ignored" this fundamental issue. The alleged issues of the old parties, particularly imperialism, were "rooted in the existing economic system" which they were pledged "to preserve and perpetuate" and which the Social Democratic Party was resolved to abolish.

The Republicans, content to rest on prosperity and their record, could afford to pay little or no attention to the upstart socialists. But a few Democrats showed signs of alarm at the inroads socialism was making into the usually Democratic urban working class. The Hearst papers, whose owner was currently making some pretensions of favoring a mild form of collectivism in espousing municipal ownership of public utilities, were notably fearful of the socialists. The *Chicago American* on one occasion carried the headline: "The Socialists Threaten and Harass the Democratic Party." As early as July, the Hearst papers were insidiously reporting that Debs would withdraw from the presidential race in favor of Bryan. Though Debs vehemently denied this canard, [46] the story persisted in the Hearst papers, and the socialist candidate was again obliged to scotch it. In a bristling letter to the press late in September, he said: "Comrade Harriman and I have been nominated as candidates for Vice-President and President respectively of the Social Democratic Party and we shall stand as such candidates to be voted upon on election day, all reports and rumors to the contrary notwithstanding."[47]

When Hearst was not taking this line of anti-socialist attack, he and his editorial writers—among whom was the Reverend Herbert N. Casson—were telling readers that Republican money was subsidizing the Social Democratic Party and the socialist press,[48] or reasoning with them that a vote for Debs was simply a vote wasted. Was it not better to have "half a loaf" voting for Bryan, they asked, than nothing at all voting for Debs? The socialists answered this question with an emphatic "No." Said J. A. Wayland: "If we vote for Bryan this year on the grounds of securing a 'half a loaf' and continue to vote for old party candidates at every election on the same grounds, how long will it be before we can carry an election? . . . Cast your vote for principle this year and put up the beacon light to guide the nation through its coming perils."[49]

In addition to Casson, the Democrats had the backing of such "non-partisan" socialists as Mayor Samuel Jones, Eltweed Pomeroy, Frank Parsons, and B. O. Flower. When Jones wrote to Debs that he was supporting Bryan not as a Democrat but as a non-partisan and as an anti-imperialist, Debs answered that if he did not know the Toledo mayor better, he would doubt the honesty of his motivation.[50] A. M. Simons of the Chicago *Workers' Call* was less charitable to Jones. What else might one expect from one who "could see no classes in society," he asked. If Jones

[46]*People*, July 29, 1900.
[47]*Social Democratic Herald*, Sept. 29, 1900.
[48]*Appeal to Reason*, Aug. 18, 1900.
[49]*Ibid.*, July 28, Oct. 20, 1900.
[50]*Social Democratic Herald*, Sept. 22, 1900.

believed in the equality of man, how could he favor a Democratic Party which was primarily instrumental in denying it to millions of people in the South? And if Jones opposed militarism and imperialism, how could he countenance "Colonel" Bryan, who was among the first to rush to arms?[51]

Insofar as the Social Democrats were concerned, the crowning blow of the campaign was an open letter sent to Debs on the very eve of the election, asking him to withdraw in the interests of reform. The letter was signed by Flower, Parsons, and Pomeroy. The *Social Democratic Herald* branded it the "quintessence of impudence" and "one of the most disgusting tricks yet played on Socialism in any campaign on record."[52] J. A. Wayland characterized the authors of the letter as Democratic "stool pigeons"[53] and refused thereafter to publish articles by non-partisan socialists in the *Appeal*. "Political bushwackers are not welcome here," he wrote.[54] After the election returns were in, the *People* caustically inquired of the same reformers: "You 'practical' fellows, who admitted that Socialism was a good thing, and that you would like to see the Social Democratic Party succeed, but 'did not want to throw your vote away,' and therefore voted for Bryan—how do you feel now?"[55]

What remained of DeLeon's Socialist Labor Party also competed for socialist votes in 1900. Having eliminated from its ranks those who leaned toward revisionism, the SLP at its 1900 national convention dropped from its platform all immediate demands[56]—a move dispelling any lingering doubts as to the party's revolutionary character. At the same time, support of the Socialist Trade and Labor Alliance was reaffirmed and the convention voted to exclude from party membership any organizer of a trade or labor union other than the ST and LA.[57] The activities of the latter organization were lauded, though its membership was dwindling commensurately with that of the par-

[51]*Workers' Call*, Sept. 22, 1900.

[52]*Social Democratic Herald*, Nov. 10, 1900.

[53]*Appeal to Reason*, Nov. 17, 1900.

[54]*Ibid.*, Nov. 24, 1900.

[55]*People*, Nov. 11, 1900.

[56]*Proceedings of the 10th National Convention of the Socialist Labor Party*, pp. 113, 255-56.

[57]*Ibid.*, p. 200.

ent organization.[58] That such actions made the Socialist Labor Party less attractive to the masses did not concern DeLeon. Better to have a small, tightly-knit party, which made no compromises, he believed, than a large, amorphous, undisciplined organization.

The Socialist Labor Party's candidates in the election were Joseph Francis Malloney, a machinist from Massachusetts, and Valentine Remmel, a glassworker from Pennsylvania. Before the campaign began, the DeLeon edition of the *People* predicted that "the wretched Debserie" would suffer "the fate of the jackdaw in the fable: plucked of its borrowed feathers" by the Populists and Democrats, "sneered at" by the Republicans, and "its 'socialism' proven to be dishwater by the Socialist Labor Party." "Debsism" would "stand out as a shivering monument to politico-economic imbecility."[59] Once the campaign got under way in earnest, however, DeLeon ignored the Social Democratic Party completely, lest he dignify it with his attention and advertise it by publicity.

The Social Democratic vote in the 1900 election did not measure up to the expectations of the more sanguine socialist enthusiasts. Nevertheless, it gave some cause for optimism as to the movement's future. The total vote cast for socialist candidates in 1900 nearly quadrupled the number polled by the Socialist Labor Party in the 1896 presidential election. Although Debs and Harriman received only 94,777 votes—as against 7,219,530 for McKinley and Roosevelt, and 6,538,071 for Bryan and Stevenson—they outstripped the Populist candidates, Barker and Donnelly, by nearly 45,000 votes, and the Socialist Labor Party standard bearers, Malloney and Remmel, by over 60,000.[60] In none of the thirty-four states in which the Social Democratic Party was registered did the size of the socialist vote decrease. The greatest Social Democratic electoral strength was in New York, where the party received 12,869 votes. This total did not loom especially impressive, however, considering that DeLeon's ramshackle party polled 12,622 votes. Debs and Harriman obtained 9,716 votes in Massa-

[58]Hillquit, *History of Socialism in the United States,* p. 304.

[59]*People,* May 20, 1900.

[60]Samuel E. Morison and Henry S. Commager, *The Growth of the American Republic* (New York, 1934), p. 927.

chusetts, 9,687 in Illinois, 7,572 in California, 7,095 in Wisconsin, and 6,128 in Missouri.[61]

The election results drew mixed reactions from the Social Democrats. The *People*, organ of the dissident Socialist Laborites, believed that the Social Democratic Party had made a creditable though hardly brilliant showing. According to its analysis, three major obstacles had confronted the party in the election. First, as in 1896, American radicals wanted to vote for a winner and therefore supported Bryan in the vain and delusive hope that he could defeat McKinley. Second, the division among the socialists discouraged those who were sympathetic but still only lukewarm to the cause. And third, the retention of the old Socialist Labor Party name and symbol by the DeLeonites caused many less informed socialists to vote for it rather than for the Social Democratic Party.[62] The New York *Jewish Daily Forward* was more emphatic and optimistic. "A start has been made," it declared. "The capitalist frost has been disintegrated and the radiant, bright concepts of socialism begin to cast their glow upon the laboring masses." This view was shared by J. A. Wayland. The election returns, instead of discouraging the Kansas editor who had campaigned for a million Social Democratic votes, almost seemed to well up in him a positive euphoria. "At last," he wrote, "the decks are cleared for action. All middle ground reform parties met their Waterloo on November 6th and from this time on the battle will be between the advocates of public and private ownership of the means of production and distribution."[63]

The *Social Democratic Herald*, on the other hand, complained that the socialist vote was far too low and placed the responsibility directly on the Springfield Social Democratic organization. It maintained that the "factionalism" created by the Springfield group had split badly the socialists in New York, Massachusetts, and Illinois. Harriman's departure for Paris a few days before the end of the campaign was criticized unmercifully, notwithstanding the fact that he had gone for the sole and express purpose of preventing DeLeon's followers from being

---

[61]*People*, Dec. 30, 1900.

[62]*Ibid.*, Nov. 11, 1900.

[63]*Jewish Daily Forward*, Nov. 8, 1900; *Appeal to Reason*, Nov. 17, 1900.

accepted as the American representatives at the International Socialist Congress.[64] The *Herald* also charged the Springfield organization with using money collected for the campaign to fortify its position among the Social Democrats.[65] The campaign had taught hundreds of socialists to bury their differences in the interests of harmony. Yet the leaders of the Chicago group, like the Bourbons, seemingly had forgiven nothing and forgotten nothing, an attitude that caused Thomas J. Morgan to sever his "long and friendly acquaintance" with Corinne Brown and Jesse Cox.[66] In December, when John C. Chase was beaten for reelection as mayor of Haverhill, the *Herald* vindictively attributed the socialist disaster to Social Democratic disunity.[67] In point of truth, Chase's defeat resulted from an electoral coalition of local Republican and Democratic leaders who were determined to crush once and for all the upstart Social Democratic administration.

Within a few weeks after the election, the cry for socialist unity was again taken up, with the loudest and most cogent pleas emanating from George D. Herron and the Christian Socialist radicals associated with the Social Crusade. Herron made the first call in a speech on November 18 before a mass meeting of Chicago socialists. Only by being itself united, said the former Grinnell professor of Applied Christianity, could the Social Democratic Party gather up and fuse the "untaught and undisciplined American discontent which probably represents one third of the nation's voters." Herron professed to fear that unless the socialists came to an agreement immediately, they might well find both the disgruntled independent voters and their own supporters going over to the Democratic Party. The latter, he said, was at the crossroads. It would have to go radically either to the right or to the left if it hoped to remain a force in American political life. Signs were already evident that the Democrats were planning to transform their organization into some sort of a radical party "with semi-Socialist propositions and tendencies." Herron warned that "this new radical [Democratic] party will certainly appear unless Socialists lay aside all factional differ-

[64]For Harriman's report, see *International Socialist Review*, I (1900), 305-9.
[65]*Social Democratic Herald*, Nov. 10, 1900.
[66]Morgan to H. D. Lloyd, Dec. 3, 1900. Lloyd Papers.
[67]*Social Democratic Herald*, Dec. 15, 1900.

ences and enter the national political field with a unity and dignified action that shall win this discontent and discipline it for intelligent and constructive effort on the basis of the International Socialists' program."[68]

Upon learning that the National Executive Board had called a convention of its followers for January 15, 1901, in Chicago, the Springfield Committee sent it an open letter which once again pleaded for union. Frankly suspicious that the convention was another move to "head off the threatened avalanche in favor of union," the Springfield officials stated that they felt compelled to present their views before the nation's socialists. The recently concluded campaign, they argued, indicated that the rank and file apparently wanted union more than did their leaders. The letter called attention to the fact that Debs himself had suggested amalgamation of the socialist forces soon after the election. Expressing a willingness to forget "many unpleasant incidents" of the past and to surrender all its power and mandates at a joint convention of the two Social Democratic groups, the Committee urged the Board to accept its bid for union. At the same time, however, unity was held to be impossible if personal abuse and controversy persisted.[69]

To pave the way for a national convention which would include Social Democrats from both factions, the Springfield Committee again polled its followers on the question of socialist unity. It asked for suggestions for a meeting place in the event that the Chicago faction showed an inclination to co-operate. And it inquired if the membership was willing to acquiesce in all decisions made at the proposed convention. All of the propositions were approved overwhelmingly. Indianapolis was selected as the best convention site.[70]

The Chicago convention heard one tirade after another against the Springfield socialist organization. Few among the eighty-nine delegates found little that was good in the rival faction. But the increasing rank-and-file demands for socialist unity could not be ignored. Some gesture toward unity had to be made

---

[68]*People*, Dec. 2, 1900. The text of Herron's speech also appears in the *International Socialist Review*, I (1900), 321-28.

[69]*People*, Dec. 23, 1900.

[70]*Ibid.*, Mar. 17, 1901.

lest the Chicago-Milwaukee group leave itself open to the charge of obstructionism. Accordingly, a resolution was introduced and passed by a large majority, calling for a convention of all the country's socialists on September 10 at Indianapolis. The resolution, however, first had to be submitted to the party membership for approval.[71]

The Berger-Stedman-Heath triumvirate was again elected to the party's National Executive Board. Mrs. Corinne Brown of Chicago and Isadore Ladoff of Milwaukee were elected to replace Jesse Cox and Eugene Debs. Theodore Debs continued as party secretary and A. S. Edwards once again was chosen to edit the *Social Democratic Herald*.[72]

When the membership of the Chicago faction voted late in March its approval of the unity resolution adopted at the convention, the stage was set for the beginning of new discussions between the rival Social Democratic camps. These were opened by a letter dated March 28, sent by Theodore Debs to Butscher, informing him of the decision of the Chicago group to call a convention, not only of all Social Democrats but also of all socialists in the United States. The plan for representation at the convention was similar to the one already approved by the membership of the Springfield faction in its own unity referendum. Each delegate was allowed to bring with him the proxy votes of the members of his own particular branch, or of any other Social Democratic organization in the vicinity. Independent socialist groups were to be similarly represented. The findings of the convention were to be submitted for the approval of each Social Democratic group by separate referendum.[73]

Butscher, in the name of the Springfield Committee, answered Debs's letter immediately and approved of all save two of the Chicago group's recommendations. He believed the September date too late, not only because it delayed socialist unity but also because it failed to give the party sufficient time to organize for the autumn elections. And he objected to the holding of separate referendums by each of the Social Democratic organizations for the purpose of approving the convention's work. The Committee

---

[71]*Social Democratic Herald*, Jan. 26, 1901.
[72]*Ibid.*
[73]*Worker*, May 5, 1901.

recalled only too well the consequences of the 1900 Indianapolis convention and desired, therefore, that all decisions reached be final.[74]

Little opposition came from the Chicago faction to the suggestion to advance the date of the convention; it was agreed to move the date up to July 29. It was adamant, however, on retaining the referendum. Rather than jeopardize the holding of the convention by debating the issue, the Springfield group gave way.[75] Eugene Debs sought to clear the air even further by appealing to the Social Democrats of both groups to sink their differences. But not all of the members of the Chicago Board shared his optimism as to the outcome of the convention. "It will be hard for me to forget," said Corinne Brown, "that these people who have cried so lustily for unity and amity have been unceasing in their efforts to disrupt our party."[76]

Illness in the family prevented Debs from attending the unity convention when it opened as scheduled on July 29 at the Indianapolis Masonic Hall.[77] Sicknesses seemingly had a habit of coming to Debs or his family when unpleasantries at socialist gatherings threatened to develop. But an impressive total of 128 delegates from 20 states and Puerto Rico were on hand to hear George D. Herron call the assembly to order. "I take it you are all here for just one purpose," Herron told the delegates. "You are here to nationalize the socialist movement of America."

Representatives of the Springfield faction were in the majority, with 72 delegates holding 5,155 unit votes. The Chicago group had 49 delegates with 1,403 unit votes. Seven "independents," claiming 382 votes, were also present. The convention was dominated by lawyers, editors, and writers. Representatives of the laboring class, as such, were almost distinguished by their absence. Likewise, the foreign-born element was definitely in the minority. This factor caught the attention of Morris Winchevsky, who wrote of the gathering: "Fully four-fifths of the delegates were American-born, the Germans and Jews for once—and I am

[74]*Ibid.*

[75]*Ibid.*, June 2, 1901

[76]*Social Democratic Herald,* July 27, 1901.

[77]*Ibid.*, Aug. 17, 1901.

afraid for all time now—taking a back seat."[78] Similar sentiments were expressed by A. M. Simons. "The number of young
American-born delegates," he wrote, "was a source of frequent
comment. It is safe to say that there was a much larger percentage of such men than would be found at any old party convention. A large majority of those who came from the West and
Southwest were descendants . . . of hardy fighting pioneers."[79]
Three Negroes, William Costley of California and John H.
Adams and Edward D. McKay of Indiana, were accredited
delegates. The Negro delegates, according to Max Hayes, "surprised some of their white brethren with their logic and understanding of the socialist movement."[80] As a whole the representatives were young men and women, although a few oldsters, like
Julius Vahlteich of Illinois who had been a Socialist member
of the German Reichstag in 1874, were also in attendance.

The *Indianapolis Journal*, expecting to find visible evidence of
the internecine socialist fight at the convention, was astounded
to note the "warm feeling" which members of the Springfield and
Chicago factions showed toward each other. It also noted that
there was no separate seating of the two groups. The debates,
moreover, were to disclose that both sides were in a mood to compromise. Old adversaries like Hillquit, "the little Napoleon of
Croker's town," and the pugnacious Berger were frequently found
fighting shoulder to shoulder on the same issue. The recriminations and personal vendettas which had appeared in the *Social
Democratic Herald* and the *People* had no place on the convention floor. The whole issue of socialist unity was hardly discussed because it was, from the first, assumed.[81]

At the insistence of Berger, backed by Hillquit, the Chicago
and Springfield factions were given equal representation on the
various committees. The independents were also represented on
each committee. Since the debates showed that factional lines

---

[78] *Jewish Daily Forward,* July 31, 1901; *Worker,* Aug. 11, 1900.

[79] *International Socialist Review,* II (1901), 235.

[80] *Cleveland Citizen,* Aug. 3, 1901.

[81] All references to the convention's proceedings, unless otherwise noted, are
taken from "Proceedings of the Socialist Unity Convention, Indianapolis,
July 29, 1901." (Hereafter cited as "Proceedings.") The copy used for this
study is on deposit in the Sterling Memorial Library at Yale University. It is
mimeographed and bound in two volumes, with continuous pagination.

were extremely loose, there is little reason to suppose that they were any tighter in the committee discussions. Early in its business the convention decided to ban minority committee reports and this undoubtedly helped to prevent debates along purely factional lines.

The sharpest argument in the early discussions was occasioned by Berger's demand that voting be carried out on the basis of factions.[82] Hillquit strongly opposed this procedure, pointing out that if the Chicago organization submitted a report which was defeated by the vote of the convention, it might then present a minority finding to its membership for a referendum vote. By such a maneuver, the will of the convention could easily be subverted. "If this is to be a unity convention," said Hillquit, "the only thing to do is to act as one body, and adopt one set of resolutions, one constitution and one platform."[83] Job Harriman also opposed voting by factions, but G. A. Hoehn of the Springfield organization voted for it, along with Margaret Haile, George Goebel, and Emil Seidel of the Chicago group. The matter was ultimately settled by the adoption of Frederic O. MacCartney's compromise proposal, which allowed separate voting but forbade the issuance of minority reports.[84]

The convention's second day was largely given over to a tumultuous debate, carried on in an "electrically charged atmosphere," on whether the socialist platform should abandon its immediate political and economic demands in favor of its long-run revolutionary program. This strategy had been adopted the year previous by the Socialist Labor Party, and it duly acknowledged that various reform groups and the Democratic Party had grafted many socialist demands onto their own platforms. The problem, of course, was not unique to the United States; socialists in several European countries were badly split on the issue.

The immediate-demands issue, in truth, brought out the inherent socialist dilemma, one that plagued the movement from the very start in the United States. By spurning capitalism, the socialists rejected the pressing contemporary issues which arose

[82]"Proceedings," p. 38.
[83]*Ibid.*, p. 39.
[84]*Ibid.*, p. 57.

out of the existing political and economic society. Yet the very problems that created these issues had to be faced, for socialist political organizations could not maintain their memberships by dwelling in the never-never land of doctrinal purity. The coming co-operative commonwealth could be guaranteed, but its delivery date was a matter for the forces of history to determine. In the meanwhile, there was the matter of practical politics within a system that was not constructed for the type of political isolationism espoused by most socialists. The dilemma was never satisfactorily reconciled, and within it may be found the basic ideological and methodological difficulty of American socialism.

In general, the Chicago faction favored retention of the immediate demands while the Springfield supporters wavered. In the debate factional lines were crossed on many occasions, with C. G. Clemens, M. J. McSweeny, and E. Backus of the Chicago organization arguing for elimination of the demands, while Harriman, Hillquit, Hoehn, Morgan, and Sieverman of the Massachusetts group asked for their retention in the party platform.[85]

Those seeking to eliminate the immediate demands found the United States, of all the countries of the world, most ripe for socialism, not only in the light of Marxian law of economic development, but also by the express opinion of Friedrich Engels.[86] Nowhere else, said A. M. Simons, had the struggle between capital and labor narrowed down to as clear-cut an issue. It was

---

[85] The immediate demands to which opposition developed were: 1. The public ownership of all means of transportation and communication and all other public utilities, as well as of all industries controlled by monopolies, trusts, and combines. No part of the revenue of such industries to be applied to the reduction of taxes on the property of the capitalist class, but to be applied wholly to the increase of wages and shortening of the hours of labor of the employees, to the improvement of the service and diminishing the rates to the consumers. 2. The progressive reduction of the hours of labor and the increase in wages in order to decrease the share of the capitalist and increase the share of the worker in the product of labor. 3. State or national insurance of working people in case of accidents, lack of employment, sickness and want in old age. The funds for this purpose to be collected from the revenue of the capitalist class and to be administered under the control of the working class. 4. The inauguration of a system of public industries. Public credit to be used for that purpose in order that the workers be secured the full product of their labor. 5. The education of all children up to the age of 18 years; and state and municipal aid for books, clothing and food. 6. Equal civil and political rights for men and women. 7. The initiative and referendum, proportional representation and the right of recall of representatives by their constituents. *Social Democratic Herald*, Aug. 17, 1901.

[86] Engels to H. D. Lloyd, May 23, 1893. Lloyd Papers.

foolhardy for socialists to attempt to achieve their aims on the basis of outbidding the older parties with promises to the workers. Since American capitalism was already showing signs of cracking and collapsing under its own weight, the immediate demands would only divert the working class and thereby help delay the advent of socialism.[87] J. W. Saunders spoke similarly. Workingmen could obtain nothing of importance from the capitalist class, he held, even if they succeeded in electing a few "Careys and MacCartneys." As long as capitalism remained, conditions would be "just the same."[88]

The present was no time for palliatives, exclaimed Gaylord Wilshire, "for we are not going to get them. We are right now in the throes of a great economic revolution which is simply coming before the great social revolution."[89] Max Hayes, with a penchant for historical analogy, declared: "They did not make immediate demands in the old abolition movement. They did not say, 'Let us set free one slave at a time.' You all know the trouble that they had with the Nebraska and Missouri compromises."[90] C. G. Clemens, who only a few years before had supported the Social Democracy–colonization faction, declared: "When you put in those specific demands, you justify the position of the People's Party and the fusion parties . . . that half a loaf is better than none."[91] Another representative, E. Backus, had the simplest argument of all. "I want a platform," he said, "that is composed of so few words that it can be printed at the top of a newspaper and on my envelopes and letterheads."[92]

Those seeking adoption of the immediate demands did not contest the long-range goals of the revolutionaries. But practicality came first. That the co-operative commonwealth was only a few years or a decade distant was sorrowfully but frankly doubted, especially by men like Thomas J. Morgan who had been struggling valiantly for socialism for nearly a quarter of a century. While the road to socialist success showed promise of becoming

---

[87]"Proceedings," pp. 1-7, 205-6.
[88]*Ibid.*, p. 253.
[89]*Ibid.*, p. 167.
[90]*Ibid.*, p. 275.
[91]*Ibid.*, p. 185.
[92]*Ibid.*, p. 202.

somewhat less rocky, the mere prospect of eventual victory in itself was insufficient to maintain the allegiance of, or attract new
members from, the working class. To ignore problems demanding immediate correction was to adopt an essentially anarchistic
attitude.

The Reverend Frederic O. MacCartney likened Wilshire, Simons, and the other socialist left-wingers to the millenarians
who had carelessly disposed of their possessions in order to prepare for the coming of the Lord. "Let us be the party of the
ideal," MacCartney pleaded, "but let us also be the party of the
actual." If socialists lacked a working program, he and Carey
could not conscientiously propose educational and labor reform
bills in the Massachusetts legislature.[93]   Another revisionist,
George Goebel, attacked from a different quarter. He denied
sharply that the increasing poverty, allegedly attendant upon
capitalism, would bring workingmen into socialism. "My experience is that the man who works for the fewest hours and
has the best wages and the most money for books is the man . . .
I have the best chance with," said Goebel. "The only revolution that you will get from the sweat shop is the revolution of
murder and arson and things of that kind, and I don't believe
in that."[94]

Two socialist veterans, Thomas J. Morgan and G. A. Hoehn,
also pleaded for immediate demands. Morgan warned that
socialism was under the twin assault of reformers on the right
who compromised on anything, and anarchists on the left who
repudiated everything. He was particularly concerned lest the
party's left-wing soapbox orators alienate organized labor by
their attitude of contempt and repudiation.[95]   Hoehn was no
less forthright on this latter point. Socialist agitators, instead
of going into labor unions and telling workers where the Social
Democratic Party stood, had habitually set up shop on the street
corners where they appealed to "hoodlums" who would "never
amount to anything" insofar as the socialist movement was concerned.[96] American socialists, said Hoehn, had good reason to

[93]*Ibid.,* pp. 187-90.
[94]*Ibid.,* p. 237.
[95]*Ibid.,* p. 287.
[96]*Ibid.,* p. 420.

pause. "Talk about the co-operative commonwealth, talk about scientific socialism, talk about our present state of society, and then you request the American wage working class to make a big jump, to jump from your revolutionary nonsense right into the co-operative commonwealth." The only place that it would land was in the lap of the anarchists. The dire days of the socialist movement in the early eighties, he said, served as an object lesson, since the movement nearly fell apart upon adopting a straight revolutionary program. Hochn declared that he personally could not and would not "stand or fight" on a platform without immediate demands.[97]

It was Morris Hillquit who most forcefully stated the case for the inclusion of the immediate demands in the platform:

> If we ever attempt to go before the working class and promise them the co-operative commonwealth in three or four or five years, and if they wait six and ten and see no chance of its realization, then we will be much worse off for they will lose faith in your propaganda. On the contrary, if you show to the working man, what we know perfectly well and understand, that we are dealing with the complex problem of social evolution and that we do not know whether or not the ultimate end in which we believe and for which we are working will be reached today, tomorrow, or in ten years or half a century—if you show them, in other words, that all we know is the general tendency and all we can do is work along these lines and that all we can call upon them to do is to co-operate with us along these lines, the real progress is begun.[98]

When the convention finally voted on the immediate-demands issue, the result was 5,358 to 1,325 for their inclusion in the platform, with the Chicago faction voting at an approximate ratio of 10 to 1 and the Springfield group 3 to 1.[99] At Herron's suggestion and over Berger's opposition, the convention agreed to attach the following statement to that part of the platform concerned with the immediate demands:

> But in advocating these measures as steps in the overthrow of capitalism and the establishment of the Co-operative Commonwealth, we warn against the so-called public

[97] *Ibid.*, p. 164.
[98] *Ibid.*, p. 182.
[99] *Ibid.*, p. 367.

ownership movements as an attempt of the capitalist class to secure government control of public utilities for the purpose of obtaining greater security in the exploitation of other industries and not for the amelioration of the conditions of the working class.[100]

The scrapping of the farmers' demands in 1899 had left many Middle Western Social Democrats highly disgruntled. It was no surprise, therefore, that several attempts should be made to insert into the new party platform proposals for governmental economic assistance to the farmers. Stedman and Berger of the Chicago faction and Simons of the Massachusetts group teamed up to lead the debate in favor of these proposals while Carey, Harriman, and Hoehn headed the opposition.

Stedman reminded the convention that the agrarian class had traditionally stood in the forefront of American radicalism and to ignore this historical fact would be inexcusably shortsighted.[101] Simons, finding no inconsistency in opposing immediate demands while urging state assistance to farmers, agreed that farmers as a class could not be given cavalier treatment by the socialists, if for no other reason than that they constituted approximately forty per cent of the nation's population. Such a group ought not only to be reckoned with but utilized.[102] Without its assistance, socialism could never become a reality in the United States.

Simons denied that the evolutionary trend in American agriculture was toward the bonanza farm. The average farmer, he said, only laughed when socialists made this doctrinaire claim.[103] Similarly, Berger pointed out that census statistics showed that the average size of farms was, in fact, decreasing. The Milwaukee editor revealed that the Dakota Dalrymple bonanza farms were virtually bankrupt and that the large farms of Southern California, often used as examples of agricultural concentration, were in reality atypical. He further pointed out that farm wage-workers were not a standing peasant class in the

---

[100]*Ibid.*, pp. 415-16.
[101]*Ibid.*, p. 385.
[102]*Ibid.*, p. 350.
[103]*Ibid.*, p. 346.

United States as they were in Germany where orthodox Marxian economics, consequently, might have greater application.[104]

Proponents of the farmers' planks sought to identify the interests of the farmer and the industrial worker, in that the former had no more control over the price of his commodities than the latter had over his labor-power and wages. "The man who is forced by economic necessity to sell his labor in the abstract and the farmer who is forced by economic necessity to sell his in the concrete to middle-men are exactly in the same economic condition," said Stedman.[105] Likewise, Simons argued that farmers actually owned few of the means of production and storage and that they were completely dependent on the railroads. In many cases, their income amounted to only $200 a year. "If he [the farmer] does not get the product of his labor," said Simons, who had spent twenty of his still-young years on a farm, "then there is nothing left to be accounted for as a capitalist, and his interest lies just the same as the day laborer in getting the full product of what his labor creates."[106]

Opponents of the proposals, while acknowledging that the farmer might be less prosperous than other members of the capitalist class, nevertheless claimed that his orientation and values were capitalistic. "To approach the farmer from his economic position would be as serious a mistake," said Carey, "as it would be to approach the decaying small manufacturer or the small capitalist. . . . Go to the farmer as a farmer, and you will find that in the last analysis his economic interest will place him exactly where the economic interest of the small manufacturer will place him."[107] C. G. Clemens who, as a Kansan, demanded a respectful hearing, said that most of the socialists in his state were farmers and that he had never known of a man who had come into the socialist movement because "he had been convinced that it was to his own selfish interest to become a socialist." With a good deal of truth, Clemens maintained that the average socialist came into the movement "with his heart first" and afterwards "educated his head."[108]

---

[104]*Ibid.*, pp. 359-61.
[105]*Ibid.*, p. 384.
[106]*Ibid.*, p. 350.
[107]*Ibid.*, p. 366.
[108]*Ibid.*, p. 392.

The St. Louis socialist editor, G. A. Hoehn, sought to refute the arguments of Stedman and Simons. As soon as a farmer employed another man, he said, his interests became different from those of the worker. While conceding that the majority of farmers were worse off than the wage earners, he held that socialists ought not to appeal to them on the basis of their economic status. Hoehn used the not entirely economically sound argument that the price which the farmer obtained for his products was dependent upon what the wage earner ultimately would pay for them. Hence, he claimed, the farmer and worker were, in reality, in direct economic conflict.[109]

In the end, another compromise was reached in which it was agreed to exclude the farmers' planks from the platform. However, a committee consisting of Harriman, Berger, Hillquit, Stedman, Simons, Clemens, and Hampton framed a manifesto which pointed out to the farmers that they were being stripped of their holdings by new financial and technological changes and that, therefore, their interests were the same as those of the wage earners.[110]

After long and acrimonious debates, the convention agreed on resolutions pertaining to the position of the party toward Negroes and trade unionism. The resolution on Negro rights condemned acts of violence and lawlessness against the colored population. Negroes were invited to join the party where their interests as wage earners were the same as other members of the working class.[111] With respect to trade unions, the following resolution was adopted unanimously by the delegates:

> The formation of every trade union, no matter how small or conservative it may be, will strengthen the power of the working class.
>
> By this class struggle so nobly carried on by the trade union forces today, the exploitation of labor will only be lessened, not abolished. The exploitation of labor can only be done away with entirely when society takes possession of all the means of production for the benefit of all the people.

[109]*Ibid.*, pp. 346, 353.
[110]*Ibid.*, p. 539.
[111]*Ibid.*, pp. 557-58, 695-96.

The socialist or co-operative system can be brought about by the independent political organization and united action of the working class, and all those that recognize and sympathize with the economic and historical mission of the proletariat.

Make the members of the trade unions acquainted with the principles of Socialism and induce them to work for and affiliate with the Socialist Party.

Trade unions are by economic and historical necessity organized on neutral grounds as far as political affiliation is concerned.[112]

After the problems of party doctrine and program were disposed of, the convention set about reorganizing the Social Democratic Party. The first thing to go was the name. The committee appointed to draw up a constitution for a unified party recommended adoption of the name "Socialist Party of America." Berger objected immediately and offered as an alternative "Social Democratic Party." Again his old adversary, Hillquit, supported him, as did Hoehn, who had been a frequent victim of Berger's invective. Carey led the fight for the new name, which was ultimately adopted, 79 to 19.[113]

On the convention's final day, another long debate was held regarding the site of the party headquarters. Several cities were suggested, but the choice narrowed down to Chicago and St. Louis. While it was generally agreed that the former city was preferable, there was also a widespread feeling that the party headquarters should not be located in one of the sites of the old factional difficulties. St. Louis, therefore, was selected.[114]

No officer of the Chicago or Springfield groups was given an executive position under the new organization of the party. Leon Greenbaum of St. Louis, who had not been involved in the old factional disputes, was unanimously elected National Secretary. He was to be assisted in his work by a National Executive Committee composed of Hoehn, E. Val Putnam, L. E.

---

[112]*Ibid.,* p. 529.

[113]*Ibid.,* p. 448. In a telegram to the convention, Debs said that he was satisfied that the word "Democrat" had been dropped, since it freed the Socialists from any connection with the capitalistic Democratic Party. *Social Democratic Herald,* Aug. 17, 1901.

[114]"Proceedings," p. 691.

Hildebrand, M. Ballard Dunn, and W. H. Baird, all of St. Louis.[115]

When the convention closed with the singing of the "Marseillaise," socialist unity had been substantially achieved. Neither the Chicago nor the Springfield faction was in control of the party. Not all of the delegates were in complete agreement on matters of doctrine. Not all of the old ill-feeling and rancor had been dissolved, and a sizable group of DeLeonite socialists still remained in splendid isolation outside the fold. But a national Socialist party had been created, and it was a party that subsequently was to play a significant role in the country's political history.

In evaluating the labors of the 1901 unity meeting, Simons wrote: "We believe that the future historian of the Socialist movement of this country will agree that the most important thing he has to chronicle up to the present day is the work of the convention that met at Indianapolis during the closing days of July."[116] While Mr. Simons may have been substantially correct, it must also be remembered that the convention represented the culmination of a dozen years of active socialist education, agitation, and organization.

---

[115]*Ibid.*, pp. 729, 730.
[116]*International Socialist Review,* II (1901), 233.

Bibliographical Essay

Since the completion of the main body of this study in May, 1952, a highly important contribution to the literature of American socialism has been published by the Princeton University Press. It is entitled *Socialism and American Life*. Editors of this two volume work are Stow Persons and Donald Drew Egbert. Feature of volume one is a colorful 190-page interpretive study by Daniel Bell entitled "The Background and Development of Marxian Socialism in the United States." Though written entirely independently of each other, Mr. Bell's history and my own are in basic agreement on many points. On the other hand, differences of emphasis also appear, particularly because I have sought to incorporate in my account a study of some of the non-Marxist elements of the general socialist movement. Also, Mr. Bell's essay carries the socialist movement to the present day. My study terminates in 1901.

Volume two of *Socialism and American Life* is devoted completely to bibliography, and to my knowledge it is the only such work of its kind. Professor T. D. Seymour Bassett, the bibliographer, has done such a thorough and competent job that I feel altogether free to refer readers to his volume for general information of a bibliographical nature.

My intention here, therefore, is not to attempt to do what Professor Bassett has done so capably nor to re-list the sources already mentioned in the footnotes. Rather, I prefer to use this opportunity to comment briefly on the types of material used in the preparation of this study, their general character and relative value, and, if and when necessary, their location. Persons interested in specific bibliographical information, consequently, would do well to refer to the footnotes. I have sought to keep the latter as free as possible not only from secondary works, whose authors frequently copy uncritically one from another, but also from obscure and non-essential sources.

Newspapers and magazines have constituted my principal fount of information. I have consulted, I believe, every important and still available socialist newspaper and magazine of the period. On occasion I have used the non-socialist press, and a word with respect to it is perhaps in order.

Any attempt to follow the development of the late nineteenth-century socialist movement from news items in the orthodox press would produce a distressingly vague and, even worse, a distorted picture. In New York, for instance, such solid dailies as the *Herald*, the *Times*, and the *Sun* seemed either utterly unaware of the existence of the socialists or considered them unworthy of news coverage. The *World* and the *Journal*, catering more to a working-class clientele, took greater cognizance of socialist affairs, though their relevant news articles were hardly models of impartial or accurate reporting. As a rule, the Chicago press found socialist activities newsworthy but rarely to the extent of meriting a front-page column. This, conceivably, was because the acrid smell of dynamite left by the Haymarket riot had not completely disappeared. The trauma of the bomb left ugly scars on the Middle Western metropolis, and if Chicago papers took any interest in socialism it was with malice aforethought and with the end goal of disparagement.

The socialist press was equally opaque in its own peculiar way. It reflected the character of the socialist movement itself. If the Fabians showed some awareness of the undeniable advantages of the existing social order, the same could hardly be said of the Marxists, who contemplated the world around them through the darkest of glasses. The Marxists, ever frustrated, dwelt in a self-contained, pristine pure microcosm within the greater macrocosm of a capitalistic society. Correlatively, the Marxist press, save for its constant preoccupation with the trade-union movement, was singularly divorced from the daily events of the contemporary world. It trained its sights on the future and discussed interminably the Marxist glory road that would take the faithful straight to the co-operative commonwealth. The sense of mission that was ever pervasive in the socialist papers deprived them of that saving grace of being able occasionally to laugh at themselves. It would not be remiss to say that the success of J. A. Wayland's journalistic ventures rested partially on their earthiness, their sense of the contemporary, and their rare and heavy-handed efforts at humor.

If parochialism characterizes the Marxist press, so does querulousness. A large percentage of its articles were attacks upon or defenses of particular assumptions, policies, and methods. Indeed, the line between news articles and editorial opinions in socialist papers would be difficult to define. The art of the polemic reached almost heroic proportions when used, for example, by Daniel DeLeon. J. A. Wayland heaped scurrility and defamation primarily on the capitalist "oppressors" of the workingmen and farmers. DeLeon reserved its use almost entirely for heretics within the movement.

Still available for scholarly research are unbroken files of such important socialist newspapers as *The Workmen's Advocate*, *The People*, *The Social Democrat*, *The Social Democratic Herald*, *New Yorker Volkszeitung*, and *Appeal to Reason*. Many of these papers, unfortunately, are in a bad state of repair, and their pages, yellow and brittle with age, crumble to the touch and in some instances defy microfilming. Persons allergic to dust or to musty smells would do well to avoid them. Some libraries have taken considerable pains to preserve these newspapers, and particularly to be singled out for commendation are the State Historical Society of Wisconsin, the Library of Congress, and the Boston Public Library. Files of less prominent socialist newspapers, if they exist, have escaped my notice. Suffice it to say, it was always an abiding satisfaction to discover in various libraries scattered issues of the less prominent socialist newspapers such as the San Francisco *Class Struggle*, *The Cleveland Citizen*, and *St. Louis Labor*.

While newspapers tell most clearly the Marxist side of the socialist story, weekly and monthly magazines provide the best source of information for the non-Marxists, including the Nationalists, the Fabians, and the Christian Socialists. It was not until 1900, in fact, that the Marxists could claim a journal faintly comparable to the German socialist review, *Die Neue Zeit*. This was *The International Socialist Review* which was edited by that pioneer Marxist interpreter of American history, A. M. Simons. Two other "scientific" socialist magazines also began publication at the turn of the century. They were Gaylord Wilshire's *The Challenge* (subsequently renamed *Wilshire's Month-*

ly) and *The Comrade*, which was published by a group of New York left-wing intellectuals including Leonard D. Abbott, George D. Herron, John Spargo, William Mailly, Morris Winchevsky, Algernon Lee, and Peter Burrowes.

In a sense, the difference in the principal editorial media indicates the particular types of reading audiences to which each socialist group was addressing its appeal. The Marxists, always self-consciously directing their message to the wage-earner class, approached the worker through what was frequently his only reading medium, the newspaper. The non-Marxists, frankly acknowledging that their gospel was aimed at the educated and humanitarian-minded middle class, framed it more often than not in the form of highly literate and semi-scholarly periodical articles. The tone of the Fabian and Christian Socialist reviews was notable for its moderation. The non-Marxist socialists were seldom very angry with anyone, and the only point on which they displayed real vehemence was in their condemnation of the class-struggle theory.

If one wished to follow the course of Fabian socialism in the United States, he would do well to begin with *The Nationalist*, the first organ of the movement, and then wend his way through *The New Nation*, *The American Fabian*, *The Commonwealth*, *Twentieth Century*, and finally *The Socialist Review*, subsequently rechristened *The Bellamy Review*. The Christian Socialist movement was represented by several journals, the most prominent of which were *The Dawn*, which echoed the Reverend W. D. P. Bliss's temperate gospel of social Christianity, and *The Kingdom*, which provided an outlet for the more radical views of the Reverend George D. Herron.

Manuscript material is of secondary importance in this study. While I would not suggest that it has not broadened and enriched it, I believe that an adequate account of American socialism during the 1880's and 1890's could be written without use of manuscripts. Judging from the number of letters that came to editors of the socialist press for publication, the socialists themselves were never reticent to take pen in hand. Yet manuscript sources, paradoxically enough, are not plentiful. To write letters and to keep them are two different things. Unfortunately, the socialists were deficient in the latter respect.

The most fruitful manuscript collection that I have consulted is the Henry Demarest Lloyd Papers at the State Historical Society of Wisconsin. Lloyd had the good sense—from the selfish point of view of the historian—to keep most of the letters that he had received and to make carbon copies of many that he sent. Lloyd's correspondence, previously used by several other scholars including his daughter, Caro, who built a two-volume biography largely upon it, constitutes a veritable treasure house for researchers in the field of late nineteenth-century liberalism and radicalism. Also at the State Historical Society are a considerable number of letters and reports written to and by Daniel DeLeon. These are supplemented by what appears to be a part of the Socialist Labor Party's official correspondence covering the period 1889-1902. The official records of the Socialist Party are at Duke University. Party secretary William Butscher kept a letterbook which was particularly useful. It contains several letters giving pertinent insights into the behind-the scenes dickerings among the socialists during the 1900 campaign. The Joseph A. Labadie Papers at the General Library of the University of Michigan are of greater use to the student of anarchism than to the researcher in socialism. The general Labadie collection of materials on labor, socialism, and anarchism, incidentally, is one of the most neglected of its kind, and I would even conjecture that the library officials themselves are unaware of its real value. Finally, attention is called to the letters which Mr. Frederic Heath of Milwaukee graciously permitted me to see and use. The fact that some of Eugene Debs's letters to Mr. Heath were highly critical of his views did not in the least deter him from showing them to me.

The proceedings of the various conventions constitute one last important source of primary material deserving of mention. Beginning with the convention of the Workingmen's Party in 1876 through the unity convention of the Socialist Party in 1901, the proceedings have usually, though not always, been published. More often than not during the formative years of the party the proceedings were recorded and published in German.

Nor should one by-pass the proceedings of the annual conventions of the American Federation of Labor, for here, as nowhere else, the issue of socialism versus trade unionism was hammered out in glowing rhetoric, harsh polemics, and brilliant debate.

Abbot, Willis J., 264, 265, 269

Abbott, Leonard, 353

Abendblatt (New York), 171, 172

Abolitionist movement, 50, 72, 103, 248, 252, 381

Academic freedom, 262, 264, 264n., 275

Adams, John H., 378

Albertson, Ralph, 131

Allen, William V., 215, 235

Altgeld, John Peter, 33, 207, 328

Altruist, The, 125

Altrurian League (New York), 121-22

American Book Company, 130-31

American Co-operative Union, 284

American Economic Association, 92

American Fabian, The, 121, 122-23, 241, 242, 247, 252, 253, 255, 270, 272

American Federation of Labor, 13, 37, 56, 85, 124, 125, 150, 152, 153, 160, 161, 162, 163, 164, 165, 166, 167, 168, 174, 201, 215, 219, 225, 332, 333; resistance to socialist "boring from within," 59-60; acceptance of industrial capitalism, 60; espouses "pure and simple" trade unionism, 60; ex-Marxists in membership, 60; controversy with New York Central Labor Federation, 61-62; Gompers upheld at 1890 convention, 62-63; convention of 1892 rejects socialism, 64; panic of 1893 strengthens socialist element, 64; flirtations with Populists, 65; convention of 1893 approves socialist political program, 65-67; socialist debacle at 1894 convention, 69-70, 71, 215; New York convention (1896), 161, 165-66; conflict with ST and LA, 165-77; relationship with Social Democratic Party, 330-31; Kansas City Convention (1898), 331, 333

American Federationist, The, 67, 68, 166, 330

American Institute of Christian Sociology, 132, 139

American Railway Union, 69, 115, 197, 280, 281, 288, 289, 291, 292, 294, 299, 310, 317, 348

Anarchism and anarchists, 16, 19, 22, 33, 51, 77, 106, 116, 133, 184, 213, 258, 310, 311, 314, 382, 383

Andrews, Stephen Pearl, 9

Appeal to Reason, 175, 194, 195, 196, 197, 199, 200, 201, 203, 204, 205, 208, 212, 232, 323, 324-25, 369, 371

Arbeiter-Zeitung (Chicago), 16, 25

Arbeiter-Zeitung (Milwaukee), 286

Arbeiter-Zeitung (New York), 172, 341

Arbeiter-Zeitung Publishing Co., 172

Arena, The, 259, 324

Arthur, Peter M., 201

Austin, Henry, 96

Aveling, Edward, 30, 31, 32, 303

Aveling, Eleanor Marx, 30, 31

Bachman, M., 17

Backus, E., 380, 381

Baird, W. H., 388

Bandlow, Robert, 171

Barnes, J. Mahlon, 161, 162, 335, 343n.

Barondess, Joseph, 317, 320n., 359

Baxter, Sylvester, 79, 87, 90

Bellamy, Edward, 6, 143, 144, 176, 183, 185, 197, 199, 200, 212, 216, 217, 219, 223, 233, 240, 242, 249; influenced by Gronlund, 30; influence of, 72-73; 105; career, 73-74, 101-2, 222, 273; literary works, 74-75; appeals to middle class, 77-78, 79; knowledge of Marxism, 78; against competitive principle, 78-79; role in Nationalist movement, 79, 80-81, 91, 100; rejects term "socialism," 86;

on Nationalism and Marxism, 87; stresses gradualism, 88, 93; patriotic and nationalistic sentiments, 89-90; belief in equality of pay 90; opposes communitarian socialism, 91; explains Nationalism, 91-93; sets forth attainable objectives, 93-94; against independent Nationalist politics, 94; publishes *New Nation*, 95, 218; favors direct legislation, 98; on Henry George's doctrines, 98-99; views on labor organizations, 99-101; suspends publication of *New Nation*, 101-2, 222; attitude toward People's Party, 218, 220, 221-22, 237, 245; writes Equality, 273, 276

Bellamy, Francis, 112

Bellamy Review, The (formerly *The Socialist Review*), 136, 270, 272

Bemis, Edward W., 233, 262, 264, 265-6, 266n.

Benham, G. B., 335, 343n., 345, 346, 348, 351, 353, 355, 356, 360, 362

Berger, Victor, 230, 231, 280, 282, 285-87, 288, 289, 290, 292, 295, 299, 306, 307, 308, 309, 311, 312, 314, 316, 317, 320, 320n., 322, 329, 331, 338, 339, 340, 344, 345, 347, 348, 351, 354, 355, 356, 357, 358, 361, 362, 363, 366, 376, 378, 379, 383, 384, 386, 387

Berkman, Alexander, 101

Bernstein, Eduard, 286, 321, 333

Bevan, Charlie, 188, 194, 200

Bible Plan for the Abolition of Poverty, The, 105

Black International; *see* International Working People's Association

Blatavsky, Helen, 81

Bliss, William Dwight Porter, 127, 134, 249, 251, 255, 273; on Bellamy, 72; member of Nationalist Club, 80, 111; critical of Nationalists, 90, 114-15; youth and education, 109; joins Episcopal Church, 109-10; apprenticeship years, 110; embraces Christian Socialism, 110; approves Fa-bian methods, 110-11, 113, 199; associated with CAIL, 111; founds Christian Socialist Society, 111-12; approves SLP platform, 114, 124, 187; defends strikers, 115; on futile strikes, 115-16; efforts to organize Christian Socialist league, 116; publishes *Dawn*, 117; founds Mission of the Carpenter, 117; organizes Brotherhood of the Carpenter, 117; desires Christian fellowship community, 118-19; lecturer for Christian Social Union, 119-20; on need for spiritual reawakening, 120; visits Europe, 120; efforts to organize an American Fabian League, 121-22; relinquishes editorship of *American Fabian*, 123, 253; attempts to organize National Educational and Economic League, 124-25; criticizes SLP, 124, 222-23; criticized by H. D. Lloyd, 125; described by Longley, 126; spokesman for clerical radicals, 126, 141; favors political action, 116, 148, 222, on People's Party, 222-24; supports 1896 Populist-Democratic fusion, 237, 240-41; controversy with British Fabians, 241-42; reaction to 1896 election, 243-44, 245, 247-48; leader of Union Reform League, 256-61; supports Democratic Party, 261, 267; relationship with Social Reform Union, 264, 267; disillusioned with Democratic Party, 273

Block, George G., 48, 49

Bloor, Ella Reeve, 304n.

Borland, W. P., 303, 304, 315, 316, 317, 318

Boston Post, 219

Bowers, Charles E., 80

Bradfield, William, 179

Breidenthal, John W., 265

Brewster, E. V., 353

Brook Farm, 118

INDEX

Brooklyn Socialist Labor Federation, 160

Brooklyn Trolley Strikes: of 1895, p. 115; of 1899, p. 326

Brotherhood of the Carpenter, 117-18, 119, 121

Brotherhood of the Co-operation Commonwealth, 6, 282-85, 288, 291, 291n., 293, 318

Brower, William L., 158, 161, 167

Brown, C. O., 133

Brown, Corinne, 83, 220n., 374, 376, 377

Brown, William Thurston, 140, 266n.

Bryan, William Jennings, 176, 208, 233, 234, 236, 239, 240, 243, 244, 247, 252, 268, 269, 281, 288, 327, 328, 329, 370, 371, 373

Buchanan, Joseph, R., 21, 68, 249, 263

Buffalo Switchmen's Strike, 68, 148

Bureau of Nationalist Literature, 102

Burns, John, 70

Burns, William E., 294, 295, 299, 310, 311, 313n.

Busche, J. F., 25, 53, 54, 55, 56, 58, 59

Butscher, William, 320n., 347, 351, 359, 362, 363, 366, 367, 368, 376

Byron, Thomas, 212

Cahan, Abraham, 300, 301

Caldwell, J. W., 264

California Nationalist, 84n.

Campbell, Helen, 80

Carberry, W. J., 320n.

Carey, James F., 169, 311, 320n., 324, 325, 331, 333, 339, 345, 347, 348, 351, 353, 354, 359, 362, 381, 384, 385, 387

Carl, Conrad, 7

Carnegie, Andrew, 4, 68

Carnegie Steel Co., 101, 115

Cass News, 177, 178

Casson, Herbert N., 168-69, 197, 244, 251-52, 255, 263, 270, 271, 272, 278, 327, 370

Casson, Lydia Commander, 270

Challenge, The, 267, 268

Chase John C., 324, 325, 347, 352, 362, 363, 368, 374

Chicago American, 369-70

Chicago Socialist, The (later *The Workers' Call*), 197

Chicago Times-Herald, 296-97

Chicago Tribune, 296-97, 316

Childs, H. C., 305, 306

Chipman, John, 131

Christian Commonwealth Colony, 131-32, 139, 282

Christian Labor Union, 105, 110

Christian Social Union, 119, 132, 256, 259

Christian Socialism, 175, 211, 222, 247, 256, 259; as represented by Jesse Jones, 105-6; Franklin Monroe Sprague, 107-8; Vida D. Scudder, 108-9; W. D. P. Bliss, 109-20, 266; George D. Herron, 126-39

Chubb, Percival, 120

Church Association for the Advancement of the Interests of Labor (CAIL), 111

Church Social Union (Great Britain), 119

Cincinnati *Brauer-Zeitung,* 359

Claflin, Sumner, 186, 187n.

Claflin, Tennessee, 10

Class Struggle, The (San Francisco), 346, 360, 369

Class struggle doctrine, 5, 78, 87-88, 106, 126, 147, 150, 168, 203-4, 251, 252, 254-55, 269, 273, 277, 295, 309, 312, 317, 345

Clemens, C. G., 380, 381, 385, 386

Cleveland Central Labor Union, 171

Cleveland Citizen, The, 232n., 328

Coeur d'Alene Strike (1892), 68, 148

Coming Crisis, The (formerly *The Colorado Worker*), 180

Coming Light, The, 270

Coming Nation, The, 175, 181, 182, 183, 185, 186, 187, 188, 189, 190, 191, 192, 193, 194, 195, 197, 200, 203,

INDEX

205, 209, 212, 233, 243, 251, 253, 270, 284, 285, 320

Commons, John R., 259, 262, 264

Commonwealth, The, 225, 226, 242, 253, 270

Communist Manifesto, 7, 10, 297

Communitarian settlements, 5-6, 90-91, 189-94, 246, 282-83, 291n., 318

Congress of Industrial Organizations, 152

Cook, Joseph, 4

Cooperative Commonwealth, The, 28-30, 78, 180, 185

Co-operative Commonwealth Co., 306

Corrigan, Michael A., 44

Costley, William, 378

Coulter, Charles, 325

Cox, Jesse, 83, 228, 245, 299, 320, 320n., 344, 357, 374, 376

Dague, R. A., 266n.

Damon, William 131

Darrow, Clarence, 83, 131, 230

Davidson, Thomas, 83, 118, 143

Davis, Kate Buffington, 84-85

Dawn, The, 112, 115, 116, 117, 119, 120, 121, 223

Dayton *Daily Press,* 196

Dean, J. E., 285

Debs, Eugene V., 73, 115, 127, 134, 137, 138, 182, 196, 197, 198, 208, 209, 220n., 232, 232n., 251, 267, 268, 307, 308, 316, 323-24, 328, 329, 330, 331, 352, 353, 355, 360, 361, 376, 387n.; refuses Populist candidacy in 1896, pp. 235-36, 236n.; at Woodstock jail, 280-81; supports Populists, 281, 282; conversion to socialism, 281-82; association with Brotherhood of the Co-operative Commonwealth, 282, 285, 288; organizes Social Democracy, 289-94; on nature of Social Democracy, 295, 310; on futile strikes, 296; as socialist proselytizer, 302-3; role at Social Democracy Convention of 1898, pp.

311-314; supports Social Democracy bolters, 314-15, 317, 320; and SLP, 335, 340, 358; on union with SLP "Kangaroo" faction, 339, 340, 341, 345, 347, 357-58, 362, 365-67, 375, 377; as Social Democratic presidential nominee in 1900, pp. 348-49, 356, 363, 365, 366, 368, 369, 370, 372

Debs, Theodore, 320, 320n., 376

DeLeon, Daniel, 43, 59, 63, 70, 115, 126, 185, 201, 207, 208, 212, 216n., 223, 237, 251, 290, 326, 339, 354, 358, 359; on *Looking Backward,* 73, 86; association with Nationalists, 83, 142, 143, 144, 337; joins SLP, 142, 144; called "Loeb," 142, 167; early career, 142-43; supports Henry George, 143, 337; on Haymarket Affair, 143-44; intellectual integrity and stature, 144, 145-46; rise in SLP, 145; candidate for political office, 145, 337; editor of *The People,* 145; criticisms of, 145, 160, 167, 332, 335, 337-38; on SLP trade unionism *vs.* political action controversy, 146; guides new SLP policies, 147-52; efforts to capture K of L, 153-60; on People's Party, 155, 156, 180, 187, 217; opposes AF of L and the K of L, 160, 164; role in ST and LA, 162-68; purges party, 168-73, 304; fails to "Americanize" socialist movement, 174; and J. A. Wayland, 199-200, 335; tours West, 238; and Debs, 282, 298, 340; on Social Democracy, 297-98, 301-2, 305, 316; attacks SLP critics, 333-34; "deposed" by "Kangaroos," 336; and presidential campaign of 1900, pp. 371-72

DeLeon, Solon, 146

Democratic Party, 42, 50, 52, 149, 183, 198, 212, 214, 216, 220, 227, 229, 234, 235, 237, 239, 242, 243, 244, 261, 262, 263, 288, 308, 326, 327,

INDEX

328, 337, 358, 369, 370, 371, 372, 374, 380, 387n.

Denver *Labor Enquirer,* 21

Devereaux, Arthur F., 80

Diaz, Abby Morton, 80

Dietzgen, Eugene, 335, 353

Dietzgen, Joseph, 25

Direct legislation (initiative and referendum), 230, 246, 248, 249-50, 258, 260, 262, 263, 269, 279, 327, 329-30

Dr. Heidenhoff's Process, 74

Dodge, E. W., 195

Doerfler, John, 320n.

Donnelly, Ignatius, 232, 372

Douai, Adolph, 15, 49

Doubleday, Abner, 83

Douglass, Frederick, 10

Drummond, Henry, 78

Dunn, M. Ballard, 388

Dupuy, Jean, 253-54

Easterling, T. C., 270

Eaton, Rice H., 270

Edwards, A. S., 188, 189, 193, 197, 200, 285, 320, 320n., 323, 345, 348, 356, 357, 376

Eight-hour day, 30, 56, 61, 65, 100, 103, 110, 143, 325

Ely, Richard T., 22, 132, 233, 245, 250

Ely, Robert E., 263

Encyclopedia of Social Reform, 121, 260

Engels, Friedrich, 3, 10, 35, 185, 380

Equal Rights Party, 10

Equality, 93, 197, 273, 274-75, 276

Equality Colony, 291n., 318

Equity, 106

Fabian Socialism (Great Britain), 81, 84, 88, 89, 90, 101, 109, 110, 111, 120, 126, 234, 251, 253, 278, 330; London Fabian Society, 80, 83, 105, 122, 122n., 241, 242; *Fabian Essays* ("tracts"), 105, 108, 122n.; *Fabian News,* 122n.

Fabian Socialism (United States), 211, 241, 278-79; American Fabian League, 121, 124, 266; Fabian societies, 121, 122, 123, 299; tracts, 121, 122; proposed program, 122-23n.; and party politics, 247, 248, 250-54, 364; emphasis on education and organization, 251-54; rejection of "class struggle," 251, 252, 254-55; middle-class status, 255-56; criticized, 255, 295

Fales, Imogene, 83, 283, 284, 328-29, 330

Farmer, W. E., 331, 345, 365

Farmer's Tribune, The, 212

Farmers' Alliances, 96, 211, 213

Federation of Organized Trades and Labor Unions (later AF of L), 26, 60

Feigenbaum, Benjamin, 334

Fellowship of the New Life, 83, 118

Fenner, C. E., 343n., 364

Flower, Benjamin O., 185, 370, 371

Foster, Frank K., 67, 68

Fourier, Charles, 5

Franz, J. F., 359

Freiheit, Die, 310

Freuder, Samuel, 83

Frick, Henry Clay, 68, 101, 115, 205

Fritsche, F. W., 18

Garland, Hamlin, 80

Gates, Thomas A., 130, 131, 266n.

General German Workingmen's Union, 9

George, Henry, 39, 44, 45, 48, 51, 75, 78, 81, 98, 99, 105, 109, 114, 143, 178, 219, 229, 237, 252; mayoralty campaign, 3, 31, 35, 37, 38, 40, 41, 42, 43, 47, 61; attitude toward socialists, 38-39, 43, 46, 47, 48, 49, 51; socialist attitude toward, 40, 41, 43, 44, 45, 46, 48, 49, 50, 51, 53; role at United Labor Party convention of 1887, pp. 45, 46, 47-48; decline in popularity, 52

INDEX

Gerau, Franz, 59
Gerecke, Adolph, 56
German Workingmen's Alliance, 7
Ghent, William J., 123, 225, 263
Gibson, George Howard, 131, 212
Gifford, O. P., 112
Gilman, Nicholas Paine, 82, 219
Gladden, Washington, 106
Gleason, Herbert W., 130
Goebel, George, 379, 382
Goldman, Emma, 311
Gompers, Samuel, 60n., 95, 201, 202, 216n., 332, 333; controversy with N. Y. Central Labor Federation, 61-62; upholds trade unionism against socialism, 62-63; criticizes existing economic system, 65; editor of *American Federationist,* 67; successful strategy against socialists, 69; deposed as AF of L president, 69-70; commits AF of L to opportunism, 71; on ST and LA, 165-66; attacks DeLeon, 166, 167; and Social Democratic Party, 330-31, 331n.
Goodwin, Roy M., 294, 295, 299, 310
Gordon, F. G. R., 320n., 329, 347, 355, 356, 357, 359
Green, Mason A., 219
Greenback Party, 18
Greenbaum, Leon, 387
Grinnell College (formerly Iowa College), 130, 132, 139, 374
Gronlund, Laurence, 28, 29, 30, 38, 44, 48, 78, 80, 82, 87, 89, 90, 122, 180, 185, 195, 197, 224, 240, 273, 277, 278, 303, 317-18
Grottkau, Paul, 17, 21, 230, 308

Haack, Fred, 309
Haile, Margaret, 311-12, 314, 317, 320n., 339, 347, 350, 352, 353, 354, 357, 359, 362, 363, 379
Hale, Edward Everett, 80
Hall, Bolton, 262
Hall, J. Edward, 50, 55

Hampton, S. J., 386
Hanford, Ben, 353, 366
Hanna, Marcus Alonzo, 212, 244, 261
Hardie, Keir, 280
Harriman, Job, 164, 267, 335, 343n., 344, 345, 346, 348, 349, 351, 352, 353, 354, 355, 356, 360-61, 363, 365, 366, 367, 368, 372, 373, 379, 380, 384, 386
Haskell, Burnette G., 20, 21, 52, 84, 85
Hayes, John W., 154, 159, 160
Hayes, Max S., 171, 328, 335, 343n., 344, 346, 347, 348, 351, 353, 355, 366, 378, 381
Haymarket Affair, 3, 17, 22, 30, 32-35, 51, 77, 103, 116, 133, 258, 293, 314
Haynes, John R., 259
Hearst, William Randolph, 207, 208, 251, 369, 370
Heath, Frederic, 209, 282, 285, 287-88, 289, 290, 299, 307, 320, 320n., 344, 345, 347, 348, 350, 351, 352, 353, 354, 356, 359, 361, 363, 366, 367, 376
Herron, George D., 263, 266n.; called a prophet, 126; criticism of, 127, 132-33, 136-37; early career, 127; seminal ideas, 128-29; appointed at Grinnell, 130; alienation from wife, 130; relationship to Christian Commonwealth Colony, 131-32; a founder of American Institute of Christian Sociology, 132; criticizes churches, 133-34; espouses Marxism, 134-36, 278; inspires Social Crusade, 137; criticism of marriage institution, 139; resigns from Grinnell, 139; marriage to Carrie Rand, 140; expulsion from ministry, 140; as socialist martyr, 140-41; emigration to Italy, 141; attacks imperialism, 262; ideas propagated by National Christian Citizenship League, 266; role in Social Democratic Party, 134, 136, 266-67, 273, 369, 374-75, 377, 383

Hess, Rousseau, 188, 191
Hewitt, Abram S., 41
Hicks, Henry, 225
Higginson, Thomas Wentworth, 80, 84
Hildebrand, L. E., 388
Hillquit, Morris, 335, 336n., 339, 341, 342, 343, 343n., 344, 345, 346, 347, 348, 351, 352, 354, 355, 356, 360, 362, 364, 378, 379, 383, 386, 387
Hinton, Richard J., 48, 303-4, 305, 307
Hintze, William, 56
Hoelm, Gustav A., 169, 170, 311, 320n., 330, 347, 351, 353, 354, 379, 380, 382, 384, 386, 387
Hoffman, C. B., 265
Hogan, James, 294, 295, 310, 311, 313, 313n., 314, 315, 316, 319
Holmes, Bayard, 233
Holmes, David, 70
Homestead Strike (1892), 68, 101, 115, 147, 148
Hourwich, Isaac, 294, 297, 301, 306, 311, 314, 317
Howe, Julia Ward, 80
Howells, William Dean, 78, 80
Hughes, Thomas, 305
Humanity, 292n.
Hunger, Jacob, 317, 320n.
Hunter, B. Franklin, 102, 285
Huntington, E.S., 80
Hussey, George, 325

Imperialism, 262-63, 369, 371
Independent Labor Party (Great Britain), 278, 318
Industrial Brotherhood, 292n.
Industrial Commonwealers, 69, 184-85
Industrial Unionism, 150, 152
Industrial Workers of the World, 165
Ingalls, J. S., 311, 318
Initiative; see Direct legislation
Insufficiency of Henry George's Theory, The, 44

International Socialist and Trades Union Congress: of 1891, pp. 63, 145; of 1896, pp. 250, 322; of 1900, pp. 353, 374
International Socialist Review, 268
International Typographical Union, 368
International Working People's Association (Black International), 19, 21, 24, 35
International Workingmen's Association (Marxist), 3, 8, 9, 10, 11, 12, 13-14, 20, 57
International Workingmen's Association (Red International), 20, 21, 35, 52, 84

Jaurès, Jean, 73
Jewish Daily Forward (New York), 173, 300, 339, 359, 368, 373
Jewish Socialists (New York), 171-73, 172n., 300-2, 338, 339, 359
Jonas, Alexander, 15, 25-26, 49, 55, 56, 144
Jones, Frederick D., 259
Jones, Jesse, 105-6, 110, 213
Jones, Mary Harris ("Mother Jones"), 293, 320n.
Jones, S. M., 363
Jones, Samuel ("Golden Rule"), 137, 207, 208, 260, 264, 266n., 267, 268, 270, 271-72, 327, 328, 364, 370
Journal of the Knights of Labor, 154, 156, 157, 158, 159, 260

Kansas State Agricultural College, 264, 265
Kansas State Christian Socialist Society, 116
Kapital, Das, 28
Kaplan, Morris, 364
Kautsky, Karl, 185
Kaweah Colony, 282
Keep, Arthur, 158, 173
Keliher, Sylvester, 294, 310, 311, 312, 313, 313n., 316, 317, 319
Kelly, Florence, 83

INDEX

Kent, Alexander, 105
Kingdom, The, 130, 131, 132, 139
Kingdom of Heaven, The, 105
Kingdom Publishing Co., 131
Knight, William H., 259
Knights of Labor, 21, 26, 27, 52, 61, 86, 106, 110, 152, 153, 154, 155, 156, 157, 158, 159, 160, 161, 163, 164, 172, 174, 219, 221, 225, 231, 289, 300
Koop, George, 320n.
Kuhn, Charles, 317, 320n.
Kuhn, Henry, 147, 153, 199, 238, 297, 332

Labadie, Joseph, 139, 140
Labor Balance, The, 106, 112
Labor Church (Lynn, Mass.), 168, 244
Labor Party of Illinois, 13
Ladoff, Isadore, 376
Land and Labor Clubs, 47
Lassalle, Ferdinand, 8, 26
Leader, The, 43, 44, 45, 47, 303
Lee, Algernon, 83, 338, 341
Legate, Henry R., 219, 222, 234
Lehr und Wehr Verein, 16, 17
Leonard, John W., 266n.
Lermond, Norman Wallace, 283, 284, 285, 291n., 318
Levine, Samuel, 317, 320n.
Liebknecht, Wilhelm, 30, 31, 32
Livermore, Mary A., 80, 112
Lloyd, Harry, 124, 125
Lloyd, Henry Demarest, 28, 138, 197, 222, 240, 246, 260, 283, 285, 306; early critic of the trusts, 27; claims treachery at AF of L convention of 1894, p. 70; on Bellamy, 72; critical of Bliss, 124-25; supports Christian Commonwealth Colony, 132; role in Chicago Populist movement, 228-30; at Populist convention of 1896, pp. 233-36; disgust with Populists, 236-37; votes SLP in 1896, pp. 238-39; on dilemma of reform movement, 244-45; opinion of SLP, 245; critical of direct legisla-

tion, 250; aids Gronlund, 276; and Social Democracy, 294, 297, 303
Lloyd, John F., 299, 310, 311, 312, 314, 316
Loebel, Oscar, 320n.
London, Meyer, 301, 345, 347, 348, 359
Lonergan, William, 347, 362, 363
Longley, Alcander, 91, 126, 284
Looking Backward, 30, 72, 73, 74, 75-77, 78, 79, 80, 86, 88, 90, 93, 94, 95, 107, 114, 176, 179, 183, 185, 189, 273, 326
Lovell, John W. Co., 25

Maguire, Matthew, 173, 174, 239
Mailly, William, 320, 320n., 347, 348
Malkiel, Leon A., 340
Malloney, Francis, 372
Mann, Prestonia, 123, 253, 253n.
Martin, Charles R., 289, 320n., 359
Martyn, Carlos, 105
Marx, Karl, 3, 8, 10, 28, 31, 35, 40, 78, 135, 144, 146, 185, 200, 351
Mass and Class, 123n.
Massachusetts Labor Party, 110
Matchett, Charles H., 149, 150, 174, 239, 244, 335, 353
Matthews, Charles B., 226
McBride, John, 70
McCaddin, George W., 155, 158
MacCartney, Frederic O., 325, 347, 348, 357, 359, 379, 382
McCormick Harvester Co., 32-33
McGlynn, Edward, 42, 44, 143, 221
McGuire, P. J., 13, 85
McKay, Edward, 378
McKinley, William, 224, 239, 240, 241, 244, 247, 250, 261, 262, 267, 272, 285, 368, 372, 373
McMackin, John, 46
McNeill, George E., 110, 115, 117, 124, 125
McSweeney, M. J., 380
Mead, Edwin D., 265
Meier, C. F., 320n.

402

Meister, Herbert, 308
"Message of Jesus to Men of Wealth, The," 128-29
Meyer, Reinhardt, 58
Meyer, Siegfried, 7
Miller, Hugo, 320n.
Miller, John, 256
Miller, Louis F., 301, 320n.
Mills, B. Fay, 261
Milwaukee Federated Trades Council, 230, 308, 369
Mission of the Carpenter, 117, 118, 120, 124
Moerschel, George, 317, 320n.
Mohr, August, 309
Molly Maguires, 14
Morgan, Thomas J., 63, 64, 66, 67, 68, 69, 125, 138, 188, 228, 229, 280, 369, 374, 380, 381, 382
Most, Johann, 20, 21, 23, 25, 310
Mrs. Ludington's Sister, 75
Muckrakers, 27, 95, 278
Murphy, Patrick J., 154, 159

National Christian Citizenship League, 266, 266n.
National Co-operative Congress, 283, 284
National Direct Legislation League, 249
National Economist, The, 211
National Educational and Economic League, 124-25
National Labor Union, 9
National Social and Political Conference: of 1899, pp. 262-64, 329; of 1901, pp. 267-70
Nationalist Magazine, The, 80, 82, 83, 84, 87, 90, 95, 97, 98, 99, 100, 101
Nationalist movement, 6, 230, 254, 276, 279, 292, 324; founding of Boston Nationalist Club, 79-80, 304; Declaration of Principles, 81; organization of clubs, 82; character of membership, 82-86; SLP overtures spurned, 86; rejects "class struggle," 87-88; stresses gradualism, 88; independent political action, 88-89, 94, 217-18; champions patriotism, 89; and communitarian socialism, 90-91; Bellamy's immediate goals, 93-94; social and political reform activities, 95-98; relations with single taxers, 98-99; stand on organized labor, 99-101; weakness of movement, 101; and the People's Party, 101, 211, 217-22; contributions to the American reform tradition, 102; criticized by Christian Socialists, 114-15; deterioration of movement, 120, 126, 175; favors direct legislation, 249
Natural Law in the Spiritual World, 78
Nelson, N. O., 83, 263
Neue Zeit, Die (Stuttgart), 321
New Bedford Textile Strike (1898), 166
"New Democracy, The," 9
New Economy, The, 273, 276, 277-78, 317
New Nation, The, 95, 97, 99, 101, 218, 219, 221
New Rugby Colony, 305
New York Central Labor Federation, 61, 62, 63, 160, 167, 326, 369
New York Central Labor Union, 37, 43, 45, 50, 61, 297, 326
New York Central Railroad Strike (1890), 115
New York Communist Club, 7, 9
New York Journal, 207, 270, 276, 289
New York Times, 31
New York World, 49, 162
New Yorker Volkszeitung, 15, 25-26, 40, 46-47, 54, 55, 56-57, 58-59, 332-35, 339
Newark Central Labor Federation, 160
Newton, R. Heber, 106, 114, 143

O'Connor, John H., 174
O'Loughlin, Daniel, 225, 242-43, 244

INDEX

Oneal, James, 360
One-Hoss Philosophy, 197n.
O'Reilly, John Boyle, 80
Our Benevolent Feudalism, 123n.
Owen, Robert, 5

Pacific Union, The, 84n.
Pallas, J. J., 297
Panic: of 1873, p. 12; of 1893, pp. 37, 64, 68, 120, 173, 175, 181, 188, 227
Paris Commune, 3, 11
Parker, Joseph, 268
Parsons, Albert R., 17, 21, 33, 293
Parsons, Frank, 250, 259, 264, 266n., 283, 285, 291, 370, 371
Parsons, Lucy, 293
Pease, Edward R., 120, 122n., 241-42
Peck, Harry Thurston, 95
Peebles, H. P., 72
Peffer, William A., 215, 215n.
People, The, 64, 70, 126, 145, 148, 149, 150, 154, 155, 156, 158, 168, 169, 170, 172, 173, 180, 185, 186, 197, 200, 216, 223, 282, 302, 332, 333, 334, 336, 337, 340, 358, 360, 369, 371, 372, 373
People's Church (Boston), 265
People's Church (Washington, D. C.), 105
People's Party (Populism), 64-65, 67, 68, 101, 120, 148, 154, 155, 157, 158, 168, 171, 175, 176, 179, 180, 183, 184, 187, 188, 195, 196, 199, 237, 239, 243, 244, 245, 246, 250, 252, 260, 263, 265, 281, 282, 288, 293, 295, 297, 308, 315, 322, 340, 358, 368, 372, 381; against socialism, 211, 213, 214, 229, 230, 232; Omaha platform (1892), 213, 214, 220, 224, 228, 249; political co-operation with Chicago socialists, 212, 213, 214, 227-30; political co-operation with Milwaukee socialists, 212, 213, 230-31, 286; presidential election of 1892, pp. 213, 221, 223; free-silver issue, 213, 214, 217, 221-22, 223, 224, 232, 233, 240, 241; criticized by

SLP, 215-17; New York Populists, 217, 224-27; Massachusetts Populists, 218-20, 221, 227; and Christian Socialists, 222-24; convention of 1896, pp. 230, 233, 234-36, 238, 242, 283, 284
"Permeation socialists," 211-12, 217, 251, 254
Philadelphia Tageblatt, 300, 306
Phillips, I., 320n., 345, 359, 363
Pine, Max, 301, 359
Pingree, Hazen S., 252
Pinkerton detectives, 101, 115, 225
Pittsburg Kansan, 190, 232n.
Pomeroy, Eltweed, 83, 138, 220n., 249, 250, 251, 261, 325n., 370, 371
Populism; *see* People's Party
Porter, Elizabeth G., 325
Porter, Winfield P., 326
Post, Louis F., 44, 47, 266n.
Powderly, Terence V., 154, 156, 159, 201, 202
Presidential election: of 1888, p. 55; of 1892, pp. 64-65, 148, 149-50, 179, 213, 216, 221, 223; of 1896, pp. 215, 231, 238-43, 247, 250, 277, 281, 285, 286, 328, 368; of 1900, pp. 138, 272, 368-73
Preston, John, 123, 271, 272
Preston, Thomas S., 42
Progress and Poverty, 38, 39-40, 43
Progressive Review, The, 234
Progressive Labor Party, 50, 52, 53
Prohibition Party, 220, 226, 263
Protestant churches: social attitude of, 103, 104, 107; criticism of, 104, 105, 107, 113, 133-34, 275
Public Ownership Clubs, 122
Pujo Committee report, 97
Pullman Strike, 69, 115, 280, 304, 316, 330, 348
Putnam, E. Val, 347, 359, 387
Putney, Squire, 347

Racowitza, Helena von, 26
Railroad Strike of 1877, pp. 14, 15, 103

404

INDEX

Railway Times, The, 197, 295
Rainsford, W. S., 124
Rand, Carrie, 129, 130, 137, 139, 140
Rand, Mrs. E. D., 129, 130, 139
Rand School of Social Science, 83
Recent American Socialism, 22
Red International; *see* International
  Workingmen's Association
Redpath, James, 143
Reed, Myron, 285
Referendum; *see* Direct legislation
Remmel, Valentine, 372
Republican Party, 7, 50, 52, 149, 183,
  198, 201, 212, 214, 216, 220, 224,
  227, 247, 260, 261, 262, 263, 272, 295,
  308, 326, 327, 328, 337, 369, 370,
  372, 374
Republik der Arbeiter, Die, 7
Revisionist Socialism, 286, 293, 321,
  333, 371
Revolutionary Clubs, 19
Revolutionary Socialist Party, 20
Robinson, Harry W., 149
Robinson, Leila J., 85
Rogers, Louis W., 296
Roosevelt, Theodore, 41, 372
Rosenberg, W. L., 25, 32, 53, 55, 56,
  57, 58, 59, 173
Rothschild, House of, 183, 205
Ruskin Colony, 192-93, 195, 233, 285
Ruskin Co-operative Association, 192,
  193, 282
Ruskin, John, 105, 185
Ruskin Magazine Quarterly, 192, 197n.

St. Louis Brauer-Zeitung, 299, 351
St. Louis Labor, 170
St. Louis Trades and Labor Council,
  369
Sanderson, Albert, 169-70
San Francisco Tageblatt, 300
Sanial, Lucien, 59, 62, 63, 83, 145, 147,
  153, 156, 157, 161-62, 237, 332
Saunders, J. W., 381
Sauter, Joseph, 56
Scates, Louis M., 324, 325, 326

Schevitsch, Serge, 25, 44, 45, 47, 48,
  51, 303
Schilling Robert, 231
Schindler, Solomon, 80, 89
Schlüter, Hermann, 144, 332, 333
Scott, Joseph E., 241n., 248-49, 250-
  51, 256, 257, 259
Scudder, Vida D., 72, 108-9, 134
Seidel, Emil, 379
Seidenberg Strike, 166-67
Seven Financial Conspiracies, 180
Shaw, George Bernard, 80, 123
Shibley, George, 265
Sieverman, Frank J., 343n., 380
Sillence, William E., 116
Simons, A. M., 175, 267-68, 269, 329,
  335, 360, 370, 378, 380, 382, 384,
  385, 386, 388
Single tax, 41, 47, 48, 98, 99, 219, 229,
  230
Slobodin, Henry L., 336, 364
Smith, Anna F., 320n.
Social Crusade, 137, 138, 139, 374
Social Crusader, The, 137, 138
Social Democracy of America, 6, 253,
  319, 381; declaration of principles,
  292-93; immediate demands, 293,
  321; officers, 294; colonization *vs.*
  political action, 294-95, 309-10, 314;
  position regarding trade unions,
  296; criticism of, 296-98; and SLP,
  297-98, 299, 300; organizational activities, 298-303; work of colonization commission, 303-6, 314, 318;
  convention of 1898, pp. 306, 310-
  15; colonization commission criticized, 306-7; political activity, 307-
  9; colonizationist faction gains control, 314; "American methods" of
  colonizationists, 315-17; collapse,
  318
Social Democrat, The (formerly *The
  Railway Times*), 295, 296, 298, 304,
  304n., 307, 309, 315, 316, 317, 318
Social Democrat, The (Haverhill),
  359

405

Social Democratic Federation, 287, 299

Social Democratic Herald, 197, 200, 263n., 320, 322, 323, 325, 326, 328, 329, 330, 331, 340, 344, 345, 353, 357, 358, 359, 360, 363, 364, 368, 369, 371, 373-74, 376

Social Democratic Party, 73, 83, 136, 138, 200, 261, 263, 263n., 268, 273, 318; in presidential campaign of 1900, pp. 134, 196-97, 266-67, 365-71, 372-74; opposes "non-partisan" socialists, 251, 327-30; organized, 314, 320; platform, 320-321, 353, 380n.; repudiates dual unionism, 321, 322; follows revisionist policies, 321, 380n.; "farmers' demands," 321, 322-23, 345, 346, 384-86; and New York Independent Labor Party, 326-27, 345; and SLP, 327; and AF of L, 330-31; national convention of 1900, pp. 343, 344-49, 377; 1st unity conference with "Kangaroo" SLP, 350-53; conference repudiated by National Executive Board, 354-55; 2d unity conference, 361-63; referenda on unity, 354, 361, 363-64; union with "Kangaroo" SLP, 339, 342, 344, 346-49, 350-68, 374-78; party name issue, 344, 346-47, 351, 351n., 352, 354, 355, 356, 357, 360, 361, 363, 364, 387, 387n.

Social Democratic Party Unity Convention (1901), 269; membership, 377-78; immediate demands issue debated, 379-84, 379n.; "farmers' demands" rejected, 384-86; Negro rights, 386; trade unions, 386-87; new party name and headquarters, 387-88

Social Democratic Workingmen's Party of North America, 13

Social Economist, The (formerly *The Socialist* of San Francisco), 250, 251, 253, 256, 270

Social Forum, The 131, 266n., 364

Social Gospel movement, 104, 105, 106, 112, 128, 130, 131, 132, 275, 282

Social Reform Union, 263-70, 278

Social Revolutionaries, 16, 17, 18, 19, 20, 21, 22, 23, 24, 33, 106

Social Unity, 270, 273

Socialism from Genesis to Revelation, 107-8, 185

Socialist, The (San Francisco), 232n., 241n., 248, 250

Socialist Co-operative Publishing Co., 332, 334

Socialist Labor Party (formerly Socialistic Labor Party), 85, 106, 114, 117, 124, 134, 142, 144, 145, 172n., 179, 187, 188, 199, 200, 212, 222, 223, 226, 227, 232, 239, 244, 245, 246, 251, 252, 253, 258, 260, 261, 289, 304, 307, 317, 324, 326, 344, 358; conventions, (1877) 15, (1879) 17, (1881) 18, (1883) 24-25, (1885) 27, 53, (1887) 32, 33-34, 52, (1889) 58, (1893) 169, 173, 215, (1896) 163, 164, 165, 169, 170, 171, 172, 237-38, (1900) 371; opposes *Lehr und Wehr Verein,* 16; relations with social revolutionaries and anarchists, 17, 19, 21, 24-25, 33-35; presidential campaigns, (1880) 17-18, (1888) 55, (1892) 148-50, 216, (1896) 237, 381, (1900) 371-72; party decline, 18-25; influence of *Volkszeitung* group, 26; position on trusts, 27-28; sponsors Liebknecht-Aveling tour, 30-32; party's status in 1866, pp. 35-36; and United Labor Party, 38, 45, 46, 46n., 47, 48, 50; and the Progressive Labor Party, 51, 53; Lassallean-*Volkszeitung* factional controversy, 51-59, 146, 287, 335, 339; the "perambulating faction," 59, 173, 287; changes in party policies, 59, 147-152; response to AF of L anti-Socialist policies, 63-

INDEX

64, 70; overtures to Nationalists, 86; "New Trade Unionism" policy, 150-52; internal disharmony, 168-73, 299, 300-2, 324; failure to capture K of L, 153-60; sponsors ST and LA, 162-65; opposition to dual unionism, 164, 170, 171, 172, 173, 333; party weakness, 174; and the People's Party, 215-17, 237, 238; and the Social Democracy 293, 294, 297-98, 299, 300, 301-2, 308, 316; "revolt" against DeLeonism, 332-38, 341; retains party name and symbol, 337, 373; party paper renamed *The Weekly People*, 338; and Social Democratic Party, 348, 372; drops "immediate demands" from platform, 371, 379-80

Socialist Party of America, 135, 200, 278, 319, 350, 387; *see also* Social Democratic Party Unity Convention (1901)

Socialist Review, The, 270

Socialist Trade and Labor Alliance, 162-168, 171, 172, 300, 333, 371

Society of Christian Socialists, 112-17

Somerby, Charles, 225, 226, 242, 243, 254, 255, 270

Sorge, Friedrich A., 3, 7, 9, 35, 63

Sotheran, Charles, 68, 83, 155, 307

Sovereign, John R., 154, 155, 156, 157, 159

Sozialist, Der, 25, 53, 57

Spahr, Charles, 259

Spanish-American War, 196, 206

Spencer, Herbert, 38, 102

Spies, August, 21, 24, 33

Sprague, Franklin Monroe, 107-8, 109, 185

Sprague, Philo W., 112

Stahl, Henry, 334, 336n.

Standard, The, 44, 51

Standard Oil Co., 133, 226, 268, 293

Star and Kansan, 212

Stauber, Frank A., 17

Stedman, Seymour, 285, 288, 289, 299, 308, 317, 320, 320n., 322, 331, 344, 347, 348, 350, 352, 353, 354, 362, 363, 376, 384, 385, 386

Stetson (Gilman), Charlotte Perkins, 123

Stephens, Uriah S., 159-60

Steward, Ira, 65

Stone, Lucy, 80

Stone, N. I., 338, 343n., 351, 352, 363

Strasser, Adolph, 13

Strickland, Frederick G., 266n.

Strobell, George H., 365

Strong, Josiah, 132

Swift, Morrison I., 255, 256, 271, 285

Swinton, John, 50, 144

Sylvis, William H., 9

Syracuse University, 264

Tammany Hall, 42, 46, 225-26, 226n., 337

Taubeneck, Herman E., 214, 215, 233

Taylor, C. F., 83, 194, 265

Ten Men of Money Island, 180

Texas "Socialist Party of America," 331-32

Theory of the Leisure Class, The, 273

Theosophy (Theosophists), 79, 80, 81, 83, 98, 100, 111, 304

Thomas, Elizabeth H., 316, 357

Tobin, John F., 161, 162, 331n.

Tolstoi, Leo, 131

Tracy City, Tennessee, labor disturbances, 68, 148

Trade unionism: Marxist position on, 8, 58; Lassallean attitude toward, 8, 54, 58; Lassalleans accused of antagonizing, 56; found insufficient by Gronlund, 30; political parties and central labor unions, 62; Nationalists' attitude toward, 99-101; Christian Labor Union, 105; Social Gospel position on, 106; Bliss on, 110, 114-15, 124-25; DeLeon's criticism of, 147, 150-51; SLP "New Trade Unionism," 150-52,

407

INDEX

163-68; Wayland on, 200-1; Social Democracy on, 296; SDP repudiation of dual unionism, 321, 322, 330-31; SLP "Kangaroo" faction on "New Trade Unionism," 341-42; Socialist Party on, 386-87

Truth, 20

Tucker, Gideon J., 143

Twentieth Century, 225, 242, 244

Tyner, Paul, 122, 256, 257, 259, 324

Union Labor Party, 219, 230, 328

Union Reform League, 256-61, 263, 266, 324

Union Reform Party, 260, 263

United Automobile W o r k e r s of America, 152

United Hebrew Trades, 153, 155, 160, 341

United Labor Party (New York), 37, 38, 41, 42-50, 52

United Steel Workers of America, 152

University of Chicago, 264

University of Nebraska, 132

Urner, Benjamin, 249

Utopian Socialism, 5-6, 8, 144, 318, 319

Vahlteich, Julius, 378

Van Patten, Philip, 15, 16, 17, 18-19, 23, 24

Veblen, Ellen, 73

Veblen, Thorstein, 72, 273

Viereck, Louis, 18

Vogt, Hugo, 48, 63, 147, 153, 163, 165, 332

Volkanswalt, Der (Cleveland), 300

Voraussetzungen des Sozialismus und die Aufgaben der Sozialdemokratie, Die, 321

Vorbote, Der (Chicago), 16

Vorwaerts, Der, (New York), 199, 332, 334

Vrooman, Carl, 266

Vrooman, Harry C., 116

Vrooman, Walter, 48

Wahrheit, Die (Milwaukee), 354

Wahrheit, Die (New York), 301

Waite, Davis H., 179, 180

Wakeman, Thaddeus B., 80, 217, 225, 243

Walker, Francis A., 86

Walker, Ryan, 197

Ward, Duren H., 262, 264

Wardell, Alonzo, 284

Warren, Fred D., 208-9

Washburn, George F., 219, 265

Watson, Tom, 232

Wayland, Julius A., 127, 212, 371; on *Looking Backward,* 73, 183; as socialist propagandist, 175, 181-82, 185-86, 195-98, 209; ideological position, 175-76, 198, 207-8; becomes a socialist, 176, 179; successful businessman, 177, 177n., 178, 181; on the People's Party, 179-80, 183, 187, 188, 232-33, 239; criticizes De-Leon and SLP, 180, 188, 200, 208, 335; founds *Coming Nation,* 181; content of newspapers, 182-87, 197; on trade unions, 183, 184, 200-1; controversy with A. S. Edwards, 188-89; ostracized by neighbors, 189; 195; defends communitarian settlements, 189-90; association with Ruskin Colony, 190-93; founds *Appeal to Reason,* 194; locates in Girard, Kan., 195; cynical of average voter, 198; belief in socialist political action, 199; on socialism and the farmer, 202; on the class struggle, 203-4; as an Anglophobe, 205-6; believes socialism inevitable, 206-7; gives up editorial direction of *Appeal,* 208-9; supports SLP in 1896, p. 239; and the Social Democratic Party, 323, 324-25, 370, 373

Wealth-Makers, The, 212, 232n.

Weaver, James Baird, 18, 65, 215, 221

Webb, Sidney, 80, 81, 93, 120, 250

408

INDEX

Wedemeyer, Joseph, 7
Weekly People, The, 338
Weitling, Wilhelm, 7
Wendell Phillips Union, 119
West, William, 9
Western Federation of Miners, 165, 368
Western Labor Union, 165
"What Means This Strike?", 166
White, W. E., 343n., 364
Will, Thomas E., 262, 264, 266n.
Willard, Cyrus Field, 79-80, 85, 90-91, 96, 303, 304, 305, 306, 311, 314, 315, 316, 317, 318
Willard, Frances E., 73-74, 80
Williams, George Fred, 266n.
Wilshire, H. Gaylord, 84, 267, 268, 269, 381, 382
Wilson, J. Stitt, 137, 138, 139
Winchevsky, Morris, 301, 317, 320n., 327, 377

Wing, Simon, 149, 150
Wingate, Charles F., 143
Winn, Henry, 219, 220, 221
Wisconsin Vorwaerts (formerly *Milwaukee Arbeiter-Zeitung*), 286, 300, 306
Woodhull, Victoria, 10, 11
Woodhull and Claflin's Weekly, 10
Workers' Call, The (formerly *The Chicago Socialist*), 369, 370
Working Class Movement in America, The, 31
Workingmen's Party of the United States, 13-15
Workmen's Advocate, 25, 31, 40, 43, 46, 49, 51, 52, 53, 54, 57, 59, 64, 86, 117, 144

Young, H. W., 212

Zametkin, Michael, 300, 301

409